# THE MUMMY

Ptaḥ-Seker-Ȧusȧr figure
which held the papyrus of Anhai,
a priestess of Ȧmen, about B.C. 900.

# THE MUMMY

## FUNEREAL RITES & CUSTOMS IN ANCIENT EGYPT

ERNEST A. WALLIS BUDGE

SENATE

*The Mummy*

First published in 1893 as *The Mummy: Chapters on Egyptian Funereal Archaeology* by The University Press, Cambridge

This edition published in 1995 by Senate, an imprint of Studio Editions Ltd, Princess House, 50 Eastcastle Street, London W1N 7AP, England



ISBN 1 85958 071 8
Printed and bound in Guernsey by
The Guernsey Press Co. Ltd

# CONTENTS

CONTENTS.

CONTENTS.

CONTENTS.

CONTENTS.

# PREFACE

THE chapters contained in this book were originally written to form the *Introduction* to the *Catalogue of the Egyptian Collection in the Fitzwilliam Museum, Cambridge*, which I wrote for the Syndics of that institution; they are intended to supply the information necessary for understanding the object and use of the antiquities described therein. In the hope, however, that they may be of service to all such as are interested in the antiquities of Egypt, it has been decided to publish them in a separate form.

The monuments and remains of ancient Egypt preserved in the great museums of Europe and Egypt are chiefly of a sepulchral character, and we owe them entirely to the belief of the Egyptians that the soul would at some period revivify the body, and to the care, consequent on this belief, with which they embalmed the bodies of their dead, so that they might resist the action of decay, and be ready for the return of the soul. The preservation of the embalmed body, or mummy, was the chief end and aim of every Egyptian who wished for everlasting life. For the sake of the mummy's safety tombs were hewn, papyri were inscribed with compositions, the knowledge of which would enable him to repel the attacks of demons, ceremonies were performed and services were recited; for the sake of the comfort of the mummy and his *ka*, or genius, the tombs were decorated with scenes which would remind him of those with which he was familiar when upon earth, and they were also provided with many objects used by him in daily life, so that his tomb might resemble as much as possible his old home. Following up the idea that the mummy is the most important of all objects, I have given an account of the various methods of embalming; of the amulets and other objects which formed the mummy's dress; of the various kinds of coffins and sarcophagi in which he was laid; of the *ushabtiu* and other figures, stelæ, vases, etc., which formed the furniture of a well appointed tomb: and also of the most important classes of tombs hewn or built in different dynasties. In the series of articles which form this account I have given the information which the experience gained from the service of some years in the British Museum has shown me to be the most needed both by those who, though possessing no special knowledge of Egyptian antiquities, are yet greatly interested in them, and by those who have formed, or who are about to form, Egyptian collections. Frequent reference has been made to the great national collection in the British Museum because the antiquities there are accessible to all. With a view of applying the facts stated in these articles to a particular case, an account of an Egyptian funeral beginning with the process of mummifying the body and ending with its deposit in the tomb has been added.

In the somewhat lengthy chapter on the Rosetta Stone, the evidence of the principal Greek writers on Egyptian hieroglyphics is brought together. The statement of the facts connected with the history of Egyptian decipherment, as well as the extracts from the papers on this subject collected by Leitch in his edition of the *Miscellaneous Works by the late Thomas Young*, London, 1855, and by Dean Peacock in his *Life of Thomas Young*, London, 1855, seems to show that the labours of Akerblad and Young were of more importance than is usually attributed to them; the views of Egyptologists quoted at the end of that chapter will indicate the prevailing opinion of experts on this matter.

E. A. WALLIS BUDGE.

# THE HISTORY OF EGYPT.[1]

THE date of the period when the land of Egypt was taken possession of by the race of people which we are accustomed to call Egyptian is unknown. None of the researches which have been carried on by historians, philologists, anthropologists and archæologists has, up to the present, given us any information from which we may reasonably hope to arrive at a decision as to the time when this event took place. And just as we know nothing of the period of the advent of the invaders, so also we know nothing of the aboriginal people whom we may assume they found living there when they arrived. The Egyptian aborigines are thought by some to have been a dark-skinned race, and to have belonged to the negro family. Whatever may be the truth on these points, it is pretty clear that no traces of their works or buildings have come down to us, and as skulls belonging to their time have not been found, any statement as to their race characteristics must be based on pure assumption.

**Antiquity of Egyptians.**

About the race to which the Egyptian known to us from mummies and statues belongs and his characteristics, there is

[1] Among the books which derive their information about the history of Egypt from native sources, and are all important for the study of Egyptian History, must be mentioned:—Champollion-Figeac, *Egypte Ancienne*, Paris, 1839; Rosellini, *Monumenti Storici*, Pisa, 1832–1844; Bunsen, *Aegyptens Stelle in der Weltgeschichte*, Gotha, 1844–1857 (English translation with supplementary additions by the late Dr. Birch, Vols. 1–5, London, 1857); Lepsius, *Chronologie der Aegypter*, Berlin, 1849; Lepsius, *Königsbuch*, Berlin, 1858; Brugsch, *Geschichte Aegyptens*, Leipzig, 1859 (English translation by Danby Seymour and Philip Smith, B.A., 2 vols., 2nd ed., London, 1881); Birch, *Egypt from the earliest Times to* B.C. 300, London, 1880; Wiedemann, *Aegyptische Geschichte*, Gotha, 1884; Meyer, *Geschichte des alten Aegyptens*, Berlin, 1887, with *Einleitung. Geographie des alten Aegyptens, Schrift und Sprache seiner Bewohner*, by Dümichen; and Mariette, *Aperçu de l'Histoire Ancienne d'Egypte*, Paris, 1867. Interesting and popular works on this subject are contained in Maspero, *Histoire Ancienne des Peuples de l'Orient*, 1st ed., 1875, and Lenormant, *Histoire Ancienne de l'Orient*, Paris, 1882.

Asia the original home of the Egyptians.

no doubt whatever. He was a Caucasian, and it would seem that he came to Egypt from an original home in Asia. He wandered, or was driven, forth from there, and travelling in a south-westerly or westerly direction, after a number of years arrived at a place to the north of the Red Sea, probably the Isthmus of Suez, the "bridge of nations." Of the time occupied by the immigrant in making his way from Asia to Egypt nothing can be said; it is quite certain, however, that when he arrived he brought a high civilization with him. Following the statement of Diodorus Siculus,[1] it was the fashion some years ago to state in books of history that the ancient Egyptian was a negro, and some distinguished historians still make the statement that "the fundamental character of the Egyptian in respect of physical type, language, and tone of thought, is Nigritic."[2] That neither the Egyptian nor his civilization is of Nigritic origin is proved by the inscriptions and by the evidence of an ever-increasing number of statues of kings, and of high officials in their service, who lived during the earliest times of the rule of the invaders over Egypt. Prof. Owen's opinion on this subject is as follows: "Taking the sum of the correspondence notable in collections of skulls from Egyptian graveyards as a probable indication of the hypothetical primitive race originating the civilized conditions of cranial departure from the skull-character of such race, that race was certainly not of the Australioid type, is more suggestive of a northern Nubian or Berber basis. But such suggestive characters may be due to intercourse or 'admixture' at periods later than [the] XIIIth dynasty; they are not present, or in a much less degree, in the skulls, features, and physiognomies of individuals of from the IIIrd to the XIIth dynasties."[3] If the pure ancient Egyptian, as found in mummies and represented in paintings upon the tombs, be compared with the negro, we shall find that they are absolutely unlike in every particular. The negro is prognathous, but the Egyptian is orthognathous; the bony structure of the

Evidence of skulls and antiquities.

[1] Bk. iii. 3. 1. (ed. Didot, p. 128).

[2] G. Rawlinson, *Ancient Egypt*, 1887, p. 24.

[3] *Journal of the Anthropological Institute of Great Britain and Ireland*, Vol. IV. p. 239.

negro is heavier and stronger than that of the Egyptian; the hair of the negro is crisp and woolly, while that of the Egyptian is smooth and fine. The Egyptian was usually of slender build, with broad shoulders, sinewy arms and legs, and long hands and feet. His head was small, with large eyes, full cheeks, broad mouth, lips inclined to be full, and square chin. The nose was short and not aquiline. It will be observed, too, that if we add that the Egyptian was dark complexioned, the above particulars will agree very well with their general description by Ammianus Marcellinus (xxii. 16, 23): "Homines autem Aegyptii plerique subfusculi sunt et atrati[1] magis quam maesti oris, gracilenti et aridi, ad singulos motus excandescentes ......" When an Egyptian had an aquiline nose, it indicated that he had Semitic blood in his veins; the aquiline nose was hardly ever met with in Upper Egypt.[2] But it is quite as impossible to show that the Egyptian was a Semite, as some have attempted to do, as that he was a negro.

Features of the Egyptian.

The language of the Egyptian as known to us by the inscriptions which he left behind him belongs wholly neither to the Indo-European nor to the Semitic family of languages. The only known language which it resembles is Coptic, and this is now pretty well understood to be a dialect of the language of the hieroglyphics. Benfey[3] endeavoured to show that the Egyptian had sprung from a Semitic stock, and De Rougé,[4] Ebers and Brugsch[5] have followed in his steps.

Opinions of scholars on the affinity of Egyptian.

[1] See also Herodotus, ii. 104.

[2] Here and elsewhere I have reproduced passages from my *Prefatory Remarks on the unrolling the Mummy of Bak-ran*, privately printed, London, 1890. See Ebers, *Aegypten und die Bücher Moses*, i. p. 46 ff. and Wiedemann, *Aegyptische Geschichte*, p. 25.

[3] The whole of the facts which favour the theory that the Egyptian is allied to the Semitic languages are collected in his work *Ueber das Verhältniss der Aegyptischen Sprache zum Semitischen Sprachstamme*, Leipzig, 1844.

[4] *Mémoire sur l'inscription du tombeau d'Ahmès*, p. 195. "...... et presque toujours un fait curieux a été mis en évidence, à savoir, que la grammaire de la langue antique se rapproche bien plus décidément des caractères propres aux idiomes sémitiques."

[5] *Wörterbuch*, I. Vorrede, ss. 9-12. "Es steht mir nämlich fest, dass die altägyptische Sprache, d. h. die älteste Gestaltung derselben, im Semitischen wurzelt und dass wir von hieraus alle jene Erscheinungen zu erklären haben, welche sonst ohne jede Ausflösung dastehen würden."

Barthélemy, de Guignes, Giorgi, de Rossi and Kopp proclaimed unhesitatingly the identity of Coptic with Hebrew,[1] but Quatremère in his *Recherches critiques et historiques sur la langue et la littérature de l'Egypte*, p. 16, declared that Coptic was without affinity with any other language, and that it was a mother tongue. Dr. Lepsius tried to show by the names of the numerals and alphabets that the Indo-European, Semitic and Coptic families of languages were originally identical,[2] and Schwartze[3] asserted that Coptic was analogous to the Semitic languages in its grammar, and to the Indo-European languages by its roots; but that it was more akin to the Semitic languages in its simple character and lack of logical structure. Bunsen and Paul de Lagarde thought that the Egyptian language represented a pre-historic layer of Semitism, and tried to show that the forms and the roots of the ancient Egyptian could be explained neither by Aryan nor Semitic singly, but by both of these families together, and that they formed in some way the transition from one to the other.[4] Stern in his *Koptische Grammatik*, p. 4, says:—"Es besteht eine alte Verwandtschaft zwischen der aegyptischen, welche dem hamitischen Stamme angehört, und den semitischen Sprachen, wie sich unverkennbar noch in der pronominalbildung und in manchen gemeinsamen Wurzeln zeigt; doch scheint sich das aegyptische von den asiatischen Schwestern früh getrennt zu haben und seinen eigenen Weg gegangen zu sein..... Die allgemeine Stammverwandtschaft der beiden Sprachen ist durch weitgehende Lautverschiebungen und Veränderungen verdeckt." Prof. W. Wright thought that "we have not a few structural affinities, which may perhaps be thought sufficient to justify those linguists who hold that Egyptian is a relic of the earliest age of Semitism, or of Semitic speech as it was before it passed into the peculiar form in which we may be said to know it historically." (*Comparative Grammar of the Semitic Languages*, p. 34.)

[1] Renan, *Histoire Générale des Langues Sémitiques*, p. 80.

[2] *Ueber den Ursprung und die Verwandtschaft der Zahlwörter in der Indo-Germanischen, Semitischen und Koptischen Sprache*, Berlin, 1836.

[3] *Das alte Aegypten*, pp. 976, 1033.

[4] Renan, *op. cit.*, p. 82.

Quite recently Dr. Erman has discussed[1] the question of the affinity of the language of the hieroglyphics with the Semitic dialects, and he is of opinion that a relationship undoubtedly exists. To support this view he prints a list of Egyptian words with what he and I believe to be their Semitic equivalents, and he thinks that the number of such words might be considerably increased if we were able to recover the radicals which are hidden in their hieroglyphic forms. His arguments are carefully thought out and his facts ably put together, and he has made an important contribution towards the settlement of a difficult subject.

On the other hand Renan, Max Müller, and others, do not admit the connexion between Egyptian and the Semitic languages in any way whatever. Renan does not seek to deny that the proposed relationships between Coptic and Semitic dictionaries have something seductive about them, but he cannot admit that they form any scientific proof; he considers them to be accidents rather than organic analogies, as shown by the following list:—[2]

| | Egyptian. | | | Coptic. | Hebrew. |
|---|---|---|---|---|---|
| Sing. 1. |  *ànuk* | I | | ⲁⲛⲟⲕ | אָנֹכִי |
| „ 2. m. |  *entuk* | thou | | ⲛ̄ⲑⲟⲕ | אַתָּה for אַנְתָּה أَنْتَ *anta* |
| „ 2. f. |  *entut* | thou | | ⲛ̄ⲑⲟ | אַתְּי for אַנְתִּי أَنْتِ *anti* |
| „ 3. m. |  *entuf* | he | | ⲛ̄ⲑⲟϥ | |
| „ 3. f. |  *entus* | she | | ⲛ̄ⲑⲟⲥ | |

[1] *Z.D.M.G.*, Band XLVI. pp. 93–129.

[2] See however Wright (*Comparative Grammar*, p. 33), "An examination of the Coptic alone readily suggests several considerations in support of this view [*i.e.*, that Egyptian is descended from the same stock as the Semitic languages]. For example, there is the marvellous similarity, almost amounting to identity, of the personal pronouns, both separate and suffixed—a class of words which languages of radically different families are not apt to borrow from one another"

| | EGYPTIAN. | | | COPTIC. | HEBREW. |
|---|---|---|---|---|---|
| Plur. 1. | 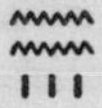 | *enen* | we | ⲁⲛⲟⲛ | אֲנוּ , אֲנַחְנוּ |
| " 2. |  | *entuten* | you | ⲛ̄ⲑⲱⲧⲉⲛ | אַתֶּם for אַנְתֶּם أَنتُم *antum* |
| " 3. |  | *entu* | they | ⲛ̄ⲑⲱⲟⲩ | |

The identity of the pronouns, and especially the manner in which they are treated in the two groups of languages, he considers a remarkable fact, and goes on to say that this identity is observed even in the details which seem the most secondary. Several apparent irregularities of the Semitic pronoun, as for example, the changing of the ת into ך in the affix, even find in the theory of the Coptic pronoun a satisfactory explanation. The analogies of the nouns of number pointed out by Lepsius are not less striking, for example :—

| EGYPTIAN. | | | COPTIC. | | |
|---|---|---|---|---|---|
| 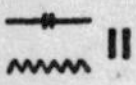 | *sen,* | two | ⲥⲛⲁⲩ | (masc.) | שְׁנַיִם |
|  | *suu* or *sas,* | six | ⲥⲟⲟⲩ | | שֵׁשׁ |
|  | *sexef,* | seven | ϣⲁϣϥ | | שֶׁבַע |
| 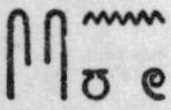 | *xemennu,* | eight | ϣⲙⲏⲛ | | שְׁמֹנָה |

Egyptian and Coptic. The conjugation itself is not without some analogies in the two languages; the present tense in Coptic, like the imperfect of the Semitic languages, is formed by the agglutination of the pronoun at the beginning of the verbal root, and the other tenses are formed by means of a composition like those which the Aramean languages make use of. Having admitted these facts, Renan goes on to say that the problem whether these resemblances are merely such things as are to be found in all languages, or analogies which spring from a common origin is, to say the truth, almost unsolvable.

Egyptian and "Hamitic." We must then make for the language and civilization of Egypt a family by itself, which may be called *Hamitic.*[1]

[1] Renan, *op. cit.*, pp. 84, 85, 89.

**Max Müller's views.**

According to Prof. Max Müller and others, "the Egyptian and the Semitic languages belong to quite different stages of language, the former to what Prof. Max Müller calls the second or Terminational, the latter to the third or Inflexional stage. In the Terminational stage, two or more roots may coalesce to form a word, the one retaining its radical independence, the other sinking down to a mere termination. The languages belonging to this stage have generally been called agglutinative. Now the Egyptian language has indeed reached this stage as regards the pronominal and one or two other suffixes. But in all other respects it most nearly resembles the languages of the first or Radical stage, in which there is no formal distinction between a root and a word."[1] A theory has been put forth by Dr. Strassmaier that a relationship exists between the Accadian and Egyptian languages, and he printed a small list of Egyptian, Coptic and Accadian words which he thought to be identical. If Egypt and Mesopotamia were conquered by branches of the same Accadian-speaking race this is only what might be expected. See his paper, *Akkadisch und Aegyptisch*, in the *Album*[2] presented to M. Leemans.

**Egyptian, Coptic, and Accadian.**

**Country of Egypt.**

The **land of Egypt** was commonly called by its inhabitants  *Kamt*, because of the dark colour of the soil, and if the colour of the ground for a few miles on each side of the Nile be compared with the Arabian and Libyan desert the appropriateness of the name Kam or Kamt is at once evident. Another old name of Egypt is *Ta-merà*, "the land of the inundation," 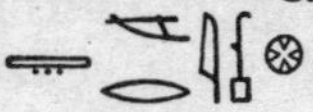, 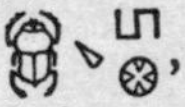, or ; two other names for the country are  *Beqet*, apparently having reference to Egypt as an olive-bearing land, and

[1] Renouf, *Hibbert Lectures*, pp. 55–61. The question of *Pronominal forms in Egyptian* has been discussed by this writer in the *Proceedings of the Society of Biblical Archæology*, March, 1888, pp. 247–264, and in this paper he states that pronouns like *ànuk*, *entuk*, *entuf*, etc., are formed of a series of demonstrative elements; ànuk = à + nu + k, entuk = en + tu + k, entuf = en + tu – f.

[2] *Etudes Archéologiques*, *Linguistiques et Historiques*, dédiées à Dr. C. Leemans, Leide, 1885, pp. 105–107.

*Baqet.* Upper Egypt was commonly called *Ta-res* or *Ta-qemā*, "the land of the South," and Lower Egypt *Ta-meḥ*, "the land of the North." Upper and Lower Egypt were represented in the inscriptions by the following: , , , , , .

Native names of Egypt.

The Hebrews called Egypt "Mizraim," and the Assyrians and Babylonians *Muṣur;* it is given this latter name in the cuneiform despatches of Tushratta, King of Mitani, about B.C. 1550. Upper Egypt extended from Aswân (Syene) to Memphis, and Lower Egypt, beginning at Memphis, included the Delta and sea-coast.

Nomes of Egypt.

From the earliest times Egypt appears to have been divided into a series of districts which the Egyptians called *ḥesp*, and the Greeks Νομοί or **Nomes.** Each nome had its capital city and temple for worship, its own feasts, its own sacred animals and trees, and its own protecting deity. The limits of each nome were most carefully marked, and the amount of cultivated land, the amount of land available for agricultural purposes after a high Nile, and the canals with their various branches, were all known.[1] Each nome with its independent administration, formed, practically, a small but complete state.

The number of the nomes according to classical authors varies; Diodorus, who says (i. 54) that the nome dates from the time of Sesostris, gives thirty-six, Pliny[2] forty-five. The number usually given in Egyptian lists is forty-two: twenty-two in Upper Egypt, and twenty in Lower Egypt. Heptanomis, or Middle Egypt, appears to have been the district between the Thebaid and the Delta; its seven nomes are said to have been Memphites, Heracleopolites, Crocodilopolites, Aphroditopolites, Oxyrhynchites, Cynopolites, Hermopolites. The Greater and Lesser Oases were considered to be parts of Heptanomis.

[1] A list of the nomes is given at the end of the chapter on Egyptian History.

[2] He calls them *praefecturas oppidorum*, (v. 9, 9). The nomes and their chief towns are given by Ptolemy, *Geographiae*, iv. 5, ed. Mercator, pp. 105–108.

Over the early **history** of Egypt there hangs a mystery greater than that which shrouds the origin and home of the Egyptian; of the period which preceded Menȧ (Menes), the first historical king of Egypt, nothing is known. According to **Manetho** a race of demi-gods and kings from This, near Abydos, and from Memphis ruled over Egypt before the advent of Menȧ, and these may possibly correspond with the *shesu Ḥeru* or "followers of Horus" of the Turin papyrus, the list of kings on which begins with god-kings and ends with the rule of the Hyksos at the end of the XVIIth dynasty or about B.C. 1700. The work of Manetho of Sebennytus on Egyptian history is, unfortunately, lost. He was alive about B.C. 271, and is said to have been a contemporary of Ptolemy I.; his Egyptian history was composed during the reign of Ptolemy II. Philadelphus, B.C. 286–247. Extracts from this work are given us by **Josephus** (*contra Apion.* I., 14), which refer to the reigns of the kings of the XV—XIXth dynasties. In **Eusebius** and **Julius Africanus** (fragments of whose work πενταβιβλίον χρονολογικόν are preserved in Eusebius) there are given a list of Egyptian dynasties, and the number of the years of the reign of each king. This list is one of the most valuable documents which have come down to us, for Manetho, by reason of his position as priest and his knowledge of the ancient Egyptian language, had access to, and was able to make use of, the ancient Egyptian literature in a way which no other writer seems to have done. The thirty **dynasties** of Egyptian kings he divides into three periods, thus: Dynasties I.—XI., Dynasties XII.—XIX., and Dynasties XX.—XXX. It must, however, be understood that the Egyptian did not group the kings into dynasties, and this fact is evident from the **Tablet of Abydos** and the **Tablet of Ṣaḳḳârah.** The **Tablet of Abydos,** discovered by Dümichen in the Temple of Osiris, at Abydos, in 1864, gives the names of seventy-five kings, beginning with **Menȧ** or **Menes,** and ending with Seti I., the father of Rameses II.; it is not a complete list, and there is nothing to show why certain names are omitted. The **Tablet of Ṣaḳḳârah,** discovered by Mariette at Ṣaḳḳârah, was inscribed during the reign of Rameses II., and it gives

The mythical period in Egyptian History.

Early historians.

Lists of Kings.

the names of forty-seven kings, agreeing closely, in the matter of selection of names, with the Tablet of Abydos. The name of Mer-ba-pen, the sixth king of the Ist dynasty, is that which begins this list. The **Tablet of Karnak** was discovered at Karnak by Burton and was taken to Paris by Prisse. It was inscribed during the reign of Thothmes III., and contains the names of sixty-one kings. Notwithstanding the fact that in the arrangement no chronological order has been followed, the tablet is of great value, for it mentions the names of some of the kings of from the XIIIth to the XVIIth dynasties, and gives the names of those of the XIth dynasty more fully than any other list. The names of the kings in Manetho's list are in many instances corrupt; by the help of the monuments, however, the greater number can be corrected, and the value of the document is the more assured as more of the historical inscriptions become known.

**Uncertainty of Egyptian Chronology.**

The **chronology** of Egypt has been, and must be for some time yet, a subject of difficulty and of variety of opinion. The fixed points in Egyptian history are so few and the gaps between them so great, that it is quite impossible to establish an accurate system of chronology: approximate dates are all that can be hoped for at present. Nearly every student of Egyptian chronology arrives at conclusions different from any of his predecessors, and how widely different they are is seen from the fact that the date given for Menes by Champollion-Figeac is 5867, by Böckh 5702, by Bunsen 3623, by Lepsius 3892, by Lieblein 3893, by Mariette 5004, and by Brugsch 4400. The system of chronology by Brugsch, which is based on the calculation of three generations to a century, is generally used throughout this book.

## DYNASTIES I–VI.

**B.C. 4400**

**Menȧ** or Menes, the first historical king of Egypt, came from This near Abydos in Upper Egypt. He left This, and journeying northwards, arrived at the head of the Delta, where, having turned the Nile out of its course, he founded the city of Memphis and built the temple of Ptah.

**Founding of Memphis.**

The name Memphis, in Egyptian 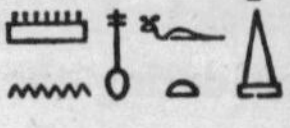 *Men-nefert*, means the "fair site"; the sacred name of the place is 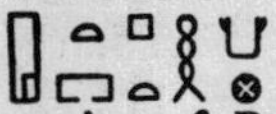 *Ḥet-Ptaḥ-ka,* and means "the temple of the genius of Ptaḥ"; from this name it seems that the Greek name for Egypt Αἴγυπτος is derived. The worship of the gods, the temple services, and the cult of Apis were introduced by Menes, who is said to have been devoured by a crocodile.

B.C.

**Tetȧ** wrote a book on anatomy, and continued building at Memphis. 4366

**Ȧta.** In the reign of this king a great famine happened. 4300
He is said to have built pyramids at Kochome near Ṣaḳ- Famine in Egypt.
ḳarah, but there is no evidence that he built the famous Step Pyramid[1] there.

**Ḥesep-ti.** The 64th chapter of the Book of the Dead is 4266
said to have been found at Denderah during his reign, and Antiquity of Book of the Dead.
the 130th chapter also dates from that period.

**Mer-ba-pen.** With this king's name the Tablet of Ṣaḳ- 4233
ḳârah begins.

During the second dynasty an earthquake swallowed up a great many people at Bubastis, and the succession of females to the throne of Egypt was declared valid. **Sent**, the last 4000
king of this dynasty, revised a work on medicine, and he Early medical knowledge in Egypt.
appears to be the first king of whom contemporaneous monuments remain.

During the rule of **Nefer-ka-Seker,** the first king of the IIIrd dynasty, the tribes of the land to the north-west of the Delta rebelled: according to Manetho's statement, the moon Eclipse o the moon
first grew very large and bright, and then became dark, and the rebels were so terrified that they fled away in terror.

The monuments of the IVth dynasty are numerous, and the tombs of this period, particularly, show to what a high state of culture and civilization the Egyptians had attained. Of the first king, **Seneferu,** very little is known: he invaded 3766

[1] The steps are six in number, and are about 38, 36, 34½, 32, 31 and 29½ feet in height; the width of each step is from six to seven feet. The lengths of the sides at the base are: north and south, 352 feet; east and west, 596 feet, and the actual height is 197 feet. The shape of the pyramid is oblong, and the arrangement of the chambers inside is peculiar to itself.

the peninsula of Sinai, and having conquered the hostile tribes there, established copper mining at Wâdy Ma'ârah. He dug wells, and built forts and temples there for the use of the miners and overseers, and from the remains of the working of his mines, which may be seen there to this day, it is clear that the copper industry must have been very large at that period in Egypt. Sinai was called  *Mafkata,* "the land of the bluish-green stone." Seneferu is said to have built the Pyramid of Mêdûm, called in Egyptian  *Chā*, and in Arabic *El-Haram el-Kaddâb*, "the false

Copper mines worked in Sinai.

Pyramid of Mêdûm.

The Pyramid of Mêdûm.

pyramid." This pyramid is about 115 feet high, and is built in three stages; the first is 70, the second 20, and the third about 25 feet high. It was never completed.

B.C. 3733

**Chufu**, or **Cheops,** the next king of Egypt, is more famous as the builder of the great pyramid of Gîzeh than as a warrior, and little more is known of his military expeditions than that he continued the wars against the tribes of Sinai which his predecessor Seneferu had so ably begun. He appears to have built many towns, and the famous temple of Denderah is said to have been founded during his reign. As the pyramids were tombs, they will be described in the chapter relating to tombs.

Great pyramid built and Denderah founded.

Statue of Chephren, King of Egypt, B.C. 3666 [Museum of Gizeh].

B.C. 3666

**Chāfrā**, or **Chephren**, is also more famous as the builder of the second pyramid than as a warrior, and with his name is coupled that of the Sphinx.

The Sphinx.

The age of the **Sphinx** is unknown, and few of the facts connected with its history have come down to these days. Some years ago it was generally believed to have been made during the rule of the kings of the Middle Empire over

Repairs to the Sphinx.

Egypt, but when the stele which recorded the repairs made in the temple of the sphinx by Thothmes IV., B.C. 1533, came to light, it became certain that it was the work of one of the kings of the Ancient Empire. The stele records that one day during an after-dinner sleep, Harmachis appeared to Thothmes IV., and promised to bestow upon him the crown of Egypt if he would dig his image, *i.e.*, the Sphinx, out of the sand. At the end of the inscription part of the name of Chā-f-Rā or Chephren appears, and hence some have thought that this king was the maker of the Sphinx; and as the statue of Chephren was subsequently found in the temple close by, this theory was generally adopted. An inscription found by Mariette near one of the pyramids to the east of the pyramid of Cheops shows that the Sphinx existed in the time of Chu-fu or Cheops. The Egyptians called the Sphinx *ḥu* 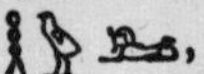, and he represented the god Harmachis, *i.e.*, *Ḥeru-em-chut* , "Horus in the horizon," or the rising sun, the conqueror of darkness, the god of the morning. On the tablet erected by Thothmes IV., Harmachis says that he gave life and dominion to Thothmes III., and he promises to give the same good gifts to his successor Thothmes IV. The discovery of the steps which led up to the Sphinx, a smaller Sphinx, and an open temple, etc., was made by

Caviglia excavates Sphinx.

Caviglia, who first excavated this monument; within the last few years very extensive excavations have been made round it by the Egyptian Government, and several hitherto unseen parts of it have been brought to view. The Sphinx is hewn out of the living rock, but pieces of stone have been added where necessary; the body is about 150 feet long, the paws are 50 feet long, the head is 30 feet long, the face is 14 feet wide, and from the top of the head to the base of the monument the distance is about 70 feet. Originally there probably were ornaments on the head, the whole of which was covered with a limestone covering, and the face was coloured red; of these decorations scarcely any traces now remain, though they were visible towards the end of the last century. The condition in which the monument now appears is due to the savage destruction of its features by the Muḥammadan rulers of Egypt, some of whom caused it to be used for a target. Around this imposing relic of antiquity, whose origin is wrapped in mystery, a number of legends and superstitions have clustered in all ages; but Egyptology has shown, I., that it was a colossal image of Rā-Harmachis, and therefore of his human representative upon earth, the king of Egypt who had it hewn, and II., that it was in existence in the time of, and was probably repaired by, Cheops and Chephren, who lived about three thousand seven hundred years before Christ.[1]

The Sphinx the emblem of Rā-Harmachis.

B.C. 3633

**Menkaurā** or **Mykerinos** is famous as the builder of the third pyramid at Gîzeh. The fragments of his inner wooden coffin and a small fragment of his basalt sarcophagus are preserved in the British Museum, together with the remains of a human body which were found with them in the third pyramid at Gîzeh. The reputation which this king left behind him is that of a good and just ruler.

The oldest coffin in the world.

The kings of the Vth like those of the IVth dynasty are famous rather as builders than as warriors. The rule of the first king, **Userkaf**, extended as far as Elephantine. **Saḥurā**, the second king, suppressed revolts in the Sinaitic peninsula and founded a town near Esneh. **Ȧn**, **Ḥeru-men-kau**, and **Ṭeṭ-ka-Rā** also made expeditions into Sinai, and caused reliefs to be cut on the rocks with the usual inscriptions in which they are called the conquerors of the land. In the reign of this last named king **Ṭeṭ-ka-Rā** or **Ȧssȧ** was written the famous work entitled the "**Precepts of Ptaḥ-Ḥetep.**" A single complete copy of this work, dating from the XIth or XIIth dynasty, is extant; it is preserved in the Bibliothèque Nationale in Paris, where it was brought by Prisse.[2] If all

3566

3400

Copper mines worked in Sinai.

3366

[1] Budge, *The Nile, Notes for Travellers in Egypt*, 2nd ed., pp. 194, 195.

[2] The hieratic text has been published by Prisse, *Facsimile d'un Papyrus Egyptien*, Paris, 1847. The best analyses of the text are by Chabas in *Revue Arch.*, Série I. t. xv., p. 1 ff. and in *Aegyptische Zeitschrift*, June and July, 1870.

The Shêkh el-Beled. From Ṣaḳḳârah [Gizeh Museum, No. 492].

other monuments of the great civilization of Egypt were wanting, these "Precepts" alone would show the moral worth of the Egyptians, and the high ideal of man's duties which B.C.
they had formed nearly 5500 years ago. Of **Unȧs**, the last 3333
king of the Vth dynasty, we know little except that he built a pyramid at Ṣaḳḳârah, which was opened in 1881.

The kings of the VIth dynasty seem to have extended their operations further south, for their names are found at El-kab, Abydos, Aswân, and elsewhere. **Tetȧ** and **Pepi I.** 3266-3233
built each a pyramid at Ṣaḳḳârah, and the rule of the latter seems to have embraced all Egypt. He renewed the Egyptian rule over the Sinaitic peninsula, and the inscriptions at Wâdy Ma'ârah show that copper mining was carried on there during his reign as busily as ever. Among Pepi's staff was a young man called **Unȧ**, who had been a favoured servant of Tetȧ; Pepi employed him in many ways and distinguished him by entrusting the care of an expedition against the Āāmu and Ḥeru-shā, who are supposed to be Semitic and Asiatic enemies of Egypt respectively. Troops were brought from Ethiopia and led against them by Unȧ; the Egyptians were successful in defeating them, and having wasted their land, they returned to Egypt bringing many captives with them. To quell the tribes in revolt to the north of the Ḥeru-shā territory it was necessary to send troops in ships. As a mark of the king's favour Unȧ was sent to the quarries of Ṭurah (in Eg.  *Re-āu*) to bring back a block of stone suitable for the king's sarcophagus. The ability and fidelity of Unȧ made him an acceptable officer to **Merenrā**, the successor of Pepi I., who 3200
sent him to the quarries to bring back a block of stone for the royal sarcophagus, to Aswân and Elephantine for granite to build a shrine and to make the doors of his pyramid, and to Alabastron for a large slab of fine white limestone. **Nefer-ka-Rā**, or **Pepi II.**, succeeded his brother Merenrā; he built a pyramid and made an expedition to Sinai. The last ruler of the sixth dynasty, **Nitȧqert** (Nitocris), was a queen; she 3133
enlarged the pyramid of Mykerinos and covered it over with slabs of granite, and the remains of a fine basalt sarcophagus which were found in a chamber near that of Mykerinos seem to indicate that the queen's body had been laid there.

The career of Unȧ.

Working of the copper mines of Sinai.

During the first six dynasties it is clear that the Egyptians were masters of the copper mine district in Sinai, that they were able to beat off the tribes on their western borders, that they defeated the two great warlike bodies of the Āāmu and the Ḥeru-shā, and that they were at peace with the Ethiopians, upon whom they could call for assistance in time of war. As builders they were unequalled, and their art had advanced so far that they were never successfully imitated by later generations. Their religion and government were well founded, and their education was of a very high character. So far as is known there was no other nation, except the Babylonians under Naram-Sin and Sargon, which was so highly civilized at this remote period.

## DYNASTIES VII–XI.

Unknown period in Egyptian history.

Of the history of Egypt of this period nothing is known; the names of the kings who reigned cannot even be arranged in accurate chronological order. Towards the end of this period a number of kings named **Ȧntef** and **Menthu-ḥetep** ruled; they appear to have been of Theban origin. **Menthu-ḥetep**, with the prenomen of **Neb-taui-Rā**, is styled, on a stele on the island of Konosso, the conqueror of thirteen nations, and his name appears on rocks which lie beside the old road from Coptos to the Red Sea through the valley of Hammâmât. The mightiest king of this period seems to
B.C. 2500 have been **Seānchkarā**, who was able to send forth an expedition to the land of **Punt**, the land of the gods, the peculiar home of the god Bes , and the land of sweet spices. The expedition set out in the eighth year of the king's reign, under the leadership of Ḥennu; it consisted of 3000 men, among whom were stone-cutters, soldiers, etc. On their road they dug four wells, and having arrived safely on the shores of the Red Sea, they took ship and sailed probably for the southern part of the Arabian peninsula. The expedition returned successfully, bearing with it great quantities of spices, precious stones, and other products of the East.

Great expedition to Punt.

## XIITH DYNASTY.

2466 The kings of this dynasty, like the Ȧntefs and Menthuḥeteps, were of Theban origin, and under their rule Egypt comes forth into the light of day as a mighty power. As they were able to defend their country from the assaults of their hereditary foes in Ethiopia, and from the tribes on their eastern and western borders, the arts and sciences flourished, and large works connected with the storage of Nile water were undertaken. The period of their rule, following as it did absolute anarchy, is one of the most interesting in the history of Egypt; and Thebes, which hitherto had not been the seat of government, became the chief city of the Egyptian empire. Thebes becomes capital of Egypt.

**Åmenemḥāt I.** made himself master of Egypt after very hard fighting, and during his rule of twenty-nine years he defeated the Uauat, an Ethiopian tribe, the Matui, a people who lived in the desert to the west of Egypt, and the Asiatics. He wrote a series of "Instructions" for his son Usertsen, whom he seems to have associated with him in the rule of the kingdom during the last ten years of his life. Conspiracies were formed against him, and he relates that his foes crept into his chamber at night to kill him. Åmenemḥāt I. is famous as the founder of the temple of Åmen-Rā, "the king of the gods," at Thebes, but although he beautified Thebes by this temple, he did not forget to establish another at Memphis, and at the other venerable cities of his kingdom. He followed the custom of the kings of the earlier dynasties and built a pyramid for his tomb. During his reign the story of Senehet was written. For an account of this remarkable papyrus see the article by Goodwin in *Fraser's Magazine*, No. 422, 1865, and for a translation see *Records of the Past*, 1st ed., Vol. VI., pp. 131–150. The original is preserved in Berlin, and a facsimile was published by Lepsius, *Denkmäler*, Abth. VI., Bl. 104 ff. B.C. 2466

**Usertsen I.** is famous as being the king who set up obelisks at Heliopolis and who beautified that city by building splendid temples there. These works were undertaken by him after taking counsel with his chief advisers, and in the record[1] of the proceedings of the solemn assembly at which this took place, Usertsen's orders for the prompt 2433 Rise of On or Heliopolis.

[1] The leather roll giving this interesting text was purchased by Brugsch in 1858, and is now preserved at Berlin.

The entrance to the tombs at Beni-Hasan. XIIth dynasty.

building of temples to the sun are preserved. Fragments of an obelisk set up by this king still exist near the modern town of Begig in the Fayyûm, and portions of inscriptions remain at Karnak, which show that he continued the building operations which his father began there. In the forty-third year of his reign **Ȧmeni Ȧmenemḥāt**, a high official, set out for Ethiopia with four hundred soldiers to quell a rebellion which had broken out there. This expedition was perfectly successful, and having smitten all the tribes of Kash without losing a man, returned to the leader's city in the nome of Meḥ, near Beni-ḥasân of to-day, bringing much gold with them. Ȧmeni Ȧmenemḥāt was one of the feudal lords of Egypt, and he led this expedition in the place of his father, who was too old to go on military service. Another high official called Mentu-ḥetep built a well at Abydos, of which, however, no trace has been found. Like so many of the kings who went before him, Usertsen caused the mines in the Sinaitic peninsula to be regularly worked.

**Tombs at Beni-ḥasân.**

B.C. 2400

**Ȧmenemḥāt II.** sent men to Nubia to dig for gold, and he opened the mines in the valley of Ḥammâmât; he appears to have lived some time at Tanis and to have had building operations carried on there like Usertsen I. In the nineteenth year of this king's reign Chnemu-ḥetep became governor of Menāt-Chufu, near Beni-ḥasân, an office held before by his father and grandfather. In the thirty-third year of Ȧmenemḥāt's reign he associated his successor Usertsen II. with him in the rule of the kingdom.

2366

In the sixth year of **Usertsen II.** thirty-seven people belonging to a branch of the Semitic race called Āāmu, in the country of Absha, brought a gift of eye-paint to **Chnemu-ḥetep**, in whose tomb this interesting scene is depicted. Some writers have seen in this a representation of the visit of Jacob's sons to Egypt to buy corn, but there is no ground whatever for this opinion. Of the wars of this king nothing is known, and of his buildings only one mention is made, and that is on a slab in the temple of Ptaḥ at Memphis.

**Visi of Semitic peoples to Egypt.**

2333

With the coming to the throne of **Usertsen III.** a new period of prosperity began for Egypt. He recognized very soon that the tribes of Nubia had to be put down with a

Egyptians conquer Nubia.

strong hand, and he marched into that country, and did not leave it until he had wasted the land, destroyed the crops and carried off the cattle. In the labours of Usertsen III. to suppress these peoples we have the counterpart of the expeditions of the English against the Mahdi and his Sudânî followers. He foresaw that it was hopeless to expect to master these people if the frontier town of Egypt was Aswân or Wâdy Ḥalfah, hence he went further south and built fortresses at Semneh and Kummeh. In spite of these, however, he himself was compelled to lead an expedition into Ethiopia in the nineteenth year of his reign, and having conquered the country he built a temple at Elephantine to the local gods and probably another at Amada. In Egypt proper he seems to have carried on building operations at Tanis and Heracleopolis.

Egyptian fortresses in Nubia.

B.C. 2300

Ancient irrigation works in Egypt.

In Åmenemḥāt III. we have the first Egyptian king who seriously set to work to make the fullest possible use of the inundation of the Nile. At the fortresses which his predecessor Usertsen III. had established, he stationed officers to record and report the increase of the Nile, and "runners" must have conveyed the information to the king in Egypt. Åmenemḥāt III. will, however, be best remembered as the builder of **Lake Moeris** in the Fayyûm. The Egyptians called the Fayyûm 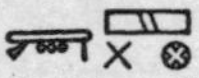 *Ta-she*, "the land of the lake"; the name Fayyûm is the Arabic form of the Coptic word ⲫⲓⲟⲙ "the water," which in turn is taken from 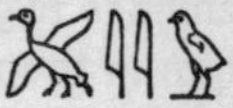  *Pa-iumā*. The Egyptian original of the name Moeris is  *mu-ur*, or  *mer-ur*, "great water." The Birket el-Kurûn to the west of the Fayyûm was originally identified with Lake Moeris, but both it and the famous **Labyrinth** were situated in the eastern part of the district. The Labyrinth was also built by Åmenemḥāt III., and is said by Herodotus (ii. 148) to have contained twelve courts, six facing the north, and six the south, and three thousand rooms: fifteen hundred above ground, and fifteen hundred below. In Egyptian it was called the "temple at the mouth of the Lake" 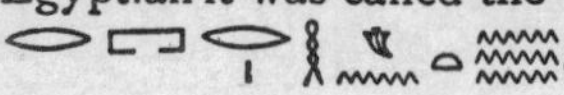, and the stone

The Fayyûm.

Building of the Labyrinth.

for building it seems to have been brought from the Valley of Ḥammāmāt. The copper mines in the mountains of Sinai were diligently worked during this reign.

B.C. 2266

**Ȧmenemḥāt IV.** reigned conjointly with his sister Sebekneferu, and beyond continuing the mining operations of his ancestors he seems to have done nothing. We may see in collecting the results of the rule of the XIIth dynasty over Egypt, that its kings had extended their sway about 250 miles south of the first cataract, and that they had lost nothing of their possessions either in the eastern desert or in the Sinaitic peninsula. Mighty public works like the Labyrinth and Lake Moeris had been successfully carried out, an active trade was carried on with the natives of Punt, and with the country to-day called Syria, and with the districts further east. Agriculture flourished, and the whole land was in a most prosperous condition. And if the living were well cared for, the dead were no less so. The tombs built for high officials and gentlemen attest the care of the sorrowing relatives, while the sculptures and paintings employed to adorn them indicate that the artistic knowledge of the Egyptians had arrived at a very high pitch.

Power of Egypt in the XIIth dynasty.

Beauty of Egyptian tombs of XIIth dynasty.

## DYNASTIES XIII–XVII.

According to Manetho these dynasties were as follows:—

The Hyksos or "Shepherd Kings."

| | | | | | | | |
|---|---|---|---|---|---|---|---|
| Dynasty | XIII, | from Thebes, | 60 | kings | in | 453 | years |
| „ | XIV, | „ Chois, | 76 | „ | „ | 484 | „ |
| „ | XV, | Hyksos, | 6 | „ | „ | 260 | „ |
| „ | XVI, | Hyksos, | 10 | „ | „ | 251 | „ |
| „ | XVII, | from Thebes, | 10 | „ | „ | 10 | „ |

There are no monuments by which these figures can be checked, and there is no other authority for them besides Manetho. The Turin papyrus gives traces of 136 names for the period corresponding to that of the XIIIth and XIVth dynasties. Among the rulers of the XIIIth and XIVth dynasties were many who were not of royal descent. **Semench-ka** is known to us by his statues found at Tanis, and according to Mariette he seems to have been an officer who rebelled and then seated himself on the throne. **Sebek-**

**ḥetep II.** was the son of a private individual, and **Nefer-ḥetep's** parents appear not to have been royal. This latter king built largely at Abydos, and as a worshipper of the local gods he is represented at Konosso and the islands of the first cataract. Of **Sebek-ḥetep III.**, brother of **Sebek-ḥetep II.**, **Sebek-ḥetep IV.**, and **Sebek-ḥetep V.** little is known; of **Sebek-ḥetep VI.** the best memorials are the rock tombs at Asyûṭ. The names of many kings belonging to this period are known from the monuments, but a greater knowledge of the history of that time is necessary for arranging them in chronological order. It seems pretty certain that few of the kings reigned many years, and that the country was divided into a number of little states which were always at war with each other, and against whomsoever was king. Such a condition of things was, of course, highly favourable for a foreign invader, who would naturally be attracted by reports of the wealth of Egypt. The hardy tribes of desert dwellers, Semites and others, who crowded on the eastern and western borders of Egypt, delayed not to take advantage of the distracted and divided state of the country, and making a successful attack on the north-east provinces of the Delta, they pressed in, and having taken possession of Memphis, became masters of Egypt. Their attack would probably be rendered less difficult by the fact that a great many of the inhabitants of the Delta were of Semitic origin, their ancestors having settled there in the XIIth dynasty, and their opposition to their kinsmen would be, in consequence, less stubborn. The sole authority for the history of this invasion is Josephus, who, quoting Manetho, says, "There was a king of ours, whose name was **Timaus.** Under him it came to pass, I know not how, that God was averse to us, and there came, after a surprising manner, men of ignoble birth out of the eastern parts, and had boldness enough to make an expedition into our country, and with ease subdued it by force, yet without our hazarding a battle with them. So when they had gotten those that governed us under their power, they afterwards burnt down our cities, and demolished the temples of the gods, and used all the inhabitants after a most barbarous manner: nay, some they

**Attacks of the Semites upon the Delta.**

**Manetho on the "Hyksos."**

slew, and led their children and their wives into slavery. At length they made one of themselves king, whose name was **Salatis**; he also lived at Memphis, and made both the upper and lower regions pay tribute, and left garrisons in places that were the most proper for them. He chiefly aimed to secure the eastern parts, as foreseeing that the Assyrians, who had there the greatest power, would be desirous of that kingdom and invade them; and as he found in the Saite [Sethroite] Nomos a city very proper for his purpose, and which lay upon the Bubastic channel, but with regard to a certain theologic notion was called **Avaris**, this he rebuilt, and made very strong by the walls he built about it, and by a most numerous garrison of two hundred and forty thousand armed men whom he put into it to keep it. Thither Salatis came in summer time, partly to gather his corn and pay his soldiers their wages, and partly to exercise his armed men, and thereby to terrify foreigners. When this man had reigned thirteen years, after him reigned another whose name was **Beon** for forty-four years; after him reigned another, called **Apachnas**, thirty-six years and seven months: after him **Apophis** reigned sixty-one years, and then **Jonias** fifty years and one month; after all these reigned **Assis** forty-nine years and two months.

**"Hyksos" kings.**

"And these six were the first rulers among them, who were all along making war with the Egyptians, and were very desirous gradually to destroy them to the very roots. This whole nation was styled **Hycsos**, that is, **'Shepherd-kings'**; for the first syllable HYC, according to the sacred dialect, denotes *a king*, as is SOS, *a shepherd*—but this according to the ordinary dialect; and of these is compounded HYCSOS: but some say that these people were Arabians." Now, in another copy it is said, that this word does not denote *kings*, but on the contrary, denotes *Captive Shepherds*, and this on account of the particle HYC; for that HYC, with the aspiration, in the Egyptian tongue again denotes SHEPHERDS, and that expressly also; and this to me seems the more probable opinion, and more agreeable to ancient history. [But Manetho goes on]:—"These people whom we have before named *kings*, and called *shepherds* also, and their descendants,"

**Manetho on the derivation of "Hyksos."**

as he says, "kept possession of Egypt five hundred and eleven years."[1] On the whole it seems that these observations of Manetho are correct. Of Salatis, the first Hyksos king, nothing is known historically, and there are no monuments known which can correctly be asserted to be the work of the kings of the first Hyksos dynasty. The country from which the **Hyksos** came, also, is unknown. Some Egyptologists consider the Hyksos to be Cushites, and some think they are to be identified with the Accadians; others, again, believe them to be Phœnicians or Semites. The features of the statues that have come down to us which are attributed to the Hyksos, have the following characteristics: The eyes are comparatively small, the nose is broad but aquiline, the cheek bones are prominent and the cheeks thick, the mouth is broad, the lips thick, and the chin protrudes slightly. From these facts some have stated decidedly that the Hyksos cannot have been Semites, but it must be proved that the monuments attributed to the Hyksos were really made by them, before this question can be considered to be definitively disposed of. Of the two meanings of the name Hyksos put forth by Josephus, the first being Manetho's explanation, and the second that of Josephus, based on another copy of Manetho's work seen by him, the former seems to be the more correct, and we may perhaps give the Egyptian  *Ḥequ-shaȧsu*, as an equivalent of it. The Shaȧsu are a well known enemy of Egypt, who came from the deserts east and north-east of Egypt, and "Ḥequ-shaȧsu" or "princes of the Shaȧsu" would be a name such as we might expect the Egyptians to bestow upon the invaders, just as they spoke of *Ḥeq Cheta*, "Prince of Cheta."

The "Shepherd Kings."

Hieroglyphic equivalent of 'Hyksos."

The kings belonging to this period, made known to us by the Egyptian monuments, are Ȧpepȧ I., Ȧpepȧ II., and Nubti. Of **Ȧpepȧ I.** very little is known, but of **Ȧpepȧ II.** a number of monuments remain, and among others one which records the submission to him of a number of Ethiopian tribes. **Bar-Hebraeus** relates that there "reigned in Egypt the fourth king of the Shepherds called **Ȧpapus,** fourteen years.

[1] Josephus, *Contra Apion*, i. 14, translated by Whiston, p. 610.

It was this king who dreamed dreams, and who made **Joseph** ruler — according to the writings of Chaldeans — and it seems that these kings were called "Shepherd Kings" because of Joseph's brethren."[1] It is known from a granite stele[2] found at Tanis, a city formerly inhabited by the Ȧpepȧ kings, that the four hundredth year from the reign of **Nubti** fell in the reign of Rameses II. Dr. Birch,[3] Wiedemann[4] and other Egyptologists, compare this period of 400 years with the 430 years of the bondage of Israel in Egypt, and, as the Exodus probably took place during the reign of the immediate successor of Rameses II., we may assume that the statement of Bar-Hebraeus was based on some trustworthy tradition. It has also been pertinently remarked that it would be easier for Joseph to hold high office under the Shepherd kings than under the rule of an ancient hereditary aristocracy. The Shepherd kings worshipped a god called **Sut** or **Sutech**, who was to the Egyptians a veritable abomination. They lived in the cities of Tanis and Avaris, on the east side of the Pelusiac arm of the Nile. They adopted the manners and customs and writing of the Egyptians, and whatever may have been their severity when they first began to rule, they were of great service to the Egyptians. It is doubtful, however, how far south their rule extended. The names of a number of kings whom Wiedemann attributes to this period are to be found in his *Geschichte*, pp. 295–297.

**Joseph in Egypt.**

**Israel in Egypt.**

**Joseph and the "Shepherd Kings."**

The kings of the XVIIth dynasty were of Theban origin, and are famous as those who defeated the Shepherd kings and expelled them. According to Manetho, "under a king whose name was **Alisphragmuthosis,** the shepherds were subdued by him, and were indeed driven out of other parts of Egypt,

**The kings of Thebes expel the Hyksos.**

[1] ܘܐܡܠܟ ܗܘܐ ܒܡܨܪܝܢ ܡܠܟܐ ܗܘ ܕܐܪܥܝܐ ܕܪ̈ܥܘܬܐ ܐܦܦܘܣ
ܦܢ̈ܐ ܐܪܥܝܣܛܪ̈ܐ: ܗܢܐ ܐܝܬܘܗܝ ܕܚܠܡ ܚܠܡ̈ܐ ܘܐܫܠܛܗ ܠܝܘܣܦ
ܐܝܟ ܡܟܬܒܢܘܬܐ ܕܟܠܕ̈ܝܐ: ܘܕܡܟܝܠ ܕܡܛܠ ܐܚ̈ܘܗܝ ܕܝܘܣܦ
ܐܬܩܪܝܘ ܗܠܝܢ ܡܠܟ̈ܐ: ܡܠܟ̈ܐ ܕܪ̈ܥܘܬܐ.

[1] Ed. Bruns, p. 14, at the top; ed. Bedjan, p. 13, at the top.
[2] An English translation is given by Birch in *Records of the Past*, V., p. 33 ff.
[3] *Egypt*, p. 76. [4] *Aeg. Geschichte*, p. 294.

but were shut up in a place that contained ten thousand acres: this place was named Avaris." Manetho says that "the Shepherds built a wall round all this place, which was a large and strong wall, and this in order to keep all their possessions and their prey within a place of strength, but that **Thummosis** the son of **Alisphragmuthosis** made an attempt to take them by force and by siege with 480,000 men to lie round about them; but that, upon his despair of taking the place by that siege, they came to a composition with them, that they should leave Egypt, and go without any harm to be done them, whithersoever they would; and that, after this composition was made, they went away with their whole families and effects, not fewer in number than 240,000, and took their journey from Egypt, through the wilderness, for Syria: but that, as they were in fear of the Assyrians, who had then the dominion over Asia, they built a city in that country which is now called Judea, and that large enough to contain this great number of men, and called it Jerusalem."[1]

Retreat of the "Hyksos."

Of more value than this account of Josephus for the expulsion of the Shepherd kings, is the mutilated papyrus[2] in the British Museum which treats of **Àpepà** and the native Theban king **Tau-āa-qen** or **Seqenen-Rā III.** According to it, Egypt belonged to her foes and had no king, although Seqenen-Rā, who is described as a *ḥeq* or prince, was master of a town in the south. Àpepà received tribute from all parts of the Delta, and part of it he devoted to building temples to his god Set. He wished all Egypt, both south and north, to worship this god, and to pay tribute to himself, and he sent a messenger from Avaris to Thebes requiring Seqenen-Rā to worship Set alone. This king returned answer saying that he could worship no god but Àmen-Rā. Some time after another messenger of Àpepà arrived with threats, which caused Seqenen-Rā much trouble, and he gathered together his generals and councillors to decide upon a plan of action. What the decision was the mutilated state of the papyrus prevents us from knowing, but there is no doubt about the ultimate result of their deliberations. One of the officers of

Seqenen-Rā III.

[1] *Contra Apion.* I. 14, Whiston's translation, p. 611.

[2] For the text see *Select Papyri*, ed. Birch, pl. 2.

**Seqenen-Rā** was called Baba, the son of Re-ȧnt, and he had a son called **Ȧāḥmes** who was born in the city of Eileithyia. This Ȧāḥmes became an officer on board a ship of war called the "North," and in the inscription on the walls of his tomb it is said that he went with the king to besiege the city of Avaris. He was next promoted to a ship called Chā-em-Mennefer, and he took part in the battle fought upon the canal of Pat'etku of Avaris. Here he performed mighty deeds of valour, and he distinctly says, "We took Avaris, and I carried off as captives from thence one man and three women, in all four heads."[1] The war of independence begun by Seqenen-Rā III., was brought to a successful issue by Ȧāḥmes or Amāsis I., and Egypt was delivered. Seqenen-Rā probably lost his life in battle with the enemy, and must in any case have been seriously wounded, judging by the smashed skull and broken bones which his mummy exhibits.

Ȧāḥmes the general.

Egyptians defeat the Hyksos.

## DYNASTY XVIII.

B.C. 1700

**Ȧāḥmes I.**, son of Ka-mes and his wife **Ȧāḥ-ḥetep**, was the first king of the XVIIIth dynasty, and the first native ruler of all Egypt for a period of about five hundred years. Having captured Avaris, Amasis marched into Asia, where he captured the town of Sharhana, the שָׁרוּחֶן of Joshua xix. 6, and made himself master of the land of T'ahi. Returning to Egypt he marched into Nubia and defeated several tribes who had rebelled systematically for many years past. Having made the borders of his country safe from invasion, Amasis began to build at Memphis and Thebes and other places. Thebes, the home of the kings who had expelled the Hyksos, became the first town in Egypt, and Ȧmen-Rā, who hitherto had enjoyed the reputation of a mere local god, became the head of Egyptian deities. **Amenophis I.**, son of Amāsis I., marched into Nubia, and brought it into subjection to him, and in the north of Egypt he defeated a people called the Āāmu-kehak. In the reign of this king the horse is first represented on the monuments.

Egyptian conquests in Asia and Nubia.

1666

[1] *Records of the Past*, VI. p. 8.

B.C. 1633 **Thothmes I.**, like his father Amenophis I., marched into Nubia[1] and defeated the rebel tribes; he made the people slaves and carried off much spoil to Thebes. Soon after his return to Thebes he set out with his army on an expedition to Mesopotamia, passing through the Arabian desert and Palestine by the way, and finally arrived on the banks of the Euphrates and Tigris. This expedition was the last in which the officer Ȧāḥmes took part, and he again distinguished himself by his personal bravery as on former occasions. To commemorate this expedition Thothmes I. set up two stelæ near the Euphrates to mark the limits of Egyptian territory.

**Limits of Egyptian territory in Asia.**

It would seem that no Egyptian king ever possessed permanent hold upon the country of Mesopotamia, 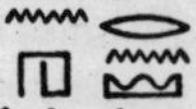 *Nehern* (compare ܒܝܬ ܢܗܪ̈ܝܢ or ܒܝܬ ܢܗܪ̈ܘܬܐ), and it is clear that Egypt only held even a nominal dominion over it as long as each king on his accession marched into the country to terrify the nomad tribes afresh, and to decide what amount of tribute each petty king or head of a tribe should pay to Egypt. The governors of cities in Mesopotamia and Ruthen, or Syria, made treaties among themselves and planned wars against each other, or a common foe, without any reference to the authority of Egypt over them. Each king of Assyria, if he wished to maintain his authority, found it necessary on his accession, or soon after, to undertake a series of military expeditions to punish the peoples who, on the death of a king, always revolted. If this were necessary for a power actually resident in Mesopotamia, how much more necessary would it be for a remote and shadowy power like that of Egypt. Thothmes I. continued the buildings at Thebes, and set up two granite obelisks. Towards the end of his reign he associated his daughter Maāt-ka-Rā, or Ḥāt-shepset, with him in the rule of the kingdom.

1000 **Thothmes II.** married his sister **Ḥātshepset** and became king of Egypt. The tribes of Nubia were again re-conquered, and the Shaȧsu were once more defeated. After a short reign, the greater part of which was occupied in continuing the buildings at Karnak, the king died and Ḥātshepset his sister-

[1] The office of "Prince of Cush" is first mentioned in the reign of Thothmes I.

wife reigned in his stead. This queen was one of the most capable women who ever reigned in Egypt; she is famous as the builder[1] of the beautiful temple at Dêr el-Baḥari, and for the remarkable expedition to **Punt** planned by her and carried out in the ninth year of her reign. Ships were made ready and sailors collected; a multitude of gifts were stowed in each ship, and the necessary guard of soldiers for each told off; a number of Egyptian ladies and high officials prepared to accompany the expedition, and the direction of the whole was put into the hands of the queen's most beloved servant. The inhabitants of Punt received the expedition in a very friendly manner, and having loaded the servants of Ḥātshepset with rich gifts of gold, ivory, balsam, precious stones, plants, trees, ebony, apes, greyhounds, etc., etc., sent them back to Egypt. When these things had been safely brought back to Thebes, Ḥātshepset received them with joy, and dedicated the greater part of them as an offering to her father Åmen-Rā. In the sixteenth year of her reign **Thothmes III.** became associated with her in her rule over Egypt. At Karnak she set up two magnificent granite obelisks in memory of her father Thothmes I. According to an inscription on the base of the one still standing, the granite for it was hewn out of the quarry in Aswân, and was brought to Thebes, and was polished and inscribed and set up within seven months. The height of this obelisk is 105 feet, and if the weight be taken into consideration, and the difficult site, among a crowd of buildings, upon which it was to be set up, it will be easy to judge of the resources and skill of the Egyptian architect and mason of that period. Of the end of Ḥātshepset nothing is known. During her lifetime she wore male attire, and put on the robes and ornaments which belonged to kings only. In the inscriptions she is always described as king "of the North and South, Maāt-ka-Rā, son of the Sun, Ḥātshepset," and the verbs and pronouns relating to her are masculine. After her death her brother Thothmes III. caused as many traces of her rule as possible to disappear.

Ḥātshepset builds Dêr el-Baḥari.

Expedition to Punt.

Obelisks at Karnak.

[1] The statue of her architect Sen-mut is preserved at Berlin.

**Thothmes III.** was one of the mightiest kings who occupied the throne of Egypt, and during his long reign of fifty-three years[1] he carried the arms of Egypt to the uttermost parts of the world as known to the Egyptians, and showed himself to be a wise and great king. While Ḥāt-shepset was amusing herself with her expedition to Punt and the building of her temple at Dêr el-Bahari, the desert tribes on her eastern and western borders were making preparations ready to revolt, and they showed their contempt for the authority of Egypt by refusing to pay tribute. The Mesopotamians, over whom the power of Egypt must ever have been of a shadowy nature, boldly declared themselves free, and their neighbours and kinsmen living in Syria and in the districts to the north and north-east of Damascus followed their example. The conquests made by Amāsis I. and Åmenḥetep I. were all forgotten, and Thothmes III. had practically to reconquer the world. In his twenty-second year he set out from Tanis, and passing through the desert of Sinai he marched to Gaza, a city which had remained faithful to his authority. A few days later he set out for Megiddo, which he found to be occupied by the governor of Kadesh, who had made a league with all the tribes living between the Mediterranean and Nineveh. Sixteen days after Thothmes left Gaza he engaged the enemy, who seeing that the Egyptian king himself was fighting against them, lost all heart, and leaping down from their chariots, decorated with gold and silver, fled to Megiddo, throwing away their arms as they went. As the gates of this town had been shut by those inside, the fugitives had to be pulled up over the walls. The number of the enemy slain by the Egyptians was enormous, and Megiddo was taken with little difficulty. The chiefs of the allied peoples seeing that their league was destroyed, and that Megiddo was in the hands of the enemy, immediately brought offerings of gold, precious stones, horses, corn, oxen, etc., etc., and submitted to Thothmes. The news of the defeat of the league reached the remote parts of Mesopotamia, and their governors, in due time, also sent gifts of

**Conquest of Western Asia by Thothmes III.**

**Fall of Megiddo.**

[1] This number includes the years which he reigned conjointly with his sister; he reigned alone thirty-one years.

propitiation to the king. The names of the places conquered by Thothmes were inscribed by his orders on some of the pylons at Karnak; of the 360 places there mentioned, comparatively few can be identified with Biblical sites with any certainty. For the next few years the Retennu or Syrians and the Babylonians brought their appointed tribute regularly, and to make the relations between himself and the former nation of an amicable character, Thothmes married a princess of their country. In the twenty-ninth and thirtieth years of his reign he marched again to Syria and captured Tunep, Aradus, Carchemish and Kadesh on the Orontes. The remaining years of his life he employed in making expeditions against the Retennu and the Mesopotamians, into whose country he marched as far as Nī. The tribes of Ethiopia and Sinai sent him valuable gifts, which are duly enumerated in the inscriptions containing the annals of this king. A good idea of the different objects of the tribute sent from the various countries may be obtained from the paintings on the tomb of Rech-mȧ-Rā at Thebes, where we see depicted horses and chariots, collars of gold, vases weighing 2,821 pounds of gold, tables of cedar, plants, ivory, ebony, corn, cattle, copper, lapis-lazuli, silver, iron, wine, etc., etc. On the south the Egyptian empire reached to the southern confines of Nubia, on the north-east to Lake Van, on the east to the Tigris, and on the west to the great desert on the left bank of the Nile. Notwithstanding the warlike activity of Thothmes III., he was able to carry on great buildings at Heliopolis, Memphis, Thebes, Elephantine and nearly every town in Nubia. Four of the obelisks set up by Thothmes have come down to us: one is now near the Lateran at Rome, one at Constantinople, one in London, and one in New York.

**Defeat of the Syrian league.**

**Ȧmen-ḥetep II.** had been associated with Thothmes III. in the rule of the kingdom, and immediately he began to reign alone he found himself plunged in wars with the tributary peoples, who on the death of Thothmes III. declared themselves free. He marched into Mesopotamia and captured Nī and Akati; he made war on the Shaȧsu and the Nubians, and defeated both peoples. B.C. 1566

**Conquest of Western Asia.**

**Thothmes IV.** maintained the authority of Egypt from 1533

Mesopotamia to the borders of Nubia, but he is better known as the repairer of the Sphinx at Gîzeh. In the first year of his reign he removed the sand which had covered up the monument, in consequence of an after-dinner sleep in which Ḥarmachis appeared to him and promised to bestow upon him the crown of Egypt if he would dig his image, *i.e.*, the Sphinx, out of the sand. Thothmes set up between the paws of the Sphinx a tablet about fourteen feet high, in which he inscribed an account of this vision and a statement of the works which he carried out at Heliopolis and Memphis.

**The Sphinx repaired.**

**B.C. 1500**

In **Åmen-ḥetep III.**, or Amenophis, the **Memnon** of the Greeks, the successor of Thothmes IV., Egypt gained a king having some of the ability and energy of Thothmes III. In the fifth year of his reign he marched into Nubia to quell a mighty rebellion which had broken out against the Egyptian rule among a number of confederate tribes. He also held the Mesopotamians in subjection, for we learn from large scarabs inscribed during his reign that his empire extended from Neherna, or Mesopotamia, to Karei, or the land south of Nubia. From these same scarabs we learn that Amenophis was a "mighty hunter," and that during the first ten years of his reign he slew 102 lions with his own hand. He built the oldest part of the Serapeum at Ṣaḳḳârah, a temple to Åmen-Rā at Karnak, a larger temple to the same god at Luxor, with an avenue of Sphinxes leading to it, and the temple of Mut to the south of Karnak. On the western bank of the river he built a large temple, the dedication of which was described on a stele found behind the Colossi, which also were set up by this king. These wonderful statues were about 60 feet high, and from that on the north, called the Colossus of Memnon, a sound was said to issue each morning when the sun rose. The upper part of it was thrown down by an earthquake, it is said, about B.C. 27; the damage was partially repaired during the reign of Septimius Severus, about A.D. 160 who restored the head and shoulders of the figure by adding to it five layers of stone; but after that Memnon's Colossus spake no more. At El-Kab, Aswân, and Soleb Amenophis III. also built temples. Four important events in the life and reign of this king are recorded by large steatite scarabs. The

**Conquest of Nubia and Western Asia.**

**Serapeum at Ṣaḳḳârah.**

**The Colossi.**

The Colossi set up in honour of Amenophis III. Thebes.

Historical scarabs of Amenophis III.

first records his lion hunts; the second the coming of Thi, the daughter of an Asiatic father, to Egypt, accompanied by 317 of her women; the third the marriage of Amenophis and Thi, and the fourth the building of a large lake 3,600 cubits long by 600 cubits wide for his queen near the town of T'ārucha, which the king opened on the 16th of Choiak in the eleventh year of his reign, by sailing across it in his barge called Åten-neferu. The tablets inscribed in cuneiform recently found at

The Tell el-Amarna tablets.

Tell el-Amarna prove that Amenophis III. married a sister and daughter of Kallimma-Sin, king of Karaduniyash, a country probably lying to the north-east of Syria; Gilukhîpa the sister of Tushratta, king of Mitani, and Sâtumkhîpa

Marriage with Thi.

daughter of Tushratta; and Thi the daughter of parents who were not royal. The country of Mitani also lay to the north-east of Syria, and we know that like Tiglath-Pileser I., king of Assyria, about B.C. 1120, Amenophis III. went thither frequently to hunt lions.[1] The kings and governors of places as remote as Babylon promptly claimed the friendship of their new kinsman, and their letters expressing their willingness to make alliances offensive and defensive, are some of the most interesting objects of the "find" at Tell el-Amarna.

B.C. 1466

Of **Åmen-ḥetep IV.**, or **Chu-en-âten,** the son of Åmen-ḥetep III. and the Mesopotamian lady Thi, very little is known; he built a temple at Heliopolis, another at Memphis, one at Thebes, and some in Nubia. He is famous, however,

Heresy of the disk worshippers.

as the leader of the heresy of the "disk worshippers," that is to say of those people who worshipped the disk of the sun, Åten 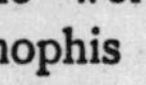, in preference to Åmen-Rā, the national god of Egypt. He showed how much he detested the god Åmen, by setting aside his name Åmen-ḥetep and adopting that of Chu-en-âten, "the brilliance of the disk." The worship of the disk was of some antiquity, and seems to have been a monotheistic worship of Rā which originated in Heliopolis. Amenophis III. seems to have encouraged this form of religion somewhat, and it is certain that he named his barge Åten-neferu, "the most beautiful disk." The native Egyptian

[1] See *The Tell el-Amarna tablets in the British Museum*, by Bezold and Budge, p. xviii.

priesthood disliked the foreign queen, and the sight of her son with his protruding chin, thick lips, and other characteristics of a foreign race, found no favour in their eyes; that such a man should openly despise the worship of Åmen-Rā was a thing intolerable to them. In answer to their angry words and acts, the king ordered the name of Åmen-Rā to be chiselled out of all the monuments, even from his father's name. Rebellion then broke out, and Chu-en-åten left Thebes and founded a new city for himself at a place between Memphis and Thebes, now called Tell el-Amarna. After a few years the queen Thi came to live there, and there Chu-en-åten passed the rest of his life with his wife and seven daughters. In the twelfth year of his reign he celebrated his victories over the Syrians and Ethiopians, but it is doubtful if they were of any importance.

**Amenophis IV. quarrels with the priests.**

**Founding of city at Tell el-Amarna.**

After the death of Amenophis IV. there is some confusion in Egyptian history; the immediate successors of the "heretic king" were **Se-āa-ka-Rā, Tut-ānch-Åmen, Åi,** of whom but little is known. The last king of the XVIIIth dynasty was **Ḥeru-em-ḥeb,** the Horus of Manetho, who seems to have been a native of Ḥet-suten, the Alabastronpolis of the Greeks, or **Tell el-Amarna.** He made an expedition into Nubia and the lands to the south of that country, and he carried on buildings at various places, and restored temples at Heliopolis, Memphis, Thebes and elsewhere.

**The "Heretic" kings.**

## THE NINETEENTH DYNASTY.

**B.C. 1400**

Of the events which led to **Rameses I.** becoming sole king of Egypt nothing whatever is known. Some suppose that he was connected with Horus, the last king of the XVIIIth dynasty, but there are no proofs which can be brought forward in support of this theory. He seems to have carried on some small war with the people of Nubia, and to have been concerned in a treaty with the Cheta; he also built a little at Thebes. He is famous, however, as the father of Seti I., and grandfather of Rameses II.; the former was probably associated with him in the rule of the kingdom, but how long it is not possible to say.

**War with Cheta.**

While Amenophis IV. was quarrelling with the priests of

**Seti I. in battle. From a bas-relief at Thebes.**

Åmen about the worship of the disk, and during the rule of his feeble successors, the peoples of Nubia and the Shaåsu and the nations of Syria and Mesopotamia became more and more independent, and as a result ceased to fear the arms of Egypt, and consequently declined to pay the tribute imposed upon them by the mighty Thothmes III. and Amenophis III. Under the rule of Rameses I. the Egyptians were forced to sign a treaty which fixed the limits of their country and those of the Cheta; hence when **Seti I.** ascended the throne he found it necessary to make war against nearly every nation that had formerly been subject to the Egyptians. From the reliefs sculptured on the walls of the temple of Åmen-Rā at Karnak we see that he attacked the people who lived north of Palestine, the Retennu or Syrians, the Shaåsu, the Cheta, and in returning to Egypt passed through the land of Limanen. At the city of Chetam, on the frontier of Egypt, he was received by the priests and nobles of Egypt, who said to him: "Thou hast returned from the lands which thou hast conquered, and thou hast triumphed over thy enemies. May thy life be as long as that of the sun in heaven! Thou hast washed thy heart on the barbarians, Rā has defined thy boundaries." Seti then sailed up to Thebes, where he presented his captives and booty to the gods in the temples there. From the lists of vanquished peoples inscribed by Seti it is found that his rule extended over Mesopotamia, Punt or Somali land, Nubia, and the lands on the west bank of the Nile. Cities like Kadesh on the Orontes, Tyre, Reseph, Migdol, etc., he not only conquered, but also built fortresses in them. During the reign of Seti the Cheta who, without, in my opinion, the slightest evidence for the theory, have been identified with the Hittites of the Bible, reappear in history. Seti set up an obelisk at Ḳanṭarah, "the bridge" uniting Asia and Africa, he built at Heliopolis, Memphis and Abydos, and at Karnak he began several buildings, some of which were finished by Rameses II. His name is often found in Nubia on rocks and stelæ, and he worked the gold mines there, and sank wells in the rock to obtain water for his workmen. Seti associated his son Rameses II. with him in the rule of the kingdom when he was but twelve years old. According to the

**B.C. 1366**

**Conquests in Western Asia.**

monuments Seti reigned about twenty-seven years. The name Seti is connected with the god Set, who though at one time worshipped by the Egyptians, was subsequently considered to be the father of all evil; in several places it is seen that his name has been carefully chiselled out.

B.C. 1333 Sesostris.

**Rameses II.**, the Sesostris of the Greeks, was perhaps the greatest king that ever ruled over Egypt. He was a man of commanding stature, of great physical strength and personal bravery, a great builder and a liberal patron of the science and art of his days. Around his name has gathered a multitude of legends, and the exploits of other warriors and heroes who reigned hundreds of years after him have been attributed to him. Before he came to the throne he led an expedition into Nubia and defeated the peoples there; and he brought back to Egypt much spoil, consisting of lions, gazelles, panthers, ebony, ivory, gold, etc., etc. In the fifth year of his reign he set out on a campaign against the **Cheta,** which was the most important event in his life; his victory over this foe was considered so great a triumph that an account of it illustrated by sculptures was inscribed upon the temples of Thebes, Kalâbshî and Abu Simbel, and a poetic description of the battle with a vivid outline of the king's own prowess was written down by **Pen-ta-urt,** a temple scribe. The Cheta were a confederation of peoples, nomad and stationary, who first appear in the time of Thothmes III., to whom they paid tribute. In the time of Rameses I. they made a treaty of friendship with the Egyptians, but in the time of Seti I. they fought with them. The kings of the Cheta at this period were **Sapalel** and his son **Maru-sar;** the latter had two sons **Māutenure** and **Cheta-sar.** Māutenure was king of the Cheta when Rameses II. marched against them in his fifth year, and Cheta-sar was king when the Cheta and the Egyptians made a new treaty in the twenty-first year of the reign of Rameses, at which time they seem to have reached the summit of their power. According to an inscription which appears to be the official statement concerning this memorable battle, Rameses II. was in the fifth year of his reign in the land of T'ah, not far from Kadesh on the Orontes. The outposts kept a sharp look-out,

Pentaurt's poem on the defeat of the Cheta.

The Cheta kings.

Rameses II., when a child.

and when the army came to the south of the town of Shabtûn, two of the spies of the Shasu came into the camp and pretended that they had been sent by the chiefs of their tribe to inform Rameses II. that they had forsaken the chief of the Cheta, and that they wished to make an alliance with his majesty and become his vassals. They then went on to say that the chief of the Cheta was in the land of Chirebu to the north of Tunep some distance off, and that he was afraid to come near the Egyptian king. These two men were giving false information, and they had actually been sent by the Cheta chief to find out where Rameses and his army were; the Cheta chief and his army were at that moment drawn up in battle array behind Kadesh. Shortly after these men had been dismissed, an Egyptian scout came into the king's presence bringing with him two spies from the army of the chief of the Cheta; on being questioned, they informed Rameses that the chief of the Cheta was encamped behind Kadesh, and that he had succeeded in gathering together a multitude of soldiers and chariots from the countries round about. Rameses summoned his officers to his presence, and informed them of the news which he had just heard; they listened with surprise, and insisted that the newly received information was untrue. Rameses seriously blamed the chiefs of the intelligence department for their neglect of duty, and they admitted their fault. Orders were straightway issued for the Egyptian army to march upon Kadesh, and as they were crossing an arm of the river near that city the hostile forces fell in with each other. When Rameses saw this, he "growled at them like his father Menthu, lord of Thebes," and having hastily put on his full armour, he mounted his chariot and drove into the battle. His onset was so sudden and rapid that before he knew where he was he found himself surrounded by the enemy, and completely isolated from his own troops. He called upon his father Åmen-Rā to help him, and then addressed himself to the slaughter of all those that came in his way, and his prowess was so great that the enemy fell in heaps, one over the other, into the waters of the Orontes. He was quite alone, and not one of his soldiers or horsemen came near him to help him.

Defeat of the Cheta.

Rameses II. the warrior.

Capture of Kadesh.

It was only with great difficulty he succeeded in cutting his way through the ranks of the enemy. At the end of the inscription he says, "Everything that my majesty has stated, that did I in the presence of my soldiers and horsemen." In the poem of Pen-ta-urt the king is said to have been surrounded by 2,500 chariots. The defeat of the chief of the Cheta and his allies was crushing, and Rameses was able to demand and obtain much tribute.

In the eighth year of his reign he led an expedition against towns in southern Syria, and Ascalon among others fell into his hands, and within a few years Mesopotamians, Syrians, dwellers on the coast, Libyans, the Shaȧsu and Ethiopians all submitted to him. In the twenty-first year of his reign he made a treaty with Māutenure, chief of the Cheta at Tanis, the favourite dwelling-place of Rameses. This treaty sets out at full length the relations which had existed between the two nations for some time before, and each party solemnly promises not to make war on the other, and to assist the other in war if required; to cement the alliance Rameses married a daughter of the chief of the Cheta called Maa-ur-neferu-Rā.

**Egyptian treaty with the Cheta.**

Notwithstanding his activity in war, Rameses II. found time to make himself famous as one of the greatest builders that ever sat on the throne of Egypt, and his name is found on stelæ, obelisks, temples, etc., etc., from Beyrût in Syria to remote Napata. He built a temple of granite at Tanis, a town which seems to have been founded four hundred years before his time by Nubti, one of the so-called Hyksos kings. Near this city ran the wall from Pelusium to Heliopolis, which Rameses is supposed to have built to keep out the Asiatics. At Heliopolis he set up obelisks, none of which has come down to our time; at Memphis he added largely to the temple of Ptaḥ; and at Abydos he completed the temple begun by his father Seti I. At Thebes he finished the buildings begun by his father and grandfather; he repaired the temples of Thothmes III. and Amenophis III., adding walls and doors, and occasionally usurping monuments of the kings who went before him; he set up statues of himself and two splendid obelisks before a building which he

**Rameses II. the builder.**

made adjoining the temple of Amenophis III.; on the western side of Thebes he finished the temple originally dedicated to Rameses I., and consecrated it to his father Seti I.; he restored the temple of Ḥātshepset at Dêr el-Baḥari; he built a temple at Medînet Habû, and at Thebes, his greatest work of all, the Ramesseum. The statues of himself which he placed in this last place are among the largest and finest known. At Bêt el-Walî at Kalâbshî in Nubia he built a beautiful little rock temple, on the walls of the court of which are some well executed sculptures representing the bringing of tribute to him by Asiatics and Ethiopians. At Abu Simbel, the classical Aboccis, he hewed out of the solid rock a large temple to Rā Harmachis to commemorate his victory over the Cheta; it is the largest and finest Egyptian monument in Nubia, and for simple grandeur and majesty is second to none in all Egypt. It is hewn out of the rock to a depth of 185 feet, and the surface of the rock, which originally sloped down to the river, was cut away for a space of about 90 feet to form the front of the temple, which is ornamented by four colossal statues of Rameses II., 66 feet high, seated on thrones, hewn out of the living rock. The large hall inside contains eight columns with large figures of Osiris about 17 feet high upon them. Among other matters the inscriptions give a list of the children of Rameses. The gold mines in the land of Akita, now Gebel Alaki, which were worked by Seti I., appear not to have been very profitable, by reason of the scarcity of water. The well which he sank to the depth of 120 cubits supplied little or no water, and the works in the mines were stopped. In the third year of his reign Rameses sent men to bore another well, and they found abundant water at the depth of twelve cubits.

Rock temple at Abu Simbel.

Rameses II. is generally thought to have been the oppressor of the Jews in Egypt, and it was probably for him that they built the treasure-cities of Pithom and Raamses.

Oppression of the Jews.

Rameses reigned sixty-seven years, and at his death he left Egypt one of the largest and most powerful kingdoms upon earth; under him this country reached its highest point of prosperity and glory. The tribute brought in by conquered nations enriched the country, the hosts of foreign workmen employed by the king produced articles of luxury and beauty, art and literature flourished unfettered, and the tombs and sepulchres of the dead were scarcely less splendid than the palaces of the king or the houses of his nobles. After the death of Rameses Egypt declined rapidly, chiefly through the inertness and want of national spirit possessed by the hosts of foreigners who lived there, and the country became a mart and a home of traders rather than of warriors.

B.C. 1300

**Mer-en-Ptaḥ**, the thirteenth son of Rameses II., had been associated with his father in the rule of the kingdom before he ascended the throne. The chief event in his reign was an expedition against the Lebu, Kehak, Māshuash, Akauasha, Tursha, Leku, Sharetana and Shekelasha in the fifth year of his reign. The Lebu, thought by some to be the Libyans, under Māroi, the son of Ṭiṭi, had advanced to the city of Pa-Bairo, and were preparing to march upon Heliopolis and Memphis; Māroi himself had reached Pa-àru-shep, when the god Ptaḥ appeared to Mer-en-Ptaḥ in a dream and promised him victory. On the third day of Epiphi the hostile forces joined in battle. Māroi fled, about thirteen thousand of his people were slain, and all his and their property fell into the hands of the Egyptians. The Akauasha have by some been identified with the Achaeans, the Sharetana with the Sardinians, the Shekelasha with the Sicilians, the Lebu with the Libyans, the Tursha with the Etruscans, the Leku with the Lycians, etc., etc. These identifications, based on a suggestion made by de Rougé, cannot be accepted, lacking as they do any historical evidence in support of them. It is quite certain, however, that the tribes against which Mer-en-Ptaḥ fought were comparatively close neighbours of Egypt. The Exodus is thought by some to have taken place during the reign of this king.

Defeat of allied tribes.

The Exodus.

Of Mer-en-Ptaḥ's successor, **Seti II.**, but little is known; his reign was very short, and was not distinguished by any remarkable event. The rule of the XIXth dynasty was brought to an end by the reigns of **Àmen-mes** and **Se-Ptaḥ.**

## THE TWENTIETH DYNASTY.

B.C. 1200

For some years after the death of Mer-en-Ptaḥ Egypt was in a state of anarchy, "each man did as he pleased, and there was no one who had authority over his fellows. The Land of Egypt was under chiefs of nomes and each fought against the other." After a time "a Syrian called Årsu,"  , arose among them and succeeded in diverting the tribute to himself and finally in making himself master of the land. Rest and peace were not restored to Egypt, however, until the gods set their son Set-Necht upon the throne, who very shortly after associated his son **Rameses III.** with him in the rule of the kingdom. On the death of Set-Necht Rameses III. reigned alone, and having established the worship of the gods in the temples, and restored the customary offerings, in the eighth year he set out with his troops for the north-eastern borders of his country to do battle against the allied forces of the Māshuash, Leku, Shekelasha and other Asiatic peoples, who had come to the land of the Amorites partly by land and partly by sea; the Egyptians were victorious and inflicted a crushing defeat on the enemy. A year or two after Rameses attacked the Māshuasha, who appear to have settled in the western part of the Delta and further south, and they were defeated with great slaughter. About this time he seems to have carried on some small wars in Nubia. In addition to his wars. he fitted out and despatched an expedition to Punt, which returned safely, bringing many marvellous things and treasures; he worked the turquoise mines in the Sinaitic Peninsula, and the copper mines in the land of Ątaka. He also opened up for trade the old road between Kosseir on the Red Sea and Coptos on the Nile. With the spoil which Rameses obtained from his successful wars, and the wealth which he gained from his mines and trading enterprises, he lavishly endowed the temples of Heliopolis, Memphis and Thebes. At Tell el-Yahûdîyeh he built a granite and limestone temple, at Heliopolis he restored temples, at Memphis he restored the temple of Ptaḥ, he added to the temple of Thothmes III. at Medînet Habû, and at the

**Egyptians defeat the allied nations.**

**Expedition to Punt, and opening of old trade routes.**

same place he built what has been generally called his "palace," and a magnificent temple to Åmen-Rā. The "palace" consisted of two square towers, the four sides of which were symmetrically inclined to a common centre. The interior chambers were ornamented with sculptures, on which were depicted scenes in the domestic (?) life of the king. The temple at Medînet Habû is of remarkable interest, and on the walls are sculptured battle scenes on land and sea, in which Rameses is victorious over his enemies. Near Karnak he built a temple to Ptaḥ, and he added buildings to the temple of Åmen-Rā there; he began to build the temple of Chonsu, and it would seem that he repaired many of the temples and shrines set up both at Karnak and Luxor. The most important document for the history of the reign of this king is the famous Harris Papyrus No. 1, now preserved in the British Museum. It was found in a box, in a rough-hewn rock chamber in the earth, near Medînet Habû. This papyrus enumerates the gifts which he made to the gods of Thebes, Heliopolis and Memphis, and concludes with a statement of the principal events of his reign. This wonderful papyrus, which measures 135 feet by 17 inches, was published in facsimile by the Trustees of the British Museum, with an introduction and translation by Dr. Birch.

**Medînet Habû and Karnak.**

**Harris Papyrus.**

**B.C. 1166–1133**

Of **Rameses IV.** little is known beyond the fact that he carried on the works in the mines in the valley of Ḥammâmât with great diligence; he was succeeded by **Rameses V.**, of whom also very little is known. Of **Rameses VI.**, the most important remains are his tomb in Bibân el-Mulûk; on the walls the risings of various stars are given and much astronomical information. This tomb was originally made for Rameses V. **Rameses VII.** and **Rameses VIII.** were the next rulers of Egypt; the most important event in the reign of **Rameses IX.** was the attempt to break into and rob the royal tombs at Thebes in his sixteenth year. The robbers were caught and prosecuted by the government, and after an official examination of the tombs had been made by the chief officers of the city, to find out exactly what damage had been done, the band of thieves were properly punished. The robbery had gone on for some years, and

**Astronomical tables at Thebes.**

**Robbery of royal tombs.**

appears to have been continued in the nineteenth year of the reign of Rameses IX. The reigns of **Rameses X.** and **Rameses XI.** are of no interest. Of the reign of their successor **Rameses XII.** an interesting though fabulous story is recorded. A stele found near the temple of Chonsu at Karnak states that the king was paying his usual visit to Mesopotamia to receive the tribute from the tribes subject to him. Each chief brought his offering of gold, etc., but the chief of Bechten brought his eldest daughter, who was a most beautiful girl, and gave her to the king. She found favour in his sight, and he married her, and gave her the official title of "royal spouse." Some time after they had returned to Egypt, a messenger came to the king from Bechten saying that a young sister of his wife Rā-Neferu, called Bentresh, was grievously ill, and entreated him to send a physician to heal her. A very learned scribe called Teḥuti-em-ḥeb was despatched, but when he arrived in Bechten he found that the illness of Bentresh was caused by an evil spirit, and he was unable to cure her. Another messenger was sent to Egypt and he asked that the god Chonsu himself might be sent to cure Bentresh, and the king having asked the god to consent to this proposition, prepared a suitable shrine and sent the god to Bechten, where he arrived after a journey of one year and five months. As soon as the god was brought into the sick maiden's chamber, he addressed the demon who possessed her and drove him out from her. The demon acknowledged the authority of the god, and promised to depart to his own place if a great feast was prepared in his honour; the chief of Bechten gladly made a feast, and the demon departed. The god Chonsu was detained in Bechten three years and nine months, and at the end of that time he returned to Egypt, his priests bringing rich gifts with them. Although it is proved now that this narrative is a romance and not history, it is nevertheless of great antiquity, and is most important as showing the belief in demoniacal possession at that remote period. The country of Bechten is unknown, but if, as is stated, seventeen months were spent in reaching it, its situation must have been very far from Egypt. With the reign of **Rameses XIII.**, the XXth dynasty comes to an end.

Princess of Bechten.

## THE TWENTY-FIRST DYNASTY.

"Priest-kings" rule over Egypt.

With the death of Rameses XIII. a new period of disorder came over the government of Egypt, and for nearly one hundred years there seems to have been no legal king seated on the throne. The chief priest of Âmen called **Ḥer-Ḥeru-se-Âmen** had little by little gathered the power of a king into his own hand, and finally he declared himself "King of Upper and Lower Egypt," and thus became the first of the so-called "priest-kings" of the XXIst dynasty. His dwelling-place was Thebes, and the buildings which he carried out there, instead of being inscribed with the records of glorious victories over the foes of Egypt, were decorated with inscriptions of a purely religious character. The tribes that were subject to Egypt, and were at that moment unprepared for war, paid their tribute to him as the successor of the Pharaohs, but it was not to be expected that a ruler who devoted more time to the service of Âmen than to war, could maintain his sovereignty over restless and warlike peoples like the Cheta, or Retennu, of whom he calls himself the conqueror. During his reign the mummies and coffins and funereal furniture of some of the kings of the XVIIth, XVIIIth and XIXth dynasties were brought from their tombs and deposited together in one place, now called in Arabic Dêr el-baḥari, where they were discovered by an Arab in 1871. For the account of the recovery of these by Brugsch-Bey and Maspero, see Maspero, *Les Momies Royales de Déir el Bahari*, fasc. 1, tom. IV., of the *Mémoires* of the French Archæological Mission at Cairo.

B.C. 1100–1000

Dêr el-Baḥari Mummies.

Ḥer-Ḥeru was succeeded by his grandson, **Pi-net'em I.**, the son of Pi-ānchi, the high-priest of Âmen, the husband of Maāt ka-Ra, a princess who belonged to the old line of kings; **Pi-net'em II.** married the royal daughter and royal wife Ḥet-Ḥert-ḥent-taui, but appears never to have been actually king. Wiedemann doubts the existence of this king.[1] Of **Paseb-chā-nut, Men-cheper-Rā** and his son **Pinetem III.** but little is known; they were succeeded by **Paseb-chā-nut II.**, during whose reign Solomon captured

[1] *Aeg. Geschichte*, p. 536.

Solomon becomes king of Palestine.

the town of Gezer, and having conquered the Canaanites there, became king of Palestine. It is thought by some that his Egyptian wife was the daughter of one of the kings of the XXIst dynasty. The history of this period is very uncertain, and definite conclusions respecting it cannot be arrived at without fuller information.

## THE TWENTY-SECOND DYNASTY.

Babylonian origin of kings of XXIInd dynasty.

Various theories have been propounded concerning the origin of the kings of this dynasty; the father of its first king Shashanq I. was called **Nemart,** a name which has been identified with that of Nimrod. From the fact that the names Usarken, Thekeleth, common to several of its kings, resemble the Assyrian and Babylonian names *Sarginu*, "Sargon," and *Tukulti*, "Tiglath," it has been generally assumed that they sprang either from a purely Semitic race in Mesopotamia itself, or from Semites who had been settled in the Delta for a considerable time. That they were of foreign extraction is certain, because the determinative placed at the end of their names is that of a man from a foreign country ;[1] and the people called Mā, of whom Nemart styles himself the prince, have been proved by De Rougé to be simply the Māshuasha.

B.C. 966–800

Conquest of Palestine and capture of Jerusalem.

**Shashanq I.**, the Shishak (שִׁישַׁק) of the Bible, the protector of Jeroboam, who lifted up his hand against Solomon (1 Kings xi. 26), led an expedition against Rehoboam, king of Judah, and took away from Jerusalem "the treasures of the house of the Lord, and the treasures of the king's house, he even took away all: and he took away all the shields of gold which Solomon had made." (1 Kings xiv. 25, 26.) The list of the cities and districts, about 138 in number, captured by Shashanq during this war is inscribed upon the south wall of the temple of Åmen-Rā at Karnak. The wife of Shashanq was called Kerāmā, and their son Åauput. Of the acts of **Usarken** (Sargon) **I., Thekeleth** (Tiglath) **I., Usarken II.**, and **Shashanq II.** but little is known, and the

[1] De Rougé, *Mélanges d'Archéologie*, t. 1, p. 87.

reigns of these kings were uneventful. During the reign of **Thekeleth II.** a rebellion broke out among the peoples to the south and north of Egypt, and it is stated that on the 25th of Mesori, in the fifteenth year of his reign, an eclipse of the moon took place. **Shashanq III.** made great gifts to the temple of Åmen-Rā at Thebes. He reigned fifty-two years; and an Apis bull which had been born in his twenty-eighth year, died in the second year of the reign of his successor **Pamȧi.** During the reign of **Shashanq IV.** three Apis bulls died, the last in the thirty-seventh year of his reign.

**Death of Apis bulls.**

## THE TWENTY-THIRD DYNASTY.

**B.C. 766**

Of the history of Peṭā-Bast, its first king, nothing is known from Egyptian monuments, and for the events of the reign of his successor, **Usarken III.**, we have to rely upon the information supplied by a stele recording the invasion and conquest of Egypt by Piānchi, king of Ethiopia. When the kings of Egypt sent to that country in the VIth dynasty, no opposition was offered by the natives to their felling trees, but in the XIIth dynasty the Egyptians found it necessary to guard against them at the first cataract by lightly-armed, swift soldiers. From the XIIth to the XXth dynasty Egypt maintained her authority over Ethiopia, and her kings built magnificent temples there, and ruled the country by a staff of officers under the direction of the "Prince of Cush." In the unsettled times which followed the death of Rameses II., the Ethiopians saw that the power of Egypt to maintain her supremacy abroad was becoming less and less. For many years they paid their customary tribute to his feeble successors, but at the same time they looked forward to a time when they could cast off the yoke of Egypt. They had adopted Egyptian civilization, the hieroglyphic form of writing, and the language and religion of Egypt; they seem to have wished to make a second Egypt in Ethiopia. When during the reigns of the kings of the XXIst and XXIInd dynasties they saw that the power of Egypt continued to decrease, they boldly resolved to found a kingdom of their own, and they chose Napata, now called Gebel Barkal, as the site of their capital. Brugsch thinks (*Egypt under the*

**Conquest of Egypt by Piānchi the Ethiopian.**

**Defection of Ethiopians.**

**Ethiopians found a kingdom.**

*Pharaohs*, 2nd ed., 1881, Vol. II., p. 235) that the founder of the kingdom was one of the descendants of Ḥer-Ḥeru, the priest-king of the XXIst dynasty, and he points out that many of them bore the name of Piānchi. Early in the eighth century before Christ Pi-ānchi was king of Napata, and his rule probably extended at least as far north as Thebes. In the twenty-first year of his reign news was brought to him that Tafnecht, prince of Saïs and Memphis, had revolted, that a league formed chiefly of governors of towns had placed him at its head, and that all Lower Egypt was in his hands.

**Piānchi's expedition to Egypt.**

Piānchi at once sent troops against the rebels, and on their way down the Nile they met a number of soldiers belonging to the army of Tafnecht, and these they defeated. The Ethiopian troops seem not to have been unvaryingly successful, for it was necessary for Piānchi himself to come to Thebes; thence he marched to Hermopolis, which surrendered after a three days' siege. Nimrod, who had defended it, delivered up to Piānchi his wives, palace, horses and everything he had. Piānchi set out once more for the north, and every city opened its gates to him until he reached Memphis. Here he met with strong opposition, for Tafnecht had brought several thousands of soldiers into the city, and every part of the wall was guarded by them. Piānchi,

**Capture of Thebes, Memphis and Saïs.**

however, brought his boats up to the very walls of the city, and after a vigorous assault captured it; there was a mighty slaughter, and it would seem that some thousands of men were slain. The rebel princes came in one by one, and tendered their submission to the Ethiopian, and thus Piānchi became master of Egypt. At Memphis, Heliopolis and Thebes he offered sacrifices to the great gods of Egypt, and no acts of wanton destruction of cities or buildings are recorded of him.

**B.C. 733**

## THE TWENTY-FOURTH DYNASTY.

**Bocchoris burnt alive.**

This dynasty is represented by a single king called **Bak-en-ren-f** (Bocchoris), who reigned but a very few years; many legends concerning him are extant in classical writers, but the Egyptian monuments scarcely mention him. According to Manetho he was burnt alive by Sabaco the first king of the XXVth dynasty.

## THE TWENTY-FIFTH DYNASTY.

B.C. 700

The kings of this dynasty were Ethiopians, who following up the success of Piānchi, made themselves masters of all Egypt. The first king, **Shabaka**, is known from the Egyptian inscriptions to have beautified the temple of Karnak, and his name is found on many buildings there to which he made additions or repairs. He is best known as being the king of Egypt to whom Hoshea (2 Kings xvii. 4), having ceased to send his customary tribute to the king of Assyria, went for help. Some think that Shabaka (Hebrew סוֹא, which Schrader would point סֶוֶא) was not king of all Egypt, because Sargon, king of Assyria (B.C. 721–705) styles him simply *shiltauna*, "prince."[1] Sabaco seems to have been known in Nineveh, for among the ruins of the palaces at Kouyunjik were found two impressions from his seal or scarab, in which he appears wearing the crown of Lower Egypt 𓋔; in his right hand he holds a stick or club, and he is in the act of slaughtering enemies. His cartouche stands above, together with his titles and the legend recording the speech of some god, "I give to thee all foreign lands."[2]

Alliance of Hoshea and Sabaco.

Egyptian scarabs found at Nineveh.

Sabaco was succeeded by his son **Shabataka**, concerning whom the Egyptian inscriptions tell us very little. During the reign of this king Sargon of Assyria died, and was succeeded by Sennacherib, who within a few years set out to suppress the rebellion which had broken out in Syria and Phœnicia. The prince of Ekron, Padi, who had been set upon the throne by Sargon, was seized by a crowd of rebels, who had obtained help from Hezekiah, king of Judah, and made prisoner; Hezekiah himself likewise appealed to the Egyptian king for assistance. Sennacherib marched on Judæa, and at Altekeh he met the allied forces of Jews and Egyptians. The battle was short and decisive, the Assyrians were victorious, and Sennacherib having wasted the country with fire, and destroyed the towns, captured and plundered Jerusalem, where Hezekiah had shut himself up "like a bird in a cage." Padi was restored to the throne of Ekron, and

Hezekiah, king of Judah, provokes the wrath of the Assyrians.

Defeat of Hezekiah and capture of Jerusalem.

[1] See Schrader, *Die Keilinschriften und das Alte Testament*, 1883, p. 269.

[2] A full description of these fragments is given in the chapter on scarabs.

Judæa became an Assyrian province. Sennacherib, hearing of the advance of Tirhakah king of Ethiopia, determined to march on the Delta, and it was during this march that an epidemic broke out among his troops, and a catastrophe destroyed nearly all of them; he returned to Nineveh without having performed upon Hezekiah the vengeance which he had threatened. The ultimate failure of his expedition probably caused his sons to despise him, and shortly afterwards two of them, Adrammelech and Sharezer, smote him with the sword, and he died (2 Kings xix. 37). Shabataka reigned twelve years, and was put to death by Tirhakah, who succeeded him.

Assyrian army destroyed.

B.C. 693

**Taharqa,** or Tirhakah תִּרְהָקָה, shortly after his accession to the throne, made an offensive and defensive alliance with the Phœnicians under Baal king of Tyre, and probably also with the people of Cyprus; Hezekiah king of Judah also joined in the league. Esarhaddon, son of Sennacherib, marched to Palestine by way of Beyrût, where on his return to Assyria he set up a memorial slab at the head of the Nahr el-Kelb side by side with those of Rameses II. Without difficulties other than those caused by thirst and heat his army marched into Egypt, and Tirhakah having fled, Memphis fell into the hands of the Assyrian king. From Memphis he marched to Thebes, and having plundered the city, and placed the rule of the whole country under twenty governors, some Assyrian, some Egyptian, he returned to Assyria laden with spoil. On the death of Esarhaddon, after a reign of thirteen years (B.C. 681–668), Tirhakah returned to Egypt and entered Memphis boldly; he drove out the Assyrians that were there, and openly attended the burial of an Apis bull in the twenty-fourth year of his reign. As soon as the news of the return of Tirhakah to Egypt reached Assurbanipal, the son of Esarhaddon, in Nineveh, he set out with his army for Egypt; he came up with the Egyptian troops at Karbanit, and completely defeated them, and Tirhakah, who had remained in Memphis, was obliged to flee to Thebes; when Assurbanipal followed him thither, he fled into Nubia. When the Assyrian king had reappointed governors over the chief towns of Egypt, and established

Alliance of Hezekiah and Tirhakah.

Capture of Memphis by Esarhaddon.

Assurbanipal's expedition to Egypt.

garrisons there, he returned to Nineveh. Soon after this Nikû, governor of Memphis, headed a rebellion against the Assyrian rule, but he was promptly sent to Nineveh in chains; Assurbanipal so far forgave him, that when he heard of new successes of Tirhakah in Egypt, he sent Nikû back to his country to rule over all Egypt under the direction of Assyria; soon after his arrival Tirhakah died. Tirhakah built a large temple at Gebel Barkal, and restored temples and other buildings at Thebes.

**Tirhakah's buildings in Nubia.**

**Ruṭ-Ȧmen,** son of Sabaco (?), succeeded Tirhakah, and in consequence of a dream, set out to regain for Ethiopia the rule over Egypt. Without very much difficulty he captured Thebes, and advanced on Memphis, where he was opposed by the Assyrian governor; in the fight which ensued Ruṭ-Ȧmen (the Urdamanah of Assurbanipal's inscriptions) was victorious, and again Memphis fell into the hands of the Ethiopians. Once more Assurbanipal marched to Egypt, where he defeated Ruṭ-Ȧmen's army, and advanced on Thebes, whither the rebel king had fled. Having arrived there, the sack and pillage of the city by the Assyrians followed. A stele found at Gebel Barkal relates that Nut-Ȧmen, a king of Ethiopia, had a dream, in consequence of which he set out to regain the rule over Egypt, and that having gained authority over Thebes and Memphis and the Delta, he returned to Ethiopia; in the Nut-Ȧmen of this stele, and the Urdamanah of the cuneiform inscriptions, we have probably one and the same king.

**Ethiopians again capture Memphis.**

**"Stele of the Dream."**

## THE TWENTY-SIXTH DYNASTY.

**B.C. 666**

**Psammetichus I.**, the first king of this dynasty, was the son of a governor (Nikû?) of Memphis and Saïs in Lower Egypt, and had been associated with Nut-Ȧmen in the rule of the country. When the Ethiopian king retired to his own land, Psammetichus became king of Egypt. He married Shep-en-ȧpt, a daughter of Piānchi, and thus secured himself from any attack by the Ethiopians; and by the help of the Ionian and Carian soldiers whom Gyges king of Lydia sent to him, he was able to overcome the Assyrian governors who, one after another, made war upon him, and resisted his

Defeat of the Assyrians.

authority. A decisive battle took place at Memphis; the Assyrians were utterly routed, and Psammetichus found himself firmly seated on the throne of Egypt. A permanent settlement was assigned by him to the Ionians and Carians, and his favour to these foreign soldiers so exasperated the Egyptian troops, that 200,000 are said to have forsaken Egypt and settled in Nubia. Psammetichus appears to have decided that it was useless to attempt to make great conquests of remote countries, as did the kings of old, but set to work to consolidate his kingdom, and to defend its borders. He was a devout worshipper of the gods, and he repaired and rebuilt many of the decayed buildings at Heliopolis, Mendes, Memphis, Abydos and Thebes. He lived at his birthplace, Saïs, and made it the capital of his kingdom. He was a wise patron of the arts and sciences, and during his rule the great renaissance of art took place. The statues and wall paintings of the first empire were diligently copied, many new copies of ancient religious works were made, and the smallest and greatest monuments of this period, as well as objects of ornament, are characterized by a high finish and elaboration of detail, which was the peculiar product of this time.

Revival of arts and sciences, and literature flourishes.

B.C. 612

**Necho II.**, son of Psammetichus I. and Shepenapt, continued the policy of his father, and added a considerable number of foreign troops to his army; he gave the Greeks every facility to enter and settle in Egypt, and he assisted the commercial enterprise of the day as much as possible. With the view of joining the Mediterranean and the Red Sea, he dug a canal from a place near Pithom, a little above Bubastis, on the Pelusiac arm of the Nile, which passing first through the plain, flowed through a valley between the spurs of the Muḳaṭṭam hills, in a southerly direction, until it emptied itself into the Arabian Gulf. It was an indirect connecting of the Mediteranean with the Red Sea by means of the Nile, and did not correspond with the Suez Canal, except in the reach from the Bitter Lakes to Suez, in which it followed a somewhat similar course.[1] About 120,000 men perished during the work, and when an oracle announced that he was only working for the good of foreigners, Necho desisted from his under-

Necho's Canal.

[1] Wiedemann, *Aegyptische Geschichte*, p. 626.

taking. Necho also sent Phœnician seamen to sail round Africa, bidding them to set out from Suez and come home by way of the Strait of Gibraltar; on their return, they stated in proof of their having accomplished their task, that they had seen the sun rise on their right hand as they sailed from east to west. A few years before Nebuchadnezzar (B.C. 604–558) ascended the throne of Babylon, Necho set out on the march to Mesopotamia, and on the road was opposed by Josiah king of Judah, at Megiddo. Then Pharaoh Necho "sent ambassadors to him saying, What have I to do with thee, thou king of Judah? *I come* not against thee this day, but against the house wherewith I have war: for God commanded me to make haste: forbear thee *from meddling* with God, who *is* with me, that he destroy thee not. Nevertheless Josiah would not turn his face from him, but disguised himself, that he might fight with him, and hearkened not unto the words of Necho from the mouth of God, and came to fight in the valley of Megiddo. And the archers shot at king Josiah; and the king said to his servants, Have me away; for I am sore wounded. His servants therefore took him out of that chariot, and put him in the second chariot that he had; and they brought him to Jerusalem, and he died, and was buried in *one of* the sepulchres of his fathers."[1] Necho went on his way to Carchemish, but did not go any farther into Mesopotamia. On his return he marched to Jerusalem and deposed Jehoahaz, the son of Josiah, whom the Jews had set up as king in the place of his father, and made Eliakim (Jehoiakim), another son of Josiah, king in his stead; he also imposed a tax of one hundred talents of silver, and a talent of gold.[2] Soon after Necho had returned to Egypt he heard that a Babylonian army was marching into western Asia, and he again set out for Carchemish, where it was encamped. On his arrival there he found that the Babylonian forces were commanded by Nebuchadnezzar II., and in the battle which followed the Egyptian king was utterly defeated; his troops, Libyans, Ethiopians, and Egyptians, were slain by thousands, and Nebuchadnezzar marched through Palestine to the borders of Egypt. Necho reigned sixteen years, and was buried at

**Rise of second Babylonian Empire.**

**Death of Josiah.**

**Nebuchadnezzar II. invades Egypt.**

[1] 2 Chron. xxxv. 21–24. [2] 2 Chron. xxxvi. 1–4.

Saïs; he was succeeded by his son **Psammetichus II.**, whose reign of a few years was, comparatively, unimportant.

B.C. 591

**Apries**, in Egyptian Uaḥ-àb-Rā, Heb. חָפְרַע (Jeremiah xliv. 30), made an attack upon Tyre and Sidon by sea; Sidon was captured, and the Cyprian fleet which attempted to resist him was destroyed. The Babylonians marched to

**Capture of Jerusalem.**

besiege Jerusalem during his reign, and Nebuchadnezzar having already had Jehoiakim and Jehoiachin, kings of Judah, brought to him in fetters at Babylon, determined to punish the new king Zedekiah who had rebelled against him. Notwithstanding the presence of some troops of Apries, Nebuchadnezzar took Jerusalem, and having blinded Zedekiah and slain his sons before his eyes, set up Gedaliah as king in his stead. Multitudes of Jews flocked to Egypt, where they were received by Apries, and this act of the Egyptian king drew upon him the wrath of Nebuchadnezzar. After a siege

**Fall of Tyre.**

of thirteen years, Tyre fell into the hands of the Babylonian king, who thus became master of Phœnicia and Egypt, for Apries had no army to set in the field against him. In a dispute which broke out between the Cyrenians and the Libyans, Apries sent an Egyptian force to help the latter people, for he had a treaty with their king, Adikran. The hostile forces met in battle, but the Egyptian troops were defeated with a great slaughter, and their countrymen were enraged and asserted that Apries had intentionally sent them against the Greeks that they might be destroyed. When the troops returned to Egypt a rebellion broke out among them,

**Defection of Amāsis, and defeat of Apries.**

and Apries sent Amāsis, an officer, to put it down; but while he was addressing the disaffected troops, a soldier placed a helmet on his head, and declared him king, and all the other soldiers agreeing in this, king he became. Apries then sent Patarbemis to bring Amāsis to him, and because he was unsuccessful in his mission, he gave orders that his nose and ears should be cut off. Soon after this, Apries marched against Amāsis, and in the battle which took place at Momemphis, on the Canopic arm of the Nile, his troops were defeated, and he himself was taken prisoner and led back to his palace at Saïs; he was shortly after strangled and buried with his fathers in the temple of Neith. Before the death of

Apries Nebuchadnezzar II. is said to have invaded Egypt, and to have sailed up as far as Aswân.

B.C.

**Amāsis II.** became sole king of Egypt after the death of Apries, and as he had married Ānch-nes-nefer-âb-Rā, daughter of Psammetichus II. and of Nit-âqert, a sister of Apries, the Egyptians regarded him as, more or less, a legal successor to the throne. He continued the policy of his predecessors towards foreigners, and gave the Greeks many valuable trading privileges; in his reign Naucratis became a very important city, and the centre of Greek influence in Egypt. In addition to Ānch-nes-nefer-âb-Rā he married Ladike, said to be the daughter either of Critoboulos or Battus or Arcesilaus the Cyrenian; according to Herodotus he was the first king of Egypt who conquered Cyprus. The same historian says (III. 1) that Cambyses, king of Persia, made war upon him because, having demanded from Amāsis his daughter to wife, the Egyptian king sent to him Nitetis, the daughter of Apries, as his own daughter; when the damsel declared who she was, Cambyses was greatly enraged, and determined to invade Egypt. During his long reign of forty-five years Amāsis repaired and added to the temples in many parts of Egypt, and he worked the mines in the valley of Ḥammâmât. He did not live to see the invasion of the Persians, but he left the country in such a flourishing condition that it formed very rich spoil for them. 572

**Greeks admitted in Egypt and rise of Naucratis.**

**Psammetichus III.**, together with his army, formed of Greek and Egyptian troops, marched against the Persians and did battle with them at Pelusium, but he was utterly routed, and the conquering host took possession of Egypt, and marched on to Memphis, whither the remainder of the Egyptian army had fled for protection. The reign of Psammetichus lasted but a few months, and he was taken captive to Persia, where he suffered a miserable death. 528

**Egyptians defeated by Cambyses.**

## THE TWENTY-SEVENTH DYNASTY.

**Cambyses**, the first king of the Persian dynasty, seems to have been of a revengeful disposition, for, according to legend, when he arrived at Saïs he is said to have ordered the mummy of Amāsis to be dragged from its tomb, and having caused it 527

Desecration of mummies and tombs by Cambyses.

to be illtreated had it burned. Tradition, in general, states that this king caused many barbarous acts to be performed by his soldiers, and the wrecking of many tombs and statues in Egypt is said to date from his reign. His expeditions against the Nubians and the people of the Oasis proving disastrous, he returned to Memphis in exasperation and grief, and finding the whole town in festival, on account of the appearance of a new Apis bull, he ordered this god to be brought to him, and, in a fit of rage, stabbed it in the thigh. Another view of the character of Cambyses is, however, given by an inscription on the statue of a naval commander under Cambyses and Darius, preserved in the Vatican. This officer, called Ut'a-Ḥeru-en-pe-resu, states that when Cambyses came to Saïs he ordered the temple of Neith to be cleansed, he restored its revenues and sacred festivals, he performed all the rites there, and established the offerings according to what the kings before him had done. When Darius was king of Egypt the same official was appointed by him to re-establish the school of scribes in Egypt, and he seems to have had some influence in preserving Saïs from the destruction which Cambyses spread over the country, and he probably helped Darius to establish the beneficent government in Egypt for which he is famous. Cambyses died from a wound in the thigh, accidentally caused by his own dagger while mounting his horse.

Restoration of Temple of Neith at Saïs.

B.C. 521

On ascending the throne **Darius Hystaspes**, the successor of Cambyses, set to work to improve the condition of the country, and to repair the damage done to the prestige of Persian government in Egypt by Cambyses. He deposed Aryandes, the Persian satrap of Egypt, appointed by Cambyses, and caused him to be slain, because he had made an attack on Cyrene, and because of his cruelty and misgovernment. Darius established a coinage, rearranged the taxation of the country, and completed the canal to join the Red Sea and the Mediterranean which Necho had begun. The course of this canal can still be traced by the inscriptions in hieroglyphics, and in Persian, Median, and Assyrian cuneiform, which cover the rocks near which the canal passed. As stated above, Darius re-established the school of scribes in Egypt, and spared no pains to improve the condition of the people, and to increase

The coinage and good government of Darius.

Red Sea Canal.

the trade of the country by land and sea. Towards the end of his reign, while the Persians were fighting the Greeks, Egypt threw off the Persian yoke, and set up **Chabbesha** as king; Darius never recovered his hold upon Egypt, and died after a reign of about thirty-six years.

Soon after **Xerxes I.** ascended the throne, he marched to B.C. 486
Egypt to reassert the Persian supremacy; he broke through the defences which Chabbesha had set up on the mouths of the Nile and in the marshes, and taking possession of the country compelled the Egyptians to send a contigent of two hundred ships to assist him in his attack upon Greece; the crews of these ships distinguished themselves by their bravery at the battle of Artemisium. After the murder of Xerxes by
Artabanus, **Artaxerxes I.** became king of Egypt, but 465
towards the end of his reign the Egyptians, headed by Inarus, king of Lybia, assisted by a fleet of two or three hundred Athenian ships, again revolted and refused either to pay taxes, or to acknowledge the Persian authority. Artaxerxes sent a force of 300,000 or 400,000 to put down the revolt, and a battle took place near Papremis; the Persians, owing to their overwhelming numbers, were at first victorious, but were subsequently beaten, and those that escaped from the general massacre fled to Memphis for refuge, and were besieged there by the Egyptians. Soon after this Artaxerxes sent more troops to Egypt, and these having surrounded Memphis, the Athenians were compelled first to withdraw, and secondly to burn their ships; Inarus was wounded in an engagement and taken captive to Persia, where he was crucified or impaled. Amyrtaeus, the governor of a town in the Delta and an ally of Inarus, fled to the marshes, and the Persians appointed Pausiris and Thannyras, their sons respectively, rulers over the Delta in their stead. **Xerxes II.**, the next king of Egypt, was murdered by his brother Sogdianus, and towards the end of the reign of **Darius II.**, his successor, the Egyptians once more rebelled, and regained their independence under Amyrtaeus of Saïs about B.C. 405.

Persians reconquer Egypt.

Fall of Memphis.

## THE TWENTY-EIGHTH DYNASTY.

Of **Ȧmen-ruṭ** or Amyrtaeus, the only king of this dynasty, 400
very little is known; his native city was Saïs, but it is not

likely that he is identical with the Amyrtaeus who assisted the ill-fated Inarus to rebel against the Persians.

## THE TWENTY-NINTH DYNASTY.

B.C. 399 **Naifāarut I.**, or Nepherites, the first king of this dynasty, was a native of Mendes, and he associated his son Nectanebus with him in the rule of the kingdom. He supplied the Lacedæmonians with wood for building one hundred triremes and half a million bushels of grain at the time when Agesilaus was fighting against the Persians.[1] He reigned six
393 years, and was succeeded by **P-se-mut** or Psammuthis, who was in turn succeeded by **Haḳer.** Of Haḳer, or Achoris, the inscriptions say nothing, although his name is found inscribed on buildings and temples at Thebes, and in the quarries of Maʿṣara and Ṭurah. Towards the end of his reign Achoris became an ally of Evagoras, king of Cyprus, but the king of Persia, against whom they began a war, succeeded in destroying their united fleet, and shortly after Achoris died, having reigned twelve or thirteen years. He
379 seems to have been succeeded by **Naifāarut II.**, who was, however, soon deposed on account of his unpopularity with the people.

*Egyptians declare war against Persians.*

## THE THIRTIETH DYNASTY.

378 To **Necht-neb-f**, or Nectanebus I., the son of Naifāarut I., the first king of this dynasty, fell the task of continuing the war which Achoris, his predecessor, and Evagoras, king of Cyprus, had begun against Artaxerxes II. The Persian king attacked Cyprus with great determination, but Evagoras met his forces with about one hundred ships and six thousand soldiers, and succeeded in partially stopping the supplies of grain for the enemy, in consequence of which a rebellion broke out among them. He increased his fleet as much as he was able, and with the addition of fifty ships from Egypt, attacked the Persians with all haste; in the great battle which followed, however, his ships were scattered or sunk,

*Persian attack upon Cyprus.*

[1] Wiedemann thinks that the king of Egypt who assisted the Greeks in this matter is, from chronological grounds, more likely to have been Achoris. (*Aeg. Geschichte*, p. 698.)

and the Persians sailed on to attack Salamis. Evagoras fled to Egypt to obtain supplies from Nectanebus to carry on the war, but when he returned he found that his capital was besieged, and that his allies had fled. He straightway tendered his submission to the Persians, who finally decided to accept from him a yearly tribute and to consider him a vassal of Persia. The war against Evagoras being at an end, the Persian king next directed his attention to an attack upon Egypt, and placing the Persian troops under the command of Pharnabazus, and his Greek troops under that of Iphicrates, he advanced against Egypt with nearly a quarter of a million soldiers and three hundred ships of war. Nectanebus on his part fortified each of the seven mouths of the Nile, giving particular attention to strengthening the defences on the Pelusiac mouth, and he flooded the whole country round. When the Persian generals saw this they determined to make their attack by the Mendesian mouth of the Nile, and after a battle they succeeded in capturing the fort which commanded it, and reduced its defenders to slavery. A dispute next arose between Pharnabazus and Iphicrates as to an immediate attack upon Memphis, and while the former was opposing the march upon this city by the latter, the Egyptians themselves mustered a strong force there, and in the battles which followed the arrival of the allied army of Persians and Greeks were generally successful. Soon after this, owing to the inundation of the Nile, the Persians withdrew to Syria, and Iphicrates returned to Athens; thus the attack of the Persians, notwithstanding their immense army, came to nought. Nectanebus restored and added to many of the temples of Egypt, and after a reign of eighteen years was succeeded by T'cheḥrā, or Teos (Tachos), who reigned but two years; the Egyptian inscriptions make no mention of this king. From Greek historians we learn that Teos levied a tax on the Egyptians to carry on the war, and that, contrary to the advice of Agesilaus, one of his allies, he advanced to attack Phœnicia. During his absence the Egyptians revolted, and sent messengers to Syria to invite Nectanebus II., the lawful heir to the throne of Egypt, to come and take possession of his country. The allies of Teos forsook him, and

Persian attack upon Egypt.

Egyptians flood the Delta.

Retreat of the Persians.

B.C. 360

he fled to the court of Artaxerxes II. and of Ochus the Persian kings, where, after a time spent in riotous living, he died.

B.C. 358 **Necht-neb-f**, or Nectanebus II., was the last native king of Egypt, and having been helped by Agesilaus to overthrow a native of Mendes who aspired to the throne, he assumed the rule of the kingdom without further opposition. After the death of Artaxerxes II., Ochus determined to make an attack upon Egypt and Cyprus and Phœnicia, the kings of which had joined forces with each other and with the Egyptians to make themselves independent. Tennes, the king of Sidon, successfully expelled a number of Persians from Phœnicia, but when he heard that Ochus himself was coming to take vengeance upon him for this proceeding, he sent messengers to him to tender his submission, and to promise him his help in invading Egypt. The Persian king promised to overlook the past, but marched on Sidon, notwithstanding, and surrounded it; Tennes betrayed the city and led Artaxerxes and his army into it, whereupon the Sidonians destroyed their fleet and set fire to their houses with themselves and their wives and families inside them. The treachery of Tennes availed him nothing, for he was put to death by Artaxerxes. Phœnicia, and soon after Cyprus, fell into the hands of the Persian king, who now made ready in earnest to conquer Egypt. In a few small preliminary battles fought on the north-east frontier of Egypt, victory rested with the Persians, and when Nectanebus learned this, and saw that Pelusium was attacked in a systematic manner, he and his troops withdrew to Memphis; the Persians advanced through the Delta, and captured Bubastis, and their march to Memphis was a triumphal progress rather than the march of an enemy upon the capital of Egypt. Fear seized Nectanebus when he heard of the approach of the Persians, and having gathered together all the money that he could conveniently carry, he fled from his troubles, some say to Ethiopia, and some say to Macedon, where according to Pseudo-Callisthenes he became the father of Alexander the Great. Nectanebus, during his reign of seventeen or eighteen years, obtained the reputation of being a devout worshipper of the gods, and a sorcerer. The mines

Persian attack upon Phœnicia.

Persians capture Cyprus.

Persians capture Memphis.

Flight of Nectanebus.

in the valley of Ḥammâmât were worked during his reign, and he added to and repaired many of the temples at Philæ, Thebes, Edfû, Heliopolis, etc. With the flight of Nectanebus the history of Egypt as an independent country comes to an end.

## Persian Rulers of Egypt.

When **Artaxerxes III., Ochus,** became sole king of Egypt, he emulated the barbarous acts of Cambyses; the principal towns were looted and destroyed, the temples were overthrown, and their sanctuaries pillaged, the Apis bull was killed and eaten by the king and his friends, and the ram of Mendes was slain. Ochus returned to Babylon with much spoil, and after a reign of twelve years was probably poisoned by Bagoas the Egyptian, who, it is said, thus avenged the slaughter of the Apis bull. B.C. 340 Ochus plunders Egypt.

**Arses,** the youngest son of Ochus, next sat on the throne of Egypt, but in the third year of his reign he and his family were slain by Bagoas.

Arses was succeeded by **Darius III.**, who narrowly escaped poisoning by the hand of Bagoas; the plot was, however, discovered, and Darius freed himself from the traitor by causing him to drink poison, and he died. Darius was defeated by Alexander the Great at Issus, and the Greeks marched on Egypt and took possession of it without any difficulty. Defeat of Darius at Issus.

## Macedonians.

**Alexander the Great** founded the Alexandria near Rakoti, 332

Eg. 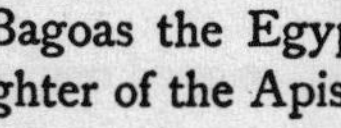 *Rāqeṭit*, Copt. ⲣⲁⲕⲟϯ, and endeavoured to make it the central market-place of the known world. He was tolerant of the Egyptian religion, and sacrificed to Âmen, the god of Libya, who greeted him as his son. After about a year spent in Egypt, Alexander set out on his expedition against Darius king of Persia. Having conquered all the east, and travelled nearly alone into China, he came back to Babylon, where he was poisoned at a banquet; his body was brought in great state to his city Alexandria and was buried there. Alexandria founded.

## PTOLEMIES.

B.C.

305 Ptolemy I., Soter, son of Lagus, founded the Alexandrian Library.

286 Ptolemy II., Philadelphus, built the Pharos, founded Berenice on the Red Sea, and Arsinoë; he employed Manetho to compile a history of Egypt and its gods from native authorities, and caused the Greek version of the Old Testament to be made.

Alexandrian Library founded. Septuagint made.

247 Ptolemy III., Euergetes I.

222 Ptolemy IV., Philopator, founded the temple of Edfû.

205 Ptolemy V., Epiphanes.

Ptolemy VI., Eupator, died in this year.

182 Ptolemy VII., Philometor.

170 Ptolemy VIII., murdered by Physcon.

Ptolemy IX., Euergetes II. or Physcon, reigned conjointly with Ptolemy VII. (B.C. 170—165).

117 Ptolemy X., Soter II., Philomètor II., or Lathyrus reigned conjointly with Cleopatra III.; he was banished B.C. 106, and recalled B.C. 87.

Ptolemy XI., Alexander I., made co-regent. He was banished B.C. 89 and slain B.C. 87.

81 Ptolemy XII., Alexander II., is slain.

Ptolemy XIII., Neos Dionysos or Auletes, became king of Egypt; he died B.C. 52.

52 Ptolemy XIV., Dionysos II., banished his co-regent Cleopatra VII., Cæsar arrived in Egypt to support Cleopatra, and Ptolemy XIV. was drowned.

Ptolemy XV., brother of Cleopatra VII., appointed her co-regent; he was murdered at her wish.

Ptolemy XVI., Cæsarion, was named co-regent.

42 Antony ordered Cleopatra to appear before him, and was seduced by her charms; he killed himself, and Cleopatra died by the bite of an asp.

Death of Cleopatra.

## ROMANS.

27 Cæsar Augustus became master of the Roman Empire, and Cornelius Gallus the first prefect of Egypt; under the third prefect, Aelius Gallus, Candace, Queen of the Ethiopians, invaded Egypt, but was defeated.

Egypt becomes a Roman Province.

A.D.

Tiberius. In his reign Germanicus went to Egypt, sailing up the Nile from the city of Canopus to Thebes, where he visited the temples of Luxor and Karnak, and heard the priest read on the pylons the names of conquered nations which still exist on them by the score. Passing over to the other side of the river, Tacitus tells us (II., 61) that he saw the stone image of Memnon, which, when struck by the sun's rays, gave out the sound of a human voice, and there is little doubt that he visited the Tombs of the Kings, the Ramesseum and the temples at Medînet Habû. He passed on to Syene, where he visited the island of Elephantine, and either going up or coming down the river, he saw Lake Moeris and the Pyramids. 14

Germanicus travels through Egypt.

Caligula. 37

Claudius. 41

Nero. In his reign Christianity was first preached in Egypt by Saint Mark. The Blemmyes made raids upon the southern frontier of Egypt. 55

Blemmyes invade Egypt.

Vespasian. Jerusalem destroyed, A.D. 70. 69

Domitian builds temples to Isis and Serapis at Rome. 82

Trajan. The Amnis Trajanus, or canal which joined the Nile and Red Sea, re-opened. 98

Hadrian. He visited Egypt twice. 117

Marcus Aurelius. 161

Commodus. 180

Septimius Severus. 193

Caracalla visited Egypt, and caused a large number of young men to be massacred in Alexandria. 211

Macrinus. 217

Elagabalus. 218

Decius. 249

Valerianus. 253

Zenobia, Queen of Palmyra, invaded Egypt. 268

Aurelian. Zenobia dethroned A.D. 273. 270

Probus. 276

Diocletian. "Pompey's Pillar" erected A.D. 302. The Copts date the era of the Martyrs from the day of Diocletian's accession to the throne (August 29). 284

Constantine the Great. 324

A.D.

337 Constantius.

379 Theodosius I., the Great, proclaimed Christianity the religion of his empire.

BYZANTINES.

395 Arcadius, Emperor of the East.

408 Theodosius II.

450 Marcianus. In this reign Silco invaded Egypt, with his Nubian followers.

474 Zeno.

481 Anastasius.

527 Justinian.

610 Heraclius expelled the Persians from Egypt after they had held it, under Chosroes, for ten years.

MUḤAMMADANS.

638 'Amr ibn el-'Âṣi conquers Egypt, and the country becomes a part of the Muḥammadan empire for about nine hundred years.

Arab conquest of Egypt.

1517 Selim I., of Constantinople, deposes Ṭûmân Bey, and Egypt becomes a Turkish Pashalik.

1798 Napoleon Bonaparte stormed Alexandria, battle of the Pyramids, and French fleet destroyed off Abuḳîr by the English.

1801 The French compelled by the English to evacuate Egypt.

1805 Muḥammad 'Ali appointed Pasha of Egypt.

1848 Ibrâhîm Pasha.

1849 Death of Muḥammad 'Ali.

1854 Sâid Pasha. During his reign the Bûlâḳ Museum was founded, and the excavation of the Suez Canal began.

1863 Ismâîl, son of Ibrâhîm Pasha, made Khedive. Suez Canal opened, 1869.

1882 Massacre of Europeans at Alexandria, bombardment of the town by the English fleet in July; Egypt was occupied by English troops, and 'Arabi Pasha defeated.

1885 Murder of Gordon, and abandonment of the Sûdân.

1892 English troops continue to occupy Egypt.

## List of Egyptian Dynasties and the Dates assigned to them by Egyptologists.

| Dynasty. | From | 1 Lepsius. | 2 Champollion Figeac. | 3 Mariette. | 4 Wilkinson. | 5 Brugsch. |
|---|---|---|---|---|---|---|
| I | Thinis... ... | 3,892 | 5,867 | 5,004 | 2,320 | 4,400 |
| II | Thinis... ... | 3,639 | 5,615 | 4,751 | 2,300 | 4,133 |
| III | Memphis ... | 3,338 | 5,318 | 4,449 | — | 3,966 |
| IV | Memphis ... | 3,124 | 5,121 | 4,235 | — | 3,766 |
| V | Elephantine ... | 2,840 | 4,673 | 3,951 | — | 3,566 |
| VI | Memphis ... | 2,744 | 4,425 | 3,703 | — | 3,300 |
| VII | Memphis ... | 2,592 | 4,222 | 3,500 | — | 3,100 |
| VIII | Memphis ... | 2,522 | 4,147 | 3,500 | — | — |
| IX | Heracleopolis | 2,674 | 4,047 | 3,358 | — | — |
| X | Heracleopolis | 2,565 | 3,947 | 3,249 | — | — |
| XI | Thebes ... | 2,423 | 3,762 | } 3,061 | — | 2,500 |
| XII | Thebes ... | 2,380 | 3,703 | | — | 2,466 |
| XIII | Thebes ... | 2,136 | 3,417 | 2,851 | — | 2,233 |
| XIV | Choïs ... ... | 2,167 | 3,004 | 2,398 | — | — |
| XV | (Shepherds) ... | 2,101 | 2,520 | | 1,830 | — |
| XVI | (Shepherds) ... | 1,842 | 2,270 | } 2,214 | 1,740 | 1,800 |
| XVII | Thebes ... | 1,684 | 2,082 | | 1,651 | — |
| XVIII | Thebes ... | 1,591 | 1,822 | 1,703 | 1,575 | 1,700 |
| XIX | Thebes ... | 1,443 | 1,473 | 1,462 | 1,269 | 1,400 |
| XX | Thebes ... | 1,269 | 1,279 | 1,288 | 1,170 | 1,200 |
| XXI | { Tanis ... / Thebes ... | } 1,091 | 1,101 | 1,110 | 1,068 | 1,100 |
| XXII | Bubastis ... | 961 | 971 | 980 | 981 | 966 |
| XXIII | Tanis ... ... | 787 | 851 | 810 | 908 | 766 |
| XXIV | { Saïs ... ... / Ethiopia ... | } 729 | 762 | 721 | 812 | 733 |
| XXV | Ethiopia ... | 716 | 718 | 715 | 773 | 700 |
| XXVI | Saïs ... ... | 685 | 674 | 665 | 664 | 666 |
| XXVII | Persia... ... | 525 | 524 | 527 | 525 | 527 |
| XXVIII | Saïs ... ... | 525 | 404 | 406 | 414 | 405 |
| XXIX | Mendes ... | 399 | 398 | 399 | 408 | 399 |
| XXX | Sebennytos ... | 378 | 377 | 378 | 387 | 378 |
| XXXI | Persia... ... | 340 | 339 | 340 | 340 | 340 |

1 *Königsbuch*, Berlin, 1858, *Synoptische Tafeln*, taf. 4–8.

2 *L'Univers. Egypte Ancienne*, Paris, 1839, p. 269.

3 *Notice des Principaux Monuments du Musée à Boulaq*, Paris, 1869, p. 15.

4 *The Ancient Egyptians*, ed. Birch, 1878, Vol. I, p. 28 ff.

5 *Egypt under the Pharaohs*, ed. 1880, Vol. II, pp. 341–346.

## LIST OF NOMES

| | NOME. | CAPITAL. |
|---|---|---|
| 1. | *Ta-kens* | *Àb* |
| 2. | *Tes-Ḥeru* | *Ṭebt* |
| 3. | *Ten* | *Neχeb* or *Sent* |
| 4. | *Uast* | *Uast* or *Ànnu qemāt* |
| 5. | *Ḥerui* | *Qebt* |
| 6. | *Àati*, or | *Ta-en-tarert* |
| 7. | *Sechem* | *Ḥet* |
| 8. | *Àbṭu* | *Àbeṭ* |
| 9. | *Àmsu* | *Àpu* |
| 10. | *Uaṭet* | *Ṭebt* |
| 11. | *Sut* | *Shàs-ḥetep* |
| 12. | *Ṭu-ḥef* | *Nut-enth-bak* |
| 13. | *Àtef-chent* | *Sauṭ* |
| 14. | *Àtef-peḥ* | *Kes* |
| 15. | *Un* | *Chemennu* |

[1] See Brugsch, *Dict. Géog.*, p. 1358, f.; and Dümicher

## (UPPER EGYPT).

| GREEK NAME. | DEITY. | | |
|---|---|---|---|
| Elephantine |  | *Chnemu* | |
| Apollinopolis magna | 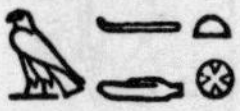 | *Ḥeru Beḥutet.* | |
| Eileithyia | 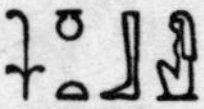 | *Neχeb.* | |
| Latopolis, Esneh | | | |
| Thebes, or |  | *Ȧmen-Rā* | |
| Hermonthis |  | *Menthu* | |
| Coptos |  | *Ȧmsu* | |
| Tentyris |  | *Ḥet-Ḥeru,* | Hathor |
| Diospolis parva |  | *Ḥet-Ḥeru,* | Hathor |
| Abydos |  | *Ȧn-ḥer* | |
| Panopolis |  | *Ȧmsu* | |
| Aphroditopolis |  | *Ḥet-Ḥeru,* | Hathor |
| Hypselis |  | *Chnemu* | |
| Hieraconpolis |  | *Ḥeru,* | Horus |
| Lycopolis, Asyût |  | *Ȧp-uat* | |
| Cusae |  | *Ḥet-Ḥeru,* | Hathor |
| Hermopolis |  | *Teḥuti,* | Thoth |

in Meyer, *Geschichte des alten Aegyptens*, p. 24, ff.

## LIST OF NOMES

| | NOME. | | CAPITAL. | |
|---|---|---|---|---|
| 16. |  | *Meḥ-maḥet* | 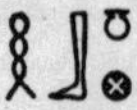 | *Ḥebenu* |
| 17. |  | ........ |  | *Ka-sa* |
| 18. |  | *Sepet* |  | *Ḥet-bennu* |
| 19. |  | *Uab* |  | *Pa-mat'et* |
| 20. |  | *Àm-chent* |  | *Suten-ḥenen* |
| 21. |  | *Am-peḥ*[1] | 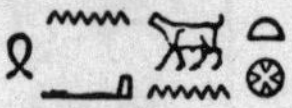 | *Śenāχent* |
| 22. |  | *Māten* |  | *Ṭep-àḥet* |

## LIST OF NOMES

| | NOME. | | CAPITAL. | |
|---|---|---|---|---|
| 1. |  | *Àneb-het'* | 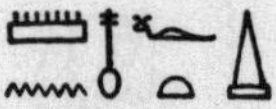 | *Men-nefert* |
| 2. |  | *Aā* | 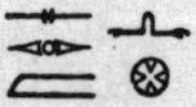 | *Sechem* |
| 3. |  | *Àment* | 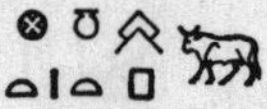 | *Nut-ent-Ḥāp* |
| 4. |  | *Sepi-res* | 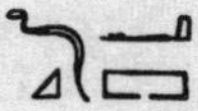 | *T'eqā* |
| 5. |  | *Sepi-meḥt* |  | *Sait* |
| 6. |  | *Ka-set* | 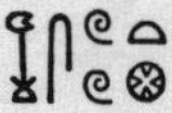 | *Chasuut* |

[1] In the western part of this nome was the Fayyûm, 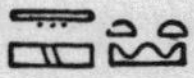 *Ta-shet.*

UPPER EGYPT)—*continued.*

| GREEK NAME. | DEITY. | | |
|---|---|---|---|
| ......... |  | *Ḥeru,* | Horus |
| Kynonpolis | 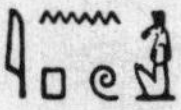 | *Ȧnpu,* | Anubis |
| Hipponus | 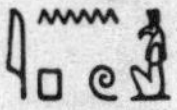 | *Ȧnpu,* | Anubis |
| Oxyrhynchus |  | *Sut* | |
| Heracleopolis Magna |  | *Her-šefiu* | |
| Nilopolis (?) |  | *Chnemu* | |
| Aphroditopolis |  | *Ḥet-Ḥeru,* | Hathor |

LOWER EGYPT).

| GREEK NAME. | DEITY. | | |
|---|---|---|---|
| Memphis |  | *Ptaḥ* | |
| Letopolis |  | *Ḥeru* | Horu |
| Apis |  | *Ḥet-Ḥeru* | Hathor |
| ......... | 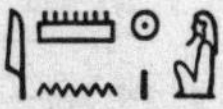 | *Ȧmen-Rā* | |
| Sais |  | *Nit* | |
| Choïs |  | *Ȧmen-Rā* | |

[2] See J. de Rougé, *Géog. Ancienne de la Basse Egypte*, Paris, 1891.

## LIST OF NOMES

| | NOME. | | CAPITAL. | |
|---|---|---|---|---|
| 7. |  | *Nefer-Ȧment* | 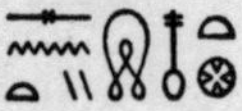 | *Sent-nefert* |
| 8. |  | *Nefer-Ȧbet* |  | *Thekut* |
| 9. |  | *Ati (or Anėt)* |  | *Pa-Ȧusȧr* |
| 10. |  | *Ka-kam* |  | *Ḥet-ta-ḥerȧbt* |
| 11. |  | *Ka-ḥebes* | 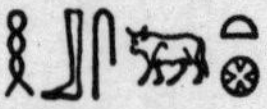 | *Ḥebes-ka* |
| 12. |  | *Teb-neter* | 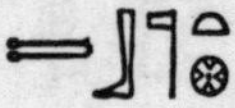 | *Theb-netert* |
| 13. |  | *Ḥeq-āṭ* |  | *Ȧnnu* |
| 14. |  | *Chent-ȧbṭ* | 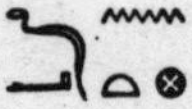 | *Ṭānt* |
| 15. |  | *Teḥuti* |  | *Pa-Teḥuti* |
| 16. |  | *Char* |  | *Pa-ba-neb-Ṭeṭṭeṭ* |
| 17. |  | *Beḥutet* | 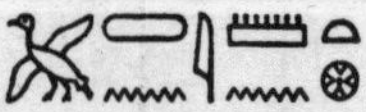 | *Pa-chen-en-Ȧmen* |
| 18. |  | *Ȧm-chent* |  | *Pa-Bast* |
| 19. |  | *Ȧm-peḥ* | 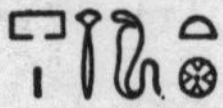 | *Pa-uaṭ* |
| 20. |  | *Sept* |  | *Peḳes* |

## (LOWER EGYPT)—*continued.*

| GREEK NAME. | | DEITY. | |
|---|---|---|---|
| Metelis |  | *Ḥu* | |
| Sethroë (?) |  | *Ȧtmu* | |
| Busiris |  | *Ȧusȧr* | Osiris |
| Athribis |  | *Ḥeru-chent-chathi* | |
| Kabasos | 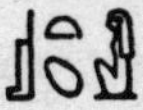 | *Ȧuset* | Isis |
| Sebennythos |  | *Ȧn-ḥer* | |
| Heliopolis |  | *Rā* | |
| Tanis |  | *Ḥeru* | Horus |
| Hermopolis |  | *Teḥuti* | Thoth |
| Mendes |  | *Ba-neb-Ṭeṭṭeṭ* | |
| Diospolis |  | *Ȧmen-Rā* | |
| Bubastis |  | *Bast* | |
| Buto |  | *Uaṭ* | |
| Phakussa |  | *Sept* | |

# LIST OF THE CARTOUCHES

### OF THE PRINCIPAL

# EGYPTIAN KINGS.

The oval in which a name of a royal person is written, is called *cartouche.* The first oval contains the prenomen, and the second the name; these are quite distinct from his titles. *suten net,* placed before the prenomen, means "King of the North and South," and *se Rā* means "Son of the Sun." Other common titles are *neb taui,* "lord of two lands," Horus, "the golden Horus," "lord of diadems," "mighty bull," "beautiful god," etc., etc. The title Pharaoh פַּרְעֹה finds its origin in , or , or

*per āa,* "great house." In the early dynasties kings' names were very simple in form, and consisted often of the prenomen only. In addition to the prenomen and name a king often had what is termed a "banner" name, which was written in a rectangular enclosure; *e.g.*:—

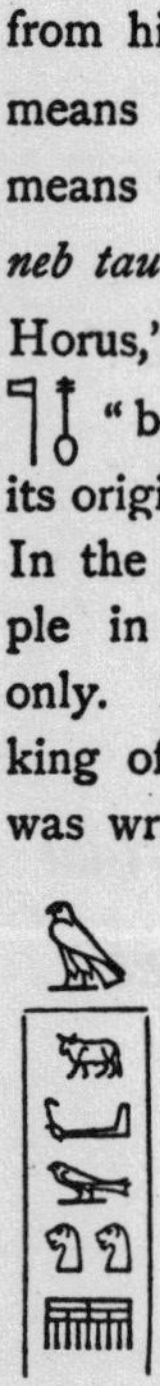

*Ḥeru ka neχt ur peḥ peḥ,* "Horus, mighty bull, great of valour," formed the "banner" name of Amenophis II.;

*āa χeperu Rā* was his prenomen; and

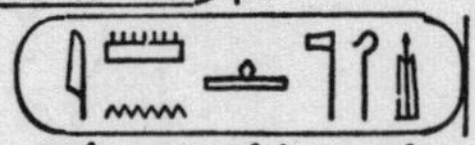

*Ȧmen-ḥetep neter ḥeq Ȧnnu,* "Amenophis, god, prince of Heliopolis," was his name. Each prenomen and name had a meaning, but many of these are very difficult to translate.

## DYNASTY* I., FROM THINIS, B.C. 4400.

1. 
Menȧ.

2. 
Tetȧ.

3. 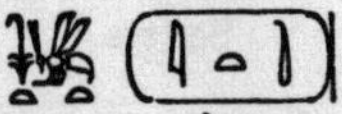
Ȧte*o*.

4. 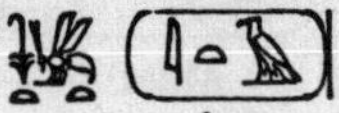
Ȧta.

5. 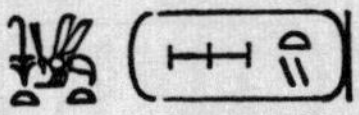
Ḥesep-ti.

6. 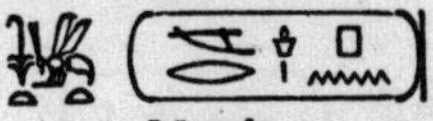
Mer-ba-pen.

7. 
Semen-Ptaḥ.

8. 
Qebḥ.

## DYNASTY II., FROM THINIS, B.C. 4133.

9. 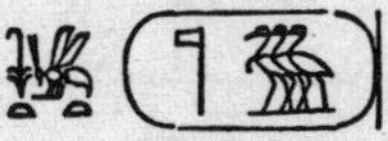
Neter-baiu.

10. 
Ka-kau.

11. 
Ba-en-neter.

12. 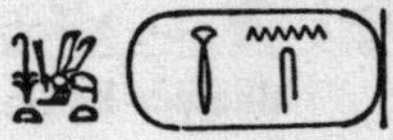
Uat'-nes.

13. 
Senṭȧ.

14. 
Per-ȧb-sen.

15. 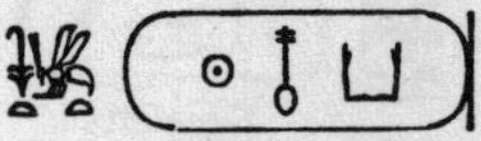
Nefer-ka-Rā.†

16. 
Nefer-ka-seker.

17. 
Ḥet'efa.

* Manetho's grouping of the kings into dynasties is only used here for convenience; the ancient Egyptians had no such division.

† Though ⊙ Rā is generally placed first in the cartouche, it is generally to be read last.

## DYNASTY III., FROM MEMPHIS, B.C. 3966.

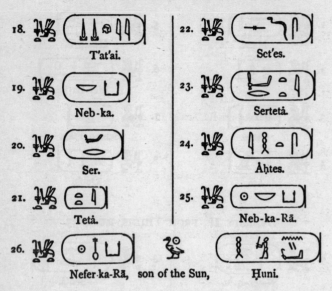

18. 
T'at'ai.

19. 
Neb-ka.

20. 
Ser.

21. 
Tetȧ.

22. 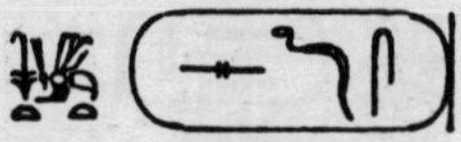
Set'es.

23. 
Sertetȧ.

24. 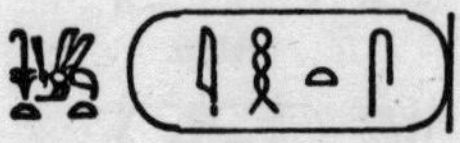
Ȧḫtes.

25. 
Neb-ka-Rā.

26. 
Nefer-ka-Rā, son of the Sun, Ḥuni.

## DYNASTY IV., FROM MEMPHIS, B.C. 3766.

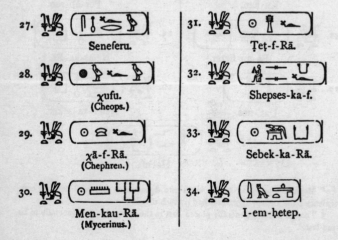

27. 
Seneferu.

28. 
χufu.
(Cheops.)

29. 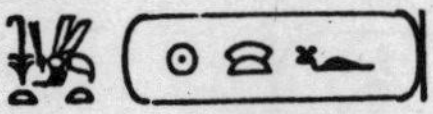
χā-f-Rā.
(Chephren.)

30. 
Men-kau-Rā.
(Mycerinus.)

31. 
Ṭeṭ-f-Rā.

32. 
Shepses-ka-f.

33. 
Sebek-ka-Rā.

34. 
I-em-ḥetep.

## DYNASTY V., FROM ELEPHANTINE, B.C. 3366.

35. 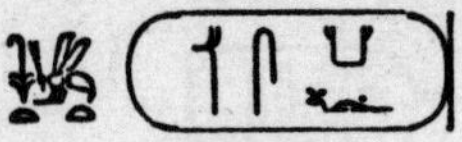

Usr-ka-f.

36. 

Saḥ-u-Rā.

37. 

Nefer-ka-åri-Rā, son of the Sun, Kakaå.

38. 

Nefer-f-Rā, son of the Sun, Shepses-ka-Rā.

39. 

Nefer-χā-Rā, son of the Sun, Ḥeru-å-ka-u.

40 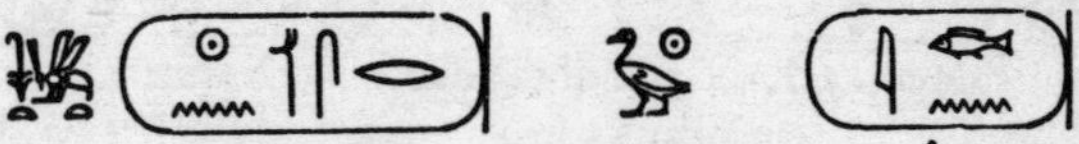

Usr-en-Rā, son of the Sun, Ån.

41. 

Men-kau Ḥeru.

42. 

Ṭeṭ-ka-Rā, son of the Sun, Åsså.

43.  Unås.

## DYNASTY VI., FROM MEMPHIS, B.C. 3266.

44 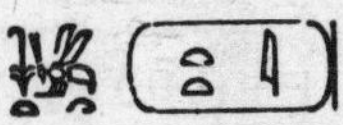 

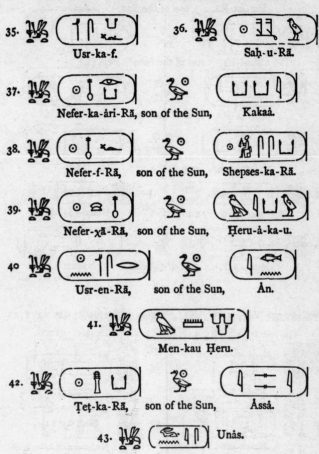

Tetå or Tetå-mer-en-Ptaḥ.
(Teta beloved of Ptaḥ.)

45. 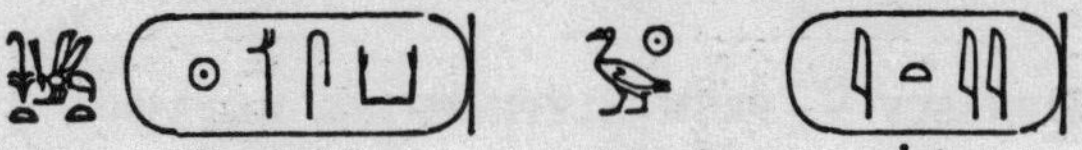
Usr-ka-Rā, son of the Sun, Åti.

46. 
Meri-Rā, son of the Sun, Pepi (I.).

47. 
Mer-en-Rā, son of the Sun, Ḥeru-em-sa-f.

48. 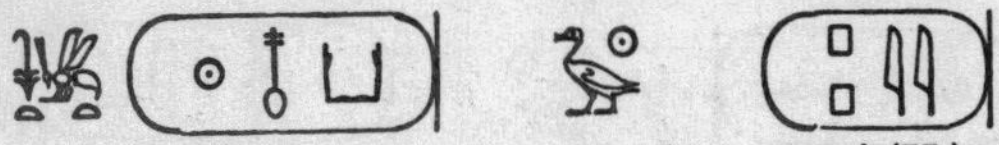
Nefer-ka-Rā, son of the Sun, Pepi (II.).

49. 
Rā-mer-en-se (?)-em-sa-f

50. 
Neter-ka-Rā.

51. 
Men-ka-Rā, son of the Sun, Netåqerti. (Nitocris.)

## Dynasties VII. and VIII., from Memphis; Dynasties IX. and X., from Heracleopolis, B.C. 3100.

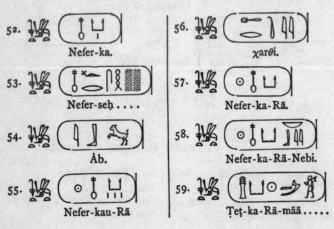

52. 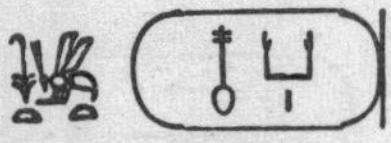
Nefer-ka.

53. 
Nefer-seḥ . . . .

54. 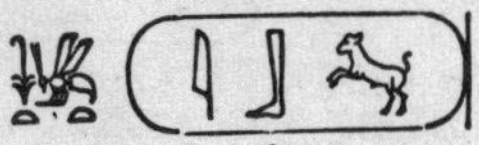
Åb.

55. 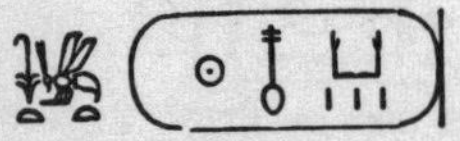
Nefer-kau-Rā

56. 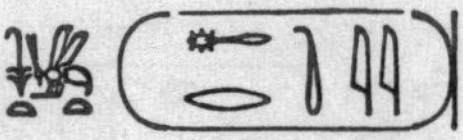
χarθi.

57. 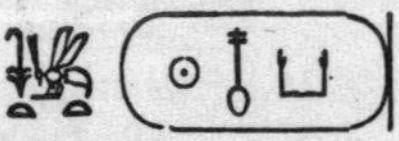
Nefer-ka-Rā.

58. 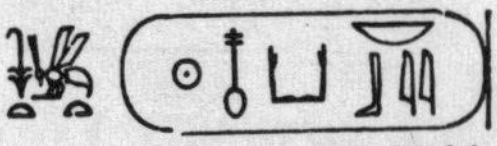
Nefer-ka-Rā-Nebi.

59. 
Ṭeṭ-ka-Rā-māā . . . . .

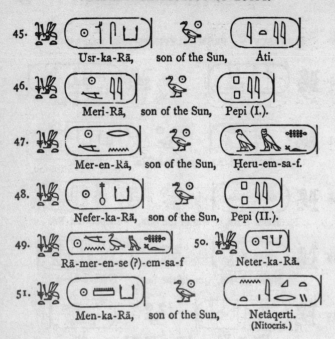

60. 

Nefer-ka-Rā-χenṭu.

61. 

Mer-en-Ḥeru.

62. 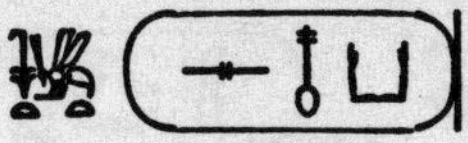 Or 

Senefer-ka. Se-nefer-ka-Rā.

63. 

Ka-en-Rā.

64. 

Nefer-ka-Rā-t-rer-l (?).

65. 

Nefer-ka-Ḥeru.

66. 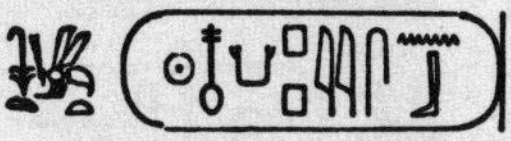

Nefer-ka-Rā-Pepi-senb.

67. 

Nefer-ka-Rā-ānnu.*

68. 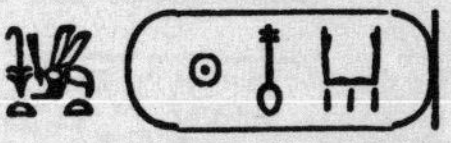

Nefer-kau-Rā.

69. 

Nefer-kau-Ḥeru.

70. 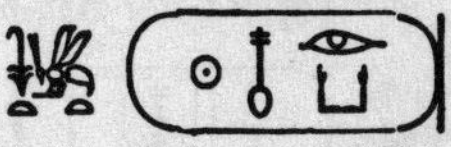

Nefer-ka-ȧri-Rā.

## DYNASTY XI., FROM THEBES.

71. 

Erpā† Ȧntef.

72. 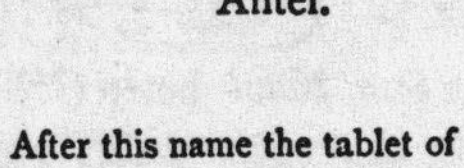

Men-[tu-ḥetep].

73. 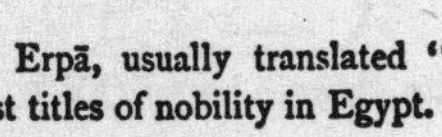

Ȧntef.

74. 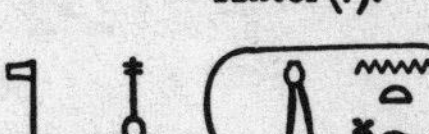

Ȧntef.

75. 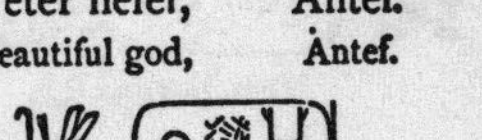

Ȧntef (?).

76. 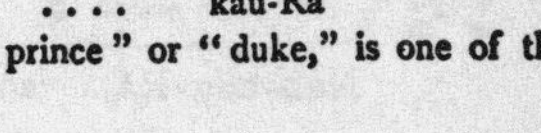

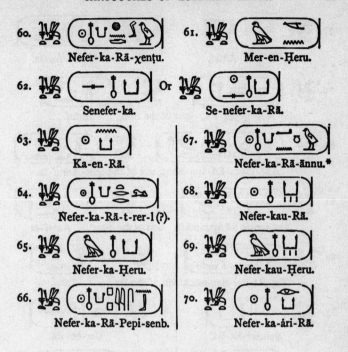

Neter nefer, Ȧntef.
Beautiful god, Ȧntef.

* After this name the tablet of Abydos had 
. . . . kau-Rā

† Erpā, usually translated "hereditary prince" or "duke," is one of the oldest titles of nobility in Egypt.

77. 

Son of the Sun Ântef.

78. 

Son of the Sun Ân-āa.

79. 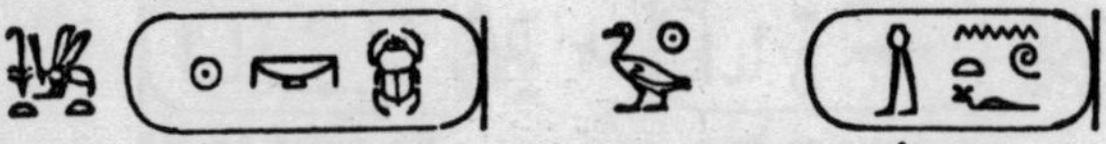

Nub-χeper-Rā, son of the Sun, Ântuf.

80. 

Āḥā-Ḥeru-Rā-âpu-maāt, son of the Sun, Ântuf-āa.

81. 

Āḥā-renpit-Rā-âput-maāt, son of the Sun, Ântef-āa.

82. 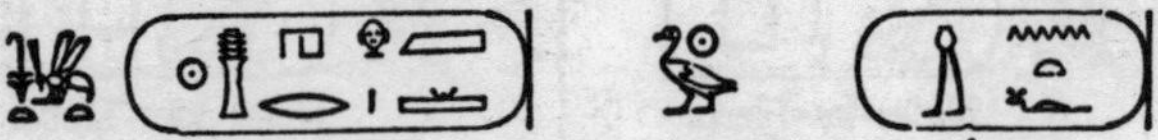

Ṭeṭ-Rā-her-ḥer-maāt, son of the Sun, Ântef.

83. 

Senefer-ka-Rā.

84. 

Rā . . . . . .

85. 

Usr-en-Rā.

86. 

Neb-nem-Rā.

87. 

Son of the Sun, Menθu-ḥetep (I.).

88. 

Se-Rā-Menθ-ḥetep (II.).

89. 

Neb-ḥetep-Rā, son of the Sun, Menθ-ḥetep (III.).

90. 

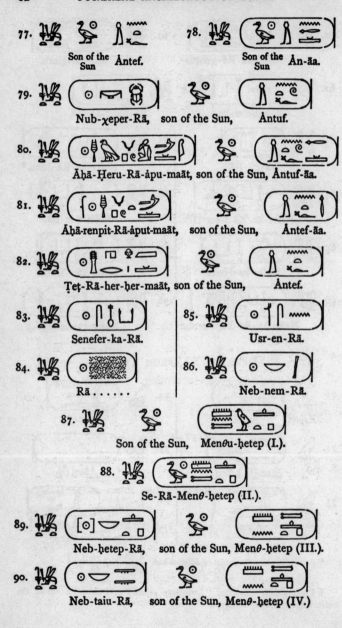

Neb-taiu-Rā, son of the Sun, Menθ-ḥetep (IV.)

91. 

Neb-χeru-Rā, son of the Sun, Menθ-ḥetep (V.).

92. 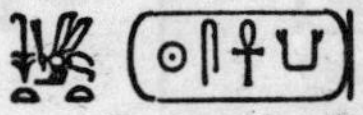

Se-ānχ-ka-Rā.

## DYNASTY XII., FROM THEBES, B.C. 2466.

93. 

Seḥetep-åb-Rā, son of the Sun, Åmen-em-ḥāt (I.).

94. 

χeper-ka-Rā, son of the Sun, Usertsen (I.).

95. 

Nub-kau-Rā, son of the Sun, Åmen-em-ḥāt (II.).

96. 

χeper-χā-Rā, son of the Sun, Usertsen (II.).

97. 

χā-kau-Rā, son of the Sun, Usertsen (III.).

98. 

Māāt-en-Rā, son of the Sun, Åmen-em-ḥāt (III.).

99. 

Māā-χeru-Rā, son of the Sun, Åmen-em-ḥāt (IV.).

100. 

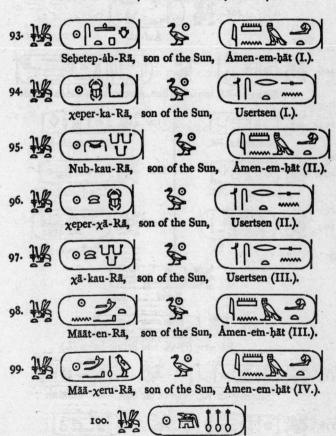

Sebek-neferu-Rā.

## DYNASTY XIII., B.C. 2233.

101. 
χu-taiu-Rā.

102. 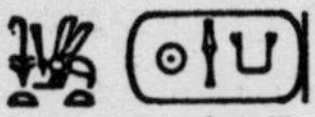
χerp-ka-Rā.

103. 
. . . . em-ḥāt.

104. 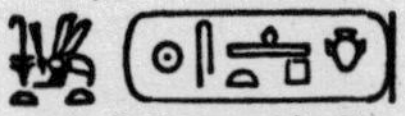
Seḥetep-àb-Rā.

105. 
Àuf-nà.

106. 
Seānχ-àb-Rā, son of the Sun, Àmeni-Àntef-Àmen-em-ḥāt.

107. 
Semen-ka-Rā.

108. 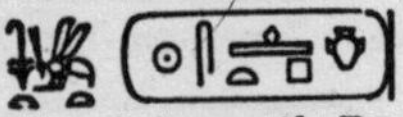
Seḥetep-àb-Rā.

109. 
. . . . . ka.

110. 
Net'em-àb-Rā.

111. 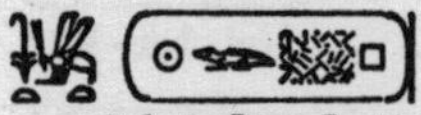
Sebek-[ḥete]p-Rā.

112. 
Ren . . . . . .

113. 
Set'ef . . . . Rā.

114. 
Rā-χerp (?)-χu-taiu Sebek-ḥetep (I.).

115. 
Semenχ-ka-Rā, son of the Sun, Mer-menfitu.

116. 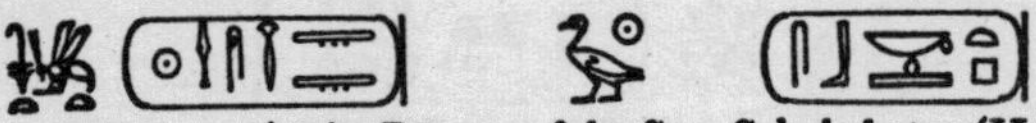
χerp-seuat'-taiu-Rā, son of the Sun, Sebek-ḥetep (II.).

117. 

χā-seshesh-Rā, son of the Sun, Nefer-ḥetep.

118. 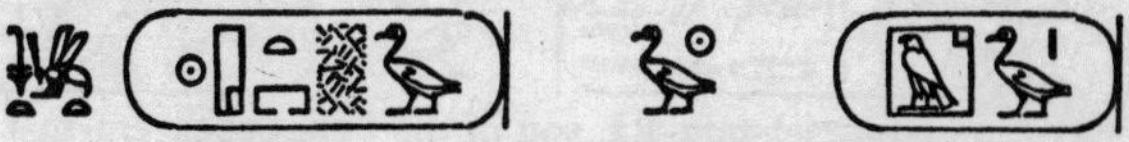

Rā-ḥet . . . . se, son of the Sun, Ḥet-Ḥeru-se.

119. 

χā-nefer-Rā, son of the Sun, Sebek-ḥetep (III.).

120. 

χā-ḥetep-Rā, son of the Sun, Sebek-ḥetep (IV.).

121. 

Uaḥ-àb-Rā-àā-àb.

122. 

χāā-χeru-Rā.

123. 

Neb-f-ā(?) a-mer-Rā.

124. 

Nefer àb-Rā.

125. 

χā-ānχ-Rā, son of the Sun, Sebek-ḥetep (V.).

126. 

Mer-χerp-Rā.

127. 

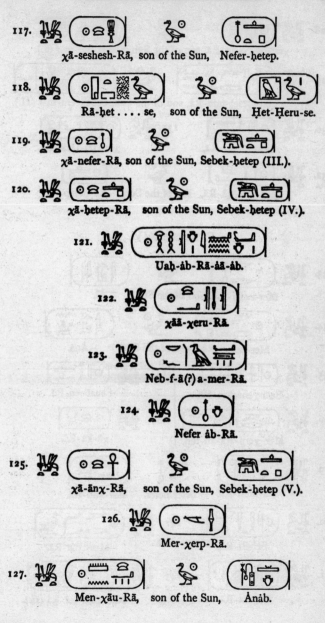

Men-χāu-Rā, son of the Sun, Ȧnȧb.

128 

χerp-uat'-χāu-Rā, son of the Sun, Sebek-em-sa-f (I.).

129. 

χerp-seśeṭ-taiu-Rā, son of the Sun, Sebek-em-sa-f (II.).

130. 

Sesusr-taiu-Rā,

131. 

χerp (?)-Uast-Rā.

132. 

χerp-uaḥ-χā-Rā, son of the Sun, Rā-ḥetep.

## Dynasty XIV.

133. 

Mer-nefer-Rā, son of the Sun, Ȧi.

134. 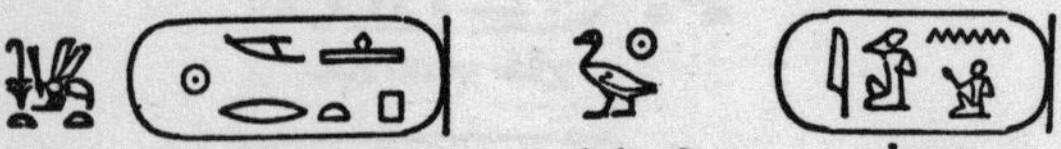

Mer-ḥetep-Rā, son of the Sun, Ȧnȧ.

135. 

Seānχenseḥtu-Rā.

136. 

Mer-χerp-Rā-ȧn-ren.

137. 

Seuat'-en-Rā.

138. 

χā-ka-Rā.

139. 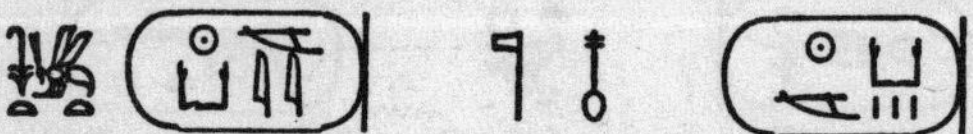

Ka-meri-Rā. neter nefer. Mer-kau-Rā.

140. 

Seḥeb-Rā.

141. 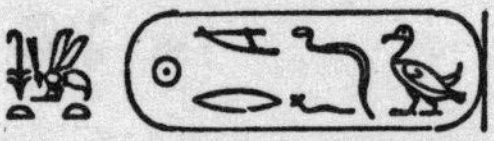

Mer-t'efa-Rā.

142. 

Sta-ka-Rā.

143. 

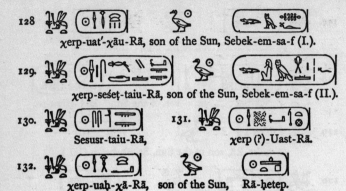

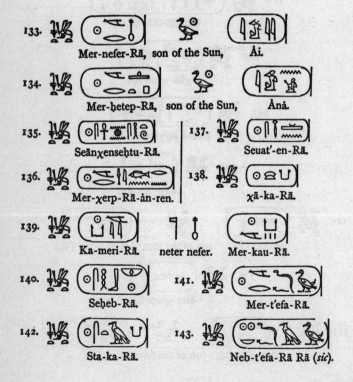

Neb-t'efa-Rā Rā (*sic*).

144. 
Uben-Rā.

145. 
Her-āb-Rā.

146. 
Neb-sen-Rā.

147. 
Seuaḥ-en-Rā.

148. 
Seχeper-en-Rā.

149. 
Ṭeṭ-χeru-Rā.

## DYNASTY XV., "SHEPHERD KINGS."

150. 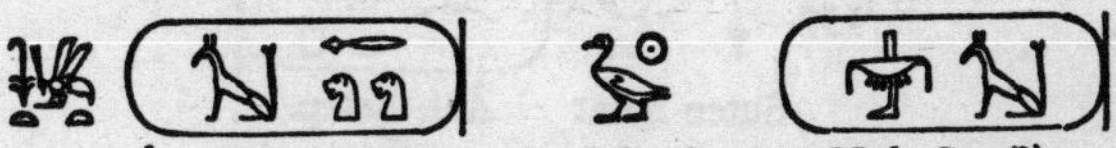
Āa-peḥ-peḥ-Set, son of the Sun, Nub-Set (?).

151. 
. . . . Bānān.

152. 
Ābeḥ (?)-en-χepeś.

153. 
Āpepā.

## DYNASTY XVI., "SHEPHERD KINGS."

154. 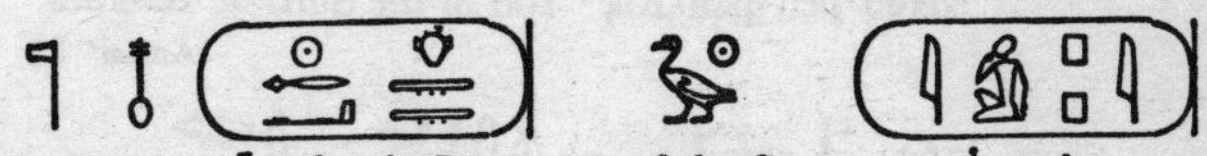
Neter nefer Āa-āb-taiu-Rā, son of the Sun, Āpepā.
Beautiful god.

*or* neter nefer Āa-qenen-Rā.

## DYNASTY XVII., FROM THEBES.

155. 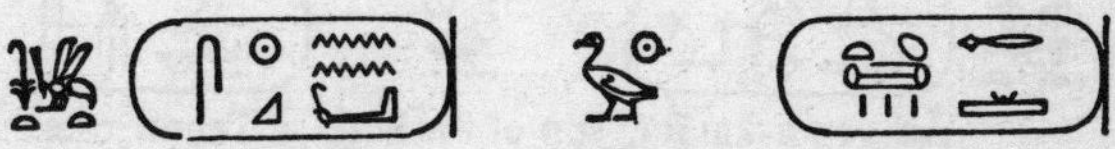
Seqenen-Rā, son of the Sun, Tau-āa.

156. 

Seqenen-Rā, son of the Sun, Tau-āa-āa.

157. 

Seqenen-Rā, son of the Sun, Tau-āa-qen.

158. 

Uat′-χeper-Rā, son of the Sun, Kames.

159. 

Suten ḥemt Āāh-ḥetep.
Royal wife.

160. 

Āāh-mes-se-pa-āri.

## DYNASTY XVIII., FROM THEBES, B.C. 1700.

161. 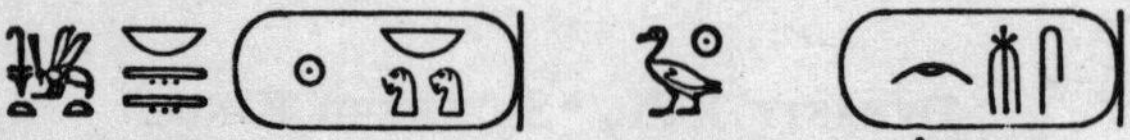

Neb-peḥ-peḥ-Rā, son of the Sun, Āāḥmes.
(Amāsis I.)

162. 

Neter ḥemt Āāh-mes-nefert-āri.
Divine wife.

163. 

Ser-ka-Rā, son of the Sun, Āmen-ḥetep.
(Amenophis I.)

164. 

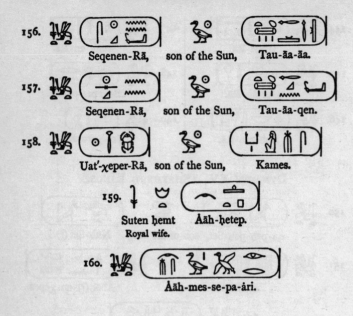

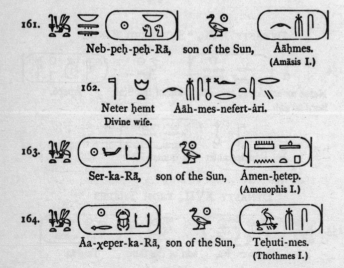

Āa-χeper-ka-Rā, son of the Sun, Teḥuti-mes.
(Thothmes I.)

165. 

Āa-χeper-en-Rā, son of the Sun, Nefer-χāu-Teḫuti-mes.
(Thothmes II.)

166. 

Māt-ka-Rā, son of the Sun, Ḥāt-shepset-χnem-Āmen.
(Queen Hatshepsu.)

167. 

Men-χeper-Rā, son of the Sun, Teḫuti-mes.
(Thothmes III.)

168. 

Āa-χeperu-Rā, son of the Sun, Āmen-ḥetep neter ḥeq Ānnu.
(Amenophis II.)

169. 

Men-χeperu-Rā, son of the Sun, Teḫuti-mes χā-χāu.
(Thothmes IV.)

170. 

Neb-māt-Rā, son of the Sun, Āmen-ḥetep ḥeq-Uast.
(Amenophis III.)

171. 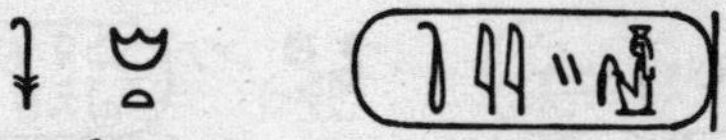

Suten ḥemt θi.
(The Mesopotamian wife of Amenophis III.)

172. 

Nefer-χeperu-Rā-uā-en-Rā, son of the Sun, Āmen-ḥetep neter ḥeq Uast.
(Amenophis IV.)

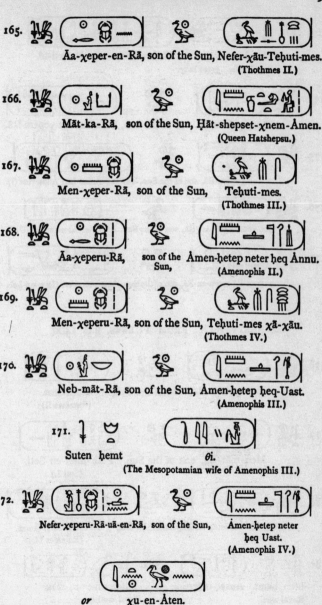

*or* χu-en-Āten.

173. 

Suten ḥemt urt Nefer-neferu-åten Neferti-ī$\theta$.

Royal wife, great lady.

174. 

Ān$\chi$-$\chi$eperu-Rā, son of the Sun, Seāa-ka-ne$\chi$t-$\chi$eperu-Rā.

175. 

Neb-$\chi$eperu-Rā, son of the Sun, Tut-ān$\chi$-Åmen ḥeq Ånnu resu (?).

176. 

$\chi$eper-$\chi$eperu-māt-åri-Rā, son of the Sun, Atf-neter Ai neter ḥeq Uast.

177. 

Ser-$\chi$eperu-Rā-setep-en-Rā, son of the Sun, Åmen-meri-en-Ḥeru-em-ḥeb.

## DYNASTY XIX., FROM THEBES, B.C. 1400.

178. 

Men-peḥtet-Rā, son of the Sun, Rā-messu.

(Rameses I.)

179. 

Men-māt-Rā, son of the Sun, Ptaḥ-meri-en-Seti.

(Seti I.)

180. 

Usr-māt-Rā setep-en-Rā, son of the Sun, Rā-messu-meri-Åmen.

(Rameses II.)

181. 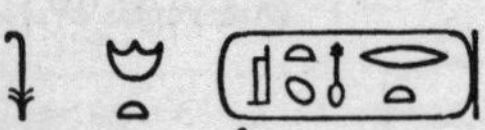

Suten ḥemt Åuset-nefert.

Royal wife.

182. 

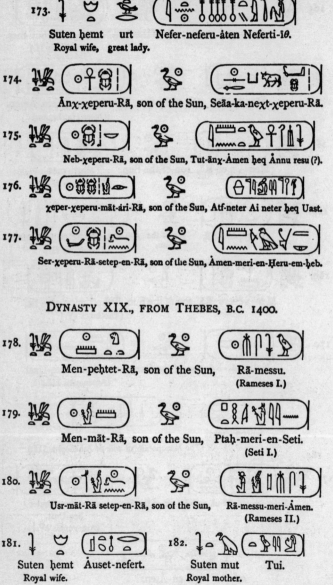

Suten mut Tui.

Royal mother.

183. 

Ba-Rā-meri-en-Åmen, son of the Sun, Ptaḥ-meri-en-ḥetep-ḥer-māt. (Meneptah I.)

184. 

Men-mā-Rā setep-en-Rā, son of the Sun, Åmen-meses-ḥeq-Uast. (Amen-meses.)

185. 

Usr-χeperu-Rā-meri-Åmen, son of the Sun, Seti-meri-en-Ptaḥ. (Seti II).

186. 

χu-en-Rā setep-en-Rā, son of the Sun, Ptaḥ-meri-en-se-Ptaḥ. (Meneptah II.)

187. 

Usr-χāu-Rā setep-en-Rā meri-Åmen, son of the Sun, Rā-meri Åmen-merer Set-neχt. (Set-Neχt.)

## DYNASTY XX., FROM THEBES, B.C. 1200.

188. 

Usr-māt-Rā-meri-Åmen, son of the Sun, Rā-meses-ḥeq-Annu. (Rameses III.)

189. 

Usr-māt-Rā setep-en-Åmen, son of the Sun, Rā-meses-meri-Åmen-Rā ḥeq māt. (Rameses IV.)

190. 

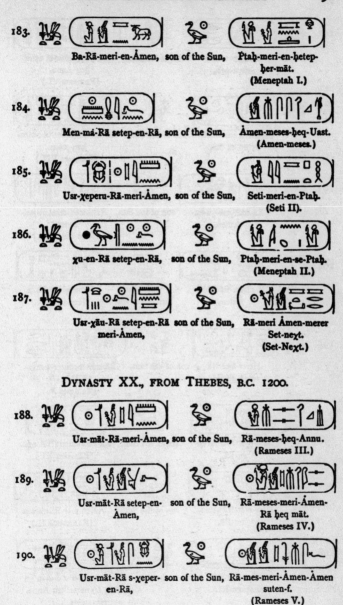

Usr-māt-Rā s-χeper-en-Rā, son of the Sun, Rā-mes-meri-Åmen-Åmen suten-f. (Rameses V.)

191. 

Rā-Ȧmen-māt-meri-neb, son of the Sun, Rā-Ȧmen-meses neter ḥeq Ȧnnu. (Rameses VI.)

192. 

Rā-usr-Ȧmen-meri-setep-en-Rā, son of the Sun, Rā-Ȧmen-meses-tȧ-neter-ḥeq-Ȧnnu. (Rameses VII.)

193. 

Rā-māt-usr-χu-en-Ȧmen, son of the Sun, Rā-Ȧmen-meses-meri-Ȧmen. (Rameses VIII.)

194. 

Neb ta Lord of the land, S-χā-en-Rā Meri-Ȧmen, neb χāu lord of crowns, Rāmeses-se-Ptaḥ. (Rameses IX.)

195. 

Nefer-kau-Rā setep-en-Rā, son of the Sun, Rā-meses-merer-Ȧmen-χā-Uast (?). (Rameses X.)

196. 

Rā-χeper-māt setep-en-Rā, son of the Sun, Rā-mes suten (?) Ȧmen. (Rameses XI.)

197. 

Usr-māt-Rā setep-nu-Rā, son of the Sun, Ȧmen mer-Rā-meses. (Rameses XII.)

198. 

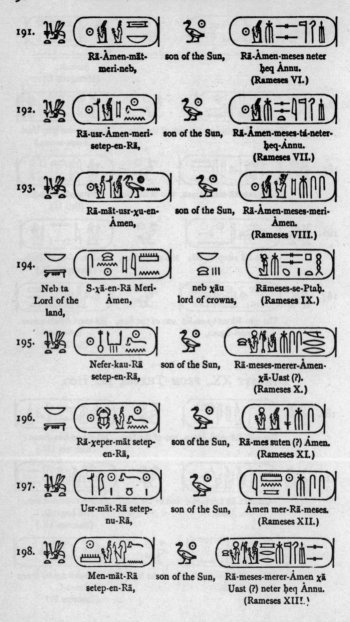

Men-māt-Rā setep-en-Rā, son of the Sun, Rā-meses-merer-Ȧmen χā Uast (?) neter ḥeq Ȧnnu. (Rameses XIII.)

## DYNASTY XXI., FROM TANIS, B.C. 1100.

### I.

199. 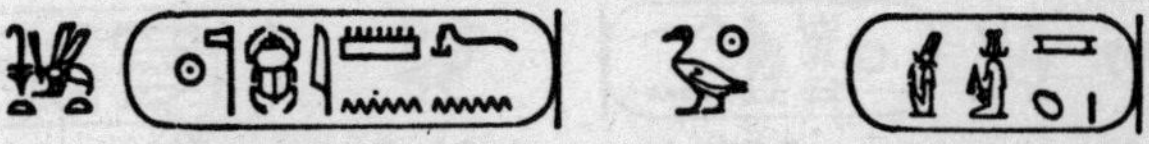

Rā-neter-χeper setep-en-Åmen, son of the Sun, Se-Mentu meri-Rā. (Se-Mentu.)

200. 

Rā-āa-χeper setep-en-Mentu, son of the Sun, Åmen-meri Pa-seb-χā-nu. (Pasebχānu I.)

201. 

Åa-seḥ-Rā, son of the Sun, . . . . . .

202. 

Setep-en-Mentu-Rā, son of the Sun, Meri-Mentu-Åmen-em-āpt. (Amenemapt.)

203. 

Ḥet' ḥeq . . . . . . . son of the Sun, Meri-Åmen Pa-seb-χā-nu. (Pasebχānu II.)

## DYNASTY XXI., FROM THEBES, B.C. 1100.

### II.

204. 

Neter-ḥen-ḥetep en-Åmen, son of the Sun, Ḥer-Ḥeru-se-Åmen. (Ḥer-Ḥeru.)
Prophet first of Amen,

205. 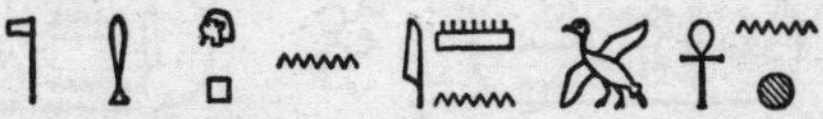

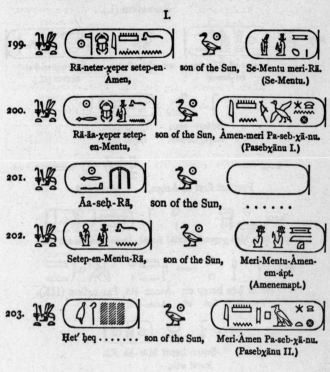

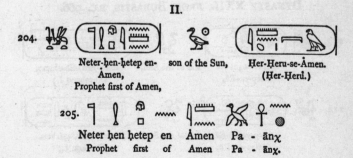

Neter ḥen ḥetep en Åmen Pa - ānχ
Prophet first of Amen Pa - ānχ.

206. 

Pai-net'em (I.).

207. 

χeper-χā-Rā-setep-en-Åmen, son of the Sun, Åmen-meri-Pai-net'em (II.).

208. 

Suten mut Ḥent-taiu.
Royal mother, Ḥent-taiu.

209. 

Prophet first of Amen, Masaherθ.

210. 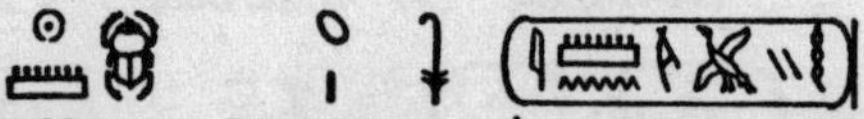

Prophet first, Men-χeper-Rā, child Royal, Åmen-meri Pai-net'em.

211. 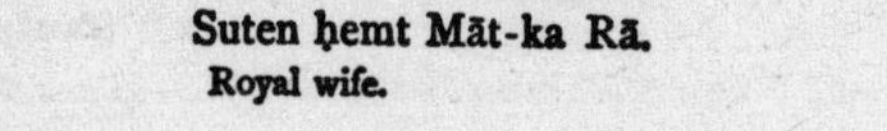

Neter ḥen ḥetep en Åmen-Rā, Pai-nat'em (III.).
Prophet first of Amen-Rā.

212. 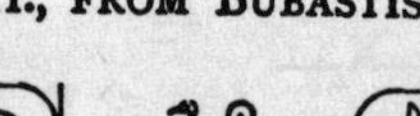

Suten ḥemt Māt-ka Rā.
Royal wife.

## Dynasty XXII., from Bubastis, b.c. 966.

213. 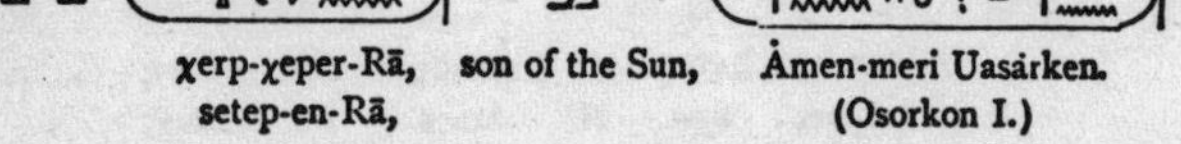

χeper-seχet-Rā setep-en-Rā, son of the Sun, Åmen-meri-Shashanq. (Shashanq I.)

214. 

χerp-χeper-Rā, setep-en-Rā, son of the Sun, Åmen-meri Uasárken. (Osorkon I.)

215. 

Ḥet'-Rā-setep-en-Åmen neter ḥeq Uast, son of the Sun, Åmen-meri Auset-meri θekeleθ. (Takeleth I.)

216. 

Rā-usr-māt setep-en-Åmen, son of the Sun, Åmen-meri Uasårken. (Osorkon II.)

217. 

χeper-seχem-Rā setep-en-Åmen, son of the Sun, Åmen-meri Shash[anq]. (Shashanq II.)

218. 

Ḥet'-χeperu-Rā setep-en-Rā, son of the Sun, Åmen-Rā-meri Åuset-meri θekeleθ. (Takeleth.)

219. 

Usr-māt-Rā setep-en-Rā, son of the Sun, Åmen-meri-se-Bast Shasha[n]q. (Shashanq III.)

220. 

Usr-māt-Rā setep-en-Åmen, son of the Sun, Åmen-meri Pa-māi. (Pa-mai.)

## DYNASTY XXIII., FROM TANIS, B.C. 766.

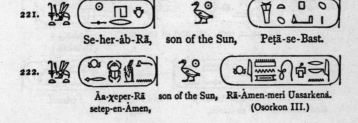

221. 

Se-her-åb-Rā, son of the Sun, Peṭā-se-Bast.

222. 

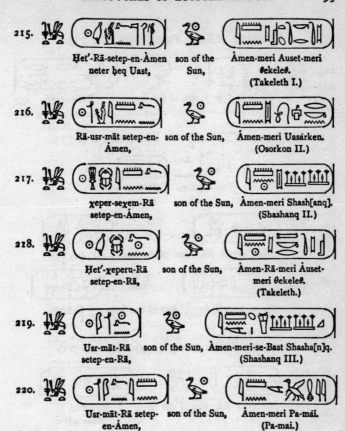

Āa-χeper-Rā setep-en-Åmen, son of the Sun, Rā-Åmen-meri Uasarkenå. (Osorkon III.)

## Dynasty XXIV., from Sais, B.C. 733.

223. 

Uaḥ-ka-Rā, son of the Sun, Bakenrenf.

## Dynasty XXIV., from Ethiopia, B.C. 733.

224. 

Suten Kaśta.
King Kashta.

225. 

Men-χeper-Rā, son of the Sun, P-ānχi.

226. 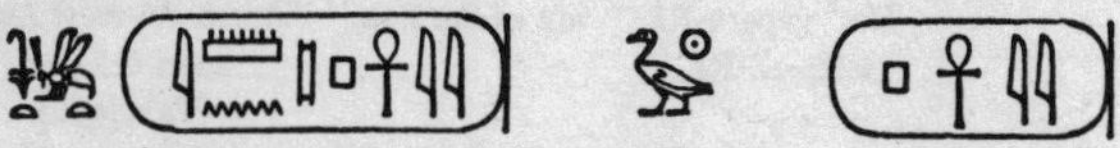

Ȧmen-meri P-ānχi, son of the Sun, P-ānχi.

## Dynasty XXV., from Ethiopia, B.C. 700.

227. 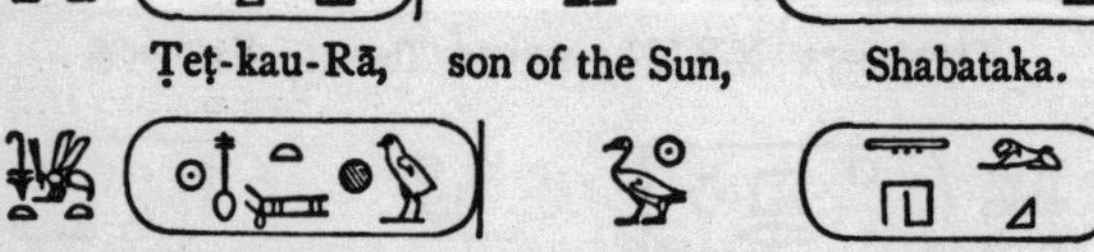

Nefer-ka-Rā, son of the Sun, Shabaka.
(Sabaco.)

228. 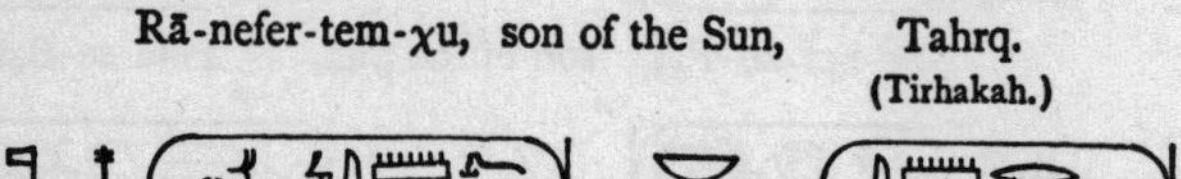

Ṭeṭ-kau-Rā, son of the Sun, Shabataka.

229. 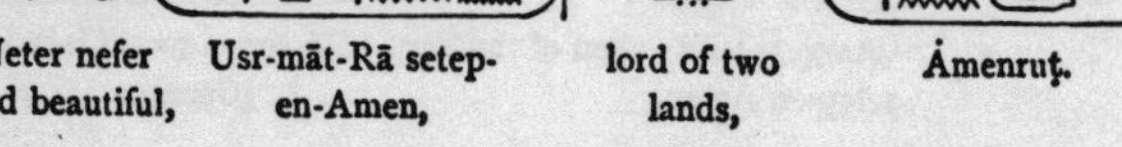

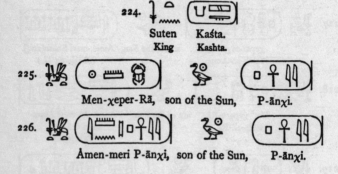

Rā-nefer-tem-χu, son of the Sun, Tahrq.
(Tirhakah.)

230. 

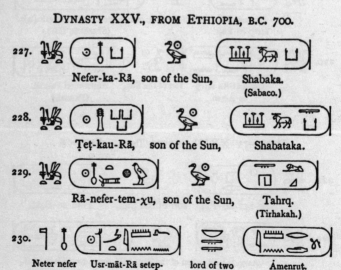

Neter nefer God beautiful, Usr-māt-Rā setep-en-Amen, lord of two lands, Ȧmenruṭ.

## DYNASTY XXVI., FROM SAIS, B.C. 666.

231. 

Uaḥ-àb-Rā, son of the Sun, Psemθek.
(Psammetichus I.)

232. 

Nem-àb-Rā, son of the Sun, Nekau.
(Necho II.)

233. 

Nefer-àb-Rā, son of the Sun, Psemθek.
(Psammetichus II.)

234. 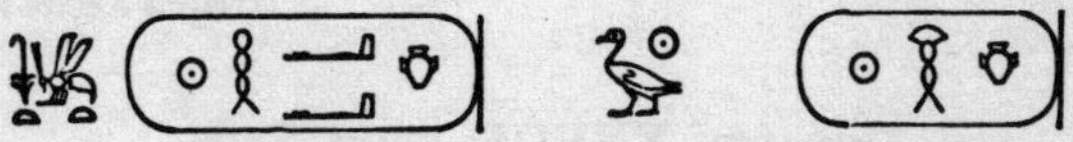

Ḥāā-àb-Rā, son of the Sun, Uaḥ àb-Rā.
(Apries.)

235. 

χnem-àb-Rā, son of the Sun, Åḥmes-se-net.
(Amāsis II.)

236. 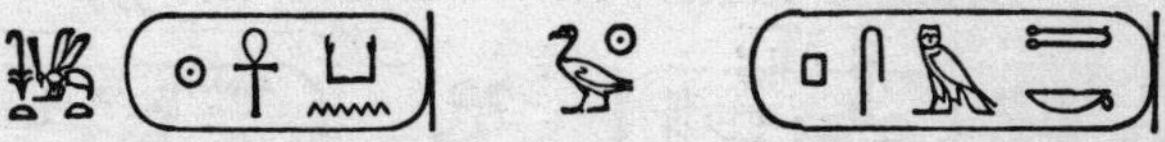

Ānχ-ka-en-Rā, son of the Sun, Psemθek.
(Psammetichus III.)

## DYNASTY XXVII. (PERSIAN), B.C. 527.

237. 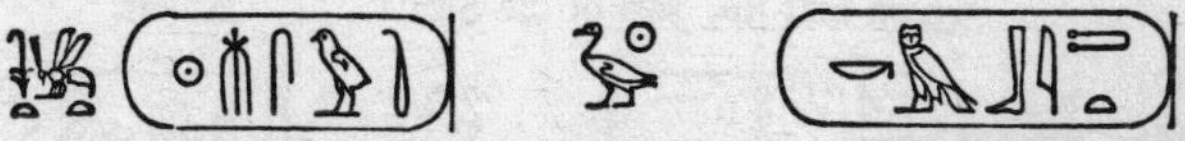

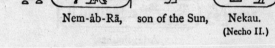

Mesuθ-Rā, son of the Sun, Kembàθet.
(Cambyses.)

238. 

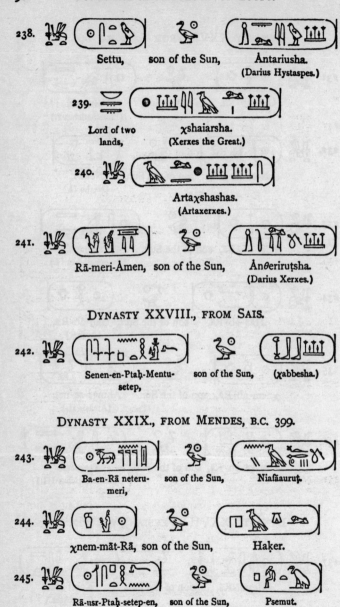

Settu, son of the Sun, Åntariusha.
(Darius Hystaspes.)

239. 

Lord of two lands, χshaiarsha.
(Xerxes the Great.)

240. 

Artaχshashas.
(Artaxerxes.)

241. 

Rā-meri-Åmen, son of the Sun, Ånθeriruṭsha.
(Darius Xerxes.)

## DYNASTY XXVIII., FROM SAIS.

242. 

Senen-en-Ptaḥ-Mentu-setep, son of the Sun, (χabbesha.)

## DYNASTY XXIX., FROM MENDES, B.C. 399.

243. 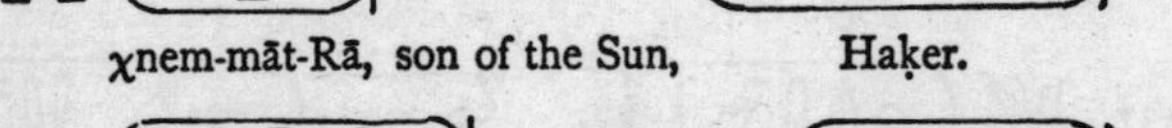

Ba-en-Rā neteru-meri, son of the Sun, Niafāauruṭ.

244. 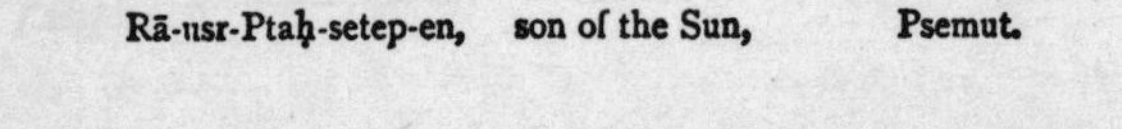

χnem-māt-Rā, son of the Sun, Haḳer.

245. 

Rā-usr-Ptaḥ-setep-en, son of the Sun, Psemut.

## DYNASTY XXX. FROM SEBENNYTUS, B.C. 378.

246. 

S-net'em-ȧb-Rā setep-en-Ȧmen, son of the Sun, Neχt-Ḥeru-ḥebt-meri-Ȧmen. (Nectanebus I.)

247. 

χeper-ka-Rā, son of the Sun, Neχt-neb-f. (Nectanebus II.)

## DYNASTY XXXI.,* PERSIANS.

## DYNASTY XXXII., MACEDONIANS, B.C. 332.

248. 

Setep-ka-en-Rā-meri-Ȧmen, son of the Sun, Aleksȧnṭres. (Alexander the Great.)

249. 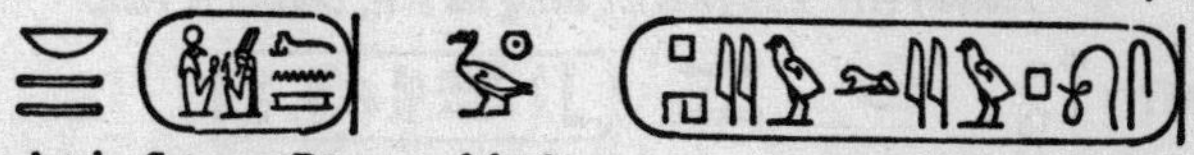

neb taiu Setep-en-Rā-meri-Ȧmen, son of the Sun, Phiuliupuas. (Philip Aridaeus.)

250. 

Rā-ḥāā-ȧb-setep-en-Ȧmen, son of the Sun, Aleksȧnṭres. (Alexander IV.)

## DYNASTY XXXIII., PTOLEMIES, B.C. 305.

251. 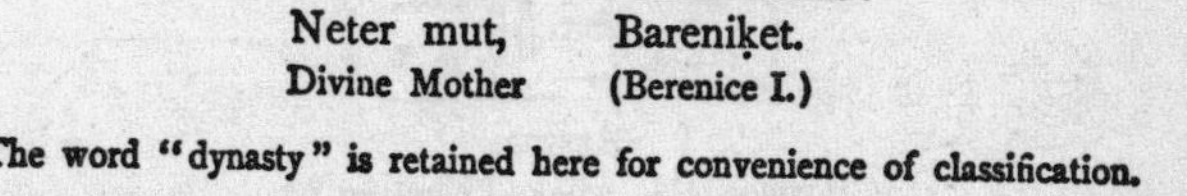

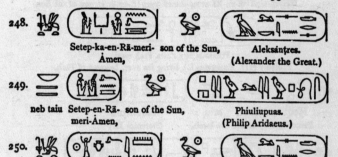

Setep-en-Rā-meri-Ȧmen, son of the Sun, Pṭulmis. (Ptolemy I. Soter I.)

252. 

Neter mut, Divine Mother Bareniḳet. (Berenice I.)

* The word "dynasty" is retained here for convenience of classification.

253. 

Rā-usr-ka-meri Åmen, son of the Sun, Ptulmis.
(Ptolemy II. Philadelphus.)

254. 

Sutenet set suten sent suten ḥemt neb taiu Årsanat.
Royal daughter, royal sister, royal wife, lady of the two lands (Arsinoë).

255. 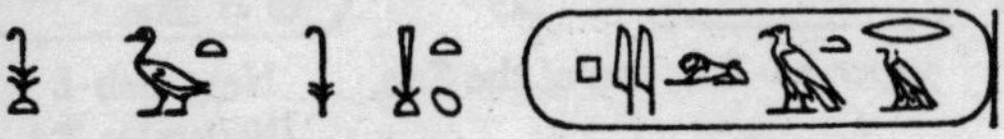

Suten set suten sent Pilatra.
Royal daughter, royal sister (Philotera).

256. 

Neteru-senu-uā-en-Rā-setep-Åmen-χerp (?)-en-ānχ, son of the Son,

Ptualmis ānχ t'etta Ptaḥ meri
Ptolemy (III. Euergetes I.), living for ever, beloved of Ptaḥ.

257. 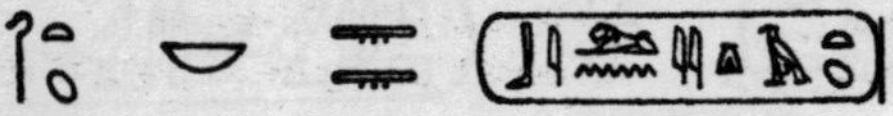

Ḥeqt nebt taiu, Bårenikat.
Princess, lady of the two lands, (Berenice II.)

258. 

Neteru-menχ-uā-[en]-Ptaḥ-setep-en-Rā-usr-ka-Åmen-χerp (?) ānχ,

son of the Sun, Ptualmis ānχ t'etta Åuset meri.
Ptolemy (IV. Philopator,) living for ever, beloved of Isis.

259. 

Suten set suten sent ḥemt urt nebt taiu
Royal daughter, royal sister, wife, great lady, lady of the two lands,

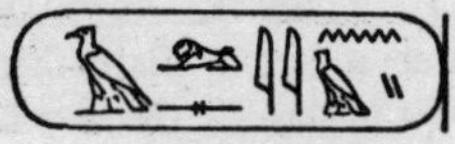

Arsinai.
Arsinoë (III., wife of Philopator I.).

260. 

Neteru-meri-uā-en-Ptaḥ-setep-Rā-usr-ka-Àmen-χerp-ānχ,

son of the Sun, Ptualmis ānχ t'etta Ptaḥ meri.
Ptolemy (V. Epiphanes) living for ever, beloved of Ptaḥ.

261. Ptolemy VI. Eupator, wanting.

262. 

Suten set sen ḥemt Qlauaperat.
Royal daughter, sister, wife, (Cleopatra I.)

263. 

Neteru-χu (?)-uā-Ptaḥ-χeper-setep-en-Rā-Àmen-àri-māt (?),

son of the Sun, Ptualmis ānχ t'etta Ptaḥ meri.
Ptolemy (VII. Philometor I.), living for ever, beloved of Ptaḥ.

264. 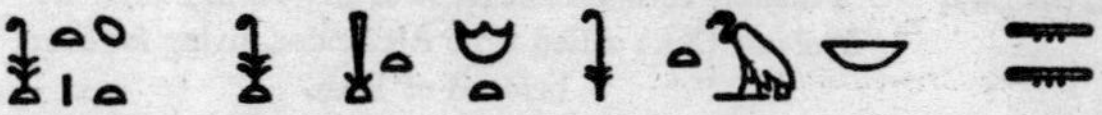

Sutenet set suten sent ḥemt suten mut neb taiu
Royal daughter, royal sister, wife, royal mother, lady of the two lands,

Qlàuapeṭrat.
(Cleopatra II. wife of Philometor I.)

265. Ptolemy VIII. Philopator II. wanting.

266. 

Neteru-χu (?)-uā-en-Ptaḥ-setep-en-Rā-Àmen-àri-māt χerp ānχ,

son of the Sun, Ptualmis ānχ t'etta Ptaḥ meri.
Ptolemy (IX. Euergetes II.), living for ever, beloved of Ptaḥ.

267. 

Suten net
King of North and South, lord of two lands,

Neteru-menχ-māt-s-meri-net-uā-Ptaḥ-χerp (?)-setep-en-Rā-Åmen-åri-māt,

Rā-se neb χāu — Ptualmis ānχ t'etta Ptaḥ meri.
Son of the Sun, lord of diadems, — Ptolemy X. (Soter II. Philometor II.)

268. 

Suten net, King of North and South, — Neteru-menχ-uā-Ptaḥ-setep-en-Rā-Åmen-åri-māt-senen-Ptaḥ-ānχ-en,

son of the Sun, — Ptualmis t'etu-nef Åleksentres ānχ t'etta Ptaḥ meri.
Ptolemy (XI.) called is he Alexander, living for ever, beloved of Ptaḥ.

269. 

Ḥeqt neb taiu — Erpā-ur-qebḥ-Båaårenekåt.
Princess, lady of two lands, — Berenice (III.)

270. Ptolemy XII. (Alexander II.), wanting.

271. 

P-neter-n-uā-enti-neḥem-Ptaḥ-setep-en-åri-māt-en-Rā-Åmen-χerp-ānχ,

son of the Sun, — Ptualmis ānχ t'etta Ptaḥ Åuset meri.
Ptolemy (XIII.), living for ever, beloved of Isis and Ptaḥ.

272. 

Neb taiu — Qlapeṭrat t'eṭtu-nes Ṭrapenet

Lady of two lands, — Cleopatra (V.), called is she Tryphaena.

273. 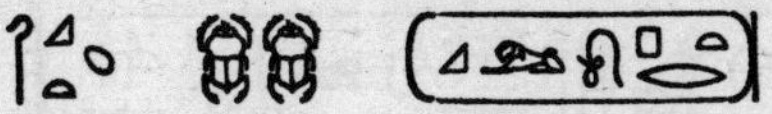

Ḥeqt — taiu — Qluapeter.

Queen — of two lands, — Cleopatra (VI.).

274. 

Suten net — neb — taiu — Ptualmis

King of North and South, — lord of — two lands, — Ptolemy (XIV.),

Rā — se — neb — χāā — Kiseres ānχ t'etta Ptaḥ Åuset meri.

son of the Sun, — lord of diadems, — Cæsar, living for ever, of Ptaḥ and Isis beloved.

## Dynasty XXXIV., Roman Emperors, B.C. 27.

275. 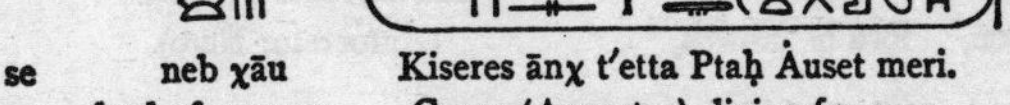

Suten net — neb — taiu — Auteqreṭer

King of North and South, — lord of — two lands, — Autocrator,

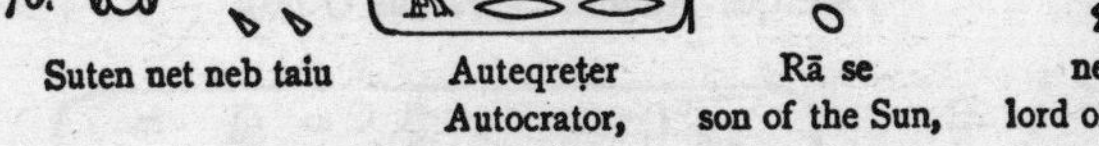

Rā se — neb χāu — Kiseres ānχ t'etta Ptaḥ Åuset meri.

Sun's son, — lord of crowns, — Cæsar (Augustus), living for ever, of Ptaḥ and Isis beloved.

276. 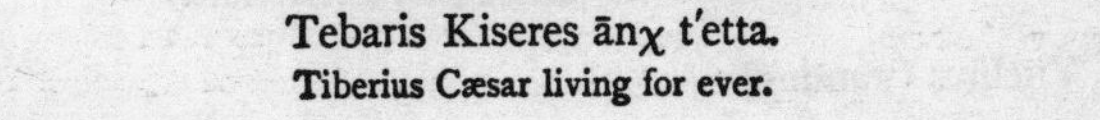

Suten net neb taiu — Auteqreṭer — Rā se — neb χāu

Autocrator, — son of the Sun, — lord of diadems,

Tebaris Kiseres ānχ t'etta.

Tiberius Cæsar living for ever.

277. 

Ḥeq ḥequ Auteḳreṭer Ptaḥ Åuset-meri son of the Sun,
King of kings, Autocrator, of Ptaḥ and Isis beloved,

Qais Kaiseres Kermeniqis.
Gaius (Caligula) Cæsar Germanicus.

278. 

Suten net neb taiu Auteqreṭer Kiseres
Autocrator Cæsar,

Rā se neb χāu Qlutes Tibaresa.
Sun's son, lord of crowns, Claudius Tiberius.

279. 

King of North and South, neb taiu lord of two lands, Ḥeq ḥequ-setep-en-Åuset meri Ptaḥ
Ruler of rulers, chosen one of Isis, beloved of Ptaḥ.

se Rā neb χāu Auteḳreṭer Anrȧni.
Sun's son, lord of crowns, (Autocrator Nero).

280. 

Merqes Auθunes (Marcus Otho).

Sun's son, lord of crowns, Kiseres netχ Autuḳreter.
Cæsar . . . . Autocrator.

281. Vitellius (wanting).

282 

Suten net (?) Auṭuḳretur Kisares

Autocrator Cæsar,

Suten net (?) Uspisines netχ

Vespasianus . . . . .

283. 

Autekretur Tetis Keseres.

Autocrator Titus Cæsar,

Sun's son, lord of crowns, Uspesines netχ.

Vespasianus . . . .

284. 

Autuḳretur Kiseres.

Autocrator Cæsar,

Sun's son, lord of crowns, Tumetines netχ.

Domitianus . . . .

285. 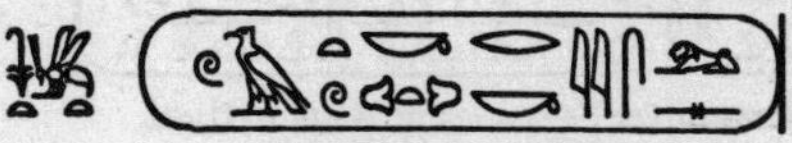 

Autukreter Kiseres. son of the Sun,

Autocrator Cæsar.

Neruȧs netχ.

Nerva . . . . .

286. 

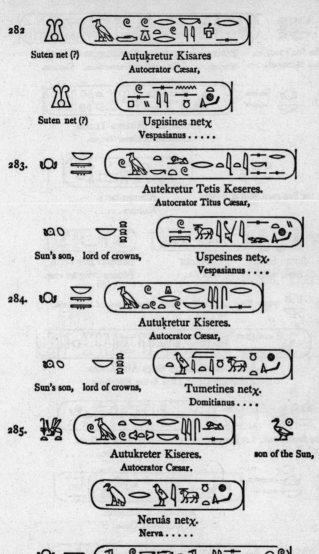

Autukreṭer Kaiseres Neruaui.

Autocrator Cæsar Nerva,

the Sun's son, lord of crowns, Trāianes netχ Arsut Kermineqsa Nteķiqes.
Trajan . . . . . (Augustus) Germanicus. Dacicus.

287. 

Autuķreter Kiseres Trinus.
Autocrator Cæsar Trajan,

the Sun's son, lord of crowns, Atrines netχ.
Hadrian. . . . .

288. 

Suten ḥemt Sābinat Sebesṭā ānχ t etta.
Royal wife, Sabina, Sebaste living for ever.

289.  King of the North and South, lord of the world,

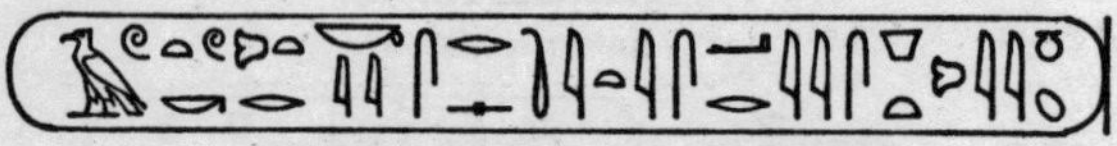

Autukreter Kiseres Θites Ālis Ātrins.
Autocrator Cæsar Titus Aelius Hadrianus,

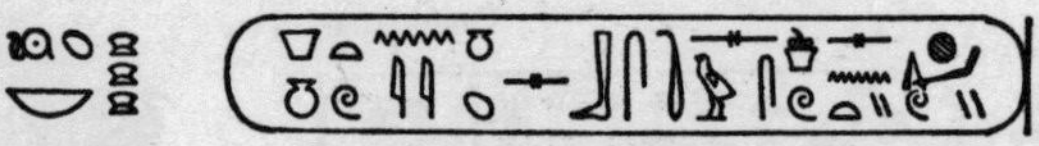

the Sun's son, lord of crowns, Āntunines Sebesθesus Baus netiχui.
Antoninus Augustus Pius. . . . . .

290. 

Autekreter Kaiseres.
Autocrator Cæsar,

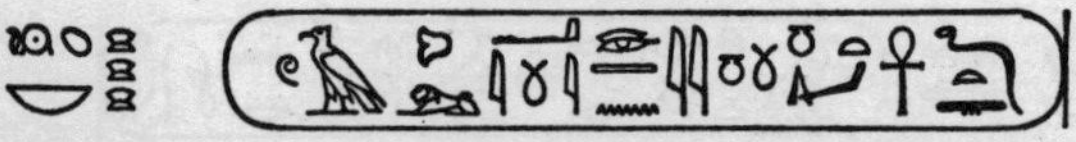

the Sun's son, lord of crowns, Aurelāis Antanines netχ ānχ t'etta.
Aurelius Antoninus, . . . . living for ever.

291. 

Autekreter
Autocrator

Ḳesers
Cæsar

Luki
Lucius

Aulli
Aelius

Uarā ānχ t'etta.
Verus, living for ever.

292. 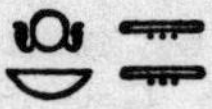

Åutekretirs Kisåures
Autocrator Cæsar,

the Sun's son, lord of crowns,

Kāmṭāus Ā-en-ta-nins neteχ.
Commodus. Antoninus . . . . .

293. Autocrator Cæsar 

Sāuris netχ.
Severus . . . .

294. Autocrator Cæsar 

Āntanenes netχ.
Antoninus [Caracalla] . . . . .

295. Autocrator Cæsar 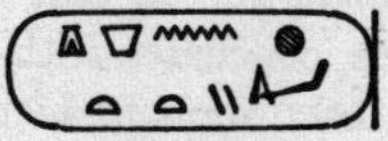

Ḳāt netiχ.
Geta . . . . .

296. Autocrator Cæsar 

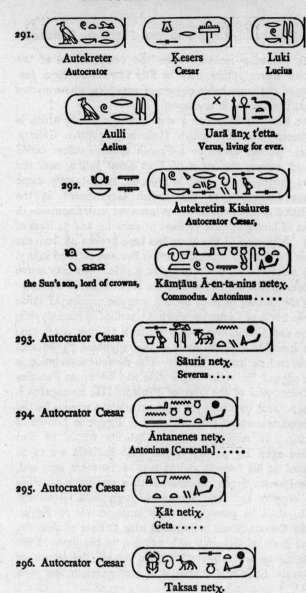

Taksas netχ.
Decius . . . . .

## THE ROSETTA STONE[1] AND THE STELE OF CANOPUS.

The following remarks upon the decipherment of the Egyptian hieroglyphics may be fitly introduced by a description of the remarkable objects of antiquity whose names stand at the head of this chapter.

**Finding of the Rosetta Stone.**

The **Rosetta Stone** is a slab of black basalt, which is now preserved in the British Museum (Egyptian Gallery, No. 24). It was found by a French artillery officer called Boussard, among the ruins of Fort Saint Julien, near the Rosetta mouth of the Nile, in 1799, but subsequently came into the possession of the British Government at the capitulation of Alexandria. It is inscribed with fragments of 14 lines of hieroglyphics, 32 lines of demotic, and 54 lines of Greek. A portion of the stone has been broken off from the top, and the right-hand bottom corner has also suffered injury. It now measures 3 ft. 9 in. × 2 ft. 4½ in. × 11 in. We may arrive at an idea of the original size of the Rosetta Stone by comparing the number of lines upon it with the number of those upon the **Stele of Canopus**, which is inscribed in hieroglyphic, demotic and Greek, measures 7 ft. 2 in. × 2 ft. 7 in. × 1 ft. 2 in., and is inscribed with 36 lines of hieroglyphics, 73 lines of demotic, and 74 lines of Greek. The demotic inscription is on the edge of the stele. This stele was set up at Canopus in the ninth year of the reign of **Ptolemy III., Euergetes I.** (B.C. 247—222), to record the decree made at Canopus by the priesthood, assembled from all parts of Egypt, in honour of the king. It records the great benefits which he had conferred upon Egypt, and states what festivals are to be celebrated in his honour, and in that of Berenice, etc., and, like the Rosetta Stone, concludes with a resolution ordering that a copy of this inscription in hieroglyphics, Greek and demotic, shall be placed in every large temple in Egypt. Now the Rosetta Stone is inscribed with 32 lines of demotic, and the Stele of Canopus with 73; but as the lines on the Rosetta Stone are rather more than double the length of those on the Stele of Canopus, it is pretty certain that each

**Stele of Canopus and Rosetta Stone compared.**

[1] A cast of the Rosetta Stone is exhibited in the Fitzwilliam Museum.

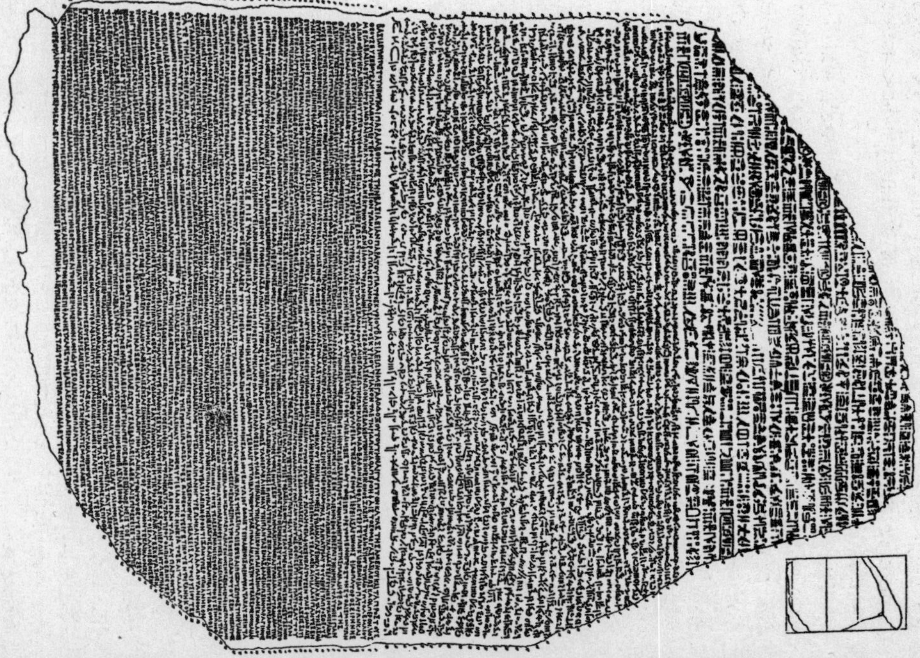

The ROSETTA STONE, inscribed with a decree of the priests of Memphis, conferring divine honours on Ptolemy V., Epiphanes, King of Egypt, B.C. 195.

document is of about the same length. The Stele of Canopus has 74 lines of Greek to 54 on the Rosetta Stone, but as the letters are longer and wider, it is clear from this also that the Greek versions occupied about the same space. Allowing then for the difference in the size of the hieroglyphic characters, we should expect the hieroglyphic inscription on the Rosetta Stone to occupy 14 or 15 lines. When complete the stele must have been about twelve inches longer than it is now, and the top was probably rounded and inscribed, like that of the Stele of Canopus, with a winged disk, having pendent uræi, that on the right wearing 𓋑, the crown of Upper Egypt, and that on the left 𓋔, the crown of Lower Egypt; by the side of each uræus, laid horizontally, would be , and above 𓋹 *tā ānch*, "giver of life."

Contents of Rosetta Stone.

The inscriptions on the Rosetta Stone form a version of a decree of the priesthood assembled at Memphis in honour of **Ptolemy V., Epiphanes**, King of Egypt, B.C. 195, written in hieroglyphics, demotic and Greek. A facsimile[1] of them was published by the Society of Antiquaries[2] in 1802, and copies were distributed among the scholars who were anxious to undertake the investigation of the texts. The hieroglyphic text has been translated by Brugsch in his *Inscriptio Rosettana*, Berlin, 1851; by Chabas, *L'Inscription hiéroglyphique de Rosette*, Paris, 1867; and by Sharpe, *The Rosetta Stone in hieroglyphics and Greek*, London, 1871, etc. The Demotic text has been studied by M. de Sacy, *Lettre à M. Chaptal sur l'inscription égypt. de Rosette*, Paris, 1802; by Akerblad, *Letter à M. de Sacy sur l'inscription égypt. de Rosette*, Paris, 1802; by Young, *Hieroglyphics* (collected by the Egyptian Society, arranged by Dr. T. Young, 2 vols., fol., 100 plates, 1823–1828), pl. x ff.; by Brugsch, *Die Inschrift von Rosette nach ihrem ägyptisch-demotischen Texte sprachlich und sachlich erklärt*, Berlin, 1850; Salvolini, *Analyse Grammaticale Raisonnée de*

Principal works on the Rosetta Stone.

[1] Other facsimiles are given in Lepsius, *Auswahl*, Bl. 18, and in Arundale and Bonomi, *Gallery of Antiquities*, pl. 49, p. 114.

[2] The Greek version of the decree of the Egyptian Priests in honour of *Ptolemy the Fifth*, surnamed *Epiphanes*, from the stone inscribed in the sacred and vulgar Egyptian and the Greek characters, taken from the French at the surrender of Alexandria. London, 1802. Nichols.

*différents textes des anciens Egyptiens*, Vol. I., *Texte hiéroglyphique et démotique de la pierre de Rosette*, Paris, 1836. This work was never finished. The Greek text has been edited by Heyne, *Commentatio in inscriptionem græcam monumenti trinis titulis insigniti ex Aegypto Londinum apportati*, in tom. xv. of *Comment. Soc. R. Sc. Gött.*, pp. 260–280; Ameilhon, *Eclaircissements sur l'inscription grecque du monument trouvé à Rosette*, Paris, 1803; Drumann, *Commentatio in inscriptionem prope Rosettam inventam*, Regiomont.. 1822; and Drumann, *Historisch-antiquarische Untersuchungen über Aegypten, oder die Inschrift von Rosette aus dem Griechischen übersetzt und erläutert*, Königsberg, 1823; Lenormant, *Essai sur le texte grec de l'inscription de Rosette*, Paris, 1842; Letronne, *Recueil des inscriptions grecques et latines d'Egypte*, Paris, 1842; by Franz in Boeckh, *Corpus Inscriptionum Græcarum*, t. iii., 1853, p. 334 ff., No. 4697, etc.

**Beneficent acts of Ptolemy V. Epiphanes.**

The inscriptions upon the Rosetta Stone set forth that Ptolemy V. Epiphanes, while king of Egypt, consecrated revenues of silver and corn to the temples, that he suppressed certain taxes and reduced others, that he granted certain privileges to the priests and soldiers, and that when, in the eighth year of his reign, the Nile rose to a great height and flooded all the plains, he undertook, at great expense, the task of damming it in and directing the overflow of its waters into proper channels, to the great gain and benefit of the agricultural classes. In addition to the remissions of taxes which he made to the people, he gave handsome gifts to the temples, and subscribed to the various ceremonies which were carried on in them. In return for these gracious acts the priesthood assembled at Memphis decreed that a statue of the king should be set up in a conspicuous place in every temple of Egypt, and that each should be inscribed with the name and titles of "Ptolemy, the saviour of Egypt." Royal apparel was to be placed on each statue, and ceremonies were to be performed before each three times a day. It was also decreed that a gilded wooden shrine, containing a gilded wooden statue of the king, should be placed in each temple, and that these were to be carried out with the shrines of the other kings in the great panegyrics. It was also decreed that ten golden crowns of a peculiar design should be made and laid upon the royal shrine; that the birthday and coronation day of the king should be celebrated each year with great pomp and show; that the first five days of the month of Thoth should each year be set apart for the performance of a festival in honour of the king; and finally that a copy of this decree, engraved upon a tablet of hard stone in hieroglyphic, demotic and Greek characters, should be set up in each of the temples of the first, second and third orders, near the statue of the ever-living Ptolemy. The Greek portion of the inscriptions appears to be the original document, and the hieroglyphic and demotic versions merely translations of it.

**Festivals in honour of Ptolemy Epiphanes.**

Although it is nearly certain that, without the aid of the Greek inscription found on the socket of an obelisk at Philæ, and the hieroglyphic inscription found on the obelisk which belonged to that socket, the hieroglyphic alphabet could never have been recovered from the Rosetta Stone, still it is around this wonderful document that all the interest in the decipherment of the Egyptian hieroglyphics clings. For many hundreds of years the interest of the learned of all countries has been excited by the hieroglyphic inscriptions of Egypt, and the theories propounded as to their contents were legion. Speaking broadly, the references to this subject by classical authors[1] are not very satisfactory; still there are some remarkable exceptions which will be referred to presently. Inasmuch as the names of Roman emperors, as late as the time of Decius, were written in hieroglyphics, it follows that the knowledge of this subject must have been possessed by some one, either Greek or Egyptian, in Egypt. "For a hundred and fifty years after the Ptolemies began to reign, the Egyptian hieroglyphics appear to have been commonly used, and the Egyptians were not prohibited from making use, so far as it seemed requisite, according to ritual or otherwise appropriate, of the native language and of its time-hallowed written signs."[2] Little by little, however, the Greek language dis-

**Rosetta Stone the base of decipherment of Egyptian hieroglyphics.**

**Late use of hieroglyphics.**

[1] See Gutschmid, *Scriptorum rerum Aegyptiacarum Series*, in *Philologus*, Bd. X., Göttingen, 1855, ss. 712 ff.

[2] Mommsen, *Provinces of the Roman Empire*, Vol. II. p. 243.

placed the Egyptian, and the writing in common use among the people, called to-day "demotic" or "enchorial," and anciently "epistolographic," completely usurped the place of the "hieratic" or cursive form of hieroglyphic writing. Although the Greeks and Romans appear not to have studied hieroglyphics thoroughly, only repeating, generally, what they were told about certain signs, nevertheless writers like Herodotus, Diodorus Siculus, Strabo, Hermapion, Chaeremon, Clemens Alexandrinus, and Horapollo, contribute information on this subject of considerable value.

**Greek writers upon Egyptian hieroglyphics.**

To **Hecataeus** of Miletus,[1] who visited Egypt between B.C. 513–501, we owe, through **Herodotus**, much knowledge of Egypt, and he must be considered the earliest Greek writer upon Egypt. **Hellanitus** of Mytilene, B.C. 478–393, shows in his *Αἰγυπτιακὰ* that he has some accurate knowledge of the meaning of some hieroglyphic words.[2] **Democritus** wrote upon the hieroglyphics of Meroë,[3] but this work is lost. **Herodotus** says that the Egyptians used two quite different kinds of writing, one of which is called sacred (hieroglyphic), the other common[4] (demotic). **Diodorus** says that the Ethiopian letters are called by the Egyptians "hieroglyphics."[5] **Strabo**, speaking of the obelisks at Thebes, says that there are inscriptions upon them which proclaim the riches and power of their kings, and that their rule extends even to Scythia, Bactria, and India.[6] **Chaeremon** of Naucratis, who lived in the first half of the first century after Christ,[7] and who must be an entirely different person from Chaeremon the companion of Aelius Gallus (B.C. 25),

[1] See *De rerum Aegyptiacarum scriptoribus Graecis ante Alexandrum Magnum*, in *Philologus*, Bd. X. s. 525.

[2] See the instances quoted in *Philologus*, Bd. X. s. 539.

[3] Περὶ τῶν ἐν Μερόῃ ἱερῶν γραμμάτων. Diogenes Laertius, *Vit. Democ.*, ed. Isaac Casaubon, 1593, p. 661.

[4] Καὶ τὰ μὲν αὐτῶν ἱρά, τὰ δὲ δημοτικὰ καλέεται. Herodotus, II. 36, ed. Didot, p. 84.

[5] Diodorus, III. 4, ed. Didot, p. 129.

[6] Strabo, XVII. 1, § 46, ed. Didot, p. 693.

[7] According to Mommsen he came to Rome, as tutor to Nero, in the reign of Claudius. *Provinces of Rome*, Vol. II. pp. 259, 273.

derided by Strabo,[1] and charged with lying by Josephus,[2] wrote a work on Egyptian hieroglyphics[3] *περὶ τῶν ἱερῶν γραμμάτων*, which has been lost. He appears to have been attached to the great library of Alexandria, and as he was a "sacred scribe," it may therefore be assumed that he had access to many important works on hieroglyphics, and that he understood them. He is mentioned by Eusebius[4] as *Χαιρήμων ὁ ἱερογραμματεύς*, and by Suidas,[5] but neither of these writers gives any information as to the contents of his work on hieroglyphics, and we should have no idea of the manner of work it was but for the extract preserved by **John Tzetzes** (Τζέτζης, born about A.D. 1110, died after A.D. 1180). Tzetzes was a man of considerable learning and literary activity, and his works[6] have value on account of the lost books which are quoted in them. In his *Chiliades*[7] (Bk. V., line 395) he speaks of *ὁ Αἰγύπτιος ἱερογραμματεὺς Χαιρήμων*, and refers to Chaeremon's *διδάγματα τῶν ἱερῶν γραμμάτων*. In his Exegesis of Homer's Iliad he gives an extract from the work itself, and we are able to see at once that it was written by one who was able to give his information at first hand. This interesting extract was first brought to the notice of the world by the late Dr. Birch, who published a paper on it in the *Transactions of the Royal Society of Literature*, Vol. III., second series, 1850, pp. 385–396. In it he quoted the Greek text of the extract, from the edition of Tzetzes' *Exegesis*, first published by Hermann,[8] and added remarks and hieroglyphic characters illustrative of it, together with the scholia of Tzetzes, the text of which he emended in places. As this extract is so important for the history of

Greek writers upon Egyptian hieroglyphics.

John Tzetzes on Egyptian hieroglyphics.

[1] Γελώμενος δὲ τὸ πλέον ὡς ἀλαζὼν καὶ ἰδιώτης. Strabo, XVII. 1, § 29, ed. Didot, p. 685.

[2] *Contra Apion.*, I. 32 ff. On the identity of Chaeremon the Stoic philosopher with Chaeremon the ἱερογραμματεύς, see Zeller, *Hermes*, XI. s. 431.

[3] His other lost work, Αἰγυπτιακά, treated of the Exodus.

[4] *Praep. Evang.*, v. 10, ed. Gaisford, t. 1, p. 421.

[5] *Sub voce* Ἱερογλυφικά.

[6] For an account of them see Krumbacher, *Geschichte aer Byzantinischen Literatur*, München, 1891, pp. 235–242.

[7] Ed. Kiessling, Leipzig, 1826, p. 191.

[8] Draconis Stratonicensis Liber de Metris Poeticis. Joannis Tzetzae Exegesis in Homeri Iliadem. Primum edidit ..... God. Hermannus, Lipsiae, 1812.

the study of hieroglyphics, it is given here, together with the scholia on it, from the excellent edition of the Greek text, by Lud. Bachmann, *Scholia in Homeri Iliadem*, Lipsiae, 1835, pp. 823, § 97 and 838, with an English translation.

Extract from Tzetzes' work on the Iliad.

Ὅμηρος δὲ, παιδευθεὶς ἀκριβῶς δὲ πᾶσαν μάθησιν ἐκ τῶν συμβολικῶν Αἰθιοπικῶν γραμμάτων, ταῦτά φησιν· οἱ γὰρ Αἰθίοπες στοιχεῖα γραμμάτων οὐκ ἔχουσιν, ἀλλ' ἀντ' αὐτῶν ζῷα παντοῖα, καὶ μέλη τούτων καὶ μόρια· βουλόμενοι γὰρ οἱ ἀρχαιότεροι τῶν ἱερογραμματέων τὸν περὶ θεῶν φυσικὸν λόγον κρύπτειν, δι' ἀλληγορικῶν καὶ συμβόλων τοιούτων καὶ γραμμάτων τοῖς ἰδίοις τέκνοις αὐτὰ παρεδίδουν, ὡς ὁ ἱερογραμματεὺς Χαιρήμων φησί·

1. καὶ ἀντὶ μὲν χαρᾶς, γυναῖκα τυμπανίζουσαν ἔγραφον·
2. ἀντὶ λύπης, ἄνθρωπον τῇ χειρὶ τὸ γένειον κρατοῦντα, καὶ πρὸς γῆν νεύοντα·
3. ἀντὶ δὲ συμφορᾶς, ὀφθαλμὸν δακρύοντα·
4. ἀντὶ τοῦ μὴ ἔχειν, δύο χεῖρας κενὰς ἐκτεταμένας·
5. ἀντὶ ἀνατολῆς, ὄφιν ἐξερχόμενον ἔκ τινος ὀπῆς·
6. ἀντὶ δύσεως, εἰσερχόμενον·
7. ἀντὶ ἀναβιώσεως, βάτραχον·
8. ἀντὶ ψυχῆς, ἱέρακα· ἔτι καὶ ἀντὶ ἡλίου καὶ θεοῦ·
9. ἀντὶ θηλυγόνου γυναικὸς, καὶ μητρὸς καὶ χρόνου καὶ οὐρανοῦ, γῦπα·
10. ἀντὶ βασιλέως, μέλισσαν·
11. ἀντὶ γενέσεως καὶ αὐτοφυῶν καὶ ἀῤῥένων, κάνθαρον·
12. ἀντὶ γῆς, βοῦν·
13. λέοντος δὲ προτομὴ πᾶσαν ἀρχὴν καὶ φυλακὴν δηλοῖ κατ' αὐτούς·
14. οὐρὰ λέοντος, ἀνάγκην·
15. ἔλαφος, ἐνιαυτόν·
16. ὁμοίως καὶ ὁ φοίνιξ·
17. ὁ παῖς δηλοῖ τὰ αὐξανόμενα
18. ὁ γέρων, τὰ φθειρόμενα·
19. τὸ τόξον, τὴν ὀξεῖαν δύναμιν· καὶ ἕτερα μυρια· ἐξ ὧν Ὅμηρος ταῦτά φησιν· ἐν ἄλλῳ δὲ τόπῳ, εἴπερ αἱρεῖσθε, ἰδὼν ἐκ τοῦ Χαιρήμονος, καὶ τὰς τῶν γραμμάτων αὐτῶν ἐκφωνήσεις Αἰθιοπικῶς εἴπω

Translation of the extract.

"Now, Homer says this as he was accurately instructed in all learning by means of the symbolic Ethiopian characters. For the Ethiopians do not use alphabetic characters, but depict animals of all sorts instead, and limbs and members of these animals; for the sacred scribes in former times desired to conceal their opinion about the nature of the gods, and therefore handed all this down to their own children by allegorical methods and the aforesaid symbols and characters, as the sacred scribe Chaeremon says."

1. "And for *joy*, they would depict a woman beating a tambourine."

Accuracy of Tzetzes' statements proved.

[The drum or tambourine was used in the temples for festival services, and a woman beating a tambourine is the determinative of the words 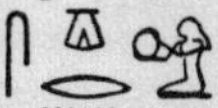 *seker*, "to beat a tambourine," and 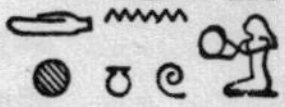 *techennu*.]

2. "For *grief*, a man clasping his chin in his hand and bending towards the ground."

[A man, seated, with his hand to his mouth,  is the determinative of the word 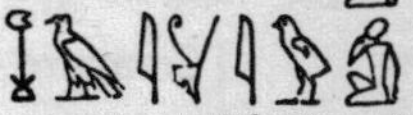 *chadnau*, "grief." A seated woman with head bent and hands thrown up before her face, is the determinative of  *hath*, "to weep."]

3. "For *misfortune*, an eye weeping."

[The weeping eye  is the determinative of the common word  *rem*, "to weep."]

4. "For *want*, two hands stretched out empty."

[Compare  *at*, "not to have," "to be without." Coptic ⲀⲦ.]

5. "For *rising*, a snake coming out of a hole."

[Compare 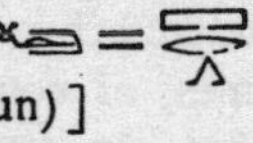 *per*, "to come forth, to rise" (of the sun)]

6. "For *setting*, [the same] going in."

[Compare 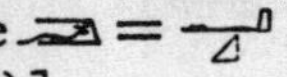 *aq*, "to enter, to set" (of the sun).]

7. "For *vivification*, a frog."[1]

[The frog  *hefennu*, means 100,000, hence fertility and abundance of life.]

[1] But compare Horapollo, (ed. Leemans, p. 33), Ἄπλαστον δὲ ἄνθρωπον γράφοντες, βάτραχον ζωγραφοῦσιν.

**Accuracy of Tzetzes' statements proved.**

8. "For *soul*, a hawk; and also for *sun* and *god*."

[Compare *ba*, "soul," *neter*, "god," and *Ḥeru*, "Horus" or "the Sun-god."]

9. "For a female-bearing woman, and *mother* and *time* and *sky*, a vulture."

[*mut*, "mother," is the common meaning of a vulture, and at times the goddess Mut seems to be identified with *nut*, "the sky." Horapollo says that the vulture also meant "year" (ed. Leemans, p. 5), and this statement is borne out by the evidence of the hieroglyphics, where we find that = *renpit*, "year."]

10. "For *king*, a bee."

[Compare *suten net*, "king of the North and South."]

11. "For *birth* and *natural growth*, and *males*, a beetle."

[The beetle *χeperà* was the emblem of the god *Cheperà*, who is supposed to have created or evolved himself, and to have given birth to gods, men, and every creature and thing in earth and sky. The word means "to become," and in late texts *cheperu* may be fairly well rendered by "evolutions." The meaning *male* comes, of course, from the idea of the ancients that the beetle had no female. See *infra*, under *Scarab.*]

12. "For *earth*, an ox."

[*àḥet* means field, and *àḥ* means "ox"; can Chaeremon have confused the meanings of these two words, similar in sound?]

13. "And the fore part of a lion signifies *dominion* and *protection* of every kind."

Accuracy of Tzetzes' statements proved.

[Compare *ḥā*, "chief, that which is in front, duke, prince."]

14. "A lion's tail, *necessity*."

[Compare *peḥ*, "to force, to compel, to be strong."]

15, 16. "A stag, *year;* likewise the *palm*."

[Of the stag meaning "year" I can give no example. The palm branch or *renpit*, is the common word for "year."]

17. "The boy signifies *growth*."

[Compare , which is the determinative of words meaning "youth" and juvenescence.]

18. "The old man, *decay*."

[Compare , the determinative of *àau*, "old age."]

19. "The bow, the *swift* power."

[The Egyptian word for bow is *peṭ*. Compare *peṭ*, "to run, to flee away."]

"And others by the thousand. And by means of these characters Homer says this. But I will proceed in another place, if you please, to explain the pronunciation of those characters in Ethiopic fashion, as I have learnt it from Chaeremon."[1]

Extract from Tzetzes.

In another place[2] Tzetzes says, "Moreover, he was not uninitiated into the symbolic Ethiopian characters, the nature of which we will expound in the proper places. All this demonstrates that Homer was instructed in Egypt," *ναὶ μὴν οὐδὲ τῶν Αἰθιοπικῶν συμβολικῶν γραμμάτων ἀμύητος γέγονε, περὶ ὧν ἐν τοῖς οἰκείοις τόποις διδάξομεν ὁποῖα εἰσί. καὶ ταῦτα δὲ τὸν Ὅμηρον ἐν Αἰγύπτῳ παιδευθῆναι παραδεικνύουσι*, and upon this the scholia on Tzetzes say:— *Περὶ τῶν Αἰθιοπικῶν γραμμάτων Διό[δωρος] μὲν ἐπεμνήσθη, καὶ μερικῶς εἶπεν, ἀλλ' ὥσπερ ἐξ ἀκοῆς ἄλλου μαθὼν καὶ οὐκ*

[1] Hermann, p. 123, ll. 2–29; Bachmann, p. 823, ll. 12–34.

[2] Hermann, p. 17, ll. 21–25; Bachmann, p. 755, ll. 9–12.

*ἀκριβῶς αὐτὸς ἐπιστάμενος [εἰ] καί τινα τούτων κατέλεξεν ὥσπερ ἐν οἷς οἶδε παῤῥησιάζεται. Χαιρήμων δὲ ὁ ἱερογραμματεὺς ὅλην βίβλον περὶ τῶν τοιούτων γραμμάτων συνέταξεν. ἅτινα, ἐν τοῖς προ[σφόροις] τόποις τῶν Ὁμηρείων ἐπῶν ἀ[κρι]βέστερον καὶ πλατυτέρως ἐρῶ.*[1] "Diodorus made mention of the Ethiopian characters and spoke particularly, yet as though he had learnt by hearsay from another and did not understand them accurately himself, although he set down some of them, as though he were talking confidently on subjects that he knew. But Chaeremon the sacred scribe compiled a whole book about the aforesaid characters, which I will discuss more accurately and more fully in the proper places in the Homeric poems." It is much to be regretted that Chaeremon's work, if he ever fulfilled his promise, has not come down to us.

Greek translation of Egyptian text by Hermapion.

One of the most valuable extracts from the works of Greek and Roman writers on Egypt is that from a translation of an Egyptian obelisk by **Hermapion,** preserved by Ammianus Marcellinus;[2] unfortunately, however, neither the name of Hermapion's work nor the time in which he lived is known. This extract consists of the Greek translation of six lines of hieroglyphics: three lines are from the south side of the obelisk, one line from the east side, and a second and a third line from the other sides. A comparison of the Greek extract with any inscription of Rameses II. on an obelisk shows at once that Hermapion must have had a certain accurate knowledge of hieroglyphics; his translation of the lines, however does not follow consecutively. The following examples will show that the Greek, in many cases, represents the Egyptian very closely.

Comparison of Greek translation with the Egyptian text.

*Λέγει Ἥλιος βασιλεῖ Ῥαμέστῃ· δεδώρημαί σοι ἀνὰ πᾶσαν οἰκουμένην μετὰ χαρᾶς βασιλεύειν, ὃν Ἥλιος φιλεῖ* = 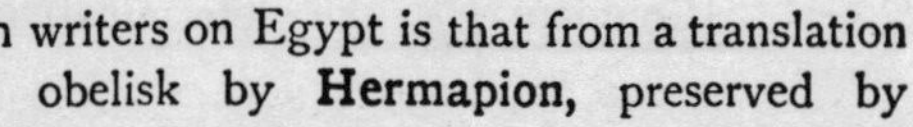

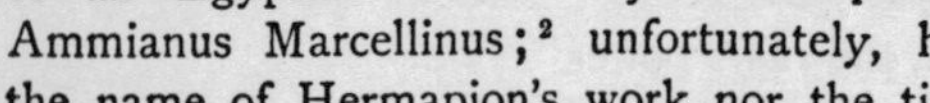 "Says Rā, I give to thee all lands and foreign countries with rest of heart, O king of the north and south, Usr-maāt-Rā-setep-en-Rā,

[1] Hermann, p. 146, ll. 12–22; Bachmann, p. 838, ll. 31–37.

[2] Liber XVII. 4.

son of the Sun, Rameses, beloved of Åmen-Rā." Θεογέννητος κτιστὴς τῆς οἰκουμένης =  "born of the gods, possessor of the two lands" (*i.e.*, the world). Ὁ ἑστὼς ἐπ' ἀληθείας δεσπότης διαδήματος, τὴν Αἴγυπτον δοξάσας κεκτημένος, ὁ ἀγλαοποιήσας Ἡλίου πόλιν =   "[the mighty bull], resting upon Law, lord of diadems, protector of Egypt, making splendid Heliopolis with monuments." Ἥλιος θεὸς μέγας δεσπότης οὐρανοῦ =  "Says Rā Harmachis, the great god, lord of heaven," πληρώσας τὸν νεὼν τοῦ φοίνικος ἀγαθῶν, ᾧ οἱ θεοὶ ζωῆς χρόνον ἐδωρήσαντο =   "filling the temple of the *bennu* (phœnix) with his splendours, may the gods give to him life like the Sun for ever," etc.

**Flaminian obelisk.**

The Flaminian obelisk, from which the Egyptian passages given above are taken, was brought from Heliopolis to Rome by Augustus, and placed in the Circus Maximus,[1] whence it was dug out; it now stands in the Piazza del Popolo at Rome, where it was set up by Pope Sixtus V. in 1589.[2] This obelisk was originally set up by Seti I., whose inscriptions occupy the middle column of the north, south, and west sides; the other columns of hieroglyphics record the names and titles of Rameses II. who, in this case, appropriated the obelisk of his father, just as he did that of Thothmes III. The obelisk was found broken into three pieces, and in order to render it capable of sustaining itself, three palms' length was cut from the base. The texts have been published by Kircher, *Oedipus Aegypliacus*, t. iii. p. 213; by Ungarelli, *Interpretatio Obeliscorum Urbis*, Rome, 1842, p. 65, *sqq.*,

[1] Qui autem notarum textus obelisco incisus est veteri, quem videmus in Circo etc. Ammianus Marcellinus, XVII. 4, § 17. It seems to be referred to in Pliny, XXXVI. 29.

[2] For a comparative table of obelisks standing in 1840, see Bonomi, *Notes on Obelisks*, in *Trans. Royal Soc. Lit.*, Vol. I. Second Series, p. 158.

plate 2; and by Bonomi, who drew them for a paper on this obelisk by the Rev. G. Tomlinson in *Trans. Royal Soc. Lit.*, Vol. I. Second Series, p. 176 ff. For an account of this obelisk, see Zoëga, *De Origine et Usu Obeliscorum*, Rome, 1797, p. 92.

Champollion's estimate of Clement's statements on hieroglyphics.

The next Greek writer whose statements on Egyptian hieroglyphics are of value is **Clement** of Alexandria, who flourished about A.D. 191–220. According to Champollion, "un seul auteur grec, ........ a démêlé et signalé, dans l'écriture égyptienne sacrée, les élémens phonétiques, lesquels en sont, pour ainsi dire, le principe vital[1] ..... Clément d'Alexandrie s'est, lui seul, occasionnellement attaché à en donner une idée claire; et ce philosophe chrétien était, bien plus que tout autre, en position d'en être bien instruit. Lorsque mes recherches et l'étude constante des monuments égyptiens m'eurent conduit aux résultats précédemment exposés, je dus revenir sur ce passage de Saint Clément d'Alexandrie, que j'ai souvent cité, pour savoir si, à la faveur des notions que j'avais tirées d'un examen soutenu des inscriptions hiéroglyphiques, le texte de l'auteur grec ne deviendrait pas plus intelligible qu'il ne l'avait paru jusque-là. J'avoue que ses termes me semblèrent alors si positifs et si clairs, et les idées qu'il renferme si exactement conformes à ma théorie de l'écriture hiéroglyphique, que je dus craindre aussi de me livrer à une illusion et à un entraînement dont tout me commandait de me défier."[2] From the above it will be seen what a high value Champollion placed on the statements concerning the hieroglyphics by Clement, and they have, in consequence, formed the subject of various works by eminent authorities. In his *Précis* (p. 328), Champollion gives the extract from Clement with a Latin translation and remarks by Letronne.[3] Dulaurier in his *Examen d'un passage des Stromates de Saint Clément d'Alexandrie*, Paris, 1833, again published the passage and gave many explanations of words in it, and commented learnedly upon it. (See also

[1] *Précis du Système hiéroglyphique des anciens Egyptiens*, Paris, 1824, p. 321.

[2] *Précis*, p. 327.

[3] See also *Œuvres Choisies*, t. I. pp. 237–254.

Bunsen's *Aegyptens Stelle*, Bd. I., p. 240, and Thierbach, *Erklärung auf das Aegyptische Schriftwesen*, Erfurt, 1846.) The passage is as follows:—

Clement of Alexandria on hieroglyphics.

αὐτίκα οἱ παρ' Αἰγυπτίοις παιδευόμενοι πρῶτον μὲν πάντων τὴν Αἰγυπτίων γραμμάτων μέθοδον ἐκμανθάνουσι τὴν ἐπιστολογραφικὴν καλουμένην, δευτέραν δὲ τὴν ἱερατικὴν, ᾗ χρῶνται οἱ ἱερογραμματεῖς, ὑστάτην δὲ καὶ τελευταίαν τὴν ἱερογλυφικὴν, ἧς ἡ μέν ἐστι διὰ τῶν πρώτων στοιχείων κυριολογικὴ, ἡ δὲ συμβολική. τῆς δὲ συμβολικῆς ἡ μὲν κυριολογεῖται κατὰ μίμησιν, ἡ δ' ὥσπερ τροπικῶς γράφεται, ἡ δὲ ἄντικρυς ἀλληγορεῖται κατά τινας αἰνιγμούς, ἥλιον γοῦν γράψαι βουλόμενοι κύκλον ποιοῦσι, σελήνην δὲ σχῆμα μηνοειδὲς κατὰ τὸ κυριολογούμενον εἶδος, τροπικῶς δὲ κατ' οἰκειότητα μετάγοντες καὶ μετατιθέντες, τὰ δ' ἐξαλλάττοντες, τὰ δὲ πολλαχῶς μετασχηματίζοντες χαράττουσιν. Τοὺς γοῦν τῶν βασιλέων ἐπαίνους θεολογουμένοις μύθοις παραδιδόντες ἀναγράφουσι διὰ τῶν ἀναγλύφων, τοῦ δὲ κατὰ τοὺς αἰνιγμοὺς τρίτου εἴδους δεῖγμα ἔστω τόδε. τὰ μὲν γὰρ τῶν ἄλλων ἄστρων διὰ τὴν πορείαν τὴν λοξὴν ὄφεων σώμασιν ἀπείκαζον, τὸν δὲ ἥλιον τῷ τοῦ κανθάρου, ἐπειδὴ κυκλοτερὲς ἐκ τῆς βοείας ὄνθου σχῆμα πλασάμενος ἀντιπρόσωπος κυλίνδει. φασὶ δὲ καὶ ἑξάμηνον μὲν ὑπὸ γῆς, θάτερον δὲ τοῦ ἔτους τμῆμα τὸ ζῷον τοῦτο ὑπὲρ γῆς διαιτᾶσθαι, σπερμαίνειν τε εἰς τὴν σφαῖραν καὶ γεννᾶν, καὶ θῆλυν κάνθαρον μὴ γίνεσθαι.[1]

Translation of extract from Clement.

"For example, those that are educated among the Egyptians first of all learn that system of Egyptian characters which is styled EPISTOLOGRAPHIC; secondly, the HIERATIC, which the sacred scribes employ; lastly and finally the HIEROGLYPHIC. The hieroglyphic sometimes speaks plainly by means of the letters of the alphabet, and sometimes uses symbols, and when it uses symbols, it sometimes (*a*) speaks plainly by imitation, and sometimes (*b*) describes in a figurative way, and sometimes (*c*) simply says one thing for another in accordance with certain secret rules. Thus (*a*) if they desire to write *sun* or *moon*, they make a circle or a crescent in plain imitation of the form. And when (*b*) they describe figuratively (by transfer and transposition without violating the natural meaning of words), they completely alter some things and make manifold changes in the form of others. Thus, they hand

[1] *Clem. Alex.*, ed. Dindorf, t. III. *Strom.* lib. v. §§ 20, 21, pp. 17, 18.

down the praises of their kings in myths about the gods which they write up in relief. Let this be an example of the third form (*c*) in accordance with the secret rules. While they represent the stars generally by snakes' bodies, because their course is crooked, they represent the sun by the body of a beetle, for the beetle moulds a ball from cattle dung and rolls it before him. And they say that this animal lives under ground for six months, and above ground for the other portion of the year, and that it deposits its seed in this globe and there engenders offspring, and that no female beetle exists."

**Three kinds of Egyptian writing.**

From the above we see that Clement rightly stated that the Egyptians had three kinds of writing:—epistolographic, hieratic and hieroglyphic. The epistolographic is that kind which is now called "demotic," and which in the early days of hieroglyphic decipherment was called "enchorial." The hieratic is the kind commonly found on papyri. The hieroglyphic kind is described as, I. *cyriologic*, that is to say, by means of *figurative phonetic characters*, *e.g.*, 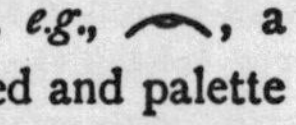 *emsuḥ*, "crocodile," and II. *symbolic*, that is to say, by actual representations of objects, *e.g.*,  "goose,"  "bee," and so on The symbolic division is subdivided into three parts: I. *cyriologic by imitation*, *e.g.*, , a vase with water flowing from it represented a "libation"; II. *tropical*, *e.g.*, , a crescent moon to represent "month," , a reed and palette to represent "writing" or "scribe"; and III. *enigmatic*, *e.g.*, , a beetle, to represent the "sun."[1] In modern Egyptian Grammars the matter is stated more simply, and we see that hieroglyphic signs are used in two ways: I. Ideographic, II. Phonetic.  *māu*, "water," is an instance of the first method, and  *m-s-u-ḥ*, is an instance of the second. Ideographic signs are used as *determinatives*, and are either *ideographic* or *generic*. Thus after  *māu*, "cat," a cat  is placed, and is an *ideographic* determinative; but , heaven with a star in it, written after  *ḳerḥ*, is a

[1] Champollion, *Précis*, p. 278.

*generic* determinative. Phonetic signs are either *Alphabetic* as *a*, *b*, *k*, or *Syllabic*, as *men*, *chen*, etc.

**Porphyry** the Philosopher, who died about A.D. 305, says of Pythagoras:[1]—

Pythagoras and hieroglyphics.

*Καὶ ἐν Αἰγύπτῳ μὲν τοῖς ἱερεῦσι συνῆν καὶ τὴν σοφίαν ἐξέμαθε, καὶ τὴν Αἰγυπτίων φωνήν, γραμμάτων δὲ τρισσὰς διαφοράς, ἐπιστολογραφικῶν τε καὶ ἱερογλυφικῶν καὶ συμβολικῶν, τῶν μὲν κοινολογουμένων κατὰ μίμησιν, τῶν δὲ ἀλληγορουμένων κατά τινας αἰνιγμούς.*

"And in Egypt he lived with the priests and learnt their wisdom and the speech of the Egyptians and three sorts of writing, epistolographic and hieroglyphic and symbolic, which sometimes speak in the common way by imitation and sometimes describe one thing by another in accordance with certain secret rules." Here it seems that Porphyry copied Clement inaccurately. Thus he omits all mention of the Egyptian writing called "hieratic," and of the subdivision of hieroglyphic called "cyriologic," and of the second subdivision of the symbolic called "tropic." The following table, based on Letronne, will make the views about hieroglyphic writing held by the Greeks plain:—

Letronne's summary.

Herodotus, Diodorus and the inscription of Rosetta divide Egyptian writing into two divisions

- I. The common, called
  - δημοτικά and δημώδη by Herodotus and Clement,
  - ἐγχώρια by the inscriptions of Rosetta,
  - ἐπιστολογραφικά by Clement of Alexandria and Porphyry.
- II. The sacred, divided by Clement into
  - 1. Hieratic, or the writing of the priests.
  - 2. Hieroglyphic composed of
    - *a.* Cyriologic, by means of the first letters of the alphabet.
    - *b.* Symbolical comprising the
      - *a.* Cyriological by imitation.
      - *b.* Tropical or metaphorical.
      - *c.* Enigmatical.

Horapollo on hieroglyphics.

The next writer of importance on hieroglyphics is **Horapollo,** who towards the close of the IVth century of our era composed a work called Ἱερογλυφικά; this book was translated into Greek by one Philip, of whom nothing is known. Wiedemann thinks that it was originally written in Coptic, which, in the middle ages, was usually called

[1] Porphyry, *De Vita Pythagorae*, ed. Didot, § 11, p. 89, at the foot.

"Egyptian," and not in ancient Egyptian.[1] In this work are given the explanations of a number of ideographs which occur, for the most part, in Ptolemaïc inscriptions; but, like the list of those given by Chaeremon, no *phonetic* values of the signs are given. Nevertheless the list is of considerable interest. The best edition of Horapollo is that of Conrad Leemans,[2] but the text was edited in a handy form, with an English translation and notes by Samuel Sharpe and Dr. Birch, by J. Cory, in 1840.

**Mediaeval writers on hieroglyphics.**

In more modern times the first writer at any length on hieroglyphics was Athanasius Kircher, the author of some ponderous works[3] in which he pretended to have found the key to the hieroglyphic inscriptions, and to translate them. Though a man of great learning, it must be plainly said that, judged by scholars of to-day, he would be considered an impostor. In his works on Coptic[4] there are, no doubt, many interesting facts, but mixed with them is such an amount of nonsense that Jablonski says touching one of his statements, "Verum hic ut in aliis plurimis fucum lectoribus fecit Jesuita ille, et fumum vendidit"; from the same writer also, Kircher's arrogant assertions called forth the remark, "Kircherus, in quo semper plus inest ostentationis, quam solidae eruditionis."[5] It is impossible to understand what grounds Kircher had for his statements and how he arrived at his results; as for his translations, they have *nothing* correct in them. Here is one taken at random from *Oedipus*

**Kircher and Jablonski.**

[1] *Aegyptische Geschichte*, p. 151. The sepulchre of Gordian was inscribed in *Egyptian*. "Gordiano sepulchrum milites apud Circeium castrum fecerunt in finibus Persidis, titulum hujus modi addentes et Graecis, et Latinis, et Persicis, et Judaicis, et Aegyptiacis literis, ut ab omnibus legeretur." Erasmus, *Hist. Rom. Scriptorum*, Basle, 1533, p. 312, at the top.

[2] Horapollinis Niloi Hieroglyphica. edidit, diversorum codicum recenter collatorum, priorumque editionum varias lectiones et versionem latinam subjunxit, adnotationem, item hieroglyphicorum imagines et indices adjecit C.L. Amstelod, 1835.

[3] *Obeliscus Pamphilius, ....... Hieroglyphicis involuta Symbolis, detecta e tenebris in lucem asseritur*, Rome, 1650, fol. *Oedipus Aegyptiacus*, hoc est, universalis hieroglyphicae veterum doctrinae, temporum injuria obolitae instauratio. Rome, 1652–54. Tomi I–IV, fol.

[4] *Prodromus Coptus*, Rome, 1636. *Lingua Aegyptiaca restituta.* Rome, 1643.

[5] Jablonski, *Opuscula*, t. I. ed. Water, 1804, pp. 157, 211.

*Aegyptiacus*, t. III, p. 431, where he gives a translation of an inscription (A) printed on the plate between pp. 428 and 429. The hieroglyphics are written on a Ptaḥ-Seker-Osiris figure and read :—

t'eṭ ȧn Ȧusȧr chent ȧmentet neter āa neb
" *Saith Osiris, at the head of the underworld, god great, lord of*

, etc.

Re-stau
*Re-stau* (i.e., *the passages of the tomb*)."

and his translation runs:—"Vitale providi Numinis dominium, quadruplicem Mundani liquoris substantiam dominio confert Osiridis, cujus unà cum Mendesio foecundi Numinis dominio, benefica virtute influente, omnia quae in Mundo sunt, vegetantur, animantur, conservantur." Other writers on hieroglyphics whose works Kircher consulted were John Peter Bolzanius Valerianus,[1] and Mercati,[2] but no good results followed their investigations. In the year 1770 Joseph de Guignes determined the existence of groups of characters having determinatives,[3] and four years later he published his *Mémoire*,[4] in which he tried to prove that the epistolographic and symbolic characters of the Egyptians were to be found in the Chinese characters, and that the Chinese nation was nothing but an Egyptian colony. In 1797 Zoëga made a step in the right direction, and came to the conclusion[5] that the hieroglyphics were letters and that the cartouches contained royal names. A few years later Silvestre de Sacy published a

De Guignes and Zoëga.

Silvestre de Sacy and Akerblad.

[1] *Hieroglyphica, seu de sacris Aegyptiorum aliarumque gentium litteris Commentatorium libri VII., duobus aliis ab eruditissimo viro annexis*, etc., Basil., 1556.

[2] *Degli Obelischi di Roma*, Rome, 1589.

[3] Essai sur le moyen de parvenir à la lecture et à l'intelligence des Hiéroglyphes égyptiens. (In *Mémoires de l'Académie des Inscriptions*, t. XXXIV. pp. 1–56.)

[4] *Ibid.*, t. XXXIX. p. 1 ff.

[5] *De Usu et Origine Obeliscorum*, Rome, 1797, fol., p. 465.

letter on the inscriptions on the Rosetta Stone,[1] and the work of this learned man was soon after followed by that of Akerblad who, in a letter to M. de Sacy[2] discussed the demotic inscription on the recently discovered Rosetta Stone, and published an alphabet of the demotic characters, from which a large number were adopted in after times by Young and Champollion. It would seem that Akerblad never gained the credit which was due to him for his really clever work, and it will be seen from the facts quoted in the following pages, how largely the success of Young's labours on the Demotic inscription on the Rosetta Stone depended on those of Akerblad. But side by side with the letters of de Sacy and Akerblad and the learned works of Young and Champollion, there sprang into existence a mass of literature full of absurd statements and theories written by men having no qualifications for expressing opinions on hieroglyphic matters. Thus the Comte de Pahlin in his *De l'étude des Hiéroglyphes*,[3] hesitated not to say that the inscription on one of the porticoes of the Temple at Denderah contained a translation of the hundredth Psalm, composed to invite all people to enter into the house of the Lord. The same author said that to produce the books of the Bible, which were written on papyri, it was only necessary to translate the Psalms of David into Chinese and to write them in the ancient characters of that language.[4] Lenoir considered the Egyptian inscriptions to contain Hebrew compositions,[5] and Lacour thought that they contained Biblical phrases.[6] Worse than all these wild theories was the belief in the works of the Kircher school of investigators, and in the accuracy of the statements made by Warburton,[7] who, it must be confessed,

**Absurd theories of the contents of Egyptian texts.**

**Warburton's views on an Egyptian alphabet.**

[1] *Lettre au Citoyen Chaptal, au sujet de l'Inscription égyptienne du Monument trouvé à Rosette*, Paris, 1802.

[2] *Lettre sur l'inscription égyptienne de Rosette*, Paris, 1802.

[3] Published at Paris in 5 vols., 1812.

[4] *Lettres sur les Hiéroglyphes*, Weimar, 1802.

[5] In *Nouvelle explication des Hiéroglyphes*, Paris, 1809–10, 4 vols.; and *Nouveaux Essais sur les Hiéroglyphes*, Paris, 1826, 4 vols.

[6] See his *Essai sur les Hiéroglyphes égyptiens*, Bordeaux, 1821.

[7] In his *The Divine Legation of Moses demonstrated, to which is adjoint an Essay on Egyptian Hieroglyphics*, London, 1738, 2 vols.

seems to have recognized the existence of alphabetic characters, but who in no way deserves the praise of Bailey, the Cambridge prize essayist, "Vir singulari quodam ingenii acumine praeditus, Warburtonus; qui primus certe recentiorum ad rectam harum rerum cognitionem patefecit viam."[1]

Here naturally comes an account of the labours of Young and Champollion, two men who stand out pre-eminently as the true discoverers of the right method of decipherment of Egyptian hieroglyphics. As much has been written on the works of these *savants*, and as some have tried to show that the whole merit of the discovery belongs to Young, and others that it belongs to Champollion, it will not be out of place here to make a plain statement of facts, drawn from the best sources, and to give the opinions of the most eminent Egyptologists on this point; a few details concerning the lives of these remarkable men must, however, be first given.

**Young and Champollion.**

**Dr. Thomas Young** was born at Milverton, in Somersetshire, on the 13th of June, 1773. His parents were both members of the Society of Friends. He lived during the first seven years of his life with his maternal grandfather, Mr. Robert Davis, at Minehead, in Somersetshire. At the age of two he could read fluently, and before he was four he had read the Bible through twice. At the age of six, he learnt by heart in six weeks Goldsmith's *Deserted Village*. When not quite seven years of age he went to a school, kept by a man called King, at Stapleton near Bristol, where he stayed for a year and a half. In March 1782, when nearly nine years of age, he went to the school of Mr. T. Thompson, at Compton, in Dorsetshire, where he remained four years. Here he read Phaedrus's Fables, Cornelius Nepos, Virgil, Horace expurgated by Knox, the whole of Beza's Greek and Latin Testament, the First Seven Books of the Iliad, Martin's Natural Philosophy, etc., etc. Before leaving this school he had got through six chapters of the Hebrew Bible. About this time he learnt to use the lathe, and he made a telescope and a microscope, and the Italian, Persian, Syriac, and Chaldee languages all occupied his attention. From 1787 to 1792 he was private tutor to Hudson Gurney, at Youngsbury, in Hertfordshire,

**Early life and studies of Young.**

**Young's oriental studies.**

[1] *Hieroglyphicorum Origo et natura*, Cambridge, 1816, p. 9.

where he seems to have devoted himself to the study of English, French, Italian, Latin, Greek, Hebrew, Chaldee, Syriac, Samaritan, Arabic, Persian, Turkish, and Ethiopic, as well as to that of natural Philosophy, Botany, and Entomology.[1] In 1792 Young began to study Medicine and Anatomy in London, and in 1793 he entered St. Bartholomew's Hospital as a pupil. In 1803 he read a paper before the Royal Society, and was elected a Fellow the following year (balloted for and elected, June 19). Shortly after he attended medical lectures in Edinburgh and Göttingen, and he subsequently went to Cambridge, where he took the degree of Bachelor of Medicine (1803), and afterwards that of Doctor of Physic (1808). In 1798 Young received a splendid bequest from his uncle Dr. Brocklesby, consisting of his house in Norfolk Street, Park Lane, his library, his prints, his pictures, and about £10,000 in money; hence he was free to form his own scheme of life. In May, 1801, he discovered the undulatory theory of light, and his paper on this subject was read before the Royal Society in the November following; in the same year he accepted the office of Professor of Natural Philosophy at the Royal Institution. In 1802 he was appointed Foreign Secretary of the Royal Society, and on the 14th of June, 1804, he married Eliza, the daughter of J. P. Maxwell, Esq., of Cavendish Square, and of Trippendence, near Farnborough, Kent. The attention of Young was called to Egyptian inscriptions by Sir W. Rouse Boughton, who had found in a mummy case at Thebes a papyrus written in cursive Egyptian characters, and to a notice of this which Young prepared for his friend, he appended a translation of the demotic text of the Rosetta Stone. As the details of his studies on the Rosetta Stone belong to the history of the decipherment of Egyptian hieroglyphics, they are given further on (p. 141 ff.), but the reader will understand Young's position better by reading Dean Peacock's chapter on "hieroglyphical researches" printed in his life of Young, pp. 258–344, and Mr. Leitch's notes in the third volume of the collected *Works of Dr. Young*. In 1816 Young was appointed

**Young's medical studies.**

**Discovers undulatory theory of light.**

**Young's study of hieroglyphs.**

[1] For the list of books read by him at this time, see the *Life of Thomas Young*, by G. Peacock, London, 1855, pp. 14–17.

Secretary to a Commission for ascertaining the length of the seconds pendulum, for comparing French and English standards, etc., and in 1818 he was appointed Secretary of the Board of Longitude and Superintendent of the Nautical Almanac. In 1825 he became Medical Referee and Inspector of Calculations to the Palladium Insurance Company. In 1826 he was elected one of the eight foreign Associates of the Academy of Sciences at Paris. In February, 1829, he began to suffer from repeated attacks of asthma, and by the April following he was in a state of great weakness; he died on the 10th of May, not having completed his fifty-sixth year. An excellent steel engraving of Young, by R. Ward, from a picture by Sir Thomas Lawrence, P.R.A., forms the frontispiece to his life by Dean Peacock, which, according to J. J. Champollion-Figeac, "exprime fidèlement la douceur, la grâce, les traits d'une figure toute rayonnante d'intelligence."[1]

**Young's death.**

**Jean François Champollion**, surnamed **le Jeune**, the immortal discoverer of a correct system of decipherment of Egyptian hieroglyphics, was born at Figeac on December 24, 1790. His family came originally from Champoléon in the High Alps, where a branch of it still holds property. As a boy he made rapid progress in classical studies, and he devoted himself at the same time to botany and mineralogy; at a very early date however he showed a natural taste for oriental languages, and like Young was, at the age of thirteen, master of a fair knowledge of Hebrew, Syriac and Chaldee.[2] In 1805 his brother J. J. Champollion-Figeac brought him to Paris, and caused him to be admitted to the Cours de l'Ecole des Langues Orientales, and introduced him to Silvestre de Sacy. Soon after his arrival in Paris Champollion turned his attention to the study of the hieroglyphic inscription on the Rosetta Stone, but his powerful friend de Sacy advised the elder brother to warn the younger off a study which *ne pouvait donner aucun résultat.* In 1812 he was nominated Professor of Ancient History to the faculty of Letters at Grenoble,

**Champollion's physical and classical studies.**

[1] *Lettre au Directeur de la Revue Britannique au sujet des Recherches du Docteur Young*, Paris, 1857, p. 11.

[2] On the subject of Champollion's studies, at Grenoble, *see Chroniques Dauphinoises*, par A. Champollion-Figeac, t. III. pp. 153, 156, 157–238.

where he still carried on his oriental studies. When he arrived in Paris he found that the old Egyptologists maintained that hieroglyphics were a symbolic language, and seeking to verify this theory, he wasted a year. He made up his mind, however, to work out this question without having regard to the theories of others, and he sketched out a plan for a large work on Egypt in several volumes. The first part of this appeared at Grenoble in 1811, entitled *Introduction;* it was never sold, for only about thirty copies were printed, but it appeared, without the analytical table of Coptic geographical names, under the title *L'Egypte sous les Pharaons*, 8vo., 2 vols., 1814. About this time Young, in England, was studying the texts on the Rosetta Stone, and had actually begun to make a translation of the demotic section, making use of the results obtained by de Sacy and Akerblad, to the latter of whom great credit is due for his acuteness and insight. Whatever may be said as to Champollion's ignorance of Young's results, it is quite certain that he must have known of those of Akerblad, and we know (see p. 135) that a printed copy of Young's paper on the Rosetta Stone had been put into Champollion's hands by de Sacy. In a very short time Champollion discovered where his predecessors had broken down, and having already written *De l'écriture Hiératique des Anciens Egyptiens*, Grenoble, 1821, on September 17, in the following year, he read his *Mémoire* on the hieroglyphics and exhibited his hieroglyphic Alphabet, with its Greek and Demotic equivalents, before the Académie des Inscriptions. Champollion's paper created a great sensation, and Louis XVIII. wished a statement concerning it laid before him, and M. le Duc de Doudeauville determined that an Egyptian Museum should be formed in the Palace of the Louvre. In the same year Champollion published his *Lettre à M. Dacier, relative à l'Alphabet des Hiéroglyphes phonétiques*, in which he showed beyond a doubt that his system was the correct one. In a series of *Mémoires* read at the Institut in April, May and June, 1823, he explained his system more fully, and these he afterwards published together entitled *Précis du Système Hiéroglyphique des Anciens Egyptiens*, Paris, 2 vols., 1824. A second edition, revised and corrected, appeared in 1828. In

Champollion's hieroglyphic and Coptic studies.

Champollion acquainted with Young's labours.

June, 1824, Champollion arrived in Turin, where he devoted himself to the study of papyri. Early in 1825 he arrived in Rome, and thence he went to Naples, where all the museums were opened for him. In 1826 he returned to Paris. In July, 1828, he set out on his long planned voyage to Egypt, and returned in March, 1830, bringing with him a fine collection of antiquities, and a number of copies of inscriptions which filled about two thousand pages. As soon as he returned to France he set to work to publish the rich results of his travels, but while occupied with this undertaking, death overtook him on the 4th of March, 1832. Louis-Philippe ordered that busts of him, executed at the expense of the civil list, should be placed in the galleries of the palace at Versailles, and in the rooms of the Egyptian Museum of the Louvre; he also ordered that marble for another bust should be given to Champollion-Figeac, and that the carving thereof should be entrusted to the famous sculptor Etex. An etched portrait of Champollion le Jeune will be found in *Les Deux Champollion, leur Vie et leurs Œuvres*, par Aimé Champollion-Figeac: Grenoble, 1887, p. 52.

Champollion's travels.

Visits Egypt.

In addition to the works of Champollion mentioned above, the following are the most important:—

Champollion's works.

*Rapport à son Excellence M. le Duc de Doudeauville, sur la Collection Egyptienne à Livourne*, Paris, 1826.

*Lettres à M. le Duc de Blacas d'Aulps relatives au Musée royal Egyptien de Turin ..... (avec Notices chronologiques par Champollion-Figeac)*: Paris, 1824–26.

*Notice sur les papyrus hiératiques et les peintures du cercueil de Pétaménoph* (Extr. de *Voyage à Meroë* par Cailliaud de Nantes), Paris, 1827.

*Notice descriptive des Monuments Egyptiens du Musée Charles X*, Paris, 1827.

*Catalogue de la Collection Egyptienne du Louvre*, Paris, 1827.

*Catalogue des Papyrus Egyptiens du Musée du Vatican*, Rome, 1826.

*Monuments de l'Egypte et de la Nubie*, iv vols., fol., 440 planches. Publié par ordre du Gouvernement, pour faire suite à l'ouvrage de l'Expédition d'Egypte, Paris, 1829–1847.

*Lettres écrites pendant son voyage en Egypte, en* 1828, 1829, Paris, 1829; 2me édition, Paris, 1833; collection complète. A German translation by E. F. von Gutschmid was published at Quedlinburg, in 1835.

*Grammaire Egyptienne, aux Principes généraux de l'écriture sacrée Egyptienne appliqués à la représentation de la langue parlée; ..... Avec des prolégomènes et un portrait de l'éditeur, M. Champollion-Figeac*, Paris, 1836–1841.

*Dictionnaire Egyptien, en écriture hiéroglyphique, publié d'après les manuscrits autographes ..... par Champollion-Figeac*, Paris, 1841.

Young's labours on the Rosetta Stone in 1814.

The results of Dr. Young's studies of the Rosetta Stone were first communicated to the Royal Society of Antiquaries in a letter from Sir W. E. Rouse Boughton, Bart.; the letter was read on the 19th of May, 1814, and was published the following year in *Archæologia*, Vol. XVIII. pp. 59–72.[1] The letter was accompanied by a translation of the demotic text on the Rosetta Stone, which was subsequently reprinted anonymously in the *Museum Criticum* of Cambridge, Pt. VI., 1815, together with the correspondence which took place between Dr. Young and MM. Silvestre de Sacy and Akerblad. In 1802 M. Akerblad, the Swedish President at Rome, published his *Lettre sur l'inscription Egyptienne de Rosette, adressée au citoyen Silvestre de Sacy*, in which he gave the results of his study of the demotic text of the Rosetta Stone; M. Silvestre de Sacy also had occupied himself in the same way (see his *Lettre au citoyen Chaptal, au sujet de l'inscription Egyptienne du monument trouvé à Rosette:* Paris, 1802), but neither scholar had made any progress in the decipherment of the hieroglyphic text. In August, 1814, Dr. Young wrote to Silvestre de Sacy, asking him what Mr. Akerblad had been doing, and saying,

Correspondence between Young and de Sacy.

"I doubt whether the alphabet which Mr. Akerblad has given us can be of much further utility than in enabling us to decipher the proper names; and sometimes I have

[1] *Letter to the Rev. S. Weston respecting some Egyptian Antiquities.* With 4 copper plates. London, 1814.

even suspected that the letters which he has identified resemble the syllabic sort of characters by which the Chinese express the sounds of foreign languages, and that in their usual acceptation they had different significations: but of this conjecture I cannot at present speak with any great confidence.".....[1] To this M. de Sacy replied: .... "Je ne vous dissimule pas, Monsieur, que malgré l'espèce d'approbation que j'ai donnée au système de M. Akerblad, dans la réponse que je lui ai adressée, il m'est toujours resté des doutes très forts sur la validité de l'alphabet qu'il s'est fait...... Je dois vous ajouter que M. Akerblad n'est pas le seul qui se flatte d'avoir lu le texte Egyptien de l'inscription de Rosette. M. Champollion, qui vient de publier deux volumes sur l'ancienne géographie de l'Egypte,[2] et qui s'est beaucoup occupé de la langue Copte, prétend avoir aussi lu cette inscription. Je mets assurément plus de confiance dans les lumières et la critique de M. Akerblad que dans celles de M. Champollion, mais tant qu'ils n'auront publié quelque résultat de leur travail, il est juste de suspendre son jugement." (Leitch, Vol. III. p. 17.) Writing to M. de Sacy in October of the same year, Young says: "I had read Mr. Akerblad's essay but hastily in the course of the last winter, and I was not disposed to place much confidence in the little that I recollected of it; so that I was able to enter anew upon the investigation, without being materially influenced by what he had published; and though I do not profess to lay claim to perfect originality, or to deny the importance of Mr. Akerblad's labours, I think myself authorised to consider my own translation as completely independent of his ingenious researches: a circumstance which adds much to the probability of our conjectures where they happen to agree. It is only since I received your obliging letter, that I have again read Mr. Akerblad's work; and I have found that it agrees almost in every instance with the results of my own

De Sacy's opinions of Akerblad's works.

De Sacy distrusts Champollion's results.

Young on Akerblad' labours.

[1] For these letters I am indebted to the third volume of the *Miscellaneous Works of the late Thomas Young*, M.D., F.R.S., &c., ed. John Leitch, London, 1855.

[2] *L'Egypte sous les Pharaons, ou recherches sur la Géographie, la Religion, la Langue, les Ecritures, et l'Histoire de l'Egypte*, Paris, 1814.

investigation respecting the sense attributed to the words which the author has examined. This conformity must be allowed to be more satisfactory than if I had followed, with perfect confidence, the path which Akerblad has traced: I must however, confess that it relates only to a few of the first steps of the investigation; and that the greatest and the most difficult part of the translation still remains unsupported by the authority of any external evidence of this kind." (Leitch, p. 18.) Nearly three weeks after writing the above, Young sent another letter to M. de Sacy, together with a Coptic and demotic alphabet derived partly from Akerblad, and partly from his own researches, and a list of eighty-six demotic words with the words corresponding to them in the Greek version. Of these words, he says: "Three were observed by de Sacy, sixteen by Akerblad, and the remainder by himself." In January, 1815, Akerblad addressed a long letter to Young, together with which he sent a translation of some lines of the Rosetta Stone inscription, and some notes upon it. Regarding his own work he says: "During the ten years which have elapsed since my departure from Paris, I have devoted but a few moments, and those at long intervals, to the monument of Rosetta..... For, in fact, I have always felt that the results of my researches on this monument are deficient in that sort of evidence which carries with it full conviction, and you, Sir, as well as M. de Sacy, appear to be of my opinion in this respect..... I must however give you notice beforehand, that in most cases you will only receive a statement of my doubts and uncertainties, together with a few more plausible conjectures; and I shall be fully satisfied if these last shall appear to deserve your attention and approbation..... If again the inscriptions were engraved in a clear and distinct character like the Greek and Latin inscriptions of a certain antiquity, it would be easy, by the assistance of the proper names of several Greek words which occur in it, some of which I have discovered since the publication of my letter to M. de Sacy, and of many Egyptian words, the sense of which is determined; it would be easy, I say, to form a perfectly correct alphabet of these letters; but here another difficulty occurs; the alphabetical characters which, without doubt, are

**Akerblad's doubts about his own labours.**

of very high antiquity in Egypt, must have been in common use for many centuries before the date of the decree; in the course of this time, these letters, as has happened in all other countries, have acquired a very irregular and fanciful form, so as to constitute a kind of running hand." (Leitch, p. 33.) In August, 1815, Young replied to Akerblad's letter, and discussed the passages where his own translation differed from that of Akerblad.

De Sacy warns Young against Champollion.

In July, 1815, de Sacy sent a letter to Young, which contains the following remarkable passages: "*Monsieur, outre la traduction Latine de l'inscription Egyptienne que vous m'avez communiquée, j'ai reçu postérieurement une autre traduction Anglaise, imprimée, que je n'ai pas en ce moment sous les yeux, l'ayant prêtée à M. Champollion sur la demande que son frère m'en a faite d'après une lettre qu'il m'a dit avoir reçue de vous. . . . . . Je pense, Monsieur, que vous êtes plus avancé aujourd'hui et que vous lisez une grande partie, du moins, du texte Egyptien. Si j'ai un conseil à vous donner, c'est de ne pas trop communiquer vos découvertes à M. Champollion. Il se pourrait faire qu'il prétendît ensuite à la priorité. Il cherche en plusieurs endroits de son ouvrage à faire croire qu'il a découvert beaucoup des mots de l'inscription Egyptienne de Rosette. J'ai bien peur que ce ne soit là que du charlatanisme; j'ajoute même que j'ai de fortes raisons de le penser. . . . . Au surplus, je ne saurais me persuader que si M. Akerblad, Et. Quatremère, ou Champollion avait fait des progrès réels dans la lecture du texte Egyptien, ils ne se fussent pas plus empressés de faire part au public de leur découverte. Ce serait une modestie bien rare, et dont aucun d'eux ne me paraît capable.*" (Leitch, p. 51.)

Young on hieroglyphics.

In a letter to de Sacy, dated 3rd August, 1815, Young says: "You may, perhaps, think me too sanguine in my expectations of obtaining a knowledge of the hieroglyphical language in general from the inscription of Rosetta only; and I will confess to you that the difficulties are greater than a superficial view of the subject would induce us to suppose. The number of the radical characters is indeed limited, like that of the keys of the Chinese; but it appears that these characters are by no means universally independent of each other, a combination of two or three of them being often employed to form a single word, and perhaps even to represent a simple idea; and, indeed, this must necessarily happen where we have only about a thousand characters for the expression of a whole language. For the same reason it is impossible that all the characters can be pictures of the things which they represent: some, however, of the symbols on the stone of Rosetta have a manifest relation to the objects denoted by them. For instance, a Priest, a Shrine, a Statue, an Asp, a Mouth, and the Numerals, and a King is denoted by a sort of plant with an insect, which is said to have been a bee; while a much greater number of the characters have no perceptible connexion with the ideas attached to them; although it is probable that a resemblance, either real or metaphorical, may have existed or have been imagined when they were first employed; thus a Libation was originally denoted by a hand holding a jar, with two streams of a liquid issuing from it, but in this inscription the representation has degenerated into a bird's foot. With respect to the epistolographic or enchorial character, it does not seem quite certain that it could be explained even if the hieroglyphics were perfectly understood, for many of the characters neither resemble the corresponding hieroglyphics, nor are capable of being satisfactorily resolved into an alphabet of any kind: in short, the two characters might be supposed to belong to different languages; for they do not seem to agree even in their manner of forming compound from simple terms." (Leitch, pp. 55, 56.) Writing to de Sacy in the following year (5th May, 1816) touching the question of the alphabetic nature of the inscription on the Rosetta Stone, he says: "Si vous lisez la lettre de M. Akerblad, vous conviendrez, je crois, qu'au moins il n'a pas été plus heureux que moi dans ses leçons Coptes de l'inscription. Mais le vrai est que la chose est impossible dans l'étendue que vous paraissez encore vouloir lui donner, car assurément l'inscription *enchoriale* n'est *alphabétique* que dans un sens très borné. . . . . . Je me suis borné dernièrement à l'étude des hiéroglyphes, ou plutôt à la collection d'inscriptions hiéroglyphiques. . . . . . Les caractères que j'ai découverts jettent déjà quelques lumières sur les antiquités de l'Egypte. J'ai reconnu, par exemple, le nom de Ptolémée dans diverses inscriptions à Philæ, à Esné et à Ombos, ce qui fixe à peu près la date des édifices où ce nom se trouve, et c'est même quelque chose que de pouvoir distinguer dans une inscription quelconque les caractères qui expriment les noms des personnages auxquels elle a rapport." (Leitch, p. 60.)

Young deciphers the name of Ptolemy.

On 10th November, 1814, Champollion sent to the President of the Royal Society a copy of his *L'Egypte sous les Pharaons*, and in the letter which accompanied it said, "La base de mon travail est la lecture de l'inscription en caractères Egyptiens, qui est l'un des plus beaux ornemens du riche Musée Britannique; je veux parler du monument trouvé à Rosette. Les efforts que j'ai faits pour y réussir n'ont point été, s'il m'est permis de le dire, sans quelques succès; et les résultats que je crois avoir obtenus après une étude constante et suivie, m'en font espérer de plus grands encore." (Leitch, p. 63.) He asked also that a collation of the Rosetta Stone with the copy of it which he possessed might be made, and suggested that a cast of it should be presented to each of the principal libraries, and to the most celebrated Academies of Europe. As Foreign Secretary of the Royal Society, Young replied saying that the needful collation should be made, and adding, "Je ne sais si par hasard M. de Sacy, avec qui vous êtes sans doute en correspondance, vous aura parlé d'un exemplaire que je lui ai adressé de ma traduction conjecturale avec l'explication des dernières lignes des caractères hiéroglyphiques. Je lui avais déjà envoyé la traduction de l'inscription Egyptienne au commencement du mois d'Octobre passé; l'interprétation des hiéroglyphiques ne m'est réussie qu'à la fin du même mois." (Leitch, p. 64.) In reply to this Champollion wrote, "M. Silvestre de Sacy, mon ancien professeur, ne m'a point donné connaissance de votre mémoire sur la partie Egyptienne et le texte hiéroglyphique de l'inscription de Rosette: c'est vous dire, Monsieur, avec quel empressement je recevrai l'exemplaire que vous avez la bonté de m'offrir." We have seen above from the extract from a letter of de Sacy that a copy of Young's work was lent to Champollion between May 9 and July 20, 1815.

Young and Champollion correspond.

Champollion acquainted with Young's work in 1815.

On August 2, 1816, Young addressed a letter[1] to the Archduke John of Austria, in which he reported further progress in his hieroglyphic studies, thus: "I have already ascertained, as I have mentioned in one of my letters to M. de Sacy, that the enchorial inscription of Rosetta contained a number of individual characters resembling the corresponding hieroglyphics, and I was not disposed to place any great reliance on the alphabetical interpretation of any considerable part of the inscription. I have now fully demonstrated the hieroglyphical origin of the running hand,[2] in which the manuscripts on papyrus, found with the mummies . . . . . ." (Leitch, p. 74.) The principal contents of Young's letters, however, incorporated with other matter, were made into a more extensive article, which was contributed to the Supplement of the *Encyclopædia Britannica*, Supplement, Vol. IV. He made drawings of the plates, which were engraved by Mr. Turrell, and having procured separate copies, he sent them to some of his friends in the summer of 1818, with a cover on which was printed the title, "Hieroglyphical Vocabulary." These plates, however, were precisely the same that were afterwards contained in the fourth volume of the Supplement, as belonging to the article EGYPT. The characters explained in this vocabulary amounted to about two hundred; the number which had been immediately obtained from the stone of Rosetta having been somewhat more than doubled by means of a careful examination of other monuments. . . . . . The higher numerals were readily obtained by a comparison of some inscriptions in which they stood combined with units and with tens.[3] Young's article in the *Encyclopædia Britannica* obtained great celebrity in Europe; and was reprinted by

**Young's work published.**

[1] This letter was printed in 1816, and circulated in London, Paris, and elsewhere; it did not appear in the *Museum Criticum* until 1821.

[2] "Que ce second système (l'Hiératique) n'est qu'une simple modification du système Hiéroglyphique, et n'en diffère uniquement que par la forme des signes." Champollion, *De l'Ecriture Hiératique des Anciens Egyptiens:* Grenoble, 1821. We should have expected some reference by Champollion to Young's discovery quoted above.

[3] Young. *An Account of some recent discoveries in Hieroglyphical Literature*, p. 17.

Leitch in the third volume of the *Works of Dr. Young*, pp. 86–197; it contains eight sections:—

I. Introductory view of the latest publications relating to Egypt.
II. Pantheon.
III. Historiography.
IV. Calendar.
V. Customs and Ceremonies.
VI. Analysis of the Triple Inscription.
VII. Rudiments of a Hieroglyphical Vocabulary.
VIII. Various Monuments of the Egyptians.

Value of Young's article in *Encyclopædia Britannica.*

This article is of very great importance in the history of the decipherment of the hieroglyphics, and had Young taken the trouble of having it printed as a separate publication, there would have been less doubt in the minds of scholars as to the good work which he did, and results borrowed from it by Champollion would have been more easily identified.[1]

Champollion on the geography of Egypt.

It has already been said (p. 130) that Champollion published at Paris in 1814 the two first parts of a work entitled *L'Egypte sous les Pharaons, ou recherches sur la Géographie, la Religion, la Langue, les Ecritures et l'Histoire de l'Egypte avant l'Invasion de Cambyse;* these parts treated simply of the geography of Egypt. In a note to the Preface he tells us that the general plan of the work, together with the introduction of the geographical section and the general map of Egypt under the Pharaohs, was laid before the *Société des Sciences et des Arts de Grenoble*, 1st September, 1807, and that the printing began on the 1st September, 1810. On p. 22 of his *Introduction*, referring to the Rosetta Stone, he says: "Ce monument intéressant est un décret des prêtres de l'Egypte, qui décerne de grands honneurs au jeune roi

[1] Ich halte mich daher verpflichtet, alles auf unsern Gegenstand bezügliche dem Leser nachträglich genau mitzutheilen und zwar mit einer um so grössern Gewissenhaftigkeit, je höher durch dessen Kenntniss die Achtung gegen den trefflichen Forscher steigen wird, der besonders in der Erklärung der symbolischen Hieroglyphen so Manches zuerst aussprach, was man ohne den Artikel der Encyclopaedie gelesen zu haben, meistens als das Eigenthum Champollion's zu betrachten gewohnt ist. Schwartze, *Das Alte Aegypten*, p. 446.

Ptolémée Epiphane. Ce décret est écrit en hiéroglyphes, en langue et en écriture alphabétique Egyptiennes, et en Grec." Now by the words "en langue et en écriture alphabétique Egyptiennes" we are clearly to understand that part of the Rosetta inscription which is written in demotic. Having referred to the studies of de Sacy and Akerblad, and spoken of the words in demotic which the latter scholar had rightly compared with their equivalents in Coptic, "que nous y avons lus ensuite," Champollion adds in a foot-note, "Ce n'est pas ici le lieu de rendre compte du résultat de l'étude suivie que nous avons faite du texte Egyptien de l'Inscription de Rosette, et de l'alphabet que nous avons adopté. Nous nous occuperons de cet important sujet dans la suite de cet ouvrage. En attendant, nous prions le lecteur de regarder comme exacts les résultats que nous lui présentons ici."

**Champollion's hieroglyphical studies in 1810.**

From this it is clear that as early as 1810 Champollion claimed to have made progress in the decipherment of the demotic text (texte Egyptien) of the Rosetta Stone, and it is now time to ask how much he was indebted to Akerblad's letter for ideas and results. A comparison of Plate II. at the end of Akerblad's *Lettre sur l'Inscription Egyptienne de Rosette*, with Plate IV. in Champollion's *Lettre à M. Dacier relative à l'Alphabet des Hiéroglyphes Phonétiques*, will show that *sixteen* of the characters of the alphabet printed by Akerblad in 1802 were retained by Champollion in 1822; also, if Akerblad's alphabet be compared with the "Supposed Enchorial Alphabet" printed at the foot of Plate IV. accompanying Young's article EGYPT, printed in 1818 and published in 1819, it will be found that *fourteen* of the characters are identical in both alphabets. Thus it seems that a greater degree of credit is due to Akerblad than has usually been awarded to him either by Young[1]

**Akerblad attributes correct values to fourteen Demotic characters.**

[1] Mr. Akerblad was far from having completed his examination of the whole enchorial inscription, apparently from the want of some collateral encouragement or co-operation to induce him to continue so laborious an inquiry; and he had made little or no effort to understand the first inscription of the pillar which is professedly engraved in the sacred character, except the detached observation respecting the numerals at the end; he was even disposed to acquiesce in the correctness of Mr. Palin's interpretation, which proceeds on the supposition that parts of the first lines of the hieroglyphics are still remaining on the stone. Young, *An Account*, p. 10.

or Champollion,[1] or, indeed, by writers on Egyptology generally.[2]

Having seen what foundations Young and Champollion had for their own works on the demotic text to rest on, we may return to the consideration of Young's hieroglyphical studies. On the four plates which appeared with his article EGYPT, he correctly identified the names of a few of the gods, Rā, Nut, Thoth, Osiris, Isis, and Nephthys, and he made out the meanings of several Egyptian ideographs. His identifications of kings' names were, however, most unfortunate. Thus of Åmenḥetep, he made Tithons; of Thi (a queen), Eoa; of Usertsen, Heron; of Psammetichus, Sesostris; of Nectanebus, Proteus; of Seti, Psammis; of Rameses II., Amasis; of Autocrator, Arsinoe, etc., etc. He correctly identified the names of Ptolemy and Berenice, although in each case he attributed wrong values to some of the hieroglyphic characters which formed these names. The hieroglyphic alphabet given by Young was as follows:— Young's hieroglyphic alphabet.

| | | | | |
|---|---|---|---|---|
| 206.[3] |  | ⲃⲓⲣ | true value | BA. |
| 207. |  | ⲉ | " | R. |
| 208. |  | ⲉⲛⲉ | " | T'. |
| 209. |  | ⲓ | " | I. |
| 210. |  | ⲕⲉ, ⲕⲏ | " | SE. |
| 211. |  |  | " | M. |

[1] "Feu Akerblad essaya d'étendre ses lectures hors des noms propres grecs, et il échoua complètement." Champollion, *Précis*, 1 éd., p. 14.

[2] See Schwartze, *Das Alte Aegypten*, pp. 160, 162.

[3] No. 205, which is omitted here, is really two demotic characters the values of which are BA and R: to these Young gave the value BERE, and so far he was right, but he failed to see that what he considered to be *one* sign was, in reality, *two*. In Nos. 213 and 214 his consonants were right but his vowels were wrong. We are thus able to see that out of a total of fourteen signs, he assigned correct values to six, partly correct values to three, and wholly wrong values to five. Champollion-Figeac in his *Lettre au Directeur de la Revue Britannique au sujet des Recherches du Docteur Young sur les Hiéroglyphes Egyptiens*, p. 5, gives Young no credit whatever for the three partly correct values assigned to hieroglyphic characters by him.

| | | | | |
|---|---|---|---|---|
| 212. |  | ⲛ | true value | N. |
| 213. |  | ⲟⲗⲉ | " | R or L. |
| 214. | 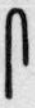 | ⲟϣ, ⲟⲥ | " | S. |
| 215. |  | ⲡ | " | P. |
| 216. |  | ϥ | " | F. |
| 217. |  | ⲧ | " | T. |
| 218. |  | ⲱ | " | CHA. |

In 1822 Champollion published his famous *Lettre à M. Dacier relative à l'alphabet des Hiéroglyphes Phonétiques*, in which he stated his discovery of the Egyptian hieroglyphic alphabet in the following words: "Vous avez sans doute remarqué, Monsieur, dans mon Mémoire sur l'écriture démotique Egyptienne, que ces noms étrangers étaient exprimés phonétiquement au moyen de signes plutôt *syllabiques* qu'*alphabétiques*. La valeur de chaque caractère est reconnue et invariablement fixée par la comparaison de ces divers noms; et de tous ces rapprochements est résulté l'alphabet, ou plutôt le syllabaire *démotique* figuré sur ma planche I., colonne deuxième. L'emploi de ces caractères phonétiques une fois constaté dans l'écriture démotique, je devais naturellement en conclure que puisque les signes de cette écriture populaire étaient, ainsi que je l'ai exposé, empruntés de l'écriture *hiératique* ou sacerdotale, et puisque encore les signes de cette écriture *hiératique* ne sont, comme on l'a reconnu par mes divers mémoires, qu'une représentation abrégée, une véritable *tachygraphie* des *hiérographes*, cette troisième espèce d'écriture, *l'hiéroglyphique* pure, devait avoir aussi un certain nombre de ses signes doués de la faculté d'exprimer les sons; en un mot, qu'il existait également une série d'*hiéroglyphes phonétiques*. Pour s'assurer de la vérité de cet aperçu, pour reconnaître l'existence et discerner même la valeur de quelques-uns des signes de cette espèce, il aurait suffi d'avoir sous les yeux, écrits en *hiéroglyphes* purs, deux noms de rois grecs préalablement connus, et contenant plusieurs lettres employées à la fois dans l'un et dans l'autre, tels que *Ptolémée* et *Cléopâtre*, *Alexandre* et *Bérénice*, etc." (p. 5). Throughout this work there

Champollion's system.

appears to be no mention whatever of Young's identification of *any* letters of the hieroglyphic alphabet, although on p. 2 Champollion says: "A l'égard de l'écriture *démotique* en particulier, il a suffi de la précieuse inscription de Rosette pour en reconnaître l'ensemble; la critique est redevable d'abord aux lumières de votre illustre confrère, M. Silvestre de Sacy, et successivement à celles de feu Akerblad et de M. le docteur Young, des premières notions exactes qu'on a tirées de ce monument, et c'est de cette même inscription que j'ai déduit la série des signes démotiques qui, prenant une valeur syllabico-alphabétique, exprimaient dans les textes *idéographiques* les noms propres des personnages étrangers à l'Egypte." That Champollion should not have known of Young's article EGYPT is a thing not to be understood, especially as advance copies were sent to Paris and elsewhere as early as 1818.

**Champollion admits value of Akerblad's and Young's labours.**

From the facts given above we are enabled to draw up the following statement as to the amount of work done in the decipherment of the Egyptian language by the early workers in this field.

**Statement of results of labours of Zoëga, Akerblad, Young and Champollion.**

Barthélemy[1] and Zoëga[2] had come to the conclusion long before the labours of Akerblad, Young, and Champollion, that the cartouches contained proper names. Akerblad drew up an alphabet of the demotic character, in which fourteen signs appear to have had correct values attributed to them. Young published a demotic alphabet in which the greater number of Akerblad's results were absorbed; he fixed the correct values to six hieroglyphic characters, and to three others partly correct values; he identified the names of Ptolemy and Alexander, the numerals and several gods' names. Champollion published a demotic alphabet, the greater part of which he owed, without question, to Akerblad, and a hieroglyphic alphabet of which six characters had had correct values assigned to them by Young, and the

[1] Caylus, *Recueil d'Antiquités Egyptiennes, Etrusques*, etc., Tom. V. p. 79.

[2] In *De Origine et Usu Obeliscorum*, p. 465. Conspiciuntur autem passim in Aegyptiis monumentis schemata quaedam ovata sive elliptica planae basi insidentia, quae emphatica ratione includunt certa notarum syntagmata, sive ad propria personarum nomina exprimenda, sive ad sacratiores formulas designandas.

values of three others had been correctly stated as far as the consonants were concerned. There is no doubt whatever that Champollion's plan of work was eminently scientific, and his great knowledge of Coptic enabled him to complete the admirable work of decipherment, which his natural talent had induced him to undertake. The value of his contributions to the science of Egyptology it would be difficult to overestimate, and the amount of work which he did in his comparatively short life is little less than marvellous. It is, however, to be regretted that Champollion did not state more clearly what Young had done, for a full acknowledgment of this would have in no way injured or lessened his own immortal fame.[1]

**Champollion's alphabet.**

Briefly, the way in which Champollion recovered the greater part of the Egyptian alphabet is as follows. It will be remembered that, on account of breakages, the only name found on the Rosetta Stone is that of Ptolemy. Shortly before Champollion published his letter to M. Dacier, he had published an account of an obelisk,[2] recently brought to London, which was inscribed with the name of a Ptolemy, written with the same characters as that on the Rosetta Stone, and also contained within a cartouche. It was followed by a second cartouche, which should contain the name of a queen. The obelisk was said to have been fixed in a socket, bearing a Greek inscription containing a petition of the priests of Isis at Philae, addressed to Ptolemy, to Cleopatra his sister, and to Cleopatra his wife. Now, he argued, if this obelisk and the hieroglyphic inscription which it bears are really the result of the petition of the priests, who in the Greek speak of the dedication of a similar monument, it follows of necessity that the cartouche must contain the name of a Cleopatra.

**The names Ptolemy and Cleopatra.**

The names of Ptolemy and Cleopatra having, in the Greek, some letters which are similar, may be used for comparing

[1] We have seen above that Champollion did know of Young's work, yet in his *Précis du Système Hiéroglyphique*, p. 18, he says that he had arrived at results similar to those obtained by Dr. Young, without having any knowledge of his opinion.

[2] *Observations sur l'Obélisque Egyptien de l'Île de Philæ*, in *Revue encyclopédique*, Mars, 1822.

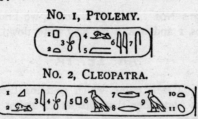

the hieroglyphics which are used in each; and if the characters which are similar in these two names express the same sound in each cartouche, their purely phonetic character is at once made clear. A previous comparison of these two names written in the demotic character shows that when they are written phonetically several characters, exactly alike, are used in each. The analogy of the demotic, hieratic, and hieroglyphic methods of writing in a general way, leads us to expect the same coincidence and the same conformity in these same names, written hieroglyphically. The names Ptolemaios and Cleopatra written in hieroglyphics are as follows:—

No. 1, Ptolemy.

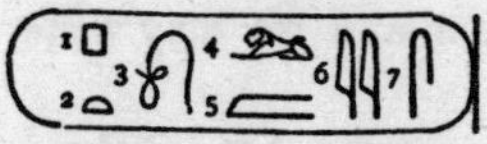


No. 2, Cleopatra.

Recovery of the Egyptian alphabet.

Now in No. 2 cartouche, sign No. 1, which must represent K, is not found in cartouche No. 1. Sign No. 2, a lion lying down, is identical with sign No. 4 in cartouche No. 1. This clearly is L. Sign No. 3, a pen, represents the short vowel E; two of them are to be seen in character No. 6 in No. 1 cartouche, and considering their position their value must be AI of *αιος*. Sign No. 4 is identical with No. 3 in No. 1 cartouche, and must have the value O in each name. Sign No. 5 is identical with sign No. 1 of No. 1 cartouche, which being the first letter of the name of Ptolemy must be P. Sign No. 6 is not found in No. 1 cartouche, but it must be A, because it is the same sign as sign No. 9, which ends the name ΚΛΕΟΠΑΤΡΑ; we know that signs 10 and 11 always accompany feminine proper names, because we see them following the names of goddesses like  Isis, and 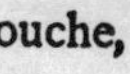 Nephthys. Sign No. 7, an open stretched out hand, must be T. It does not occur in No. 1 cartouche, but we find from other cartouches that  takes the place of , and the reverse. Sign No. 8 must be R; it is not in No. 1 cartouche, and ought not to be there. In No. 1 cartouche sign No. 7 must be S, because it ends the name which in Greek ends with S. Thus from these two cartouches we may collect twelve characters of the Egyptian alphabet, viz., A, AI, E, K, K, L, M, O, P, R, S, T. Now let us take another cartouche from the *Description de l'Egypte*, t. III. pl. 38, No. 13, and try to make it out; it reads:—

The name Alexander.

No. 3.

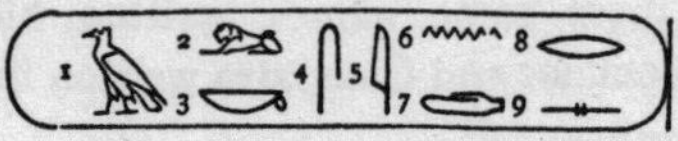

Now signs Nos. 1, 2, 4, 5, 7, and 8, we know from cartouches Nos. 1 and 2, and we may write down their values thus:—

**ΑΛ..ΣΕ..ΤΡ.**

The only Greek name which contains these letters in this order is Alexander, therefore let us assign to the signs , , and , the value of K, N and S respectively. We find on examination that the whole group corresponds, letter for letter, with the group which stands in the demotic text of a papyrus in the place of the Greek name **ΑΛΕΧΑΝΔΡΟΣ**. We have, then, gained three new phonetic signs K, N, and S, and have determined the value of fifteen in all.

Again, let us take the cartouche of another lady:—

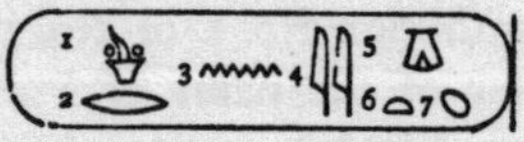

The name Berenice.

Now signs Nos. 2, 3, 4, 6, and 7 we know, and we may write them down thus:—

**. RNAI . .**

The only female name which contains these letters in this order is that of Berenice, and to  and  we may therefore assign the values B and K respectively. Thus we have gained two more signs.

If we take two other cartouches, viz. :—

 and 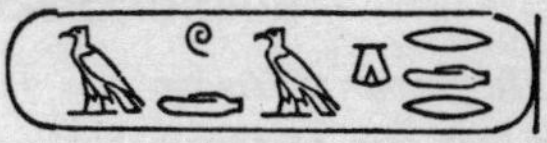

we find that we are able to read the first at once KAISRS, which is clearly *Καισαρος* or Caesar; in the second the only sign we do not know is ℮. Writing down the values we know we have A.TAKRTR, which is clearly *Αυτοκρατορ*; thus the value of the second character must be U. In this manner Champollion worked through the names of all the Ptolemies and the Roman Emperors, and eventually succeeded in making out the value of one hundred and eleven signs. At the foot of Plate I., in his *Lettre à Monsieur Dacier*, he writes his own name in hieroglyphics thus :—

SHA- M - PU - LL - I - O - N.

The following are the letters of the Egyptian alphabet with their values as now accepted by Egyptologists :—

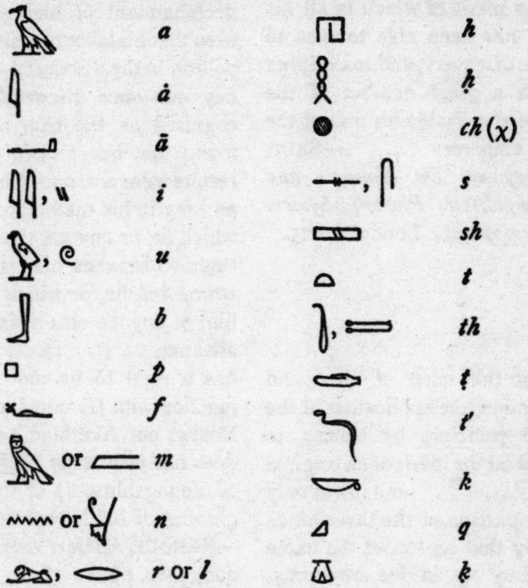

## Opinions of Egyptologists on the Labours of Young and Champollion.

*In favour of Young.*

The first idea of certain hieroglyphics being intended to represent sounds was suggested by Dr. Young, who, from the names of Ptolemy and Berenice, had pointed out nine, which have since proved to be correct; the former taken from the Rosetta inscription, and the latter deduced with singular ingenuity from the enchorial of the same monument. [M. Champollion fils seems to be unwilling to allow this: but the fact is evident; and surely he has accomplished too much to stand in need of assuming to himself the merits of another. Note 1, p. 1.] Working upon this basis, M. Champollion, with happy success, made out four or five others, as also about thirty synonymes; and by the ingenious application of these, the merit of which is all his own, he has been able to turn to effect the discovery, and to decipher therewith a great number of the names of the Ptolemies and of the Roman emperors. . . . . .—Salt, H., *Essay on Dr. Young's and M. Champollion's Phonetic System of Hieroglyphics;* London, 1825.

Amidst this mass of error and contradiction, the application of the phonetic principle by Young, in 1818, had all the merit of an original discovery . . . . . . and it was only by a comparison of the three kinds of writing that he traced the name of Ptolemy up in his own way,

*In favour of Champollion.*

His [Young's] translations, however, are below criticism, being as unfounded as those of Kircher. How far even, in the decipherment, he proceeded correctly, may be doubted. . . . But even here [in interpretation] there is much too incorrect in principle to be of real use; much of it is beneath criticism. —Birch, *Hieroglyphs*, p. 196.

It is even to this day a common habit of Englishmen to couple the name of their countryman, Dr. Thomas Young, with that of Champollion, as sharing with him the glory of this discovery. No person who knows anything of Egyptian philology can countenance so gross an error . . . . . . But it is not true that he discovered the key to the decipherment of hieroglyphics, or even that his labours assisted Champollion in the discovery. When the key was once discovered and recognized as the true one, it was found that one or two of Young's results were correct. But there was nothing in his method or theory by which he or anyone else could distinguish between his right and his wrong results, or which could lead him or anyone else a single step in advance. . . . . . . . . . If anyone has a right to be named in conjunction with Champollion, it is not Young, but Akerblad, to whom he does full justice (as he does indeed to Young himself) at the very beginning of his letter to M. Dacier. —Renouf, *Hibbert Lectures;* London, 1880, pp. 12–16.

*In favour of Young.*

from the demotic into hieratic, into hieroglyphs.—BIRCH, *Hieroglyphs*, in WILKINSON, *The Egyptians*, pp. 195, 196.

Fast gleichzeitig mit dem alten Jomard . . . . . ; hatte Dr. Young das Glück aus den hieroglyphischen Texten die Bezeichnungen für die Einer, Zehner, Hunderte, und Tausende richtig herauszuerkennen und überdies den hieroglyphischen Königsnamen—

PTOLMIS und

BRNIKA-t

ihre entsprechende griechische Form Ptolemaios und Berenike gegenüberzustellen, eine Entdeckung, die ihm **allein gebührt** und die den Ausgangspunkt der späteren Entzifferungen bilden sollte . . . . . . Dr. Young's glückliche Zusammenstellungen der oben aufgeführten ägyptisch-hieroglyphischen Eigennamen mit ihren entsprechenden griechischen Vorbildern sollten ihm plötzlich die Augen öffnen und ihn [*i.e.*, Champollion] auf den rechten Pfad führen.—BRUGSCH, *Die Aegyptologie*, pp. 9, 11.

Ein solcher Ring mit Hieroglyphen  fand sich nun auch an den betreffenden Stellen der Inschrift von Rosette und er musste den Namen des Ptolemäus bilden. Es war der bekannte englische Naturforscher Thomas Young, der im Jahre 1819

*In favour of Champollion.*

Sæculi enim hujus et initium usque quum cognitio hieroglyphorum, quibus veteres Aegyptii in sacra dialecto scribenda utebantur, densissimis tenebris scateret, ita quidem ut fere omnia, quæ antea vel eruditissimi homines summo ingenii acumine explorasse sibi visi sunt, si hodie forte legimus risum vix tenere possimus: hoc lapide detecto postquam omnium animi ad spem enucleandi tandem istud monstruosum et perplexum per tot sæcula quasi involucris involutorum genus signorum arrecti sunt, unus vir Champollio Francogallus exstitit, qui mira sagacitate incredibilique studio adjutus totam hieroglyphorum rationem nulla fere parte relicta luce clarius explanavit et exposuit. — BRUGSCH, *Inscriptio Rosettana;* Berlin, 1851, pp. 1, 2.

Unabhängig von Young kam gleichzeitig ein junger französischer Gelehrter, François Champollion, zu der gleichen Vermutung und ihm war es beschieden, sogleich ein völlig richtiges Resultat zu erhalten. —ERMAN, *Aegypten*, p. 14.

. . . . . Young, qui, le premier, fit l'application du principe phonétique à la lecture des hiéroglyphes. Cette idée fut, dans la réalité, le *fiat lux* de la science. . . . . Toutefois, malgré quelques succès remarquables, Young ne sut pas la féconder; il avait bien reconnu dans les hiéroglyphes les noms de Ptolémée et de Bérénice, mais sans réussir à assigner à chacun des signes qui les composent leur véritable valeur; ses autres lectures sont fausses, quoiqu'il ait rencontré juste dans la détermination de la valeur

*In favour of Young.*

diesen scharfsinnigen und völlig richtigen Schluss machte und wenigstens für einige Zeichen des Namens den Lautwert feststellte.—ERMAN, *Aegypten*, p. 14.

Der erste, der es that und von dem richtigen Grundsatze ausging, dass die Königsnamen alphabetisch geschrieben sein müssten . . . . . war der berühmte englische Physiker Thomas Young (geboren 1773). Er erkannte in der häufigsten in dem Dekret von Rosette vorkommenden Gruppe den Namen Ptolemäus, er vermochte ein später zum grossen Teile bestätigtes hieroglyphisches Alphabet aufzustellen und sie über das System der ägyptischen Schrift vollkommen richtige Ansichten zu bilden. So haben wir denn in Young den eigentlichen Entzifferer der ägyptischen Schrift zu sehen, wenn es ihm auch nicht gelang, der Sprache selbst Herr zu werden. — WIEDEMANN, *Aegyptische Geschichte*, p. 29.

In the first work of Champollion, his essay *De l'Ecriture hiératique des Anciens Egyptiens*, published in 1821, he recognized the existence of only the first of these three ways of representing words, supposing that all the Egyptian characters represented ideas. When he discovered the erroneousness of this opinion, he used all possible efforts to suppress the work in which he had stated it. That work, however, contained a valuable discovery. . .

*In favour of Champollion.*

alphabétique de plusieurs caractères. Quelques minces qu'ils soient, ces premiers résultats constitueraient en faveur du docteur Young un titre considérable, s'il ne les avait pas compromis lui-même en s'engageant dans une fausse voie, et en publiant des traductions tout aussi imaginaires que celles de ses devanciers. La solution du problème était réservée au génie de Champollion le jeune ; c'est un honneur que personne ne peut lui disputer. — CHABAS, *L'Inscription de Rosette*, p. 5.

Wenn wir die Frage so stellen : Wer hat zuerst einige hieroglyphische Zeichen in ihrem Lautwerthe richtig bestimmt ? oder besser gesagt, zufällig errathen, so müssen wir antworten : das war Th. Young ; den Schlüssel zur Entzifferung der Hieroglyphenschrift jedoch hat er nicht gefunden. François Champollion, geb. den 23. December 1790, gest. den 4. März 1832, er ist es, den die Wissenschaft der Aegyptologie in dankbarer Verehrung als ihren eigentlichen Begründer nennt . . . . . . .—DÜMICHEN, *Geschichte des alten Aegyptiens*, Berlin, 1878, s. 304.

Zwei grosse Männer, in England der auf vielen Gebieten des Wissens ausgezeichnete Thomas Young, in Frankreich François Champollion, begaben sich zu gleicher Zeit, aber unabhängig von einander, an die Arbeit. Beider Bemühungen lohnte schöner Erfolg. Champollion aber wird mit Recht vor seinem britischen Rivalen als Entzifferer der

*In favour of Young.*

. . . . . . In the year after this publication, Champollion published his *Lettre à M. Dacier*, in which he announced the phonetic powers of certain hieroglyphics and applied them to the reading of Greek and Roman proper names. Had he been candid enough to admit that he was indebted to Dr. Young for the commencement of his discovery, and only to claim the merit of extending and improving the alphabet, he would probably have had his claims to the preceding and subsequent discoveries, which were certainly his own, more readily admitted by Englishmen than they have been. In 1819 Dr. Young had published his article "Egypt" in the Supplement to the Encyclopædia Britannica; and it cannot be doubted that the analysis of the names "Ptolemæus" and "Berenice," which it contained, reached Champollion in the interval between his publication in 1821 and 1822, and led him to alter his views. . . . . . The *Grammaire Egyptienne* ought to have been given to the public as his *sole* bequest in the department of Egyptian philology. It was published from a manuscript written in 1831, immediately before his last illness. Shortly before his decease, having carefully collected the sheets, he delivered them to his brother, with the remark, "Be careful of this; I trust that it will be my visiting card to posterity." Even the warmest admirers of Champollion must admit that he left his system in a very imperfect state. Few, probably, will deny that he held many errors to the close of his life, both in what respects the

*In favour of Champollion.*

Hieroglyphen genannt werden müssen.—EBERS, *Aegypten in Bild und Wort;* Leipzig, 1879, Bd. ii., s. 49.

Un savant anglais du plus grand mérite, Th. Young, essaya de reconstituer l'alphabet des cartouches. De 1814 à 1818, il s'exerça sur les divers systèmes d'écriture égyptienne, et sépara mécaniquement les groupes différents dont se composaient le texte hiéroglyphique et le texte démotique de l'inscription de Rosette. Après avoir déterminé, d'une manière plus ou moins exacte, le sens de chacun d'eux, il en essaya la lecture. . . . . . Ses idées étaient justes en partie, mais sa méthode imparfaite; il entrevit la terre promise, mais sans pouvoir y entrer. Le véritable initiateur fut François Champollion. . . . . . — MASPERO, *Histoire Ancienne;* Paris, 1886, pp. 729, 730.

Ce fut en 1819, que le Dr. Young déclara le premier que les cartouches, ou encadrements elliptiques, dans le texte hiéroglyphique de l'inscription de Rosette, correspondaient aux noms propres grecs et particulièrement à celui de Ptolémée du texte grec, et aux groupes, du même nom, dans le texte intermédiaire en écriture égyptienne démotique ou vulgaire, groupes qui avaient été déjà reconnus et décomposés par MM. Silvestre de Sacy et Akerblad. Il allait encore plus loin en supposant que chaque signe du cartouche représentait un son du nom de Ptolémée et en cherchant à les définir réellement un à un par une analyse très ingénieuse. . . . . . Plusieurs signes

*In favour of Young.*

reading of the characters, and in what respects the interpretation of the texts.—HINCKS, *On the Number, Names, and Powers of the Letters of the Hieroglyphic Alphabet*, in Trans. Royal Irish Acad., Vol. XXI., Section *Polite Literature*, pp. 133, 134, Dublin, 1848.

*In favour of Champollion.*

avaient été faussement interprétés et la preuve la plus évidente en était qu'il ne réussissait pas à lire d'autres noms que ceux de Ptolémée et de Bérénice. Il faut donc avouer que, malgré cette découverte, les opinions du Dr. Young, sur la nature du système hiéroglyphique, étaient encore essentiellement fausses et que cette découverte elle-même serait probablement restée infructueuse et à peine signalée comme découverte dans la science, si on avait suivi le chemin que son auteur lui-même avait proposé.—LEPSIUS, *Lettre à M. le Professeur F. Rosellini* sur l'*Alphabet Hiéroglyphique;* Rome, 1837, p. 11.

**Seyffarth and others reject Champollion's system.**

It could hardly be expected that the system of decipherment proposed by Champollion would be accepted by those who had rival systems to put forth, hence we find old theories revived and new ideas brought to light side by side with Champollion's method of decipherment. Among those who attacked the new system were, Spolm, the misguided Seyffarth, Goulianoff and Klaproth. Spolm and Seyffarth divided hieroglyphics into emphonics, symphonics and aphonics, by which terms they seem to imply phonetics, enclitics and ideographics. Their hopelessly wrong theory was put forth with a great show of learning in *De Lingua et Literis veterum Ægyptiorum* at Leipzig, 1825–31. Goulianoff[1] did not accept Champollion's system entirely, and he wished to consider the phonetic hieroglyphics acrologic; this also was the view taken by Klaproth, who bitterly attacked Champollion in his *Lettre sur la découverte des hiéroglyphes acrologiques, adressée à M. de Goulianoff*, Paris, 1827, and also in his *Examen critique des travaux de feu M. Champollion sur les Hiéroglyphes*, Paris, 1832. To the first of these two works Champollion published a reply entitled *Analyse critique de la*

[1] See his *Essai sur les Hiéroglyphes d'Horapollon*, Paris, 1827.

*lettre sur la découverte des hiéroglyphes acrologiques par J. Klaproth* (Extr. du Bulletin de Férussac), Paris, 1827, in which he showed the utter worthlessness of the theory. In 1830, when the correctness of Champollion's system was fully demonstrated, Janelli published at Naples his *Fundamenta Hermeneutica Hieroglyphicae*, in three volumes, in which the old symbolic theory of the hieroglyphics was re-asserted! and there were many who hesitated not to follow the views of François Ricardi, feu Charles d'Oneil, the soundness of which may be estimated by the title of one of his works, "*Découverte des Hiéroglyphes domestiques phonétiques par lesquels, sans sortir de chez soi, on peut deviner l'histoire, la chronologie (! !), le culte de tous les peuples anciens et modernes, de la même manière, qu'on le fait en lisant les hiéroglyphes égyptiens selon la nouvelle méthode;*" Turin, 1824.[1] Little by little, however, Champollion's system was accepted. In 1835 Leemans published his edition of Horapollo, in which the results of the decipherment of Egyptian hieroglyphics were ably applied, and two years later Richard Lepsius published his famous *Lettre à M. F. Rosellini sur l'alphabet hiéroglyphique*, wherein he discussed the whole question of the decipherment, and showed that Champollion's method was, without any question, correct. About this time students, who worked on Champollion's plan, sprang up in Holland, Italy, France and England, and the misguided Seyffarth alone continued down to 1855 to write and protest against the new system.

**Persistence of false systems of interpretation.**

## An Egyptian Funeral.

The funeral of a poor Egyptian was, probably, very much like that of one of the present day. After the body had been steeped for a short time in bitumen or natron, or perhaps merely rubbed with these substances, the few personal ornaments of the man were placed on it, he was wrapped in one

[1] Another of his works was entitled, *Triomphe sur les impies obtenu par les adorateurs de la très-sainte Trinité et du Verbe éternel, sous le gouvernement des sixième et septième rois d'Egypte au VIe siècle après le déluge. Sculpté en signes hiéroglyphiques sur l'Obélisque Barberinus et maintenant expliqué;* Geneva, 1821.

piece of linen, and with his staff to support his steps,[1] and his sandals to protect his weary feet in the nether-world, he was laid in a hole or cave, or even in the sand of the open desert, to set out on his last journey. Trusting in the might of a few amulets that were buried with him, he feared not to meet his foes in the grave.

The funeral of a king or a member of the royal family, or of a wealthy person, was a very magnificent ceremony, and it is, perhaps, impossible to realize exactly what an imposing sight it must have been. Treating of the burial of a king in

Diodorus on Egyptian burial.

Egypt, Diodorus says (I. 72), that when a king died all the inhabitants of the country wept and rent their garments; the temples were closed, and the people abstained from sacrifices and celebrated no festival for a period of seventy-two days. Crowds of men and women, about two or three hundred in number, went round about the streets with mud on their heads, and with their garments knotted like girdles below the breasts (*σινδόνας ὑποκάτω τῶν μαστῶν*), singing dirges twice daily in praise of the dead. They denied themselves wheat, they ate no animal food, and they abstained from wine and dainty fare. No one dared to make use of baths, or unguents, or to recline upon couches, or even to partake of the pleasures of love. The seventy-two days were passed in grief and mourning as for the death of a beloved child. Meanwhile, the funeral paraphernalia was made ready, and on the last day of mourning, the body, placed in a coffin, was laid at the entrance to the tomb, and according to law, judgment was passed upon the acts of the king during his life. Every one had the power to make an accusation against the king. The priests pronounced a funeral oration over the body, and declared the noble works of the king during his life, and if the opinion of the assembled multitude agreed with that of the priests, and the king had led a blameless life, they testified their approval openly; if, on the other hand, the life of the king had been a bad one, they expressed their disapprobation by loud murmurs. Through the opposition of the people many kings have been deprived of meet and proper burial,

[1] Compare Psalm xxiii. 4.

Diodorus on Egyptian burial.

and kings are accustomed to exercise justice, not only because they fear the disapprobation of their subjects, but also because they fear that after death their bodies may be maltreated, and their memory cursed for ever.

It is very doubtful if the above description of the mourning is not somewhat exaggerated, and there appears to be no authority in Egyptian inscriptions for the statement that many kings were deprived of their meet and proper burial because of the disapproval of their past lives shown by the people. This account by Diodorus is more valuable for the indication of the great and solemn respect which was shown to dead kings, as sons of the god Rā, and as lords of the land of Egypt, than for its strict accuracy of detail. The customs observed at the burial of kings would be respectfully imitated at the funerals of the nobles and officials of his court, and the account by the same writer of what happened after the mummy of an Egyptian gentleman was prepared for burial, must next be considered.

According to Diodorus (I. 92), when the body is ready to be buried, the relatives give notice to the judges and the friends of the deceased, and inform them that the funeral will take place on a certain day, and that the body will pass over the lake; and straightway the judges, forty in number,[1] come and seat themselves in a semi-circle above the lake. Then the men who have been commissioned to prepare a boat called *βâρις*,[2] bring it to the lake, and they set it afloat under the charge of a pilot called Charon.[3] And they pretend that Orpheus travelling in Egypt in ancient times, was present at a ceremony of this kind, and that he drew his fable of the infernal regions partly from his remembrance of this

[1] Is it possible that Diodorus has confused the forty judges at the lake with the forty-two judges or assessors of the Book of the Dead, before each of whom the deceased was supposed to declare that he had not committed a certain sin?

[2] In Egyptian: 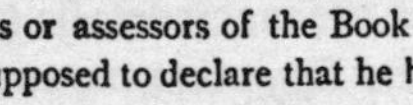 *barei.*

[3] Wiedemann compares the Egyptian *kare*, "Schiffer." The dictionaries give 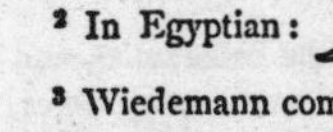 *qare*, a "ship," and 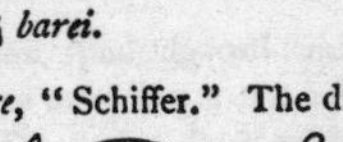 *qāre*, "coachman," "cart-driver."

Diodorus on Egyptian burial.

ceremony,[1] and partly from his imagination. Before the coffin containing the dead man was placed in the boat on the lake, every person had the right to bring accusations against the deceased. If any accuser succeeded in showing that the deceased had led a bad life, the judges made a decree which deprived the body of legal burial; if, on the other hand, the accusation was found to be unjust, the person who brought it was compelled to pay heavy damages. If no one stood forth to bring an accusation, or if an accusation seemed calumnious, the relatives of the deceased ceased to mourn and began to praise the dead man and his virtues, and to entreat the gods of the infernal regions to admit him into the place reserved for good men. The Egyptians never praised the birth of a man, as did the Greeks, for they believed that all men are equally noble. The people being gathered together, add their cries of joy, and utter wishes that the deceased may enjoy everlasting life in the underworld in the company of the blessed. Those who have private burial places lay the bodies of their dead in the places set apart for them; but those who have not, build a new chamber in their house, and set the body in it fixed upright against the wall. Those who are deprived of burial, either because they lie under the ban of an accusation, or because they have not paid their debts, are merely laid in their own houses. It happens sometimes that the younger members of a family, having become richer, pay the debts of their ancestors, secure the removal of the condemnatory sentence upon them, and give them most sumptuous funerals. The great honours which are paid to the dead by the Egyptians form the most solemn ceremonies. As a guarantee for a debt, it is a customary thing to deposit the bodies of dead parents, and the greatest disgrace and privation from burial, wait upon those who redeem not such sacred pledges.

In this account also there are many details given for which proof is still wanting from the Egyptian monuments.

[1] Thus Orpheus brought back from his travels in Egypt the ceremonies, and the greater part of the mystic rites celebrated in memory of the courses of Ceres, and the whole of the myth of hell. The difference between the feasts of Bacchus and of those of Osiris exists only in name, and the same may be said of the mysteries of Isis and those of Osiris. Diodorus, I. 96.

An attempt may now be made to describe briefly what happened after death to the body of a man of high rank who departed this life at Thebes towards the end of the XVIIIth or beginning of the XIXth dynasty, that is to say about B.C. 1400. The facts are all known, and therefore nothing need be invented; it is only necessary to gather them together and to bring them to a focus on the person of one man. We must imagine then that we are living on the east bank of the Nile, near the temple of Åmen-Rā, "lord of the thrones of the earth," in the fifteenth century before Christ. One morning before the day has dawned, even before the officials who conduct the early services in the temples are astir, we are awakened by loud cries of grief and lamentation, and on making inquiries we are told that Ani, the great scribe of the offerings of the gods in the temple of Åmen-Rā, is dead. As he was the receiver of the revenues of the gods of Abydos, as well as of Åmen-Rā of Thebes, first prophet of Åmen, and the precentor who stood on the threshold of the temple morning by morning to lead off the hymn of praise to the sun, his death naturally causes great excitement in the temples and the immediate neighbourhood; as his forefathers for five or six generations have been temple officers of the highest rank, it is certain that his funeral will be a great event, and that numbers of the hereditary aristocracy and government officials will assist at the ceremony. He leaves no wife to mourn for him, for she is already dead, and is now lying in a chamber of a splendid tomb, not yet finished, however, nine miles away across the river, awaiting the coming of her husband. She was called Tutu, and belonged to one of the oldest and most honourable families in Thebes; she was a member of the famous college of singers of Åmen-Rā, and also a member of the choir of ladies, each one of whom carried a sistrum or a tambourine in the temple of that god.

Egyptian embalmment according to the monuments.

Ani began to hew out the tomb for himself and his wife many years ago, and during his lifetime he spared neither pains nor expense in making it one of the largest and finest ever known for a person of lower rank than a king. Ani was not a very old man when he died, although his step was slow and his back somewhat bent; in stature he was of middle height, and

Tomb of Ani.

his features had a kind but dignified look, and though comparatively few loved him, all respected him for his uprightness and integrity. He was a learned man, and knew the literature of Egypt well; he himself wrote a fine, bold hand, and was no mean artist with his pencil. He was a tried servant of the king, and loved him well, but he loved his god Åmen more, and was very jealous for his honour, and the glory of his worship in the temple of the Apts. All his ancestors had been in the service of the god, and it was even said that the oldest of them had seen Åmen, who, until the expulsion of the Hyksos by the kings of Thebes, had occupied the position of a mere local deity, suddenly become the national god of Egypt. Whether Ani believed in his innermost heart any or all of the official religion is another matter; his official position brought him into contact with the temporal rather than the spiritual affairs of the Egyptian religion, and whatever doubts he may have had in matters of belief, or concerning the efficacy of the magic of his day, etc., etc., he said nothing about them to any man.

For some days past it had been seen that Ani's death was to be expected, and many of his colleagues in the temple had come to see him from time to time, one bringing a charm, another a decoction of herbs, etc., and a few had taken it in turns to stay in his room for some hours at a time. One night his illness took a decidedly serious turn, and early in the morning, a short time before daybreak, when, as the Orientals say, the dawn may be smelled, Ani died. The news of his death spreads rapidly through the quarter, for all the women of his house rush frantically through the streets, beating their breasts, and from time to time clutching at their hair, which is covered with handfuls of the thick dust of the streets, after the manner of Ånpu in the *Tale of the Two Brothers*, and uttering wailing cries of grief. In the house, parties of mourning women shriek out their grief, and all the members of the house add their tears and sobs. The steward of the house has, however, sent across the river to the *cher-ḥeb* or priest who superintends and arranges the funerals of the wealthy and great, and informed him of Ani's death, and as quickly as possible this official leaves his

Death of Ani.

house near the Valley of the Tombs of the Kings, and together with his assistants, makes his way with all haste to Ani's house. Having arrived there he takes Ani's body into his charge, and proceeds to discuss the method by which the body shall be preserved, and the style of the funeral. While his assistants are taking away the body to the embalming house, he sends quickly to the western bank of the Nile, and summons his chief mason to his presence; after a short time he arrives, and the *cher-ḥeb* instructs him to go to Ani's tomb with a body of men, and to finish hewing whatever chambers and pillars remain in a half completed state, to plaster the walls, and to paint upon them scenes for which he supplies him with details and notes. The *cher-ḥeb* knows that for many years past Ani, and one or two of his friends among the scribes, had been writing and illuminating with vignettes a fine copy of the "Book of the Dead"; he remembers that this work remains unfinished, and he therefore sets a skilful scribe to finish it in the style in which Ani would probably have finished it. Parties of professional mourners are next organized, and these go round about the city at stated times, singing in chorus, probably accompanied by some musical instrument, funereal dirges, the subjects of which were the shortness of life and the certainty that all must die, and the virtues of the dead man. These dirges were sung twice daily, and Ani's friends and colleagues, during the days of mourning, thought it to be their duty to abstain from wine and every kind of luxury, and they wore the simplest and plainest garments, and went quite unadorned.

**Ani's body given to the embalmers.**

**Dirges for the dead.**

Meanwhile it was decided that Ani's funeral should be one of the best that money could purchase, and as while he was alive he was thought to be in constant communion with the gods, his relatives ordered that his body should be mummified in the best possible way, so that his soul 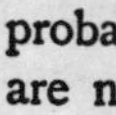 *ba*, and his intelligence 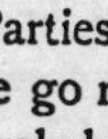 *χu*, when they returned some thousands of years hence to seek his body in the tomb, might find his 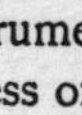 *ka* or "genius" there waiting, and that all three might enter into the body once more, and revivify it, and live with it for ever in the kingdom of Osiris. No opportunity must

**Object of embalmment.**

be given for these four component parts of the whole of a man to drift away one from the other, and to prevent this the perishable body  *χa* must be preserved in such a way that each limb of it may meetly be identified with a god, and the whole of it with Osiris, the judge of the dead and king of the nether world. The tomb must be made a fit and proper dwelling-place for the *ka*, which will never leave it as long as the body to which it belongs lies in its tomb. The furniture of the tomb must be of the best, and every material, and the workmanship thereof, must also be of the best.

The embalmment.

The *cher-ḥeb* next goes to the embalming chamber and orders his assistants to begin their operations upon Ani's body, over which formulæ are being recited. The body is first washed and then laid upon the ground, and one of the assistants traces with ink on the left side, over the groin, a line, some few inches long, to indicate where the incision is to be made in the body; another assistant takes a knife, probably made of flint, and makes a cut in the body the same length as the line drawn in ink by his companion. Whether this man was then driven away with sticks, and stones thrown after him, as Diodorus states, or not, is a moot point upon which the inscriptions give us no information. The chief intestines and the heart and lungs were then carefully taken out and washed in palm wine, and stuffed with sweet smelling spices, gums, etc. They were next smeared all over with an unguent, and then carefully bandaged with strips of linen many yards long, on which were inscribed the names of the four children of Horus[1] who symbolized the four cardinal points and of the four goddesses who took the intestines under their special protection. While this was being done a set of four alabaster jars was brought from the stores of the *cher-ḥeb's* establishment, and in each of these one of the four packets of

[1] Compare 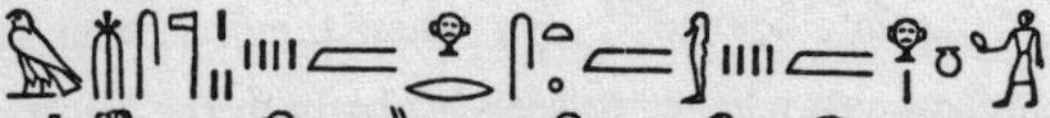
 "the four children of Horus, in the form of four figures made of metal, with the face of a man, with the face of an ape, with the face of a jackal, and with the face of a hawk."

embalmed intestines was placed. Each jar was inscribed with a formula, and all that was wanted to make it the property of Ani was to inscribe his name upon it in the blank spaces left for the purpose. Each jar had a cover made in the form of the head of the child of Horus to whom it was dedicated. The jar of Mesthȧ had the head of a man, and in it was placed the stomach; it was under the protection of Isis. The jar of Ḥāpi had the head of an ape, and in it were placed the smaller intestines; it was under the protection of Nephthys. The jar of Ṭuamāutef had the head of a jackal, and in it was placed the heart; it was under the protection of Neith. The jar of Qebḥsennuf had the head of a hawk, and in it was placed the liver; it was under the protection of Serqet. The inscriptions on the jars state that the part of the deceased in it is identified with the child of Horus to whom the jar is dedicated, and that the goddess under whose charge it is protects it. The covers of the jars are fastened on by running in liquid plaster, and they are finally set in the four divisions of a coffer on a sledge with a vaulted cover and a projecting rectangular upright at each corner. It was of the greatest importance to have the intestines[1] preserved intact, for without them a man could not hope to live again. The brain is next removed through the nostrils by means of an iron rod curved at one end, and is put aside to be dried and buried with the body; at every step in these processes religious formulæ are recited. The body thus deprived of its more perishable parts is taken and laid to soak in a tank of liquid natron for a period of seventy days. At the end of this time it is taken out and carefully washed and dried, and it is seen that it is of a greenish-grey colour; the skin clings to the bones, for the flesh beneath it has shrunk somewhat, but the hair of the body is well preserved, the nails of the hands and feet still adhere to the skin, and the face, though now drawn and very thin, has changed but little. Longitudinal slits are next made in the fingers and toes and the fleshy parts of the arms, thighs and legs, which are then stuffed with a mixture of sweet spices and natron, and sewn up again. The cavity in

Jars for intestines.

Removal of brain.

The body steeped in natron.

[1] In mummies of the best period the intestines are sometimes found in packets beneath the bandages.

the skull is now filled up with a mixture of spices, powdered plaster and natron, and the nostrils through which it was inserted are plugged up with small linen pledgets dipped in some astringent; obsidian eyes are also inserted in the eye-sockets. Large quantities of gums, spices, natron, as well as a very little bitumen, are pounded and well mixed together, and with them the breast and stomach are carefully packed through the slit in the side; while certain formulæ are being recited, a gold plate inscribed with the *utchat*, or eye of Horus, 𓂀 is laid upon it to indicate that this god watched over this body as he did over that of his father Osiris. The nails of the hands are stained with *henna* (Arab. حِنَّاء), and on the

The ornaments of the body.

little finger of the left hand is placed Ani's gold ring, in the bezel of which is mounted a handsome steatite scarab inscribed on the base with his name and titles. The ring was supposed to confer upon the deceased some power, but what that power was is not yet exactly made out; it is certain, however, that no one was buried without one or more, and if the relatives of the deceased were not able to buy them in gold or silver, they made use of faïence rings, glazed various colours, and even of small strings of beads which they tied on the fingers in lieu of rings. The legs are then brought closely together, and the arms are laid on the body with one wrist crossed over the other. The *cher-ḥeb* next provides a large and handsome scarab made of green basalt which is set in a frame of gold, over the back of it is a horizontal band of the same metal, at right angles to which, on the side of the tail of the beetle, runs another band which joins the frame; at the head of the scarab is a gold loop through which is now threaded a thick gold wire sufficiently long to go round Ani's neck. This scarab was part of the stock in trade of the *cher-ḥeb*, and all that was necessary to do to make it Ani's property was to inscribe his name and titles upon it in the blank line left for the purpose at the head of the flat base.

The scarab laid over the heart.

This done the scarab was covered with a thin gold leaf and laid upon Ani's breast at the neck.[1] The inscription upon it

[1] According to some rubrics of the thirtieth chapter the scarab was to be placed "within the heart" of a person after the ceremony of "opening the mouth"

was one of the verses of the 30th chapter of the Book of the Dead, and contained a prayer, addressed by Ani to his heart, that there might not be brought against him adverse evidence when it was weighed in the balance in the judgment hall of Osiris, that he might not be obstructed or driven back, and that his name might not be overthrown by those powers who made it their business to harass the newcomers among the dead in the nether-world. The prayer ends with a petition that no false evidence may be borne against him in the presence of the god.

Process of bandaging.

And now the bandaging begins. The body is first of all smeared all over with unguents. Pieces of linen are then torn into strips about three inches wide, and one edge of each strip is gummed. On one end of each of these the name of Ani has been written in hieratic characters to facilitate the identification of the mummy during the process of bandaging; a number of these strips are dipped in water, and the embalmers having bandaged the fingers, hands, and arms, and toes separately, begin to bandage the body from the feet upwards. The moist bandages cling tightly to the body, and the gummed edge enables each fold of the bandage to obtain firm hold; the little irregularities are corrected by small pledgets of linen placed between the folds and gummed in position. These linen bandages are also held in position by means of narrower strips of linen wound round the body at intervals of six and eight inches, and tied in a double knot. Over these fine linen bandages passages from the Book of the Dead, and formulæ which were intended to give power to the dead, are written. One end of a very thick bandage of eighteen to twenty-five folds of linen is laid under the shoulders, and the other is brought over the head and face, and rests on the upper part of the chest; this is held in position by a bandage wound round the neck, and tied in a double knot at the back of the neck. The same plan is adopted with respect to the feet, but before the bandage

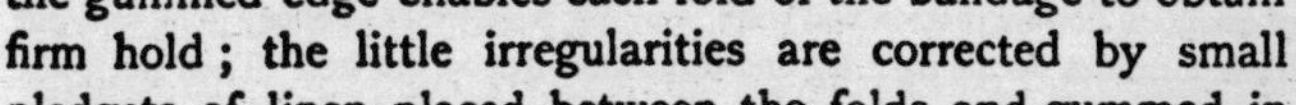
(Naville, Bd. II, 99), had been performed; this rite, however, took place in the tomb.

which secures all is tied, thick pads of linen are laid on the top of the feet to prevent any injury happening to them when the mummy is made to stand upright.[1] The bandaged arms having been pressed closely into the sides, and the fore-arms and hands having been laid upon the stomach, the bandaging goes on again, while formulæ are recited by the *cher-ḥeb.* Each bandage had a special name,[2] each bandage gave power to the deceased, and was inscribed with words and figures of gods, which also gave him power, and the adjustment of each in its proper position required both care and judgment. More folds of linen are laid on the body perpendicularly,[3]

**Process of bandaging.**

**Names of the bandages.**

[1] Referring to the embalming of the feet, the following extract is of interest. "After these things perform the embalming operations on his right and left arms, and then the . . . . . and the children of Horus, and the children of Chent-āat, shall carry out the embalming operations on the two legs of the deceased. Rub the feet, legs, and thighs of the deceased with black stone (?) oil, and then rub them a second time with the finest oil. Wrap the toes in a piece of cloth, draw two jackals upon two pieces of linen with colours mixed with water perfumed with *ānti*, and each jackal shall have his face turned towards the other; the jackal on the one bandage is Anubis, lord of Ḥert; the jackal on the other is Horus, lord of Ḥebennu. Put Anubis on the right leg, and Horus on the left leg, and wrap them up in fine linen. To complete the embalming of the legs, take six measures of *ānchamu* flowers, natron and resin, and mix with water of ebony gum, and put three measures on the right leg and three measures on the left. Then put some fresh (?) *senb* flowers made into twelve bundles (?) on the left leg, and twelve bands of linen, and anoint with the finest oil." Maspero, *Le Rituel de l'Embaumement*, pp. 43, 44, in *Mémoire sur Quelques Papyrus du Louvre* (Extrait des *Notices et Extraits des Manuscrits*, tom. xxiv., 1re partie; Paris, 1875).

[2] *E.g.*, one of the bandages of the nostrils was called  *nehi*, and the other  *smen*; a head bandage  *ḥeḥtheṭhsu*, the two bandages of the cheek 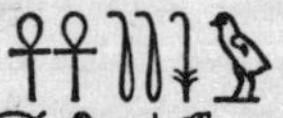 *ānchth ānchth su*, the two bandages of the top of the head  *meḥut'ati.*

[3] While the head was being bandaged the following petition was recited by one of the embalmers:—"O most august goddess, O lady of the west, O mistress of the east, come and enter into the two ears of the deceased! O doubly powerful, eternally young, and very mighty lady of the west, and mistress of the east may breathing take place in the head of the deceased in the nether world! Grant that he may see with his eyes, that he may hear with his two ears, that he may breathe through his nose, that he may utter sounds from his mouth, and articulate with his tongue in the nether world! Receive his voice in the hall of truth and justice, and his triumph in the hall of Seb in the presence of the great

and more bandages are wound round the body horizontally, until, little by little, it loses its shape beneath them. When a length of about three hundred cubits has been used in folds and bandages, a coarse piece of linen is laid on the body, and is sewn up at the back. Over this again a saffron-coloured linen sheet is laid, and this having been deftly sewn over the head, down the back, and under the feet, is finally held in position by a perpendicular bandage of brownish coloured linen, passing from the head to the feet and under them up the back to the head, and by four horizontal bandages of the same coloured linen, one round the shoulders, one round the middle of the body, one round the knees, and one round the ankles. Thus the mummy is complete.

Ani's coffin.

During the seventy days which have been spent in embalming Ani's body, the coffin makers have not been idle, and they have made ready a covering of wood to be laid on the mummy, and two beautiful coffins. The covering, in the form of a mummy, is slightly vaulted, and has a human face, bearded, on it; it is handsomely painted outside with collar, figures of Nut, Anubis, and Ap-uat, the full names and titles of Ani in perpendicular lines of inscription, the cartouches of the king in whose time he lived, and scenes in which Ani is adoring the gods. On the inside of the cover, on the purple ground, are painted in a light yellow colour pictures of the horizon, the spirits of the East, in the form of apes, adoring Rā, the lion gods of the morning and evening with a disk on their united backs, etc., etc.[1] The inner coffin is equally

---

god, lord of the west. O Osiris (*i.e.*, the deceased), the thick oil which comes upon thee furnishes thy mouth with life, and thine eye looketh into the lower heaven, as Rā looketh upon the upper heaven. It giveth thee thy two ears to hear that which thou wishest, just as Shu in Ḥebît (?) heard that which he wished to hear. It giveth thee thy nose to smell a beautiful perfume like Seb. It giveth to thee thy mouth well furnished by its passage (into the throat), like the mouth of Thoth, when he weigheth Maāt. It giveth thee Maāt (Law) in Ḥebît. O worshipper in Ḥetbenben, the cries of thy mouth are in Siut, Osiris of Siut comes to thee, thy mouth is the mouth of Ap-uat in the mountain of the west." (See Maspero, *Le Rituel de l'Embaumement*, p. 27, in *Mémoire sur Quelques Papyrus du Louvre* (Extrait des *Notices et Extraits des Manuscrits*), tom. xxiv., 1re partie; Paris, 1875).

[1] A fine example of such a covering is that of Nesi-pa-ur-shefi, preserved at Cambridge.

handsome, and carpenter and artist have expended their best labour upon it; before Ani was embalmed he was measured for it, and due allowance having been made for the bandages, it fits the mummy exactly. It is in the form of a mummy, and the sycamore planks of which it is made are about two inches thick; the bottom is in one piece, as is also each of the sides, the rounded head-piece is cut out of a solid piece of wood, and the foot-piece is also separate; all these parts are pegged together with wooden pegs about two inches long. On the cover is pegged a solid face, carved out of hard wood, which is thought to have a strong resemblance to that of

**Coffin ornamentation.**

Ani; bronze eyelids and obsidian eyes are fixed in it, and a carved wooden beard is fastened to the chin. Solid wooden hands are next fastened to the breast. The whole coffin, inside and out, is next covered with a thin layer of plaster; over this a coat of light yellow varnish is painted, and the

**Scenes painted on the coffin.**

scenes and inscriptions are painted on it in red, light and dark green, white and other colours. At the head is Nephthys, and at the foot is Isis, each making speeches to Ani, and telling him that she is protecting him. On the cover outside is Nut, and between two series of scenes in which Ani is represented worshipping the gods, are two perpendicular lines of inscriptions recording his name and titles; at the foot of these are figures of Anubis and Ap-uat. The sides of the coffin are ornamented with figures of gods in shrines, the scene of the weighing of the heart, Ani drinking water from the hands of a goddess standing in a tree, Shu lifting up Nut from the embraces of Seb, etc. Inside the coffin are painted figures of a number of gods and genii with instructions referring to them, and the goddesses Nut and Hathor; the first covers Ani with her wings, and the second, as mistress of the nether-world, receives Ani into her arms. Around the edge of the coffin near the cover, from head to foot, run two lines of inscription, one on each side, which repeat at considerable length the name and titles of Ani. The outer edge of the coffin, and the inner edge of the cover are "rabbeted" out, the one to fit into the other, and on each side, at regular intervals, four rectangular slots about $1\frac{1}{2}$in. × 2in. × $\frac{3}{8}$in. are cut; to fasten the coffin hermetically, tightly fitting wooden dowels, four inches long, are pressed into the slots in the coffin, and pegs driven from the outside of the coffin through them keep them firmly in position. Ani's body having been placed in this coffin, the cover is laid upon it, the ends of the dowels fit into the slots in the sides, and coffin and cover are firmly joined together; wooden pegs are driven through the cover and dowels, the "rabbets" fit tightly, the little space between the coffin and cover is "stopped" with liquid plaster, and thus the coffin is sealed. Any injury that may have happened to the plaster or paintings during the process of sealing is repaired, and the whole coffin is once more varnished. This coffin is, in its turn, placed inside an outer coffin, which is painted, both inside and outside, with scenes similar to those on the inner coffin; the drawing is, however, more free, and the details are fewer. The outer coffin being sealed in the same way as that inside it, Ani is now ready to be carried to his everlasting home in the Theban hills.

**The outer coffin.**

On a day fixed by the relatives and friends, all the various articles of funereal furniture which have been prepared are brought to Ani's house, where also the mummy in its coffins now lies awaiting the funeral; the *cher-ḥeb* sees that the things necessary for a great man's funeral are provided, and arranges for the procession to start on the first auspicious day. This day having arrived, the *cher-ḥeb's* assistants come, and gathering together the servants and those who are to carry burdens, see that each has his load ready and that each knows his place in the procession. When all is ready the funeral train sets out from Ani's house, while the female servants wail and lament their master, and the professional mourners beat their breasts, feign to pull out their hair by handfuls, and vie with each other in shrieking the loudest and most often. They have not a great distance to go to reach the river, but the difficulties of passing through the narrow streets increase almost at every step, for the populace of Thebes loved the sight of a grand funeral as much as that of any European country to-day. After some few hours the procession reaches the river, and there a scene of indescribable confusion happens; every bearer of a burden is anxious to deposit it in one of the boats which lie waiting in a row by the quay; the animals which

**The funeral procession**

draw the sledge, on which Ani's bier is laid, kick out wildly and struggle while being pushed into the boats, people rush hither and thither, and the noise of men giving orders, and the shouts and cries of the spectators, are distracting. At length, however, the procession is embarked and the boats push off to drop with the current across the Nile to a place a little north of the Temple of Thothmes III., opposite Asâsîf. After an hour spent in disembarking, the procession re-forms itself in the order in which it will march to the tomb, and we see for the first time what a splendid funeral has been provided.

**Funereal offerings.**

In the front walk a number of men bearing tables and stands filled with vases full of wine, beer, oil, perfumes, flowers, bread, cakes, ducks, haunches of beef, and vegetables; one man carries Ani's palette and box of instruments which he used for writing and drawing, another carries his staff, another his bed, another his chair, others bring the *ushabtiu* figures in a box with a vaulted cover and made like a tomb; and following them comes the stele recording his name and titles and prayers to the gods of the nether-world; and behind them, drawn by two men, is a coffer surmounted by a jackal, on a sledge decorated with lotus flowers, in which stand the four jars which contain Ani's intestines.

**Ani's personal property carried to the tomb.**

Next follow the men bearing everything which Ani made use of during his life, as, for example, the palette which he carried when he followed his king to war in order to keep the accounts of the army and to make lists of all the precious things which were brought to his lord as gifts and tribute, and the harp on which he played in his leisure hours. Next comes the chest , in which is laid the mummy of Ani, placed in a boat which is mounted on a sledge drawn by four oxen; at the head of the chest is a figure of Nephthys, and at the foot a figure of Isis, the boat is supplied with oars as if it were really destined to row down to Abydos, so that the body might be buried there, and its soul pass into the nether-world through the "Gap"  Peka (*i.e.*, the 'Gap') the place whence, according to the Egyptian belief, souls, under the guidance of Osiris, set out on their last journey. At the head of the boat stands a white-robed *Sam* priest wearing a panther skin; he holds a bronze

VIEW OF ANI'S FUNERAL PROCESSION
(From the Papyrus of Ani, Brit. Mus. No. 10,470, sheet 5).

instrument for burning incense in the left hand, and with the right he scatters water on the ground from a libation vase . Behind the boat follow a number of white-robed priests, one of whom has his head powdered.[1] Next follow more funereal offerings and flowers carried in boxes suspended from the ends of poles which the men who carry them balance on their shoulders. After these come a number of women with breasts uncovered and dishevelled hair, who in their wailing lamentations lament the dead and praise his virtues. Among these would probably be the female servants of Ani's house, whose grief would be genuine, for they would feel that they had lost a good master and a comfortable home.

**Ani's tomb in the mountains.**

Meanwhile the procession has moved on and has entered one of the rocky defiles to the north of Dêr el-Baḥari, whence, winding along through the valley of the kings, they hope to reach a remote place in the Western valley. The progress of the train is slow, for the ground is rough and rocky, and frequent halts have to be made; on the right hand and on the left, kings and nobles are buried in splendid tombs, and almost every hill which they climb hides the mummy of some distinguished Egyptian. A few miles further on, at some little distance upon a hill, a rectangular opening is seen, and when the procession arrives at the foot of it, a number of workmen, attendants, tomb-guardians and others are seen assembled there. The mummy in its coffin is lifted out of the chest, and carried up the hill to the rectangular opening, which proves to be the mouth of Ani's tomb; there it is set upright, and before it the attendants pile up tables with sepulchral offerings and flowers, and animals for sacrifice are also brought there. The wailing women and the distant relatives of Ani here take farewell of him, and when they have descended the hill, the coffin is let down the slanting passage by ropes into the chamber, where it is hoped that Ani's friends will bring sepulchral offerings to his *ka*, at the appointed seasons. This chamber is rectangular and has two rows of square pillars in it. From it there leads a passage about six

[1] In the papyrus of Ani, his wife is represented kneeling on the ground in grief by the side of the boat.

feet wide by seven feet high, and passing through this we see to the right and left a series of chambers upon the walls of which are painted in vivid colours the pictures of Ani and his wife Tutu making offerings to the gods, and inscriptions recording his prayers and their answers. The walls of some rooms are occupied entirely with scenes drawn from the daily events of his life. As he was a scribe, and therefore no mean artist, we are probably right in assuming that he superintended the painting of many of them himself. Some of the rooms have their walls unornamented, and it would seem that these were used for the living rooms of the priests who visited or lived in the tombs for the purpose of carrying out the various sepulchral rites at their appointed times. We pass through or by seventeen chambers, and then arrive at a flight of steps which leads down to the chamber in which the mummy and coffin are to be placed. Hewn in the wall just above the top of the flight of steps is a square niche, in which, seated on one seat, are two stone figures of Ani and his wife; he has an open roll of papyrus on his knees, and holds a palette in his hand, and she has lotus flowers in both hands, which rest on her knees. The plinth of the statues is inscribed with the names and titles of Ani and Tutu. Beneath, let into the wall, is a stone stele, the surface of which is divided into two parts; the upper part contains a representation of Ani adoring the sun-god Rā, and the lower contains about thirty lines of inscription in which Ani prays that Rā, Osiris and Anubis will cause all kinds of sepulchral goods to be supplied for his *ka* or genius; that they will grant his coming forth from and going into the netherworld whenever he pleases; that his soul may alight on the trees which he has planted; that he may drink cool water from the depths of the Nile when he pleases, etc.

**Statue and stele of Ani.**

The mummy in its coffin has been brought down the steps, and is now carried into a large chamber on the left, where its final resting place is to be. As we pass into this room we see that a part of it is already occupied with a coffin and the funereal furniture belonging to it. When we come nearer we find that it is the coffin of Tutu, Ani's wife. Close by her is a table of alabaster covered with shapely vessels of the same substance, filled with wine, oil, and other unguents;

**Tutu, Ani's wife.**

VIEW OF ANI'S FUNERAL PROCESSION
(From the Papyrus of Ani, Brit. Mus. No. 10,470, sheet 6).

each of these fragile objects is inscribed with her name. On the table are spoons made of ivory of the most beautiful workmanship. They are shaped in the form of a woman. The body is stained a deep creamy colour, the colour of the skin of the Egyptian lady, who guarded herself from the rays of the sun; the hair is black, and we see that it is movable; when we lift it off we see the name of "Tutu, the sistrum bearer," engraved beneath. On a second stand, made of wood, we find the articles for her toilet, mirror, kohl pot in obsidian, fan, etc., and close by is the sistrum which she carried in the temple of Åmen-Rā upon earth, and which was buried with her, so that she might be able to praise that god with music in his mansions in the sky. Chairs and her couch are there too, and stands covered with dried flowers and various offerings. Removing the lid of the coffin we see her mummy lying as it was laid a few years before. On her breasts are strings of dried flowers with the bloom still on them, and by her side is a roll of papyrus containing a copy of the service which she used to sing in the temple of Åmen in the Apts, when on earth. Her amethyst necklace and other ornaments are small, but very beautiful. Just over her feet is a blue glazed steatite *ushabti* figure. While we have been examining Tutu's general furniture, the servants of the *cher-ḥeb* have brought down the coffin, which is placed on a bier along the east wall, and the chairs and couch and boxes and funereal offerings, and arranged them about the chamber. In a square niche in the wall, just over the head of the coffin, Ani's writing palette and reeds are placed, and by its side is laid a large roll of papyrus nearly 90 feet long, inscribed in hieroglyphics during his lifetime and under his direction, with the oldest and most important chapters of the "Book of the Dead"; the vignettes, which refer to the chapters, are beautifully painted, and in some as many as thirteen colours are used in this chamber; and in every work connected with Ani's tomb there is a simple majesty which is characteristic of the ancient Egyptian gentleman. At each of the four corners or sides of the bier, is placed one of the so-called Canopic jars, and at the foot are laid a few stone *ushabtiu* figures, whose duty it was to perform for the deceased such

**Ani's Book of the Dead.**

labours as filling the furrows with water, ploughing the fields, and carrying the sand, if he were called upon to do them. When everything has been brought into this chamber, and the tables of offerings have been arranged, a priest, wearing a panther skin, and accompanied by another who burns incense in a bronze censer, approaches the mummy, and performs the ceremony of "opening the mouth" 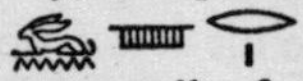 *un-re;* while a priest in white robes reads from a roll of papyrus or leather. The act of embalming has taken away from the dead man all control over his limbs and the various portions of his body, and before these can be of any use to him in the nether-world, a mouth must be given to him, and it must be opened so that his *ka* may be able to speak. The twenty-first and twenty-second chapters of the "Book of the Dead" refer to the giving a mouth to the deceased, and the vignette of the twenty-second chapter (Naville, bl. xxxiii) represents a priest called the "guardian of the scale," 

**The giving the mouth to the deceased.**

*àri māχet*, giving the deceased his mouth. In the vignette to the twenty-third chapter a priest is seen performing the operation of opening the mouth 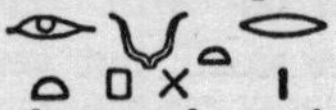 *àrit àpt re*, with the instrument 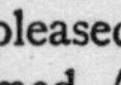, and the deceased says in the text, "Ptah[1] has opened my mouth with that instrument of steel with which he opened the mouth of the gods."[2] When the mouth of the deceased had been opened, his *ka* gained control of his speech, intelligence and limbs, and was able to hold intercourse with the gods, and to go in and out of his tomb whenever he pleased. When the formulæ are finished and all rites performed, Ani's relatives and near friends withdraw from the mummy chamber and make their way up the stairs, through the long passage and into the first chamber, where they find that animals have been slaughtered, and that many of the assistants and those who accompanied the funeral arc

**The funeral feast.**

[1] Some copies read Shu.

[2] 

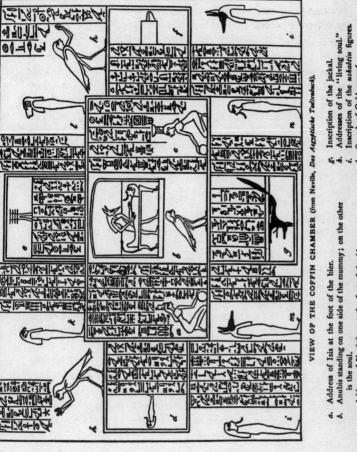

**VIEW OF THE COFFIN CHAMBER** (from Naville, *Das Aegyptische Todtenbuch*).

*a.* Address of Isis at the foot of the bier.
*b.* Anubis standing on one side of the mummy; on the other is the soul.
*c.* Address of Nephthys at the foot of the bier.
*d.* Speech of a statuette.
*e.* Inscription of the *ṭeṭ*.
*f.* Inscription of the flame.
*g.* Inscription of the jackal.
*h.* Addresses of the "living soul."
*i.* Inscription of the *ushabtiu* figures.
*k.* Speech of Qebḥ-sennuf.
*l.* Speech of Ḥāpi.
*m.* Speech of Ṭuamāutef.
*n.* Speech of Mesthȧ.

eating and drinking of the funereal offerings. When the last person has left the mummy chamber, masons bring along slabs of stone and lime which they have ready and wall it up; the joints between the stones are so fine that the blade of a modern penknife can with difficulty be inserted to the depth of half an inch. We have seen Ani's body embalmed, we have watched all the stages of the manufacture of his coffin, we have seen the body dressed and laid in it, we have accompanied him to the tomb, we have gone through it and seen how it is arranged and decorated, and we have assisted at the funereal ceremonies; in his beautiful tomb then, let us leave him to enjoy his long rest in the company of his wife. Ani did not cause such a large and beautiful tomb to be hewn for him merely to gratify his pride; with him, as with all educated Egyptians, it was the outcome of the belief that his soul would revivify his body, and was the result of a firm assurance in his mind of the truth of the doctrine of immortality, which is the foundation of the Egyptian religion, and which was as deeply rooted in them as the hills are in the earth.

## MUMMY.[1]

**Mummy** is the term which is generally applied to the body of a human being, animal, bird, fish, or reptile, which has been preserved by means of bitumen, spices, gums, or natron. As far as can be discovered, the word is neither a corruption of the ancient Egyptian word for a preserved body, nor of the more modern Coptic form of the hieroglyphic name. The word "mummy" is found in Byzantine Greek (*μουμία, μώμιον*), and in Latin,[2] and indeed in almost all European languages. It is derived from the Arabic مُومِيَا, "bitumen," and the Arabic word for mummy is مُومِيَّة, which means a "bitumenized thing," or a body preserved by bitumen. The Syriac-speaking people called it ܡܘܡܝܐ, the Greeks *πιττάσ-*

Origin of the word "Mummy."

[1] I have reproduced here many paragraphs from my *Prefatory Remarks made on Egyptian Mummies, on the occasion of the unrolling of the Mummy of Bak-Ran*, privately printed; London, 1890.

[2] It appears in Latin about A.D. 1000. Wiedemann, *Herodots Zweites Bush*; Leipzig, 1890, p. 349.

φαλτος, and the Persians call a drug used in medicine موميائى. The celebrated Arabic physician Ibn Bêtâr (died A.H. 646), quoting Dioscorides,[1] who lived in the first century of our era, says that *Mumia* is found in the country called Apollonia, and that it flows down with water from the "lightning mountains," and being thrown by the water on the sides of the water courses, becomes hard and thick, and that it has a smell like that of pitch. Having further quoted the article by Dioscorides on Pittasphaltus, he adds, "What I say on this subject is as follows: The name *mûmîa* موميائ is given to the drug of which mention has just been made, and to that which is called 'Bitumen of Judæa,' القفر اليهودى, and to the *mûmîa* of the tombs الموميائ القبورى, which is found in great quantities in Egypt, and which is nothing else than a mixture which the Byzantine Greeks used formerly for embalming their dead, in order that the dead bodies might remain in the state in which they were buried, and experience neither decay nor change. Bitumen of Judæa is the substance which is obtained from the Asphaltites Lake, بحيرة يهودا." 'Abd el-Laṭîf[2] mentions that he saw *mûmîa* or bitumen which had been taken out of the skulls and stomachs of mummies sold in the towns, and he adds that he bought "the contents of three skulls for half an Egyptian dirhem," ولقد اشتريت ثلثة اروس مملوة منه بنصف درهم مصرى, and says that it varies very little from mineral pitch, for which it can be substituted if one takes the trouble to procure it.

"Mummy" the substance used in embalming bodies.

Mummy sold as a drug.

About three or four hundred years ago Egyptian mummy formed one of the ordinary drugs in apothecaries' shops. The trade in mummy was carried on chiefly by Jews, and as early as the twelfth century a physician called El-Magar was in the habit of prescribing mummy to his patients. It was said to be good for bruises and wounds. After a time, for various reasons, the supply of genuine mummies ran short, and the

[1] *Materia Medica* (ed. Kühn, in *Medicorum Graecorum Opera*, tom. xxv., Leipzig, 1829, p. 101).

[2] See Abd el-Laṭîf, *Relation de l'Egypte*, tr. by De Sacy, Paris, 1810, p. 273, and *Abdollatiphi Historiæ Ægypti Compendium*, Ed. White, Oxford, 1810, p. 150.

Jews were obliged to manufacture them. They procured the bodies of all the criminals that were executed in gaols, and of people who had died in hospitals, Christians and others. They filled the bodies with bitumen and stuffed the limbs with the same substance; this done, they bound them up tightly and exposed them to the heat of the sun. By this means they made them look like old mummies. In the year 1564 a physician called Guy de la Fontaine made an attempt to see the stock of the mummies of the chief merchant in mummies at Alexandria, and he discovered that they were made from the bodies of slaves and others who had died of the most loathsome diseases. The traffic in mummies as a drug was stopped in a curious manner. A Jew at Damietta who traded in mummies had a Christian slave who was treated with great harshness by him because he would not consent to become a Jew. Finally, when the ill-treatment became so severe that he could bear it no longer, the slave went to the Pasha and informed him what his master's business was. The Jew was speedily thrown into prison, and only obtained his liberty by payment of three hundred pieces of gold. Every Jewish trader in mummy was seized by the local governor of the place where he lived, and money was extorted from him. The trade in mummy being hampered by this arbitrary tax, soon languished, and finally died out entirely.[1]

**End of the trade in mummy.**

The hieroglyphic word for mummy is  *Sāḥu*, and the word used to indicate the act of making a dead man into a mummy is 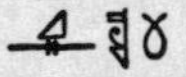 or 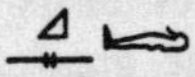 *qes*; it means to "wrap up in bandages." The Coptic forms of the latter word are ⲕⲉⲥ, ⲕⲏⲥ, ⲕⲱⲥ, ⲕⲱⲱⲥ, ⲕⲱⲱⲥⲉ, and they were used by the Copts to translate the Greek *ἐνταφιασμὸς, ταφή, ἐνταφιάζειν, θάπτειν*, etc.; the word ⲙⲓⲟ̀ⲗⲱⲛ, "mummy," is also given by Kircher, *Lingua Aegyptiaca Restituta*, Rome, 1643, p. 183, at the foot. The mummifier was called ⲣⲉϥⲕⲱⲥ; compare ⲟⲩⲟϩ ⲁⲩⲕⲱⲥ ⲙ̀ ⲡⲓⲥⲣⲁⲏⲗ ⲛ̀ϫⲉ ⲛⲓⲣⲉϥⲕⲱ̀ⲥ[2] = *καὶ ἐνεταφίασαν οἱ ἐνταφιασταὶ τὸν Ἰσραήλ*.[3]

**Egyptian name of the embalmed body.**

[1] Pettigrew on *Mummies*, p. 4.
[2] Lagarde, *Der Pentateuch Koptisch*, Gen. l. 2.
[3] Lagarde, *Librorum Vet. Test. Canon.*, Gen. l. 2, p. 51.

Whether the art of mummifying was known to the aboriginal inhabitants of Egypt, or whether it was introduced by the new-comers from Asia, is a question which is very difficult to decide. We know for a certainty that the stele of a dignitary preserved at Oxford was made during the reign of Senṭ, the fifth king of the second dynasty, about B.C. 4000. The existence of this stele with its figures and inscriptions entreating the god of the dead to grant sepulchral meals, points to the fact that the art of elaborate sepulture had reached a high pitch of perfection in those early times. The man for whom it was made was called Sherȧ, and he held the dignity of *neter ḥen* or "prophet"; the stele also tells us that he was *suten rech* or "royal relative."

**Antiquity of embalming.**

The inscriptions contain prayers asking that there may be granted to the deceased in the nether world, "thousands of oxen, linen bandages, cakes, vessels of wine, incense, etc.," which fact shows that religious belief, funereal ceremonies, and a hope for a life after death, had already become a part of the life of the people of Egypt. During the reign of king Senṭ, the redaction of a medical papyrus was carried out. As this work presupposes many years of experiment and experience, it is clear that the Egyptians possessed at a remote period ample anatomical knowledge for mummifying a human body. Again, if we consider that the existence of this king is proved by papyri and contemporaneous monuments, and that we know the names of some of the priests who took part in funereal ceremonies during his reign, there is no difficulty in acknowledging the great antiquity of such ceremonies, and also that they presuppose a religious belief in the actual revivification of the body because of which hoped-for event the Egyptians took the greatest possible care to preserve and afterwards to hide the bodies of the dead.

Though there exists, to my knowledge, no monument of a similar nature to that of the stele of Senṭ which would prove beyond doubt that mummies were made in the first dynasty, still it seems tolerably certain that they were made, and there

**Ancient Egyptian work on anatomy.**

is little doubt that the Egyptians possessed all the anatomical knowledge necessary for this purpose. We know from Manetho that Tetȧ, the second king of the first dynasty, about B.C. 4366, wrote a book upon anatomy, and that he busied himself in making experiments with drugs. The mother of this king, a lady called Shesh ,[1] earned fame for herself by inventing a hair wash. From the fact that the bodies of some ancient Egyptians who lived during the first four dynasties, have been found in a skeleton state in sarcophagi which had never been opened since the time they were cemented, some six thousand years ago, until the present day, it has been argued by some that mummification was not practised during the early dynasties in Egypt. Some system of preservation must have been adopted, however, because the bones are discoloured, and smell strongly of bitumen.

**Account of embalming by Herodotus.**

The knowledge of the way in which the ancient Egyptians mummified their dead is obtained from the works of Greek historians, and from an examination of mummies. According to Herodotus,[2] "When in a family a man of any consideration dies, all the females of that family besmear their heads and faces with mud, and then leaving the body in the house, they wander about the city, and beat themselves, having their clothes girt up, and exposing their breasts, and all their relations accompany them. On the other hand, the men beat themselves, being girt up in like manner. When they have done this, they carry out the body to be embalmed. There are persons who are appointed for this very purpose; they, when the dead body is brought to them, show to the bearers wooden models of corpses made exactly like by painting. And they show that which they say is the most expensive manner of embalming, the name of which[3] I do not think it right to mention on such an occasion; they then show the second, which is inferior and less expensive; and then the third which is the cheapest. Having explained them all, they learn from them in what way they wish the body to be prepared; then the relations, when they have agreed on the price, depart; but the embalmers remaining in the workshops thus proceed to embalm in the most expensive manner. First they draw out the brains through the nostrils with an iron hook, taking part of

**Three methods of embalming.**

**First method of embalming.**

[1] *Papyrus Ebers*, Bd. II., *Glossarium Hieroglyphicum*, by Stern, p. 47.

[2] Bk. II. 85.

[3] *i.e.*, Osiris.

it out in this manner, the rest by the infusion of drugs. Then with a sharp Ethiopian stone they make an incision in the side, and take out all the bowels; and having cleansed the abdomen and rinsed it with palm-wine, they next sprinkle it with pounded perfumes. Then having filled the belly with pure myrrh pounded, and cassia, and other perfumes, frankincense excepted, they sew it up again; and when they have done this, they steep it in natrum, leaving it under for 70 days; for a longer time than this it is not lawful to steep it. At the expiration of the 70 days they wash the corpse, and wrap the whole body in bandages of flaxen cloth, smearing it with gum, which the Egyptians commonly use instead of glue. After this the relations, having taken the body back again, make a wooden case in the shape of a man,[1] and having made it, they enclose the body; and thus, having fastened it up, they store it in a sepulchral chamber,[2] setting it upright against the wall. In this manner they prepare the bodies that are embalmed in the most expensive way.

Second method of embalming.

"Those who, avoiding great expense, desire the middle way, they prepare in the following manner. When they have

[1] Really in the form of the god Osiris.

[2] Compare *ταριχεύει δὲ ὁ Αἰγύπτιος· οὗτος μὲν γε—λέγω δ' ἰδών—ξηράνας τὸν νεκρὸν ξύνδειπνον καὶ ξυμπότην ἐποιήσατο.* Lucian, *De Luctu*, § 21 (ed. Dindorf, Paris, 1867, p. 569).

*Αἰγύπτιοι δὲ τὰ ἔντερα ἐξελόντες ταριχεύουσιν αὐτούς, καὶ σὺν ἑαυτοῖς ὑπὲρ γῆς ἔχουσιν.* Sextus Empiricus, *Pyrrhoniarum Institutionum* lib. III. cap. 24 (ed. J. A. Fabricius, Leipzig, 1718, p. 184).

Mortuos limo obliti plangunt: nec cremare aut fodere fas putant: verum arte medicatos intra penetralia collocant. Pomponius Mela, lib. I. cap. 9 (ed. Gronov., Leyden, 1782, p. 62).

Aegyptia tellus
Claudit odorato post funus stantia saxo
Corpora, et a mensis exsanguem haud separat umbram.

Silius Italicus, *Punicorum* lib. XIII. ll. 474–476 (ed. H. Occioni, Turin, 1889).

Balsama succo unguentaque mira feruntur
Tempus in aeternum sacrum servantia corpus.

Corippi, *De laudibus Justini*, lib. III. ll. 22–25 (ed. Antwerp, 1581, p. 4).

charged their syringes with oil made from cedar, they fill the abdomen of the corpse without making any incision or taking out the bowels, but inject it at the fundament; and having prevented the injection from escaping, they steep the body in natrum for the prescribed number of days, and on the last day they let out from the abdomen the oil of cedar which they had before injected, and it has such power that it brings away the intestines and vitals in a state of dissolution; the natrum dissolves the flesh, and nothing of the body remains but the skin and the bones. When they have done this they return the body without any further operation.

"The third method of embalming is this, which is used only for the poorer sort. Having thoroughly rinsed the abdomen in syrmæa, they steep it with natrum for 70 days, and then deliver it to be carried away."[1]

**Third method of embalming.**

According to Genesis l. 3, the embalming of Jacob occupied 40 days, but the period of mourning was 70 days. From Egyptian documents it is known that the length of the period from the death of a man to his burial varied; in one case the embalming occupied 16 days, the bandaging 35 days, and the burial 70 days, *i.e.*, 121 days in all. In a second case the embalming occupied 66 days, preparations for burial 4 days, and the burial 26 days; in all 96 days. Elsewhere we are told that the embalming lasts 70 or 80 days, and the burial ten months.[2]

**Period of embalmment varied in length.**

The account given by Diodorus (I. 91) agrees with that of Herodotus in many particulars, but some additional details are given. According to it, if any man died, all his relatives and friends threw dust or mud on their heads, and went round about through the town uttering cries of grief as long as the body remained unburied; during the interval between the death and the burial, they abstained from the use of baths and wine, they partook of no choice foods, and they put not on fine apparel. The methods of embalming were three in number; the most expensive, the less expensive, and the poorest of all. The first method cost one talent of silver, about

**Account of embalming by Diodorus.**

**Cost of embalming a body.**

[1] Cary's translation, pp. 126, 127.

[2] For the authorities see Wiedemann, *Herodots Zweites Buch*, p. 358.

£250; the second twenty minæ, about £60; and the third cost very little indeed. The people who practise the art of embalming belong to a class of men in whose families this profession is hereditary, and they set down in writing a statement of the various methods of embalming practised by them and the cost of each, and ask the relatives of the dead man to decide upon the method to be adopted. When this question has been settled, the embalmers take the body into their charge, and they hand it to those who are fully acquainted with the process of embalming. The first of these called the "scribe" (γραμματεὺς) makes a mark on the left side of the body, which is laid upon the ground, to indicate where the incision is to be made. Next, a man, called the "ripper up" (παρασχιστής), with an Ethiopian stone (λίθον Αἰθιοπικον) makes a cut in the side lengthwise of the size indicated by the scribe. Having done this, he flees away in all haste, pursued by his assistants, who hurl after him pieces of stone and call down curses, that vengeance may come upon him for this crime; for the Egyptians hold in abomination anyone who wounds or commits an act of violence upon the human body. The embalmers (ταριχευταὶ) are held in high honour, and are treated with much consideration, because they are friends of the priests, and are allowed to enter the sanctuary as if they were ceremonially pure. Having assembled around the body, one of them puts his hand into it through the cut that has been made, and draws out everything that he finds inside, with the exception of the heart and reins (lungs?); others clean the intestines, and wash them with palm-wine and balsams. Finally, having treated the body first with oil of cedar and other materials of this nature, and then with myrrh, cinnamon, and other sweetsmelling drugs and spices suitable for embalming purposes, they bring it into such a state of completeness, that the eye-lashes and eye-brows remain uninjured, and its form is so little changed that it is easy to recognize the features. The greater number of the Egyptians who keep the bodies of their ancestors in magnificent chambers, enjoy the sight of those who have been dead for several generations, and they feel great satisfaction in seeing the features and form of these

Details of embalming.

bodies, and look upon them, to a certain extent, as contemporaries.

With reference to the fleeing away of the paraschistes it is difficult to understand what Diodorus had in his mind. A little further on he says that the embalmers were great friends of the priests, and as this was certainly the case, the man who performed the operation probably merely fulfilled a religious obligation in fleeing away, and had very little to fear. In some particulars Diodorus appears to have been misinformed, and in any case the knowledge he possessed of mummies could hardly have been at first hand. He lived too late (about B.C. 40) to know what the well-made Theban mummies were like, and his experience therefore would only have familiarized him with the Egypto-Roman mummies, in which the limbs were bandaged separately, and the contour of their faces, somewhat blunted, was to be seen through the thin and tightly drawn bandages which covered the face. A good example of a mummy made about this date is that of the lady Mut-em-Mennu, which is preserved in the British Museum, No. 6704; in this mummy the features of the face can be clearly distinguished underneath the bandages.

**Statements of Diodorus not wholly trustworthy.**

A curious idea about the fate of the intestines taken from the body obtained among certain Greek writers. Plutarch[1] says, in two places, that when the Egyptians have taken them out of the body of the dead man, they show them to the sun as the cause of the faults which he had committed, and then throw them into the river, while the body, having been cleansed, is embalmed. Porphyry[2] gives the same account at

**Fate of the intestines.**

[1] Οἱ τὸν νεκρὸν ἀνατέμνοντες ἔδειξαν τῷ ἡλίῳ, εἶτ' αὐτὰ μὲν εἰς τὸν ποταμὸν κατέβαλον, τοῦ δὲ ἄλλου σώματος ἤδη καθαροῦ γεγονότος ἐπιμέλονται. Plutarch, *VII. Sap. Conv.*, XVI., ed. Didot, p. 188. *Cf.* also Ἐπεὶ καλῶς εἶχεν, ὥσπερ Αἰγύπτιοι τῶν νεκρῶν τὴν κοιλίαν ἐξελόντες καὶ πρὸς τὸν ἥλιον ἀνασχίζοντες ἐκβάλλουσιν, ὡς αἰτίαν ἁπάντων ὧν ὁ ἄνθρωπος ἥμαρτεν. Plutarch, *De Carnium Esu, Oratio Posterior*, ed. Didot, p. 1219.

[2] Ἐκεῖνο μέντοι οὐ παραπεμπτέον, ὅτι τοὺς ἀποθανόντας τῶν εὖ γεγονότων ὅταν ταριχεύωσιν, ἰδίᾳ τὴν κοιλίαν ἐξελόντες καὶ εἰς κιβωτὸν ἐνθέντες μετὰ τῶν ἄλλων, ὧν διαπράττονται ὑπὲρ τοῦ νεκροῦ, καὶ τὴν κιβωτὸν κρατοῦντες πρὸς τὸν ἥλιον μαρτύρονται, ἑνὸς τῶν ὑπὲρ τοῦ νεκροῦ ποιουμένου λόγον τῶν ταριχευτῶν.

greater length, and adds that the intestines were placed in a box; he also gives the formula which the embalmers used when showing the intestines to the sun, and says that it was translated by Ekphantos into Greek out of his own language, which was presumably Egyptian. The address to the sun and the other gods who are supposed to bestow life upon man, the petition to them to grant an abode to the deceased with the everlasting gods, and the confession by the deceased that he had worshipped, with reverence, the gods of his fathers from his youth up, that he had honoured his parents, that he had neither killed nor injured any man, all these have a sound about them of having been written by some one who had a knowledge of the "Negative Confession" in the 125th chapter of the Book of the Dead. On the other hand it is difficult to imagine any Greek acquainted with the manners and customs of the Egyptians making the statement that they threw the intestines into the river, for when they were not placed in jars separate from the body, they were mummified and placed between the legs or arms, and bandaged up with the body, and the future welfare of the body in the nether-world depended entirely upon its having every member complete.

**General correctness of statements of Herodotus and Diodorus.**

An examination of Egyptian mummies will show that the accounts given by Herodotus and Diodorus are generally correct, for mummies both with and without ventral incisions are found, and some are preserved by means of balsams and gums, and others by bitumen and natrum. The skulls of mummies which exist by hundreds in caves and pits at

---

῞Εστι δὲ καὶ ὁ λόγος, ὃν ἡρμήνευσεν ῎Εκφαντος[1] ἐκ τῆς πατρίου διαλέκτου, τοιοῦτος. ῏Ω δέσποτα ἥλιε, καὶ θεοὶ πάντες οἱ τὴν ζωὴν τοῖς ἀνθρώποις δόντες, προσδέξασθέ με καὶ παράδοτε τοῖς ἀϊδίοις θεοῖς σύνοικον. Ἐγὼ γὰρ τοὺς θεούς, οὓς οἱ γονεῖς μοι παρέδειξαν, εὐσεβῶν διετέλουν ὅσον χρόνον ἐν τῷ ἐκείνῳ αἰῶνι τὸν βίον εἶχον, τούς τε τὸ σῶμά μου γεννήσαντας ἐτίμων ἀεί· τῶν τε ἄλλων ἀνθρώπων[2] οὔτε ἀπέκτεινα, οὔτε παρακαταθήκην ἀπεστέρησα, οὔτε ἄλλο οὐδὲν ἀνήκεστον διεπραξάμην. Εἰ δέ τι ἄρα κατὰ τὸν ἐμαυτοῦ βίον ἥμαρτον ἢ φαγὼν ἢ πιὼν ὧν μὴ θεμιτὸν ἦν, οὐ δι᾽ ἐμαυτὸν ἥμαρτον, ἀλλὰ διὰ ταῦτα (δείξας τὴν κιβωτὸν, ἐν ᾗ ἡ γαστὴρ ἦν). Porphyry, *De Abstinentia*, lib. IV., 10, ed. Didot, p. 75.

[1] Wilkinson reads "Euphantos" (*Ancient Egyptians*, iii. 479).

[2] Wiedemann (*Herodots Zweites Buch*, p. 354) adds οὐδένα in brackets.

Thebes contain absolutely nothing, a fact which proves that the embalmers were able not only to remove the brain, but also to take out the membranes without injuring or breaking the bridge of the nose in any way. Skulls of mummies are found, at times, to be filled with bitumen, linen rags, or resin. The bodies which have been filled with resin or some such substance, are of a greenish colour, and the skin has the appearance of being tanned. Such mummies, when unrolled, perish rapidly and break easily. Usually, however, the resin and aromatic gum process is favourable to the preservation of the teeth and hair. Bodies from which the intestines have been removed and which have been preserved by being filled with bitumen are quite black and hard. The features are preserved intact, but the body is heavy and unfair to look upon. The bitumen penetrates the bones so completely that it is sometimes difficult to distinguish which is bone and which is bitumen. The arms, legs, hands, and feet of such mummies break with a sound like the cracking of chemical glass tubing; they burn very freely, and give out great heat. Speaking generally they will last for ever. When a body has been preserved by natron, that is, a mixture of carbonate, sulphate, and muriate of soda, the skin is found to be hard, and to hang loosely from the bones in much the same way as it hangs from the skeletons of the dead monks preserved in the crypt beneath the Capuchin convent at Floriana, in Malta. The hair of such mummies usually falls off when touched.

Bodies preserved by bitumen, natron, and aromatic substances.

The Egyptians also preserved their dead in honey. 'Abd el-Latîf relates that an Egyptian worthy of belief told him that once when he and several others were occupied in exploring the graves and seeking for treasure near the Pyramids, they came across a sealed jar, and having opened it and found that it contained honey, they began to eat it. Some one in the party remarked that a hair in the honey turned round one of the fingers of the man who was dipping his bread in it, and as they drew it out the body of a small child appeared with all its limbs complete and in a good state of preservation; it was well dressed, and had upon it numerous ornaments.[3] The body of Alexander the Great

Bodies preserved in honey.

[3] 'Abd el-Laṭîf, tr. De Sacy, p. 199

was also preserved in "white honey which had not been melted."[1]

Bodies preserved by bitumen and salt only.

The bodies of the poor were preserved by two very cheap methods; one method consisted of soaking in salt and hot bitumen, and the other in salt only. In the first process every cavity was filled with bitumen, and the hair disappeared; clearly it is to the bodies which were preserved in this way that the name "mummy" or bitumen was first applied. The salted and dried body is easily distinguishable. The skin is like paper, the features and hair have disappeared, and the bones are very white and brittle.

Oldest mummy in the world.

The **oldest mummy** in the world about the date of which there is no doubt, is that of Seker-em-sa-f,[2] son of Pepi I. and elder brother of Pepi II., B.C. 3200, which was found at Ṣaḳḳârah in 1881, and which is now at Gîzeh. The lower jaw is wanting, and one of the legs has been dislocated in transport; the features are well preserved, and on the right side of the head is the lock of hair emblematic of youth. An examination of the body shows that Seker-em-sa-f died very young. A number of bandages found in the chamber of his pyramid at Ṣaḳḳârah are similar to those in use at a later date, and the mummy proves that the art of embalming had arrived at a very high pitch of perfection already in the Ancient Empire. The fragments of a body which were found by Colonel Howard Vyse in the pyramid of Mycerinus at Gîzeh, are thought by some to belong to a much later period than that of this king; there appears to be, however, no evidence for this belief, and as they belong to a man, and not to a woman, as Vyse thought, they may quite easily be the remains of the mummy of Mycerinus. The skeletons found in sarcophagi belonging to the first six dynasties fall to dust when air is admitted to them, and they emit a slight smell of bitumen.

Characteristics of mummies of different periods.

Mummies of the XIth dynasty are usually very poorly made; they are yellowish in colour, brittle to the touch, and fall to pieces very easily. The limbs are rarely bandaged separately, and the body having been wrapped carelessly in a

[1] Budge, *History of Alexander the Great*, p. 141.

[2] Maspero, *Guide du Visiteur au Musée de Boulaq*, 1883, p. 347.

number of folded cloths, is covered over lengthwise by one large linen sheet. On the little finger of the left hand a scarab is usually found; but besides this there is neither amulet nor ornament. The coffins in which mummies of this period are found are often filled with baskets, tools, mirrors, bows and arrows, etc., etc.

**Characteristics of mummies of different periods.**

Mummies of the XIIth dynasty are black, and the skin is dry; bandages are not common, and in the cases where they exist they are very loosely put on. Scarabs, amulets, and figures of gods are found with mummies of this epoch.

From the XIIIth to the XVIIth dynasties mummies are very badly made and perish rapidly.

From the XVIIIth to the XXIst dynasties the mummies of Memphis are black, and so dry that they fall to pieces at the slightest touch; the cavity of the breast is filled with amulets of all kinds, and the green stone scarab inscribed with the XXXth chapter of the Book of the Dead was placed over the heart. At Thebes, during this period, the mummies are yellow in colour and slightly polished, the nails of the hands and feet retain their places, and are stained with *henna*. The limbs bend in all directions without breaking, and the art of careful and dainty bandaging has attained its greatest perfection. The left hand wears rings and scarabs, and papyri inscribed with chapters of the Book of the Dead are found in the coffins, either by the side of the mummy, or beneath it.

After the XXIst dynasty the custom arose of placing the mummy in a cartonnage, sewn or laced up the back, and painted in brilliant colours with scenes of the deceased adoring the gods and the like.

In the period between the XXVIth dynasty and the conquest of Egypt by Alexander, the decoration of mummies reached its highest point, and the ornamentation of the cartonnage shows the influence of the art of Greece upon that of Egypt. The head of the mummy is put into a mask, gilded or painted in bright colours, the cartonnage fits the body very closely, and the feet are protected by a sheath. A large number of figures of the gods and of amulets are found on the mummy itself, and many things which formed its private property when alive were buried with it. Towards the time of

Characteristics of mummies of different periods.

the Ptolemies, mummies become black and heavy; bandages and body are made by the bitumen into one solid mass, which can only be properly examined by the aid of a hatchet. Such mummies are often wrapped in coverings inscribed with scenes and texts, copied, without any knowledge of their meaning, by an artist who altered them to suit his own fancy or purpose.

About B.C. 100 mummies were very carefully bandaged; each limb was treated separately, and retained its natural shape after bandaging, and the features of the face, somewhat blunted, are to be distinguished beneath the bandages.

About A.D. 50 the desire on the part of relatives and friends to see the face of the deceased resulted in the insertion of a piece of wood, painted with his portrait, over the face of the dead man. The mummies, from this time on to the fourth century, are of little interest, for they become mere bundles; scenes were painted, athwart and along the bodies, in which the deceased is represented adoring ill-shaped Egyptian deities; but little by little the hieroglyphic inscriptions disappear, and finally those in Greek take their place.

Græco-Roman mummies.

A remarkable example of a very late Græco-Roman mummy, probably of the fourth century A.D., is British Museum No. 21,810. The body is enveloped in a number of wrappings, and the whole is covered with a thin layer of plaster painted a pinkish-red colour. Over the face is inserted a portrait of the deceased, with a golden laurel crown on his head; on the breast, in gold, is a collar, each side of which terminates in the head of a hawk. The scenes painted in gold on the body are: 1. Anubis, Isis, and Nephthys at the bier of the deceased. 2. Thoth, Horus, uræi, etc., referring probably to the scene of the weighing of the heart. 3. The soul revisiting the body, which is attempting to rise up from a bier, beneath which are two jars; beneath this scene is a winged disk. Above these scenes in a band is inscribed, in Greek, "O Artemidorus, farewell." ΑΡΤΕΜΙΔΩΡΗ, ЄΥΨΥΧΙ; and above the band is a vase , on each side of which is a figure of Maāt 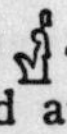. Mummies of children of this period have the hair curled and gilded, and hold bunches of flowers in their hands, which are crossed over their breasts.

In the early centuries of our era, mummies of wealthy people were wrapped in royal cloth made wholly of silk.[1] When Pisentios, Bishop of Coptos, and his disciple John took up their abode in a tomb in the "mountain of Tchêmi" (ⲡⲓⲧⲱⲟⲩ ⲛ̀ ϭⲏⲙⲓ =  the necropolis of Thebes) they found it filled with a number of mummies, the names of which were written on a parchment roll which lay close by them. The two monks took the mummies and piled them up one upon the other; the outer coffins were very large, and the coffins in which the bodies were laid were much decorated. The first mummy near the door was of great size, and his fingers and his toes were bandaged separately (ⲡⲉϥⲧⲏⲃ ⲛ̀ ϫⲓϫ ⲛⲉⲙ ⲡⲉϥϭⲁⲗⲁⲩϫ ⲕⲏⲥ ⲛ̀ ⲟⲩⲁⲓ ⲟⲩⲁⲓ); the clothes in which he was wrapped were made entirely of silk (ϩⲟⲗⲟⲥⲏⲣⲓⲕⲟⲛ[2] ⲛ̀ⲧⲉ ⲛⲓⲟⲩⲣⲱⲟⲩ).[3] The monk who wrote this description of mummies, and coffins, and silk, evidently described what he had actually seen. The huge outer coffins to which he refers belong to a very late period, as do also the highly-decorated inner coffins; the fingers and toes being bandaged separately also points to a late Roman period. His testimony

Description of mummies by Pisentios.

Silken mummy cloths.

[1] Silk, Heb. מֶשִׁי (Ezek. xvi. 10, 13), LXX., τρίχαπτον, σηρικὸς (Rev. xvii. 12), Syr. ܫܪܝܩܐ, was common in Greece and Rome at the end of the second century of our era. According to Aelius Lampridius (cap. 26), Heliogabalus was the first Roman who wore cloth made wholly of silk, *holoserica veste*, and an idea of the value of silk in the early days of its adoption in Europe is gained from the fact that Aurelian denied his wife a shawl of purple silk because a pound of silk cost one pound weight in gold (Flavius Vopiscus, *Vit. Aur.*, cap. 45). The custom of women wearing silk was railed at by Clement of Alexandria, Tertullian, Cyprian, Bishop of Carthage, Ambrose, Chrysostom and others; yet Basil, about A.D. 370, illustrated the doctrine of the resurrection from the change of the chrysalis into a butterfly. The custom in Italy of wrapping dead bodies in silk is probably not earlier than the end of the third century, and in Egypt we may place it about one hundred years later. On the use of silk by the ancients, see Yates, *Textrinum Antiquorum*, pp. 161–249, and for the collected statements of ancient authors on the subject, see G. D. Hoffman, *Observationes circa Bombyces, Sericum, et Moros, ex antiquitatum, historiarum, juriumque penu depromptæ*; Tübingen, 4to., 1757.

[2] Greek ὁλοσηρικός.

[3] For the complete text see Amélineau, *Etude sur le Christianisme en Egypte*, p. 143.

that silk was used for wrapping mummies is corroborated by the fact that within the last few years a number of mummies wrapped in cloths covered with silk[1] have been found. In the British Museum is a fine specimen (No. 17,173), in which two men on horseback, four dogs, flowers, etc., are woven in green and yellow on a reddish ground. The whole is inside a circular border ornamented with flowers. This piece of silk is sewn on a piece of fine yellow silk which is in turn sewn on a piece of ordinary mummy cloth to strengthen it.

**Mummy labels.**

Mummies of the Roman period were identified by small wooden labels, of an average size of five inches by two inches, pierced at one end, and tied to the necks of the dead. The inscriptions record the name of the deceased, and sometimes those of his father and mother, and the number of years of his life; some are in Greek only, a large number are bilingual, Greek and demotic, and a few also give the equivalent of the inscriptions in hieroglyphics. Unfortunately they are very easy to forge, for the natives use old wood from Egyptian coffins, and are able to imitate the inscriptions very closely, and many imitations are sold to tourists annually.

**Decline of embalming in Egypt due to Christianity.**

The Egyptian Christians appear to have adopted the system of mummifying, and to have mixed up parts of the old Egyptian mythology with their newly adopted Christianity. Already in the IIIrd century of our era the art of mummifying had greatly decayed, and although it was adopted by wealthy people, both Christian and Pagan, for two or three centuries longer, it cannot be said to have been generally in use at a period later than the IVth century. I believe that this fact was due to the growth of Christianity in Egypt. The Egyptian embalmed his dead because he believed that the perfect soul would return to its body after death, and that it would animate it once more; he therefore took pains to preserve the body from all destroying influences in the grave. The Christian believed that Christ would give him back his body changed and incorruptible, and that it was therefore unnecessary for him to preserve it with spices

[1] For excellent coloured representations of Byzantine mummies, see Plates A and B, in *Mémoires de la Mission Archéologique Française au Caire*, tom. iii., Paris, 1890.

and drugs. The idea of embalming the body and keeping it in the house with the living seems to have been repugnant to many famous Christians in Egypt, and Anthony the Great admonished his two faithful disciples not to allow his body to be taken into Egypt, but to bury it under the ground in a place known to none but themselves, lest it should be laid up in some dwelling. He disapproved of this custom, and had always entreated those who were in the habit of keeping the body above ground to give it up; and, concerning his own body, he said, "At the resurrection of the dead I shall receive it from the Saviour incorruptible."[1] For the description of a plaque, which must have come from the mummy of a Copt, see under "Anubis" in the article "Figures of the Gods."

## MUMMY CLOTH.

Mummy cloths were thought to be made of cotton.

The bandages with which the bodies of men and animals are wrapped were, until comparatively lately, believed to be made of *cotton*. In 1646 Greaves stated in his *Pyramidographia* that the "ribbands, by what I observed, were of *linen*, which was the habit also of the Egyptian priests," and he adds, "of these ribbands I have seen some so strong and perfect as if they had been made but yesterday." Ronelle in the *Mémoires de l'Académie R. des Sciences*, for 1750, asserted that every piece of mummy cloth that he had seen was made of *cotton*, and Forster[2] and Solander, Larcher[3] and Maty, Blumenbach[4] and others accepted this opinion.

[1] *μὴ ἀφεῖτέ τινας τὸ σῶμά μου λαβεῖν εἰς Αἴγυπτον, μήπως ἐν τοῖς οἴκοις ἀπόθωνται· τούτου γὰρ χάριν εἰσῆλθον εἰς τὸ ὄρος, καὶ ἦλθον ὧδε. Οἴδατε δὲ καὶ πῶς ἀεὶ ἐνέτρεπον τοὺς τοῦτο ποιοῦντας, καὶ παρήγγελλον παύσασθαι τῆς τοιαύτης συνηθείας. Θάψατε οὖν τὸ ἡμέτερον ὑμεῖς, καὶ ὑπὸ γῆν κρύψατε· καὶ ἔστω τὸ παρ' ἐμοῦ ῥῆμα φυλαττόμενον παρ' ὑμῖν, ὥστε μηδένα γινώσκειν τὸν τόπον, πλὴν ὑμῶν μόνων. 'Εγὼ γὰρ ἐν τῇ ἀναστάσει τῶν νεκρῶν ἀπολήψομαι παρὰ τοῦ Σωτῆρος ἄφθαρτον αὐτό.—See* Life of Antony by Athanasius.

(Migne, *Patrologiae*, Ser. Græc. tom. 26, col. 972.)

[2] *De Bysso Antiquorum*, London, 1776, pp. 70, 71.

[3] *Hérodote*, Paris, 1802, p. 357.

[4] *Beiträge*, Göttingen, 1811, pt. 2, p. 73.

Jomard thought that both cotton and linen were used for bandages of mummies;[1] Granville, in the *Philosophical Transactions* for 1825, p. 274, also embraced this view. The question was finally settled by Mr. Thomson, who after a twelve years' study of the subject proved in the *Philosophical Magazine* (IIIrd Series, Vol. V., No. 29, Nov., 1834) that the bandages were universally made of linen. He obtained for his researches about four hundred specimens of mummy cloth, and employed Mr. Bauer of Kew to examine them with his microscopes. "The ultimate fibre of cotton is a transparent tube without joints, flattened so that its inward surfaces are in contact along its axis, and also twisted spirally round its axis: that of flax is a transparent tube jointed like a cane, and not flattened nor spirally twisted."[2] The coarse linen of the Egyptians was made of thick flax, and was used for making towels, awnings and sail-cloth;[3] the fine linen, Ὀθόνη, is thought by some to be the equivalent of the אֵטוּן מִצְרָיִם of Proverbs vii. 16. The Greek Σινδών = Heb. סָדִין, was used to denote any linen cloth, and sometimes cotton cloth; but the *σινδόνος βυσσίνης* with which mummies, according to Herodotus (II. 86), were bandaged, is certainly linen. The Egyptian word usually translated by "byssus" is  *shens*, Coptic ϣⲉⲛⲥ; ordinary words for linen are  *māk*,  *mennui*, 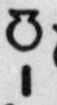 *nu*, Coptic ⲛⲁⲧ = *οθονιων βυσσινων* (Rosetta Stone, l. 17). One piece of very fine texture of linen obtained at Thebes had 152 threads in the warp, and 71 in the woof, to each inch, and a second piece described by Wilkinson (*Ancient Egyptians*, III. 165) had 540 threads in the warp, and 110 in the woof.[4] One of the cities in Egypt most

Mummy cloths made of linen.

[1] *Description de l'Egypte; Mémoires sur les Hypogées*, p. 35.

[2] *See* Yates, *Textrinum Antiquorum*; London, 1843, p. 262, where the whole subject is carefully discussed.

[3] Comp. שֵׁשׁ בְּרִקְמָה מִמִּצְרַיִם, Ezekiel, xxvii. 7.

[4] See also an interesting letter by De Fleury to M. Devéria on "Les Etoffes Egyptiennes" in *Rev. Arch.*, t. XXI, Paris, 1870, pp. 217-221.

famous for its linen industry was  Apu, the Panopolis of the Greeks,[1] the ϧⲙⲓⲙ or ϣⲙⲓⲛ of the Copts, and Akhmîm[2] of the Arabs; but as Egypt exported great quantities of this material, and also used immense quantities for bandages of mummies, it is probable that other cities also possessed large linen manufactories.[3] **Panopolis the great centre of linen weavers.**

The length and breadth of mummy bandages vary from about 3 feet by 2½ inches, to 13 feet by 4½ inches; some are made with fringe at both ends, like a scarf, and some have carefully made selvedges. Large linen sheets several feet square are also found in tombs. The saffron coloured pieces of linen with which mummies are finally covered measure about 8 feet by 4 feet. Usually two or three different kinds of linen cloth are used in bandaging mummies. Mummy cloths are with very few exceptions quite plain, and it is only in the Greek times that the fine outer linen covering is decorated with figures of gods, etc., in gaudy colours. Several square pieces of linen in the Museums of Europe are ornamented with blue stripes, and it is pretty certain that the threads which form them were dyed with indigo before they were woven into the piece. As far back as the time of Amenophis III. it was customary to inscribe texts in the hieratic and hieroglyphic characters upon mummy cloths, and at that period large vignettes accompany the chapters from the Book of the Dead; after the XXVIth dynasty hieratic only appears to have been used for this purpose, and the bandages, which are rarely more than four inches wide, are frequently so coarse that the text is almost illegible. Badly drawn vignettes, drawn in outline, usually stand at the top of each column of writing. **Mummy bandages.**

The marvellous skill which the Egyptians displayed in making linen did not die out with the fall of the native **Duration of the linen industry in Egypt.**

[1] Πανῶν πόλις, λινουργῶν καὶ λιθουργῶν κατοικία παλαιά, Strabo, XVII., l. 42.

[2] Akhmîm has a population of about 10,000 souls, and of these 1000 are Christians.

[3] In the map published by Yates (*Textrinum Antiquorum*, p. 250) to show the divisions of the ancient world in which sheep's-wool, goat's-hair, hemp, cotton, silk, beaver's-wool, camel's-wool, camel's-hair and linen are found, the only other districts where linen was made besides Egypt are Colchis, Cinyps, and a district near the mouth of the Rhine.

sovereigns of Egypt, and the Copts, or native Christians of that country, carried on the industry with splendid success until the twelfth century of our era. Although they ceased to mummify their dead, for the hope of the resurrection of the body given by Christianity practically killed the art of embalming, they continued to dress them in garments which are remarkable for the beauty of the embroidery and tapestries with which they are decorated. A great "find" of fine examples of this work was made at Akhmîm, the ancient Panopolis, in 1884. The graves at Akhmîm are about five feet deep, and are not indicated by any mound. The bodies appear to have been buried with natron sprinkled over them, for many of their garments are covered with crystals of this substance; and they appear also to have been buried with their best clothes on. The head was provided with a band or cap, and was sometimes supported on a pillow. The body wore a tunic, and the feet had stockings, sandals or shoes upon them; the head, breast, arms, and fingers were decorated with ornaments. The condition in life of the deceased was indicated by inscriptions on rectangular wooden tesseræ (see p. 188), or by his tools, which were buried with him. The body was entirely covered over with linen and laid upon a board, and thus dressed was then deposited in the earth. The chief ornaments found in the tombs at Akhmîm are: hair-pins and combs made of wood or bone; earrings of several shapes and forms made of glass; silver and bronze filigree work, gold with little gold balls, and iron with pendent agates; necklaces made of amber, coloured glass, and blue and green glazed faïence beads; torques, or neck-rings, made of bronze; bracelets, open and closed, made of bronze, iron, glass and horn; finger-rings of bronze; and bronze belt buckles made in the form of a Christian cross. A large number of ivory crosses are also found; the cross which is found so often on these objects was not used merely as an ornament, but as a special symbol and emblem of Christianity.[1] The most ancient and the greater number of the tombs which

Discovery of Christian necropolis at Panopolis.

Ornaments found upon the bodies.

Age of the necropolis.

[1] I owe these details to Forrer, Die Gräber und Textilfunde von Achmim —Panopolis. Strassburg, 1891, pp. 12, 13. This book contains 16 plates on which are photographed, in colours, 250 pictures of the textile fabrics and the other most interesting objects found at Akhmîm.

contained these belong to the second or third century after Christ, and the most recent to the eighth or ninth century;[1] they are taken from bodies of Christians and heathen which were buried with or without coffins, or in private or common burial places. The Museum of Gobelins possesses a piece of cloth, the threads of the woof of which are made of pure silk, and this is said by M. Gerspach,[2] the Director of the National Manufactory at Gobelins, to belong to a period subsequent to the eighth century, because silk does not appear in Egyptian tapestries until that century. It may then be considered that the Coptic linen work found at Akhmîm covers a period of eight centuries, viz., ii–ix. M. Gerspach adds, "Il est fort probable que les Coptes ont continué, pendant plusieurs siècles encore, une fabrication dans laquelle ils excellaient; ils ont vraisemblablement travaillé à ces milliers de pièces représentant les grands hommes de l'Islam, montrant des villes, des paysages et des animaux que possédait le calif Mostansser-Billah et qui furent brûlées au Caire en 1062 avec les immenses richesses accumulées dans le Dépôt des étendards" (p. 2). Of the character, style, design, and antiquity of Coptic linen work he says, "Le style est plus ou moins pur, mais il dénote constamment une grande liberté de composition et de facture; il est exempt de minuties et de subtilités, même lorsque nous ne comprenons pas très bien la pensée de l'artiste. Quand il ne se rattache pas à la décoration romaine ou à l'art oriental, il est original, il a un caractère propre, une saveur particulière, qu'il soit fin comme nos dentelles ou épais et obtus comme les ornements des races inférieures; il constitue alors, dans une manifestation intime et populaire, un genre spécial qu'on nommera peut-être bientôt le style copte. A première vue, en effet, on retrouve l'antiquité dans les pièces les plus simples, qui sont aussi les plus anciennes; en général, ces morceaux sont d'une seule couleur pourpre ou brune, avec

**Gerspach on Coptic linen work and designs.**

[1] According to Forrer (p. 26), the foundation of the cemetery at Akhmîm may be dated in the first or second century after Christ, and the decay of the art of the best kind is to be sought at the end of the seventh or in the course of the eighth century after Christ.

[2] *Les Tapisseries Coptes*, Paris, 1890, p. 2. This most interesting work contains 153 reproductions in one or more colours of the most important designs found on Akhmîm linen.

des filets clairs en lin écru. Le dessin est sommaire, net, sobre, bien combiné, harmonieux, d'une grande franchise plastique, dans le style qu'adoptera ultérieurement l'art héraldique; naturellement, dans la figure il est plus faible que dans l'ornement, car le tapissier, avec sa broche, ne trace pas aussi facilement que le céramiste avec son pinceau ; nous devons excuser les tapissiers Coptes, leurs successeurs de tous les temps et de tous les pays ayant comme eux fait plus ou moins de fautes de dessin ..... Les tapisseries polychromes[1] sont généralement postérieures à cette première série, mais il importe de faire remarquer que certains modèles primitifs n'ont pas été abandonnés et qu'on les retrouve dans les tissus modernes du bas Danube et de l'Orient ..... Jusqu'ici[2] le dessin est clair et lisible; maintenant nous arrivons à une suite inférieure; les lignes se compliquent et les formes deviennent épaisses; ...... l'ornement est encore dans un bon esprit, mais les figures sont faibles ...... Avec les siècles suivants, nous tombons dans une décadence relative, moins profonde que celle de la mosaïque au IXe siècle; le corps humain est contourné, strapassé ; les têtes sont bestiales ; les animaux sont difformes et fantastiques, pourvus de sortes de tentacules; ils se transforment en ornements; la flore n'est même plus ornemanisée ni conventionelle ; certains motifs sont incompréhensibles ; l'ornement, mieux tenu, présente toujours des combinaisons intéressantes; .... même dans leurs fautes, les Coptes continuent à prouver qu'ils sont décorateurs."

## Canopic Jars or Vases.

"Canopic jars" is the name given to the series of four jars in which the principal intestines of a deceased person were placed. They were thus named by the early Egyptologists, who believed that in them they saw some confirmation of the legend handed down by some ancient writers that Canopus, the pilot of Menelaus, who is said to have been buried at Canopus, in Egypt, was worshipped there under the form of a jar with small feet, a thin neck, a swollen body, and

[1] Of the fourth century.
[2] Fifth century.

a round back. Each jar was dedicated to one of the four genii of the underworld, who represented the cardinal points, and each jar was provided with a cover which was made in the shape of the head of the deity to whom it was dedicated.

**The four genii of the dead.**

The names and characteristic heads of each are:—1. Mesthȧ or Ȧmset, man-headed. 2. Ḥāpi, dog-headed. 3. Ṭuamāutef jackal-headed. 4. Qebḥsennuf, hawk-headed. Mesthȧ represented the south, Ḥāpi the north, Ṭuamāutef the east, and Qebḥsennuf the west. These four gods are, in some texts, said to be the children of Horus, and in others the children of Osiris. Each jar was hollowed out and received one of the larger intestines after it had been steeped in bitumen and wrapped up in bandages; the covers of the jars were then fastened on by plaster. Mr. Pettigrew examined the contents of one set of vases, and it was found that the vase dedicated to Mesthȧ contained the stomach and large intestines; that dedicated to Ḥāpi, the small intestines; that dedicated to Ṭuamāutef, the lungs and heart; and that dedicated to Qebḥsennuf, the liver and gall-bladder.

**Age of Canopic jars.**

Canopic jars first appear about the XVIIIth dynasty, and they continue in use until the XXVIth dynasty, after which time the Egyptians appear to have been somewhat careless about them, and either to have preferred to bury the intestines inside the body or to have forgotten the significance of their use. In the XVIIIth dynasty they are made of the most beautiful alabaster and arragonite, and fine calcareous stone; in the XXVIth dynasty they are still made of these substances, but green and blue glazed faïence and wood also appear. Later they are made of terra-cotta, and the covers are all made in the same shape; sometimes they have the shape of a vessel of the same diameter at the bottom as at the top, the gods being traced upon them, in outline, on the outside surface. Frequently the jars are made of wood, painted with bright colours, and sometimes solid wooden models only are found in the tombs, a fact which shows sometimes the poverty of the deceased, and sometimes probably the dishonesty of the funeral furnisher. When the intestines were not buried in jars they were returned to the body, and figures of Mesthȧ, Ḥāpi, Ṭuamāutef and Qebḥsennuf made of wax, sheet silver, gold or porcelain, were laid upon the parts which these gods were supposed to protect. On the alabaster and stone jars the inscriptions were incised, and on wood and faïence they were painted or traced in outline in ink. In papyri of the XVIIIth and XIXth dynasties, the vignettes of the 17th chapter of the Book of the Dead show that Canopic jars were placed in a sepulchral chest, upon the sides of which were painted figures of the four gods, in the form of men, but each having its characteristic

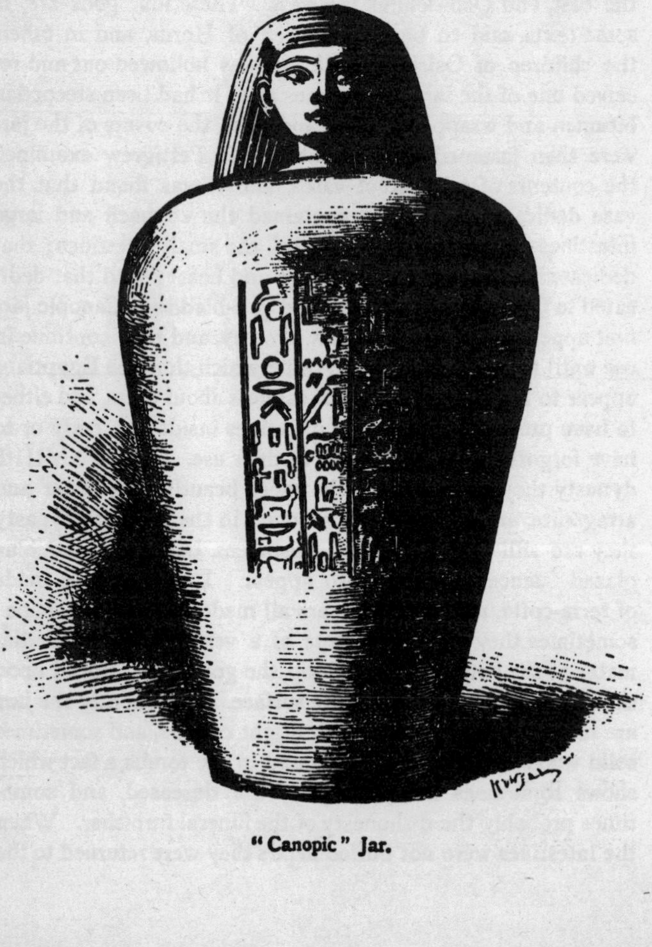

"Canopic" Jar.

head. Out of the cover there rises the sun with the head and arms of a man, and in each hand he holds ☥ *ānch*, "life." (*Papyrus of Ani*, pl. 8.) On papyri and coffins of a later period the jars are shown arranged in a row under the bier. In the 151st chapter of the Book of the Dead the four gods are shown standing in the mummy chamber, one at each corner; the inscriptions which refer to them read:—

I. 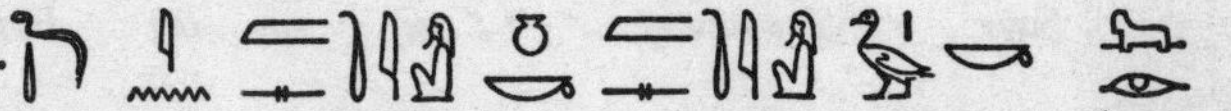

met' ȧn Mesθȧ nuk Mesθȧ se - k Ȧusȧr

*Says Mesthȧ, "I am Mesthȧ son thy, O Osiris.*

Speech of Mesthȧ.

i - ȧ un - ȧ em sau - k seruṭ - nȧ

*Come have I that may be I in protection thy. Make to flourish I*

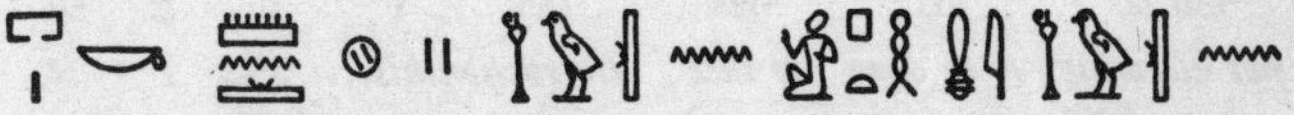

pa - k men sep sen utu en Ptaḥ mȧ utu en

*house thy, firm, firm, hath commanded Ptaḥ, as commanded*

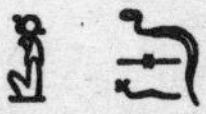

Rā t'esef

*Rā himself."*

II. 

met' ȧn Ḥāpi nuk Ḥāpi se - k Ȧusȧr

*Says Ḥāpi, "I am Ḥāpi son thy, O Osiris.*

Speech of Ḥāpi.

i - nȧ un - ȧ em sau - k θes - k

*Come have I that may be I in protection thy. Tie up [I] for thee*

ṭep āt - k ḥui nek χefta - k

*head and limbs thy, smiting down for thee enemies thy*

χer - k ertā - nȧ nek ṭep t'etta

*beneath thee. Give I to thee head [thy] for ever."*

Speech of Ṭuamāutef.

III. 

met' ȧn Ṭuamāutef nuk se - k Ḥeru

*Says Ṭuamāutef, "I am son thy Horus*

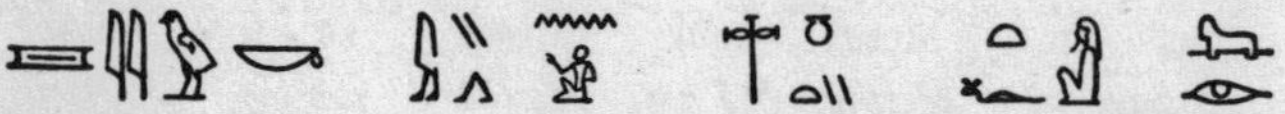

meriu - k ī - nȧ net' tef Ȧusȧr

*loving thee. Come have I to avenge father [my] Osiris,*

em ṭā ȧri nek nek - f ṭā - ȧ su

*not allowing to be done to thee destruction his. Place I it*

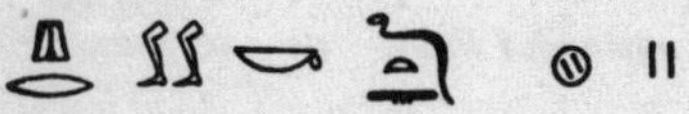

χer reṭ - k t'etta sep sen

*under feet thy for ever and ever."*

Speech of Qebḥsennuf.

IV. 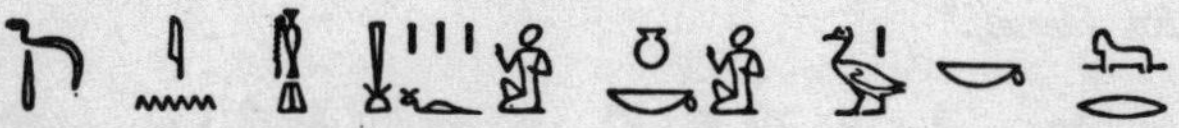

met' ȧn Qebḥ - sennuf nuk se - k Ȧusȧr

*Says Qebḥ - sennuf, "I am son thy Osiris.*

ī - nȧ un - ȧ em sau - k ṭemṭ - ȧ

*Come have I that may be I in protection thy. Gather together I*

kesu - k saq - ȧ āt - k ȧn - nȧ nek

*bones thy, collect I limbs thy, bring I for thee*

âb - k  ṭā - â  nek  su  ḥer  âuset - f  em  χat - k
*heart thy, place I for thee it upon seat its in body thy,*

seruṭ - nâ  pa - k
*make flourish I house thy."*

The inscriptions on the outsides of the jars, which are sometimes accompanied by inscribed figures of the four gods, vary considerably; some consist of a few words only, but others occupy several lines. These inscriptions show that each of the four gods was under the protection of a goddess; thus Isis guarded Mesthâ, Nephthys guarded Ḥāpi, Neith guarded Ṭuamāutef, and Selket or Serqet guarded Qebḥsennuf. The following are examples of the formulæ inscribed on these jars:—[1]

I. ÂMSET. 

met' ân Âuset  sam - â  t'et  setep - â   Speech of Isis.
*Says Isis, "Conquer I the foe, make I*

sa  ḥer  Âmseθ  enti  âm - â  sa
*protection over Âmseth who is in me. The protection of*

Âusâr  sa  Âmseθ  Âusâr  Âmseθ
*Osiris [is] the protection of Âmseth, [for] Osiris [is] Âmseth."*

[1] These inscriptions are taken from the set of Canopic jars exhibited in the British Museum, Nos. 886 to 889; they were made for the commander of soldiers

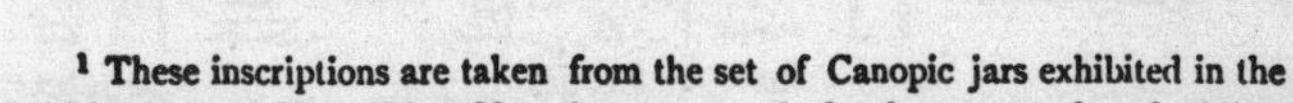

 Nefer-âb-Rā-em-χut, Psammetichus, son of Neith, son of Ta-ṭā-nub-ḥetep. See Sharpe, *Egyptian Inscriptions*, 1st Series, pl. 114.

[2] Here follow the name and titles of the deceased.

II. ḤĀPI.

Speech of Nephthys.

met' ȧn Nebt-ḥet ḥap - ȧ seśeta ȧri - ȧ

*Says Nephthys, " Hide I the secret thing, make I*

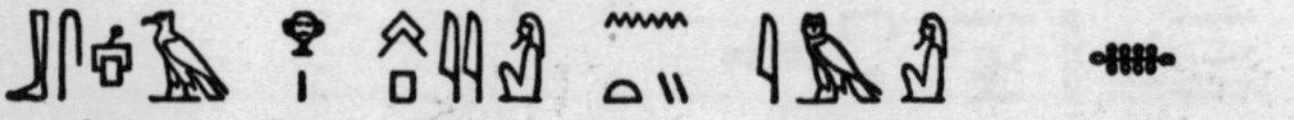

bessa ḥer Ḥāpi enti ȧm - ȧ sa

*protection over Ḥāpi who is in me. The protection of*

Ȧusȧr sa Ḥāpi Ȧusȧr pu Ḥāpi

*Osiris* [*is*] *the protection of Ḥāpi,* [*for*] *Osiris* [*is*] *Ḥāpi."*

III. ṬUAMĀUTEF.

Speech of Neith.

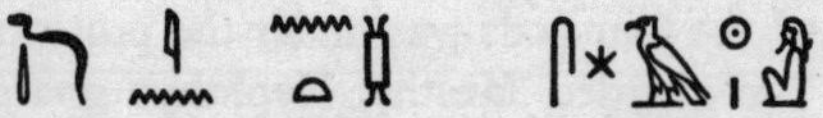

met' ȧn Net seṭua - ȧ

*Says Neith, "Make pass the morning I,*

semāśer - ȧ hru neb ḥer ȧri māket en

*make pass the night I of day every in making the protection of*

Ṭuamāutef enti ȧm - ȧ sa Ȧusȧr

*Ṭuamāutef which is in me. The protection of Osiris*

sa Ṭuamāutef Ȧusȧr pu Ṭuamāutef

[*is*] *the protection of Ṭuamāutef,* [*for*] *Osiris* [*is*] *Ṭuamāutef."*

IV. QEBḤSENNUF.

Speech of Serqet.

met' ȧn Serqet seqeṭet

*Says Serqet,* ................

sa - ȧ hru neb ȧri māket en Qebḥ-sennu-f

*"protection my day every in making protection of Qebḥ-sennu-f*

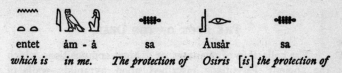

| | | | | |
|---|---|---|---|---|
| entet | ȧm - ȧ | sa | Ȧusȧr | sa |
| *which is* | *in me.* | *The protection of* | *Osiris* | [*is*] *the protection of* |

| | | | |
|---|---|---|---|
| Qebḥ-sennnu-f | Ȧusȧr | pu | Qebḥ-sennu-f |
| *Qebḥ-sennu-f*, [*for*] | *Osiris* | [*is*] | *Qebḥ-sennu-f.*" |

Frequently the first parts of these inscriptions read,  *qenȧ em āāui ḥer enti ȧm-ȧ.* "I embrace with my two arms that which is in me;" the variants for 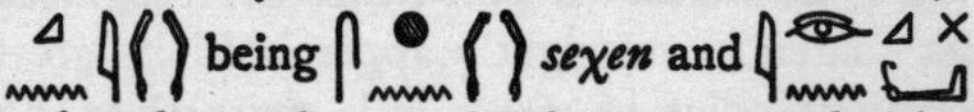 *seχen* and *ȧnq*; frequently also they only contain the names and titles of the deceased preceded by the words  *ȧmχi χer* "watchfully devoted to," which are followed by the names of the four gods. Often the same formula is repeated on all four jars. Variant readings.

## Chests for Canopic Jars. 

The chests, or coffers, which held Canopic jars were made of wood, and were usually painted black; they were fitted on a kind of sledge with two runners, the ends of which were rounded. They are about two feet square. On one end are traced in outline figures of Neith and Serqet, and on the other Isis and Nephthys; on the one side are Mesthȧ and Ḥāpi, and on the other Ṭuamāutef and Qebḥsennuf. By the side of each god is inscribed the formula which is given in the 151st chapter of the Book of the Dead, and by the side of each goddess is inscribed the formula which is found on Canopic vases. (Excellent examples of chests on sledges are Nos. 8543*a*, and 8543*b*, 3rd Egyptian Room, British Museum.) The inside of the chest is divided into four equal spaces by wooden partitions, and in each stood a jar. The use of such chests is certainly as old as the XIIth dynasty.

## THE BOOK OF THE DEAD.

The Book of the Dead not a 'Ritual.'

The collection of chapters, or distinct compositions, which the ancient Egyptians inscribed upon pyramids, walls of tombs, sarcophagi, coffins and papyri, amulets and other objects which were buried in the tombs with the dead was called "*Rituel Funéraire*" by Champollion, and this misleading name was adopted by De Rougé, who, in his *Etudes sur le Rituel Funéraire des Anciens Egyptiens*,[1] brought forward reasons for so doing, and considered that all he had said "justifie suffisamment, suivant nous, le titre choisi par Champollion." Champollion's grammar shows that he had studied every part of the so-called Ritual, and the many short passages which he translated prove that he recognized the nature of its contents, and rightly appreciated its great value from a religious point of view; it is quite clear, however, that he never completely analysed a single chapter of it, and that he never translated any passage from it of considerable length. Had this remarkable man lived to examine the work further he would have seen that it was not a "Ritual."[2] This collection of chapters was entitled "Todtenbuch" by Lepsius, in 1842, and by the name "BOOK OF THE DEAD" it is now most generally known.

Early printed copies of the Book of the Dead.

The earliest publications of parts or whole copies of the Book of the Dead were made by Cadet (J. Marc), *Copie figurée d'un rouleau de Papyrus, trouvé à Thèbes, dans un tombeau des Rois*, Strassburg, 1805; Fontana, *Copie figurée d'un rouleau de papyrus trouvé en Egypte, publiée par* Fontana *et expliquée par* Joseph de Hammer, Vienna, 1822; Sen-

1 In *Revue Archéologique*, N.S., tom. i. 1860, pp. 69–100, 234–249, 337–365.

2 Dieser Codex ist kein Ritualbuch, wofür es Champollion's Bezeichnung "Rituel Funéraire" zu erklären scheint; es enthält keine Vorschriften für den Todtenkultus, keine Hymnen oder Gebete, welche von den Priestern etwa bei der Beerdigung gesprochen worden wären: sondern der Verstorbene ist selbst die handelnde Person darin, und der Text betrifft nur ihn und seine Begegnisse auf der langen Wanderung nach dem irdischen Tode. Es wird entweder erzählt und beschrieben, wohin er kommt, was er thut, was er hört und sieht, oder es sind die Gebete und Anreden, die er selbst zu den verschiedenen Göttern, zu welchen er gelangt, spricht. Lepsius, *Vorwort* (*Todtenbuch*), p. 3.

kowski, *Exemplum Papyri Aegyptiacæ quam in peregrinatione sua repertam Universitati Cracoviensi dono dedit*, Petropoli, 1826;[1] Young, *Hieroglyphics*, London, 1823, fol., plates I.–VI.; Hawkins, *Papyri in the Hieroglyphic and Hieratic character from the Collection of the Earl of Belmore*, London, 1843, fol., plates 1–8; and Rosellini, *Breve notizia intorno un frammento di Papiro funebre egizio essistente nel ducale museo di Parma;* Parma, 1839, 8vo; *Description de l'Egypte*, ed. Jomard, *Antiquités*, tom. ii. The most important publication, however, was that of Lepsius in 1842, who under the title of *Das Todtenbuch der Aegypter*, reproduced the complete text of a papyrus at Turin, which contained 165 chapters. The custom of inscribing chapters of Books of the Dead upon the walls of the sarcophagus chambers of tombs is as old as the Vth dynasty, but at that epoch large, well-spaced hieroglyphics, arranged between lines, occupy the walls conjointly with architectural decorations;[2] towards the VIth dynasty the space allotted for decorative purposes becomes narrower, the hieroglyphics are smaller, and the inscriptions overflow into the passages and chambers, the walls of which, in earlier times, were left blank. The pyramids of the Vth and VIth dynasties which have inscriptions on their inner walls are those of Unȧs, Tetȧ, Pepi I., Pepi II., and Seker-em-sa-f; this set of inscriptions is usually called the "Pyramid Texts," and they have been published with a French translation by Maspero in *Recueil de Travaux:* Unȧs, tom. iii., pp. 177–224, and tom. iv., pp. 41–78; Tetȧ, tom. v., pp. 1–60; Pepi I., tom. v., pp. 157–199, tom. vii., pp. 145–176, tom. viii., pp. 87–119; Pepi II., tom. ix., pp. 177–190, tom. x., pp. 1–28, tom. xi., pp. 1–30, tom. xii., pp. 53–95, 136–195.

Lepsius publishes the Turin Papyrus.

The Pyramid Texts.

During the XIth dynasty the custom of writing chapters of the Books of the Dead upon wooden coffins or sarcophagi became common; examples of the texts of this period, written upon coffins in the hieratic character, have been

Texts inscribed upon coffins.

[1] This book was published at the expense of the Academy of St. Petersburg, and never came into the market.

[2] Maspero, *La Religion Egyptienne, d'après les Pyramides de la V^e et de la VI^e Dynastie* (in *Revue de l'Histoire des Religions*, Paris, 1885, p. 124).

published by Lepsius[1] and Birch.[2] At this period Books of the Dead were also written upon papyrus.[3]

Texts written upon papyri.

After the expulsion of the Hyksos from Egypt by the kings of Thebes, copies of the Book of the Dead were usually written upon papyri, and these papyri are of various lengths and widths. The roll of papyrus was often placed in a rectangular niche in the wall of the tombs, or in the coffin by the side of the mummy; sometimes it was placed between the legs, and sometimes it was fastened under the bandages. The length and style of execution of the work depended entirely upon the fancy of the relatives of the dead man. Books of the Dead, illuminated and plain, formed part of the stock in trade of the Egyptian undertaker. If the purchaser were rich he would probably select the best copy he could buy; if poor he would be content with a simple undecorated text. In these "stock" copies blank spaces were left to receive the names of the deceased for whom they were purchased. Copies are extant in which, through omission or neglect, no name whatever has been inserted. The numerous badly-written and incorrect copies which are so common in the museums of Europe are probably the result of cheap work; careless work, however, exists in the most beautiful papyri, and some of the finest known contain blunders which show not only that the scribe was careless, but also that he did not understand what he was writing. Books of the Dead are written in the hieroglyphic and hieratic characters, and are ornamented with pictures of the gods, sacred animals and birds, mythological scenes, representations of the funeral procession, etc., etc., painted, at times, in as many as thirteen colours. The titles of the chapters, catch-words, and certain passages are written in red, and the text in black. Hieroglyphic texts are usually written in perpendicular lines, and those in hieratic in horizontal lines. The vignettes and scenes were probably executed by one class of men, and the text by another, and it seems sometimes as if the relatives of the dead spent nearly all the

Vignettes and ornamentation of papyri.

[1] *Aelteste Texte des Todtenbuchs*, Berlin, 1867, 4to.

[2] *The Coffin of Amamu*, London, 1886, fol.

[3] For the fragments found with the mummy of Ȧn-Ȧntef, *see* B.M. First Egyptian Room, Case D.

money which they could afford to spend upon a copy of the Book of the Dead on the artists' work for pictures, while they left the execution of the text to an inferior scribe. Although many of the faulty readings which occur in the Book of the Dead are to be attributed to the carelessness of the scribe, it is quite certain that a very large number were the result of his ignorance, and that, at times, he did not know which was the beginning or end of the text which he was about to copy. In proof of this M. Naville[1] has reproduced from a papyrus the 77th chapter copied from the wrong end, and on the opposite page he gives the restored text in the right order. An examination of papyri shows that frequently more than one artist and scribe were employed in making a single copy of the Book of the Dead; but it is also evident that in some instances both the vignettes and the text were the work of one man.

According to M. Naville the Book of the Dead is known to us in four recensions:—

**The recensions of the Book of the Dead.**

1. That of the Old and Middle Empires, which is usually written in hieroglyphics.
2. The Theban recension, which was much used from the XVIIIth–XXth dynasty, also written in hieroglyphics.
3. The redaction closely resembling that of Thebes which obtained after the XXth dynasty, and which was written in hieratic; in it the chapters have no fixed order.
4. A text of the Saïte and Ptolemaïc periods written both in hieroglyphic and hieratic characters; this text shows that the Book of the Dead at this epoch had undergone a thorough revision, and in it the chapters have a fixed order.

The texts of the earliest recension are, for the most part, written in hieroglyphics upon tombs and sarcophagi, but texts written upon papyrus in hieroglyphic and hieratic characters took their place, probably because they cost less money, and

[1] In his *Einleitung*, pp. 42, 43.

because the relatives of the deceased could make them as long or as short as they pleased. It is probable that Books of the Dead were not written in hieratic during the XVIIIth dynasty.

A complete edition of the Book of the Dead contemplated.

In September, 1874, at a special meeting of the second International Congress of Orientalists, a resolution was passed to the effect that for the furtherance of Egyptian studies an edition of the Book of the Dead, or the "Bible of the Old Egyptians," as critical and complete as possible, should be steadily kept in view. It was further resolved that such an edition should contain the text of the Book of the Dead in three forms:—1. Under the Old Empire; 2. Under the Theban dynasties of the New Empire; 3. Under the Psammetici (XXVIth dynasty).[1] A Committee was formed which was composed of Messrs. Birch, Lepsius, Chabas and Naville, and M. Naville undertook the labour of this work. At the instance of Lepsius the Berlin Academy voted a sum of 3,000 marks for preliminary expenses, and the Prussian Government voted 4,800 thalers for its publication. When M. Naville began to collect materials for his edition, he found that the texts of the Old Empire were so few while those of the XXVIth dynasty were so many, and had so few actual variants in them, that he abandoned the idea of making an edition of the texts of the first and third recensions, and at the Fourth International Congress of Orientalists held at Florence, in September, 1878, he asked the Committee to allow him to alter the original plan, and he stated his intention of confining himself to collecting carefully all the necessary texts for a critical edition of the Theban recension of the Book of the Dead. He believed that in order to obtain a correct text of this recension, accurate copies of carefully written papyri must be published, from which, by comparison, the text may be emended. In 1886 M. Naville gave to the world the two volumes which contained the results of his twelve years' labour, under the title of *Das Aegyptische Todtenbuch der XVIII. bis XX. Dynastie*, Berlin,[2] fol. The first

M. Naville undertakes to make the edition.

Change of plan.

[1] Transactions of the Second Session of the International Congress of Orientalists, held in London, in September, 1874, London, 1876, p. 442.

[2] Lepsius unfortunately died before the work was issued. Egyptologists are indebted to Dr. Dillmann of Berlin for the issue of this valuable work.

volume contains the text[1] and vignettes which were ably drawn by Madame Naville, and the second contains the variants. In a small quarto volume published a few months later, we have four chapters in which are discussed the Theban edition of the Book of the Dead, its history, its importance and the manner in which it was written; the description of the texts used by M. Naville, remarks on each chapter of the Book of the Dead, and a list of the chapters in hieroglyphics. The texts of the Theban recension contain many corrupt readings, but it is of the greatest importance to have the material at hand from which a critical edition may one day be made, and M. Naville has rendered invaluable service to the science of Egyptology by bringing it together.[2]

Recent printed copies of texts.

Among the most valuable publications of texts of the Theban recension of the Book of the Dead must be mentioned, *Photographs of the Papyrus of Nebseni*[3] *in the British Museum*, 1876, fol.; *Facsimile of the Papyrus of Ani* (published by the Trustees of the British Museum, 1890, fol.); *Papyrus Funéraire de Nebset*, ed. Pierret, 1872; and the papyrus of Shuti-Qenna, by Leemans, *Papyrus Egyptien Funéraire Hiéroglyphique du Musée à Leide*, 1882, Livraison 5, Part III.

A useful example of a hieroglyphic text of the Book of the Dead not earlier than the XXVIth dynasty, is that which Lepsius published in 1842 from a papyrus in Turin; the text is full of blunders and difficulties but, notwithstanding this fact, the work is a standard one for reference, and is of considerable value. Of hieratic texts belonging to a period subsequent to the XXVIth dynasty, the copy published by De Rougé is an excellent example.[4]

Translations of the Book of the Dead.

An English translation of the Book of the Dead was published by Birch in the English edition of Bunsen's *Egypt's Place in Universal History*, Vol. V, pp. 161–333, and a French translation by Pierret, entitled *Le Livre des Morts des Anciens*

[1] M. Naville bases his text chiefly upon British Museum Papyrus 9,900, and the papyri which he calls C*a* and P*b*.

[2] See the review of this work by Maspero in *Revue de l'Histoire des Religions*, Paris, 1887, pp. 263–315.

[3] B.M. No. 9900.

[4] *Rituel Funéraire des Anciens Egyptiens*, Paris, 1861, fol.

*Egyptiens*, appeared in Paris, in 1882; both these were, however, made from the text of the Turin papyrus.[1] A German translation of the first fifteen chapters was published by Brugsch in *Aeg. Zeitschrift*, 1872, pp. 65–72, 129–134, and specially interesting chapters have been discussed by Birch,[2] Maspero,[3] Lefébure,[4] Guieysse,[5] Pierret,[6] and others. A number of "supplementary" chapters were published by Pleyte (*Chapitres supplémentaires du Livre des Morts*, 162, 162*, 164–174) with translation and commentary, at Leyden in 1881, and Schiaparelli has translated and commented upon a large portion of one of the Books of the Dead in *Il libro dei funerali degli antichi Egiziani*.[7]

**Antiquity of the Book of the Dead.**

The age of the Book of the Dead is unknown, but it is certain that parts of it are as old as the beginning of Egyptian civilization, and Theban tradition in Egypt asserted that the 130th chapter was as old as Ḥesep-ti,  the fifth king of the Ist dynasty; the 64th chapter is variously stated to belong to the time of this king and to that of Men-kau-Rā (Mycerinus) of the IVth dynasty.[8] The 178th chapter must also be at least as old as the time of this last king, because it is inscribed on the cover of his wooden coffin, which is now preserved in the British Museum (1st Egyptian Room, No. 6647).[9] The oldest chapters appear to have been composed at Heliopolis, the great sanctuary and home of religious learning in Egypt, which was to the

[1] A complete list of the words in this papyrus is to be found in Lieblein, *Index Alphabétique*, Paris, 1875.

[2] *The Chapter of the Pillow*, *Aeg. Zeit.*, 1868, p. 52; *the Chapter of the Heart*, *ibid.*, 1880, p. 56; and *the Chapter of the Tie*, *ibid.*

[3] *Le Chapitre de la Boucle*, in *Mémoire sur quelques Papyrus du Louvre*, Paris, 1875.

[4] *Les yeux d'Horus*, Paris, 1874.

[5] *Rituel funéraire Egyptien*, Paris, 1876.

[6] *Etudes Egyptologiques*, p. 85.

[7] *Estratto dal Volume VIII delle Memorie della R. Accademia dei Lincei*, Torino, 1882 and 1890.

[8] Naville, *Einleitung*, p. 31.

[9] I am aware that doubts have been thrown upon the age of this cover by a French writer, but it seems to me that the appearance and condition of the wood preclude any possibility of the theory that this cover was "restored" at a later period of Egyptian history being correct.

Egyptians what Jerusalem was to the Jews and Mecca is to the Mussulmans. The growth in the length of the chapters and the increase in their number was probably slow but sure; and that revisions should take place from time to time is only what was to be expected.

**Egyptian name of the Book of the Dead.**

The commonest name for the Book of the Dead in Egyptian is  *pert em hru*, which is generally translated by "coming forth, or going out, by day;" this was probably only a conventional name, and may account for the difficulty which scholars have had in agreeing as to its meaning. Another name is  *Re en seåqer χu*, "The Chapter of making strong the beatified spirit." (Naville, *Einleitung*, p. 24.) The author of the Book of the Dead was said to be the god Thoth.

The Book of the Dead is composed of a series of chapters,[1] each one of which formed a distinct composition, which could be added to or omitted from a papyrus according to the wish of those who were causing a copy to be made.[2] Champollion divided the book into three parts:—chapters 1–15, 16–125, and 126 to the end; but had this scholar lived to devote more time and attention to the subject he would have seen that these divisions[3] were purely arbitrary.

**The object of the Book of the Dead.**

The Book of the Dead treats of the dead man's journey through Amenti, and in it he speaks to the incorporeal gods and beings who reside there, uttering the formulæ which will deliver him from the foes who wish to impede his progress, reciting prayers, and chanting hymns to the great gods, with all of whom these compositions were supposed to enable him

[1] A Theban papyrus never contains more than ninety chapters.

[2] Es ist aber auch eine unrichtige Vorstellung, dass dieses Buch ein einziges Ganzes, eine in sich abgeschlossene von Anfang bis Ende fort schreitende Beschreibung der Seelenwanderung sei, welche von *einem* Verfasser so und in dieser Ausdehnung herrühre. Es ist vielmehr eine Sammlung verschiedener für sich bestehender Abschnitte, die sich auf die Zukunft der Seele beziehen, unter denen einzelne mehr oder minder wichtige Stellen einnehmen, auch im Allgemeinen nach einer gewissen Regel, die aber nicht immer unverbrüchlich ist, angeordnet sind. Lepsius.

[3] This subject is discussed by Lepsius in the *Vorwort* (p. 5) to his edition of the *Todtenbuch*.

to prevail. It contains texts which were ordered to be inscribed upon amulets and bandages for the benefit of the dead; it contains a plan of the mummy chamber and the arrangement of certain pieces of furniture in it; it contains the text of the confession of the deceased in the presence of the forty-two assessors, and the scene of the weighing of the heart in the judgment hall of Osiris; it has a representation of the Elysian Fields, etc. In our limited space here it is impossible to give the briefest summary of the chapters of the Book of the Dead and their contents; the above notes are only intended to indicate the best books and chief authorities on a work which is so often referred to in these pages.

## PILLOWS.

**Materials of which pillows are made.**

The **pillows** which the Egyptians were accustomed to put under the heads of mummies were made of wood (sycamore generally), granite, alabaster and calcareous stone. They vary from six to ten inches in height, and are often made in three pieces, viz., the curved neck-piece, the column and base. The column is usually round or square, and the base is oblong. The neck-piece is sometimes supported by two columns or pillars, fluted (B.M. No. 17,102), but it may be joined to the base by six supports (B.M. No. 2543), or even by twenty-one (B.M. No. 18,155). Pillows are made also in the shape of animals, *e.g.*, B.M. No. 20,753, which is in the shape of a stag, the horns being curved downwards to form the neck-piece. Neck-pieces and columns are sometimes ornamented with ivory studs (B.M. No. 2541). The base is frequently dispensed with, and the supports are made in the form of the necks of ducks, the ends terminating in their heads and beaks. Such examples have usually the ends of the neck-piece ornamented with carvings of figures of the god Bes (B.M. No. 18,156), and sometimes with grotesque figures (apes?) wearing plumes, and being led along by chains (B.M. No. 2256*c*). Such animals greatly resemble those represented on the Black Obelisk of Shalmaneser II. The column of a

**Ornamentation of pillows.**

wooden pillow is ornamented in various ways, and the name of the deceased is often written upon it in hieratic or hieroglyphics. One example (B.M. No. 2529*a*) is inscribed with lion-

Ushabti figure of Pa-mer-âḥu.

headed gods, , and *ut'at* and *neferu* on the front, a figure of Bes  on the back, and a dog-headed ape holding an eye  on each side. Another example (B.M. 2556*a*) is inscribed on the top of the neck-piece with lotus flowers and an *ut'at* . On each end of the base are also inscribed lotus flowers, and beneath are versions of the 55th, 61st and 62nd chapters of the Book of the Dead; this pillow was made for Āāua, the son of Ḥeru, a prophet of Menthu, lord of Thebes, the son of the lady of the house Nes-Mut. 
. The use of the pillow is very ancient, and goes back at least as far as the VIth dynasty; the beautiful example in alabaster from Abydos now in the British Museum, No. 2533, made for the high official  Àṭenȧ, probably belongs to this period. For the use of models of the pillow as an amulet, see the article "Amulets." Pillows similar in size and shape are in use to this day among the tribes of Nubia, and they are found among the natives in several places along the west coast of Africa; that the ancient Egyptians borrowed them from the peoples of the south is not likely, but that the use of them by the Ethiopians, copied from the Egyptians, spread from the Sûdân southwards is most probable.

**Inscribed pillows.**

**Antiquity of the pillow.**

## USHABTIU FIGURES.[1]

**Ushabtiu,** 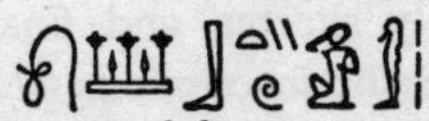 was the name given by the Egyptians to stone, alabaster, wood, clay, and glazed faïence figures of the god Osiris, made in the form of a mummy, which were deposited in the tombs either in wooden boxes or laid along the floor; sometimes they are found lying in the sarcophagi and coffins. They were placed there to do certain agricultural works for the deceased, who was supposed

**The working figures in the under-world.**

[1] Observations on these figures by Birch have appeared in *Aeg. Zeit.*, 1864, pp. 89–103, and 1865, pp. 4–20; Mariette, *Catalogue des Monuments d'Abydos*, pp. 46–48; and by Loret, *Recueil de Travaux*, pp. 90, 91.

to be condemned to sow the fields, to fill the canals with water, and to carry sand from the West to the East. The ushabtiu figures of the XIIIth dynasty are made of granite, wood, and calcareous stone; the last substance was, however, that most commonly used. The use of faïence for this purpose appears not to have been known at that epoch. Generally the hands are crossed over the breast, but sometimes they are covered up in bandages. The hands do not hold any agricultural implements as in the later dynasties; and the inscriptions upon them consist usually of the name and titles of the deceased, and resemble very closely those on the stelæ of this period. The breasts of sepulchral figures of this period are sometimes inscribed with a scarabæus having its wings outspread. Blue, green, brown, and red glazed faïence figures appear during the XVIIIth dynasty, and continue until the XXVIth dynasty, by which time this substance has taken the place of stone, wood, or metal. In this dynasty the figures first begin to carry a hoe, mattock and basket. During the XIXth dynasty the dress of these figures changes, and they are represented as wearing the garments which the people for whom they are made wore during their lifetime. In the XXVIth dynasty these figures still hold the hoe, mattock and basket, and they stand on a square pedestal and have a rectangular upright plinth down the back. They were cast in moulds, and are easily distinguishable by their light bluish-green colour. Between the XXIInd and XXIVth dynasties *ushabtiu* figures seem not to have been placed in the tombs, and after the XXVIth dynasty they are made with less care, the inscriptions grow gradually shorter, and finally the figures become very small and bear no inscriptions whatever.

Description of *ushabtiu* at various epochs.

*Ushabtiu* inscriptions.

*Ushabtiu* figures are generally inscribed with the VIth chapter of the Book of the Dead, which appears on them in three forms; the following, from Mariette, *Catalogue des Monuments d'Abydos*, p. 48, is an example of the first form:—

VIth dynasty.

The second form (Mariette, *Catalogue*, p. 58) reads:—

[name of deceased]
[Here some copies add

XVIIIth dynasty.

The third form, which agrees with the text of the 6th chapter found in papyri of the XXVIth dynasty, reads:—

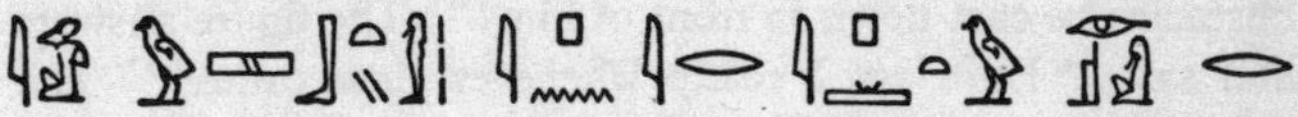

å úsabti åpen år åptu Åusår er
*O* ushabtiu *figures these, if is decreed Osiris to*

XXVIth dynasty.

årit kat nebt årit åm em neter $\chi$ert
*do labours any* [*which*] *are to be done there in the underworld,*

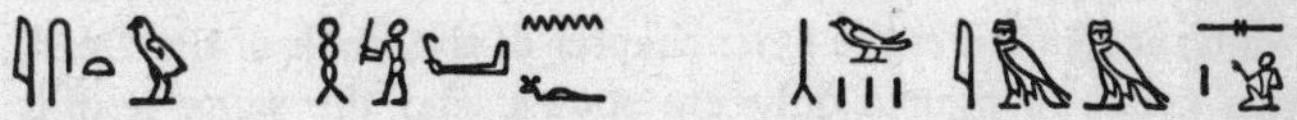

åstu ḥu - nef set'ebu åm em se
*behold, be there smitten down for him obstructions there for a person*

er χert - f māku - å ka - ten

*beneath him. Here am I* [*when*] *call ye.*

åp - tu - ten er ennu neb årit åm er

*Watch ye at moment every to work there, to*

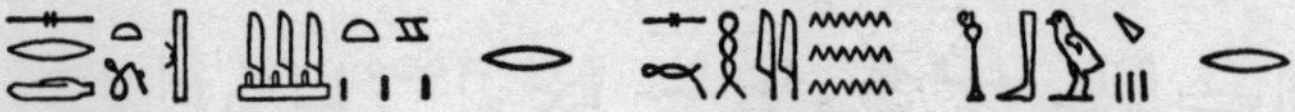

seruṭet seχet er semeḥi ut'ebu er

*plough the fields, to fill with water the canals, to*

χen śā en Åbtet er Åmentet θes rer

*carry sand of the east to west. Again*

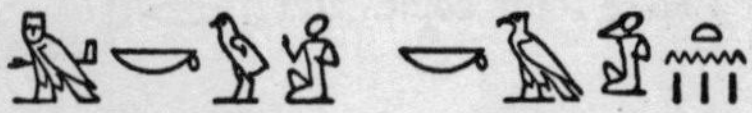

māku - å ka - ten

*here am I* [*when*] *call ye.*

That is to say, the deceased addresses each figure and says, "O *ushabtiu* figures, if the Osiris," that is, the deceased, "is decreed to do any work whatsoever in the underworld, may all obstacles be cast down in front of him!" The figure answers and says, "Here am I ready whenever thou callest." The deceased next says, "O ye figures, be ye ever watchful to work, to plough and sow the fields, to water the canals, and to carry sand from the east to the west." The figures reply, "Here am I ready when thou callest."

The 6th chapter of the Book of the Dead, which also forms a part of the 151st chapter, is part text and part a representation of the chamber in which the deceased in his coffin is laid. In the representation of the funereal chamber which accompanies the 151st chapter of the Book of the Dead, two ushabtiu figures only are shown, and the same text is written by the side of each of them. See Naville, *Das Todtenbuch*, Bl. clxxiii, *Einleitung*, p. 180.

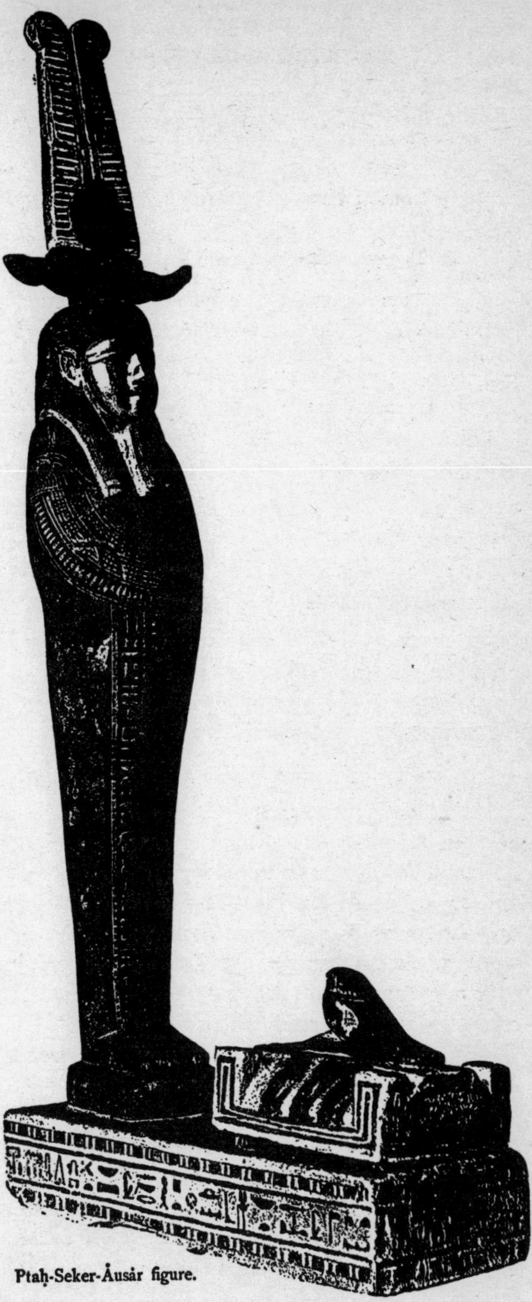

Ptaḥ-Seker-Åusår figure.

**Ushabtiu of the XXVIth and following dynasties.**

*Ushabtiu* figures were placed in tombs in large numbers; in the tomb of Seti I. nearly seven hundred were found. The figure was inscribed, in the later times, after the XXVIth dynasty, and laid in the model of a coffin or sarcophagus made of wood, terra-cotta, or stone. On the coffins were painted figures of the four genii of the underworld, Anubis and other principal sepulchral deities, with appropriate inscriptions, and these models bear a striking resemblance to the coffins made in Egypt from B.C. 500–300. The inscriptions on figures of this period are frequently written in a very cursive and almost illegible hieratic, and in demotic; sometimes, however, they have the form and brevity of those inscribed on the ushabtiu figures of the XIIIth dynasty.

## PTAḤ-SEKER-ÂUSÂR FIGURES.

**Description of figures.**

This name is given to a large class of wooden figures, standing on pedestals, made in the shape of the god Osiris as a mummy. The god wears on his head horns, the disk and plumes , his hands are crossed over his breast, and in them he holds the flail  and crook . The figures are sometimes hollowed out, and contain papyri inscribed with prayers and chapters from a late recension of the Book of the Dead. Frequently the papyri are found in hollows in the pedestals, above which stand small models of funereal chests, surmounted by a hawk; in the hollows portions of the body, mummified, were often placed. Many figures are quite black, having been covered by bitumen; others are painted in the most vivid colours, with blue head-dress with yellow stripes, green, red and yellow collar, face gilded, and body covered with wings of a blue and green colour.

The god Ptaḥ-Seker-Âusâr 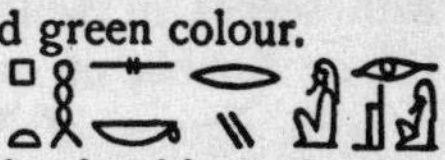 appears on stelæ in company with Osiris, Anubis and other gods of the dead, and he is addressed on figures made in his honour, because he was supposed to be specially connected with the resurrection. He is sometimes represented in the form of Osiris (Lanzone, *Dizionario*, pl. xcvii), and with all the attributes of this god; the other forms in which he appears

Forms of Ptaḥ-Seker-Ȧusȧr.

are:—1. As a little squat boy, with a beetle on his head; and 2. As a hawk wearing a crown and feathers , standing on a throne before which is a table of offerings in a shrine. In this form he is often painted on the outsides of coffins. Behind him is a winged uræus wearing a disk, and *ut'ats* . The inscriptions upon Ptaḥ-Seker-Ȧusȧr figures vary greatly in length; at times they are written in perpendicular lines down the front and back of the figure, and continue round each of the four sides of the pedestal; at others they consist of a very few words. Be the inscription long or short, the deceased prays that Ptaḥ-Seker and Ȧusȧr (Osiris) will give sepulchral meals of oxen, ducks, wine, beer, oil, and wax, and bandages, and every good, pure, and sweet thing to his *ka*. The formulæ of these figures greatly resemble those found on stelæ of a late period. The British Museum possesses a remarkably fine collection of these figures, and as they come from several distinct places, and have many varieties, they are most instructive.

Contents of inscriptions.

## SEPULCHRAL BOXES.

In addition to the chests placed in tombs to hold Canopic vases, the Egyptians made use of a smaller class of wooden boxes to hold *ushabtiu* figures, papyri, articles of dress and other things. They vary in size from six or eight inches to two feet square. Some are made perfectly square, with sides that slant slightly inwards like the pylon of a temple, being higher than they are wide: others are oblong in shape, and each end rises above the level of the cover. Some have two and others four divisions. The outsides are usually ornamented with scenes in which the deceased is represented adoring Rā, or Anubis, or one of the principal gods of the dead, and with figures of Mesthȧ, Ḥāpi, Ṭuamāutef and Qebḥsennuf, painted in bright colours upon a black or white ground. The boxes from Thebes are decorated in the same style as the coffins from that place. Frequently the ornamentation consists of , etc., etc., arranged in symmetrical rows, above them being figures of Osiris, Isis,

Ornamentation of sepulchral boxes.

Nephthys, and other gods of the dead. The inscriptions sometimes resemble those found on chests for Canopic jars, but frequently they contain prayers in which the deceased entreats the gods to give him gifts of cakes, bread, beer, wine, ducks, oxen, wax, oil, bandages, etc., etc. Such inscriptions are at times very brief, at others they cover the whole box.

**Boxes from Akhmîm.**

An interesting class of sepulchral boxes comes from Aḥmîm, the ancient Panopolis, which deserves special mention. The largest of them in the British Museum (No. 18,210) is 3½ feet long and 3 feet high. Each side tapers slightly towards the top, and is in the shape of a pylon. The hollow cornice is ornamented with yellow, black, and red lines upon a white ground. Beneath it are two rows of ornaments: the first is formed by , and the second by  repeated several times. Beneath each line is a row of five-rayed stars . The front of the box is ornamented with  and uræi wearing disks  and a winged disk . Behind is a hawk upon a pedestal, before which is an altar with offerings. On the right hand side is Thoth with both hands raised, pouring out a libation; and on the left is a hawk-headed deity with both hands raised also pouring out a libation. On the back of the box is a hawk, with extended wings, and sceptres . On the right hand side of the box is a figure of the deceased, kneeling, having his left hand raised, and above him are two cartouches . Behind him are three jackal-headed deities, each having his left arm raised, while his right hand is clenched and laid upon his stomach. On the left hand side of the box the deceased is represented in the same attitude, and behind him are three hawk-headed deities. These six gods form the vignettes of the 112th and 113th chapters of the Book of the Dead; the hawk-headed were called Horus, Mesthȧ, and Ḥāpi, and the jackal-headed Horus, Ṭuamāutef and Qebḥsennuf; they are figured in Lanzone, *Dizionario*, Tav. xxvi. In two sides of the box are two pairs of rectangular openings about six inches from each end;[1] the use of these is unknown to me.

[1] For the description of a similar box see my article in *Proc. Soc. Bib. Arch.*, 1886, pp. 120–122.

## FUNEREAL CONES.

**Loaves of bread in the shape of cones.**

This name is given to a large number of burnt terra-cotta conical objects which are found near tombs chiefly at Thebes, in the districts called 'Asâsîf and Ḳûrnah; they were used from the XIth to the XXVIth dynasties. They vary in size, but the ordinary length is ten inches, and the diameter three inches. The face, or flat part, of the cone at its thickest end contains inscriptions in relief which record the name and titles of the person in whose tomb they were found; the inscriptions appear to have been made by a stamp with the characters incuse. The inscribed end of the cone is variously coloured blue, red, or white. Dr. Birch thought[1] that they were used for working into ornamental architecture, or to mark the sites of sepulchres; it is more probable, however, that they are merely models of bread or cakes which were placed in the tomb . It is not likely that they were seals, because they have been found of a rectangular shape with several copies of the same inscription stamped upon them.

## SEPULCHRAL STELÆ OR TABLETS

**Use of stelæ.**

**Stelæ** is the name given to the tablets of granite, calcareous stone, wood, or faïence, which the Egyptians used in large numbers for inscribing with decrees and historical records of the achievements of kings, biographical notices of eminent officials, priests, and private persons, hymns to Rā and other gods, and notices of any events of importance. The greater number, however, of those which have been found belong to the class called sepulchral, and are inscribed with the names and titles of deceased persons, their pedigrees, and the principal events in their lives. They were placed inside tombs, either in the corridor leading to the mummy chamber, or at the door, or at the foot or the head of the bier, or let into the wall; sometimes they are rectangular and sometimes they are rounded at the top. The styles of stelæ, the arrangement of the scenes upon them, and the inscriptions, vary with

**Stelæ of the Ancient Empire.**

[1] Wilkinson, *Ancient Egyptians*, iii: p. 437.

Stele of Åntef, son of Åmen-set.

the different dynasties. From the Ist–VIth dynasty[1] stelæ are rectangular in form, and sometimes are made to resemble the outer façade of a temple. The inscriptions are comparatively short, and merely record the names of the relatives of the deceased who are represented on the stele, and the prayers to Osiris for cakes, bread, meat, wine, oil, milk, wax, bandages, ducks, oxen, etc., which are put into the mouth of the deceased. A remarkable inscription found in a tomb[2] of the VIth dynasty is that of Unȧ, who was born in the reign of Tetȧ, and held service under this king; under Pepi, the successor of Tetȧ, he brought stone from the quarries of Ruāu, and conducted an expedition against the nomad tribes to the east of Egypt, and in the reign of the following king, Mer-en-Rā, he died full of days and honour. During the XIth dynasty the stelæ have many of the characteristics of those of the VIth dynasty, but the execution is better. A large number of the stelæ of the XIIth dynasty are rounded, the inscriptions and scenes are carefully executed, and are often painted with many colours; sometimes on the same stele the figures are in relief, while the inscriptions are incised. As a rule the contents of the inscriptions are repetitions of the titles of the deceased, praises of the king, bald statements of the work he has done for him, prayers to the god for sepulchral meals, and an address to those who pass by the stele to make mention of the dead man in appropriate funereal formulæ. The scenes usually represent the several members of the family of the deceased bringing to him offerings of the various things for which he prays. From the XIIth–XVIIth dynasty, biographies on stelæ[3] are rare. Stelæ of the XIIIth and XIVth dynasties are characterized by their uniformity of colour, when painted; the workmanship is, however, poor, the inscriptions are badly cut, and the hieroglyphics are thin and small. The stelæ of the XVIIIth dynasty are usually rounded at the top, and have

Stelæ of the Middle Empire.

[1] The oldest stele known is preserved at Gîzeh and at Oxford, and was made for Sherȧ, a priest of Senṭ, the fifth king of the IInd dynasty, about B.C. 4000; it is figured in Lepsius, *Auswahl*, Pl. 9.

[2] Compare the interesting inscription published by Schiaparelli, *Una tomba egiziana inedita*, Rome, 1892.

[3] The inscription of Chnemu-ḥetep, one of the most valuable of this period, is inscribed on the walls of his tomb.

very little in common with those of older dynasties. In earlier times the deceased was represented as being surrounded by his parents, brothers and sisters, wife and servants, but at this epoch the gods take their places, and he stands alone before Osiris, god and judge of the dead. In many stelæ of this period the name of the god Åmen has been carefully chiselled out, by order of the "heretic king," Amenophis IV. A remarkable characteristic of stelæ at this time is the length and fulness of the inscriptions upon them. In the earlier times, private matters in the life of the deceased were passed over with little or no mention; now, however, full biographies become the rule, and the inscriptions cover not only the stelæ, but the walls of the chamber in which the mummies were laid. Sometimes such biographies are almost the only authorities for the history of a period, and the inscription of Amāsis is an example of this class of documents. Amāsis was a naval officer who was born about the time of the final war of the Egyptians against the Hyksos, and he was present at the capture of the town of Avaris, during the reign of Amāsis I., king of Egypt. He was specially honoured by this king for his prowess in battle, and he served in various campaigns undertaken by his successors, Amenophis I., and Thothmes I. The stelæ of the XIXth dynasty show a great falling off both in design and execution. The figures of men and women are poor, and their limbs are made out of all proportion to the rest of their bodies. The mode of wearing their clothes, too, has changed, a large portion of the body is entirely covered by the dress, and the figures wear a heavy head-dress, which falls squarely upon the shoulders. The hieroglyphics are carelessly engraved, and lack the spirit which indicates those of the XVIIIth dynasty. During the XXth dynasty the use of stelæ appears not to have been so general, and from about B.C. 1000–650 they almost disappear. The stelæ which belong to this period are few and small, and the designs are generally poor imitations of stelæ of an older date. The cause of this decline is not quite evident, but it may be either the result of the disquietude caused by the unsettled condition of Egypt through foreign invasions, or the consequence of some religious schism. It will be noticed

Stele of Amāsis.

**Stelæ of the New Empire.**

that *ushabtiu* figures, as well as stelæ, become fewer and poorer during this same period. The stelæ of the XXVIth dynasty exhibit the features which are characteristic of the sculptures of this period. They occur in large numbers, they are larger in size, the hieroglyphics are small, but cleanly cut, and they have a beauty which is in itself sufficient to proclaim the time to which they belong. The inscriptions are copied from ancient texts, and as neither the scribe nor the sculptor understood at times what he was writing, frequent mistakes are the result. After the XXVIth dynasty stelæ were made of all possible designs and forms; the hieroglyphics are badly cut, the inscriptions are the ordinary formulæ, in which the deceased prays for sepulchral meals, and it is quite clear that the placing of a stele in the tomb had become a mere matter of form with the greater number of the Egyptians. In Ptolemaic times ancient models were copied, but the inscriptions are as often in Greek or demotic, or both, as in hieroglyphics. Stelæ bearing bilingual inscriptions, in hieroglyphics and Greek, or hieroglyphics and Phœnician, are also known. Subsequently it became the fashion to make the figures of the gods on stelæ in high relief, and the attributes and costumes of Greek gods were applied to those of Egypt.

**Ornamentation of stelæ of the XXVIth dynasty.**

The greater number of the wooden stelæ in European museums belong to the XXVIth and subsequent dynasties. They are rounded at the top, they usually stand upon two pedestals having steps on each side, and they vary in size from 6 in. by 4 in. to 3 ft. by 20 in. The inscriptions and scenes upon them are usually painted in white, green, red, yellow, or black, upon a light or dark brown ground. On the back are at times figures of the sun shedding rays and standards of the east and west. The large tablets have three registers; in the first are the winged disk, with pendent uræi wearing the crowns of the north and south, the jackal-headed gods Anubis and Àp-uat, emblems of "life" and "power", etc.; in the second register are the boat of the sun, in which stand a number of gods, Rā, Horus, Cheperà, Maāt, Anubis, etc., and the deceased, or his soul, kneeling at a table of offerings in front of the boat in adoration of Rā; in the third register the deceased makes adoration to a number of gods, and below this comes the inscription. The smaller, and more numerous, tablets have in the rounded part, the winged disk with pendent uræi, and the inscription 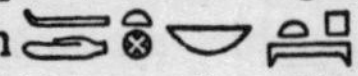 *Beḥuṭet neb pet* "[Horus of] Beḥuṭet, lord of heaven." The scene which follows is divided into two parts: in the one the deceased stands or kneels by the side of an altar in adoration before Rā-Harmachis , and in the other he adores Nefer-Åtmu. Below the scenes are two inscriptions which read from the middle of the tablet to the sides, and contain, the one an address or prayer to Rā when he rises, the other, an address to Rā when he sets. Frequently a tablet is inscribed with the prayer to Rā-Harmachis and Nefer-Åtmu for sepulchral meals.

Inlaid stelæ.

Wooden stelæ were sometimes inlaid with glass figures and hieroglyphics of various colours in imitation of the scenes and inscriptions on tablets of an earlier date. A remarkable example of this class of work is B.M. $\overset{91}{\underset{1}{5\text{—}25}}$ which, according to Dr. Birch, is inscribed with the name of Darius, and represents this king making offerings to Anubis, who is seated on a throne under a winged disk and stars; behind the god is Isis, with horns on her head, and a sceptre in her hand.

Stelæ in glazed faïence.

That sepulchral stelæ were sometimes made of glazed faïence, we know from B.M. No. 6133, a fine example of a light blue colour, in which the deceased Åmen-em-åpt, a royal scribe, is standing in adoration before the god Osiris, who holds a flail and crook. This interesting object was probably made about B.C. 1000, when the art of making glazed faïence of a fine blue or green colour was at its greatest perfection.

## VASES.

The **Vases** found in Egyptian tombs are made of alabaster, diorite, granite, basalt and other kinds of hard stone, steatite, bronze, wood, terra-cotta, faïence, and glass. The shapes of vases are various, but the following are the most common:  Vases were placed in the tombs to contain the offerings of wine, oil, unguents, spices, and other offerings made to the temples, or to the dead in their tombs. Among hard stones capable of receiving a high polish, granite, diorite and alabaster were those most commonly used for making vases. Granite and diorite vases are usually without inscriptions, and were made during all periods of Egyptian history. Vases of alabaster are very much more numerous, and as this material was comparatively easily worked, and readily lent itself to form symmetrical and beautiful shapes, it was a great favourite with the Egyptians. They were sometimes inscribed on the front, the flat part of the rim, or the top of the cover, with inscriptions recording the names and titles of the deceased persons with whom they were buried; thus they are valuable as giving the names of kings and officials of high rank, pedigrees, etc., and as showing at the same time the wonderful skill of the Egyptian alabaster worker at a period nearly four thousand years B.C. Alabaster vases were in use from the IVth–XXVIth dynasty, and the Persian kings had their names inscribed upon them in Egyptian and cuneiform. Arragonite, or zoned alabaster, was used for large vases and liquid measures; a beautiful example of this material is B.M. No. 4839, which has two handles and a cover, and is inscribed with its capacity  "eight *hen* and three quarters." Vases in glazed steatite are not common, and I believe the oldest to be B.M. No. 4762, which is inscribed with the name of Thothmes I., B.C. 1633. Vases in bronze are ancient, tolerably numerous, and of various shapes; among them must be classed those, in the shape of buckets with handles, which are ornamented with scenes in relief, in which the deceased is represented adoring various deities; they belong chiefly to the period of the XXVIth dynasty. *Models* of vases in wood were also made and placed in the tombs. They were sometimes painted to resemble glass (B.M. No. 9529*d*), and were sometimes covered with plaster and gilded, examples of which are B.M. No. 9529*e* and 9529*f*; both were made for the tomb of Rameses II.; the former is inscribed  *uatchu*,

**Use of vases.**

**Value of inscriptions on vases.**

**Models of vases.**

"stibium," and the latter 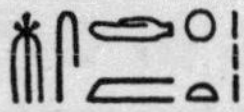 *mesṭemet*, "stibium." The use of glass for vases is very ancient, and Dr. Birch states that [1] the earliest dated example of Egyptian glass is a small dark blue fragment inscribed with the prenomen of Ȧntef III., of the XIth dynasty.

**Glass vases.**

The next oldest example is a small vase or jug with one handle, of a fine turquoise-coloured, opaque glass, ornamented in yellow, with a border round the neck, and three trees round the sides, and inscribed with the prenomen of Thothmes III.,[2] B.C. 1600; the handle has stripes of white and dark blue, and round the neck where it joins the thick part of the vase, is a row of white spots. The vase is $3\frac{1}{2}$ in. high, and its greatest diameter is $1\frac{9}{16}$ in.; the British Museum number is 4762. Vases made of variegated and striped glass are represented on the walls of tombs of the XIXth and XXth dynasties, and it seems that the terra-cotta and wood vases, or models of them, belong to that period. The next oldest examples are the small black, opaque glass vases, ▽, mottled with white spots, which formed part of the funereal paraphernalia of the princess Nesi-Chensu, about B.C. 1000.[3] Transparent glass seems not to have been made in Egypt much earlier than the XXVIth dynasty.

**Vases in glazed faïence.**

Vases in faïence glazed with a blue or green colour are at least as old as the XIXth dynasty; a beautiful example of this date is B.M. No. 4796, with lotus leaves, rosettes, and a line of hieroglyphics around the outer edge, in white or light yellow, upon a lavender-coloured glazed ground. The inscription records the name and titles of Rameses II., about B.C. 1333. About B.C. 1000, small vases ▽ and libation jars ⊽ were glazed with a beautiful light bluish-green; the vases of Nesi-Chensu are fine examples of this work (B.M. No. 17,402, and 13,152). During the XXVIth dynasty flat, circular, convex vases or bottles made of glazed faïence became common; the neck and lip were in the form of the capital of a papyrus column, with an ape at each side, and where the

[1] *Catalogue of the Egyptian Antiquities at Alnwick Castle*, p. 179, and Wilkinson's *Ancient Egyptians*, Vol. II. p. 142.

[2]  "Beautiful god, Men-cheper-Rā, giver of life."

[3] The No. of the B.M. vase is 17,043.

body of the vase joins the neck it is ornamented with rows of inscribed papyrus flowers and pendants. On the upper part of the flat band which goes round the vase, is inscribed 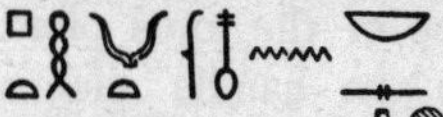 "May Ptaḥ open a happy new year for its owner," and 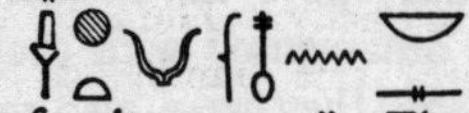 "May Sechet open a happy new year for its owner." These vases were probably given as gifts, and they all appear to come from Lower Egypt. The oldest vases known are made of terra-cotta and red earthenware, and are of various shapes and sizes. They were sometimes glazed or painted and varnished, to imitate porphyry, diorite, and variegated stone and glass, and sometimes they were ornamented with floral designs, figures of animals, geometrical patterns, etc., etc. Vases in this material were inscribed, in hieratic or hieroglyphic, with the names and titles of the persons in whose tombs they were found, and sometimes with sepulchral inscriptions. It is not possible, in the absence of inscriptions, to date terra-cotta vases accurately, and all the evidence forthcoming tends to prove that the various kinds of vases which were thought to belong to the XVIIIth or XIXth dynasty belong to the XXIInd or later.

## Objects for the Toilet.

The Egyptian lady, in making her *toilette*, made use of the following objects:—

**Mirror**, in Egyptian  *un-ḥrå*, "lifting up the face," or  *maa-ḥrå*, "object for seeing the face." The mirror was made of bronze, and in shape was nearly round (B.M. No. 2728*a*), or oval (B.M. No. 2733), or oval flattened (B.M. No. 2732), or pear-shaped (B.M. No. 2728*b*). Mirrors were kept in bronze cases or wooden boxes. The handles were made of ivory (B.M. Nos. 22, 830, 2734), wood, bronze, or faïence (B.M. No. 2736), and were usually in the shape of the lotus in flower . Wooden handles were inlaid with gold (B.M. No. 2728*a*), or were painted with the colours of the lotus plant and flower (B.M. No. 18,179); they

Egyptian mirrors.

**Description of mirrors.**

were sometimes square, and sometimes terminated in a hawk's head (B.M. No. 2733), or they were carved in the shape of a figure of Bes (B.M. No. 2728*b*). Bronze handles of mirrors were also made in the shape of the lotus plant and flower, but the flat space where the handle widens out into the flower was ornamented with the head of Hathor in relief (B.M. No. 2728*a*); they were also made in the form of figures of women, with their arms raised (B.M. Nos. 20,773, 2718*a*). The mirror was further ornamented by supporting the bronze disk on each side with a pair of uræi (B.M. No. 20,756), or with a hawk of Horus (B.M. No. 2731). The metal of which mirrors are made has been shown to be almost pure copper, a very small percentage of tin and other substances being present. The use of mirrors in Egypt appears to be of great antiquity, but the date of their first appearance is not known exactly. The greater diameter of the mirror varies from three to twelve inches.

**Tweezers.** Pairs of tweezers, for removing hairs from the head or face, were made of bronze, the ends being, at times, in the form of human hands; they vary in length from about two to six inches.

**Hair-pins** are usually made of wood, bone, ivory, metal, or alabaster, and vary in length and thickness; the heads are sometimes ornamented with gold and silver bands or heads, and sometimes terminate in the figure of an animal or bird.

**Combs** are made of wood or ivory, and when they have but a single row of teeth the back is carved into serrated edges, and its sides are ornamented with various devices, annular or otherwise. Double combs, *i.e.*, combs with two rows of teeth, have the one row of teeth thicker and longer than the other. Combs used for merely ornamental purposes terminate with figures of animals, etc., etc. The date of the first appearance of combs in Egypt is unknown, and it has been thought that they were not introduced until a comparatively late period.

**Fan.** The feathers of the fan were inserted in a handle made of wood or ivory, or both, having the same shape as the handles of mirrors ; both sides of the handle were sometimes ornamented with heads of Hathor in relief (B.M. No. 20,767).

Stibium vases and tubes.

**Kohl pots.** Of all the necessaries for the toilet these objects are the most commonly found, and the varieties known are very many and very interesting. The object of the *kohl* jar was to hold the *kohl*, or stibium, or antimony, or copper, with which ladies were wont to stain the eyelids and eyebrows. The simplest form consisted of a hollow tube of alabaster, steatite,[1] glass,[2] wood, or ivory, from three to six inches high; alabaster tubes are usually uninscribed (B.M. No. 2574), wooden tubes are made in the shape of a column with a palm leaf capital (B.M. No. 2591), ivory or bone tubes are sometimes made in the form of figures of Bes (B.M. No. 2571), and sometimes are ornamented with spirals (B.M. No. 6184). Faïence tubes are white, blue, or green, and have inscriptions on them in black; fine examples of this class are B.M. No. 2572*b*, inscribed with the prenomen of Amenophis III., and the name of his wife Thi; and B.M. No. 2573, inscribed with the prenomen of Tut-ānch-Åmen, and the name of his wife Ānch-nes-Åmen. B.M. No. 2589, is a fine example of kohl tube in glass, made in the form of a column with a palm leaf capital. Kohl tubes were sometimes made of the common reed, and carried in a leather bag (B.M. No. 12,539); the single tube was sometimes represented as being held by a monkey or some other animal (B.M. No. 21,895). The tube was often formed of a hollow sunk in a jar made of alabaster, stone, steatite, granite, or porphyry; steatite jars are glazed, and ornamented with  and  in hollow work (B.M. No. 2645). Such jars often had the rim, which supported the cover, turned separately, and in the centre of the cover, inside, a small boss was made to enable it to rest firmly on the jar; these jars rested upon square stands supported by four legs. The outsides of porphyry jars are sometimes ornamented with raised figures of apes and uræi. Kohl jars had sometimes two tubes, and

Different forms of stibium vases.

Stibium vases having more than one tube.

[1] B.M. No. 2736 is inscribed  "Menthu-em-ḥāt, son of Ḥeq-āb, lord of watchful devotion."

[2] See B.M. No. 24,391, made of light blue glass banded with gold.

were made of wood, with a movable cover on a pivot (B.M. No. 2595), of obsidian, with a figure of Bes in relief (B.M. No. 2599), of ivory, with each tube in the form of a lotus column (B.M. 22,839), and of stone. Kohl pots with three tubes were also made, and an interesting example in terra-cotta is B.M. No. 2612, which is in the form of a "triple" crown. Kohl pots with four and five tubes are very common in wood, and several examples exist in faïence. B.M. No. 2605 is inscribed on each tube,[1] and contains two, or more, different powders; and B.M. 2606*a*, with five tubes, probably a votive offering by a friend or relative of the deceased Amāsis, a scribe and overseer of works, is inscribed :—

**Different kinds of eye-paint used at different seasons of the year.**

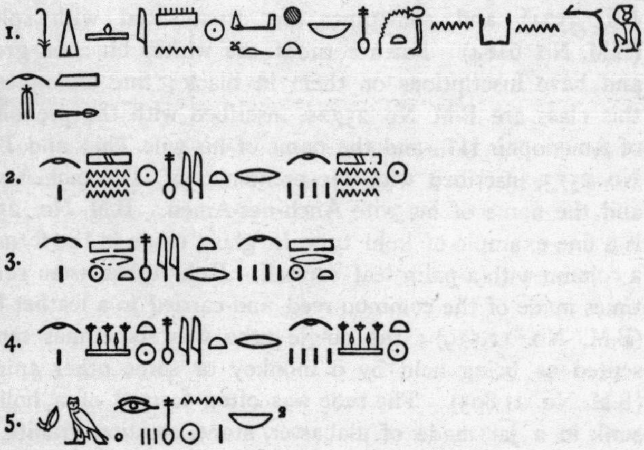

The following texts are inscribed upon a remarkable brown wood stibium-holder, in the possession of Sir Francis Grenfell, G.C.B. It contains five tubes, each of which held

[2] These inscriptions show that one kind of eye-paint was to be used from the first to the fourth month of the inundation season; a second from the first to the fourth month of the season of coming forth; a third from the first to the fourth month of the period of growing; and also that a fourth was to be used every day.

a different coloured substance; on one side is a full-face figure of Bes, and on the other an ape. It came from Dêr el-baḥari.

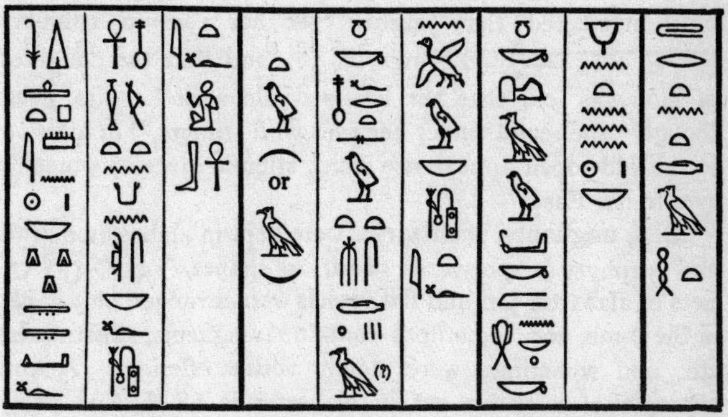


A set of four or more kohl tubes were also formed by the compartments of a wooden box which was generally inlaid with ivory. The studs in kohl tubes were used for fastening the cover.

**The *kohl* stick.**

The stick with which the kohl was applied to the eyes was made of wood, bronze, glass, etc., and was thicker and more rounded at one end than at the other. The thick end was moistened, and dipped in the powder in the tube, and then drawn along the eyelid; the stick generally remained in the tube, but often a special cavity, either between or behind the tubes, was prepared for it.

The black powder in the tube was called in Egyptian *mesṭem* (var. *mest'emut*), Copt. ⲥⲑⲏⲙ, ⲥⲧⲏⲙ, Arab. كحل, whence the word *Kohl*, Gr. στίμμι, stibium; it seems to have been the sesquisulphuret of antimony, but sulphide of lead, oxide of copper, black oxide of manganese, and other powdered substances were also used. The act of painting the eyes with kohl was called *semṭet*, and the part painted *semti*. The custom of painting the eyelids, or the parts immediately under them, is contemporary with the earliest dynasties,

Antiquity of use of eye-paint.

and we know that in the XIIth dynasty[1] *mestchem* was brought from the land of Ȧbsha, by people of the Āāmu, as an acceptable gift to the king of Egypt. This custom seems to have been common all over the East, and it will be remembered that Jezebel "set her eyes in stibium" (וַתָּשֶׂם בַּפּוּךְ עֵינֶיהָ 2 Kings ix. 30), and that the daughter of Zion was told that her lovers would seek her life, even though "she rent asunder her eyes with stibium,"[2] in allusion to the wide open appearance which stibium gives to women's eyes in the East.

**Oils, unguents, scents,** etc., were kept in alabaster, diorite and porphyry jars, or vases, of various shapes, 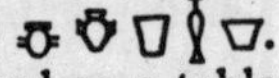. Sets of alabaster jars and flat vessels were arranged on a table in the tomb, and sometimes contained unguents, sweetmeats, etc., and sometimes were merely votive offerings. A fine example of a votive set in alabaster is (B.M. No. 4694) inscribed with the name Ȧtenā, from Abydos, which comprises a wide mouthed jar on a stand, five smaller jars with pointed ends, and four flat saucers, the whole standing on a circular table of the same material. The shapes of the jars are of great beauty, and the alabaster is of the finest. The custom of placing alabaster jars in tombs is, at least, as ancient as the IVth dynasty, and it lasted until the XXVIth dynasty; examples are known inscribed with the names of Unȧs (B.M. No. 4602), Pepi I. (B.M. No. 22559), Mentu-em-sa-f (B.M. No. 4493), Amāsis I. (B.M. No. 4671*a*), Thothmes III. (B.M. No. 4498), Amenophis II. (B.M. No. 4672), Rameses II. (B.M. No. 2880), Queen Ȧmenȧrṭās (B.M. No. 4701), etc.

Alabaster vases of Ȧtenā.

## Necklaces, Rings, Bracelets, etc.

Judging by the enormous quantity of beads which are found in Egyptian tombs, Egyptian ladies must have thought very highly of the necklace as an ornament. Beads are of all shapes, round, rectangular, oval, and oblong, and were made of

[1] In the sixth year of Usertsen II. The scene of the presentation of the *mestchem* is painted on the walls of the tomb of Chnemu-ḥetep at Beni-Hasân; *see* Lepsius, *Denkmäler*, II. ff. 131–133.

[2] כִּי־תִקְרְעִי בַפּוּךְ עֵינַיִךְ Jeremiah iv. 30.

mother-of-emerald, carnelian, agate, lapis-lazuli, amethyst, rock crystal, onyx, jasper, garnet, gold, silver, glass, faïence, clay, and straw. The necklace was ornamented with pendants made in the form of figures of the gods, or of animals sacred to them, or of amulets to which magical powers were attributed. Each kind of stone was supposed to possess special properties, and the Egyptians arranged their necklaces in such a way that the wearer was supposed to be protected from the attack of all evil powers and baneful beasts. Breasts of mummies and mummy cases are painted in imitation of rows of beads of various precious stones, or of collars made of beads, interspersed with pendants in the shape of flowers, etc.

**Egyptian jewellery.**

Rings were made of gold, silver, bronze, precious stones or faïence; sometimes the bezels were solid and did not move, sometimes they were inlaid with scarabs, inscribed with various devices, or the name of the wearer, and revolved. During the XVIIIth dynasty, a very pretty class of ring was made at Tell el-Amarna, in blue, green, and purple glazed faïence; examples are very numerous, and every Egyptian collection of importance contains several.

Bracelets were made of gold or silver, and were at times inlaid with precious stones and coloured paste; after the XXVIth dynasty the ends of bracelets, owing to Phœnician influence, terminated in lions' heads.

## Scarab.

**Description of Egyptian beetle.**

**Scarab**,[1] or Scarabæus,[2] is the name given by Egyptologists to the myriads of models of a certain beetle, which are found in mummies and tombs, and in the ruins of temples and other buildings in Egypt and other countries, the inhabitants

[1] Scarab, from the Greek *σκάραβος*, or *σκαράβειος*, perhaps a transcription of the Latin *scarabaeus*; compare *δηνάριον*, a transcription of *denarius*. The Copts called this beetle ϭⲁⲗⲟⲩⲕⲥ, and the Arabs خُنْفُسَآء, plur. خَنَافِس, جُعَل, plur. جِعْلَان and ذُرَّاح, plur. ذَرَارِيح. See also Payne Smith, *Thes. Syr.*, col. 1188, and Duval, *Lex. Syr.*, col. 714.

[2] The old plural *scarabees* we find in "You are scarabees that batten in dung." *Elder Brother*, Beaumont and Fletcher.

of which from a remote period had trading and other relations with the Egyptians. The beetle which was copied by the Egyptians in this manner belongs to the family called by naturalists *Scarabæidæ* (Coprophagi), of which the *Scarabæus sacer* is the type. These insects compose a very numerous group of dung-feeding Lamellicorns, of which, however, the majority are inhabitants of tropical countries. The species are generally of a black hue; but amongst them are to be found some adorned with the richest metallic colours. A remarkable peculiarity exists in the structure and situation of the hind legs, which are placed so near the extremity of the body, and so far from each other, as to give the insect a most extraordinary appearance when walking.

**Habits of the Egyptian beetle.**

This peculiar formation is, nevertheless, particularly serviceable to its possessors in rolling the balls of excrementitious matter in which they enclose their eggs; whence these insects were named by the first naturalists Pilulariæ. These balls are at first irregular and soft, but, by degrees, and during the process of rolling along, become rounded and harder; they are propelled by means of the hind legs. Sometimes these balls are an inch and a half, or two inches in diameter, and in rolling them along the beetles stand almost upon their heads, with the heads turned from the balls. These manœuvres have for their object the burying of the balls in holes, which the insects have previously dug for their reception; and it is upon the dung thus deposited that the larvæ, when hatched, feed. It does not appear that these beetles have the instinct to distinguish their own balls, as they will seize upon those belonging to another, in case they have lost their own; and, indeed, it is said that several of them occasionally assist in rolling the same ball. The males as well as the females assist in rolling the pellets. They fly during the hottest part of the day.[1] Latreille, in the Appendix to Cailliaud's *Voyage à Méroé*, Paris, 1823–27,[2]

[1] See J. O. Westwood, *An Introduction to the Modern Classification of Insects;* London, 1839, Vol. I. p. 204 ff.

[2] Tom. ii. p. 311. "Cet insecte est d'un vert parfois éclatant; son corselet est nuancé d'une teinte cuivreuse à reflet métallique." Compare Ælian, *De Nat. Animal.*, iv. 49; Aristotle, *Hist. Animal.*, iv. 7; Pliny, *Nat. Hist.*, xi. 20 ff., and xxix. 6.

considers the species which he has named *Ateuchus Aegyptiorum*, or ἡλιοκάνθαρος, and which is of a fine greenish colour, as that which especially engaged the attention of the early Egyptians; and Dr. G. W. Clarke affirms that it is eaten by the women of Egypt because it is considered an emblem of fertility. Horapollo, and other[1] ancient writers, state that a female scarabæus does not exist. According to Horapollo (ed. Leemans, p. 11), a scarabæus denotes an *only begotten*,[2] *generation*, *father*, *world*, and *man*. It represents an *only begotten*, because the scarabæus is a creature self-produced, being unconceived by a female. The male, when desirous of procreating, takes some ox dung, and shapes it into a spherical form like the world. He next rolls it from east to west, looking himself towards the east. Having dug a hole, he buries it in it for twenty-eight days; on the twenty-ninth day he opens the ball, and throws it into the water, and from it the scarabæi come forth. The idea of *generation* arises from its supposed acts. The scarabæus denotes a *father* because it is engendered by a father only, and *world* because in its generation it is fashioned in the form of the world, and *man* because there is no female race among them. Every scarabæus was also supposed to have thirty toes, corresponding with the thirty days' duration of the month.[3] Latreille thinks that the belief that one sex only existed among scarabæi arose from the fact that the females are exceedingly like the males, and that both sexes appear to divide the care of the preservation of their offspring equally between them.

Description of the beetle by Horapollo.

[1] Ὁ κάνθαρος ἄθηλυ ζῶόν ἐστι, Aelian, *De Natura Animal.*, x. xv. ed. Didot, p. 172, Κάνθαρος γὰρ πᾶς ἄῤῥην, Porphyry, *De Abstinentia*, iv. 9, ed. Didot, p. 74.

[2] For the word *scarabeus* applied to Christ compare, "Vermis in cruce: scarabeus in cruce: et bonus vermis qui haesit in ligno bonus scarabeus qui clamavit è ligno. Quid clamavit? *Domine, ne statuas illis hoc peccatum.* Clamavit latroni: *Hodie mecum eris in paradiso.* Clamavit quasi scarabeus: *Deus, Deus meus, quare me dereliquisti?* Et bonus scarabeus qui lutum corporis nostri ante informe ac pigrum virtutum versabat vestigiis: bonus scarabeus, qui de stercore erigit pauperem." See the exposition of St. Luke, by Ambrose, Bishop of Milan (*Opera*, Paris edition, 1686, tom. I. col. 1528, No. 113).

[3] "En comptant pour un doigt chaque article des tarses, on reconnaîtra que cet insecte avait été bien attentivement examiné." Mulsant, *Histoire Naturelle des Coléoptères de France*, Lamellicornes; Paris, 1842, p. 48.

**Egyptian name for the beetle.**

The Egyptians called the scarabæus 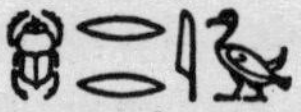 *Chepera*, and the god whom this insect represented was called 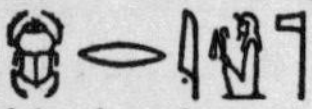 *Cheperà.* This god usually wears a beetle on his head, and sometimes he has a beetle, with or without outstretched wings, in the place of a head.[1] The god

**The scarab an emblem of Cheperà.**

Cheperà was the "father of the gods," and the creator of all things in heaven and earth. He made himself out of the matter which he himself produced. He was identified with the rising sun, and thus typified resurrection and new birth generally. The word 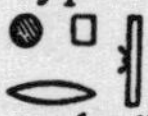 which is usually translated "to exist, to become, to make," also means "to roll," and the "roller," or "revolver," was a fitting name for the sun, according to the Egyptian ideas of that luminary. The abstract noun  *cheperu*, may very well be rendered by "evolutions."

**Classes of scarab.**

Scarabs may, for convenience of consideration, be divided into three classes:—1. Funereal scarabs; 2. Scarabs worn for ornament; 3. Historical scarabs. Of the first class the greater number found measure from half to two inches in length, and they are made generally of faïence or steatite, glazed blue or green; granite, basalt, jasper, amethyst, lapis-lazuli, ruby, carnelian, and in the Roman period glass also, are often used. Upon the flat base of the scarab the Egyptians engraved the names of gods, kings, priests, officials, private persons, monograms, and floral and other devices. Sometimes the base of the scarab takes the form of a heart, and sometimes the scarab is united with the *u'tat* 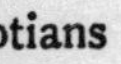, or eye of Horus; it is also found united with a frog, the emblem of "myriads" and of "revivification." Rarely the back of the scarab is ornamented with a pattern made up of a number of small scarabs. Such small scarabs were set in rings, and placed upon the fingers of the dead, or were wrapped up in the linen bandages with which the mummy was swathed over the heart. They represented the belief of the Egyptians in the revivification of the body, and

[1] See Lanzone, *Dizionario*, pl. cccxxix.

in the renewed life after death, which was typified by the Sun, who renewed his life daily.

*Description of funereal scarab.* Among funereal scarabs must be mentioned those of green basalt, which were specially made to be laid upon the breasts of mummies. Of this class there are many varieties, but the form most approved by the Egyptians seems to have consisted of a scarab of fine, hard basalt, let into a gold border, to which was attached a fine gold wire for hanging round the neck. The folds of the wings of the beetles were indicated either by lines of gold painted on the back, or by pieces of gold inlaid therein. Occasionally, the scarab itself is let into a mount of solid gold (B.M. No. 7876), and sometimes the scarab is joined to a heart, and pierced for suspension, the heart being ornamented with hieroglyphics meaning "life, stability, and protection"  (B.M. No. 7925). On the back of the scarab we at times have a figure of a *bennu* bird and the inscription 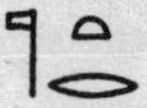  "the mighty heart of Rā" (B.M. No. 7878), at others the boat of the Sun , *ut'ats* , the *bennu* or phœnix , and Rā (B.M. No. 7883); and sometimes the scarab is human-headed (B.M. Nos. 15,516 and 7999). One instance is known where the back of the scarab is ornamented with incised figures of Greek deities (B.M. No. 7966). In late times this class of scarab was made of blue and green faïence, and inserted in pectorals of the same material, upon which were painted the boat of the sun, and figures of Isis and Nephthys, one at each end of the boat; the scarab occupied the middle of the boat (B.M. Nos. 7864 and 7865). The bases of large funereal scarabs were usually inscribed with the text of the 30th chapter of the Book of the Dead, but this was not always the case. Some scarabs have only scenes of the deceased adoring Osiris (B.M. No. 7931), and others figures of Osiris, Isis, and Nephthys (B.M. Nos. 7930, 15,500 and 15,507). *Description of funereal scarabs.* At times the inscriptions are merely written with gold or ink (B.M. Nos. 7915 and 15,518). As such scarabs formed part of the stock-in-trade of the Egyptian undertaker, the names

of the persons with whom they were buried are not found inscribed upon them, although blank spaces are left (B.M. No. 7877); frequently scarabs have neither figures nor inscriptions upon their bases. A remarkable example of funereal scarab is B.M. No. 18,190, which was taken from the mummy of Thothmes III., found at Dêr el-Baḥari. This object is made of steatite, glazed a greenish (purple in some places) colour. A frame of gold runs round the base, the two sides of which are joined by a band of the same metal across the back; a thin layer of gold covered the back, but parts of this are hidden by the remains of the mummy cloth which adhere to it. The base is inscribed with a figures of Thothmes III., kneeling; on his head is the crown , in the right hand he holds the whip , and with the left he is making an offering. Before him is a dog (?) seated, and behind him a hawk. Above is the sign  *nefer*, and the legend "Rā-men-cheper, triumphant before the gods for ever." 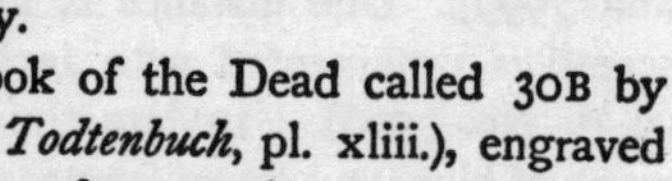
The surface of the base was covered with a layer of gold, parts of which still remain. This scarab is 3 inches long. On the upper end of the gold frame was a loop by which the scarab, by means of a chain, was attached to a bronze collar round the neck of the mummy.

**The chapters of the heart.**

The chapter from the Book of the Dead called 30B by M. Naville (*Das Aegyptische Todtenbuch*, pl. xliii.), engraved upon scarabs, is one of a series of seven chapters, relating to the heart, which are entitled:—

Chap. 26. Chapter of giving a heart to N.[1] in the underworld.

Chaps. 27, 28 and 29. Chapter of not allowing his heart to be carried off from him in the underworld.

Chap. 29B. Another chapter of a heart of carnelian.

Chaps. 30A and 30B. Chapter of not allowing to be repulsed the heart of N. in the underworld. According to a papyrus in Berlin, *Ba* in Naville's edition, chap. 26 is entitled "Chapter of a heart of lapis-lazuli (

[1] N. = name of the person for whom the scarab or papyrus was made.

*chesbeṭ*)"; chap. 27, "Chapter of a heart of opal (?), ([1] *neshem*)"; chap. 29 B, "Chapter of a heart of carnelian (?) ( *sehert*)"; and chap. 30 B, "Chapter of a heart of green jasper ( *meḥt*)." The most important of these chapters is the 30th, which exists in two different versions, called 30 A and 30 B, but it appears that the former was never inscribed upon scarabs. According to the rubric found in a papyrus at Parma (see Naville, *Todtenbuch*,[2] Bd. ii. bl. 99), this chapter was found during the reign of Mycerinus in Hermopolis, under the feet of the majesty of this god, by Ḥeru-ṭā-ṭā-f his son.

This interesting text reads:—

The finding of a chapter of the heart.

meṭ ḥer χeper en meḥ - f mesesbeb em
*To be said over a scarab of green jasper bound round with*

smu ānt - f em ḥet' erṭāu en
smu *metal, ring its [being] of silver, to be placed on*

χu er χeχ - f qementu re pen em
*a blessed one*[3] *over throat his. Was found chapter this in*

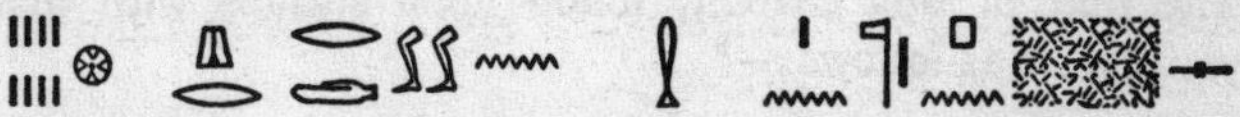

χemennu χer reṭ en ḥen en neter pen -s
*Hermopolis under the feet of the majesty of god this,* {*[inscribed was] it*}

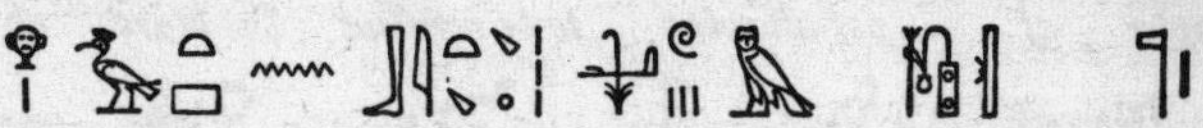

ḥer ṭebt en bȧt qemāu em nā neter
*upon a slab of steel of the south with the writing of the god*

[1] Quoted by Birch in *Aeg. Zeitschrift*, 1867, p. 17.
[2] First published by Birch in *Aeg. Zeitschrift*, 1867, p. 54.
[3] *I.e.*, the deceased.

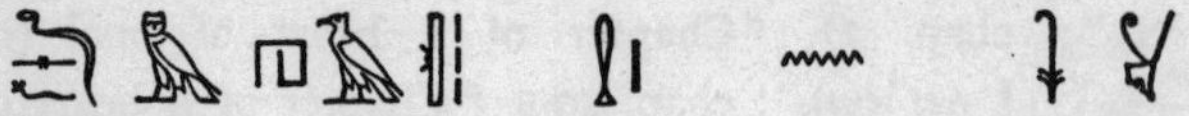

t'esef em ha ḥen en suten net

*himself in the time of the majesty of the* {*King of the North and South,*}

Rā-men-kau maātχeru ȧn suten se Ḥeru - ṭā - ṭā - f

{*Men-kau-Rā (Mycerinus)*} *triumphant, by the royal son Ḥeru - ṭāṭā - f.*

qem su em ua - f er ȧrit sȧp

*Found he it on way his to make inspection*

em er pau

*of the temples.*

According to some copies of the 30th, or 64th chapter,[1] at the end of which this statement is sometimes added, it was found during the reign of Ḥesep-ti, the fifth king of the first dynasty.

The chapter of the heart.

Chapter 30 B belongs to the Psychostasia, in which the heart of the dead man is weighed against the feather, , emblematic of Law; in the vignette which sometimes accompanies this chapter, the deceased is seen being weighed against his own heart, in the presence of Osiris, the pointer of the scales being watched by the cynocephalus ape of Thoth. The text of this chapter, found upon scarabs with many variants, is as follows :—[2]

re en tem erṭāt χesef ȧb en

*Chapter of not allowing to be repulsed the heart of*

[Name]

em neter χert t'eṭ - f ȧb - ȧ en

{Here comes name of deceased} *in the underworld. Says he, " O Heart mine of*

[1] Goodwin, *On a text of the Book of the Dead belonging to the Old Kingdom*, in *Aeg. Zeitschrift*, 1866, p. 55; Lepsius, *Das Todtenbuch*, p. 12.

[2] Naville, *Das Todtenbuch*, bl. xliii.

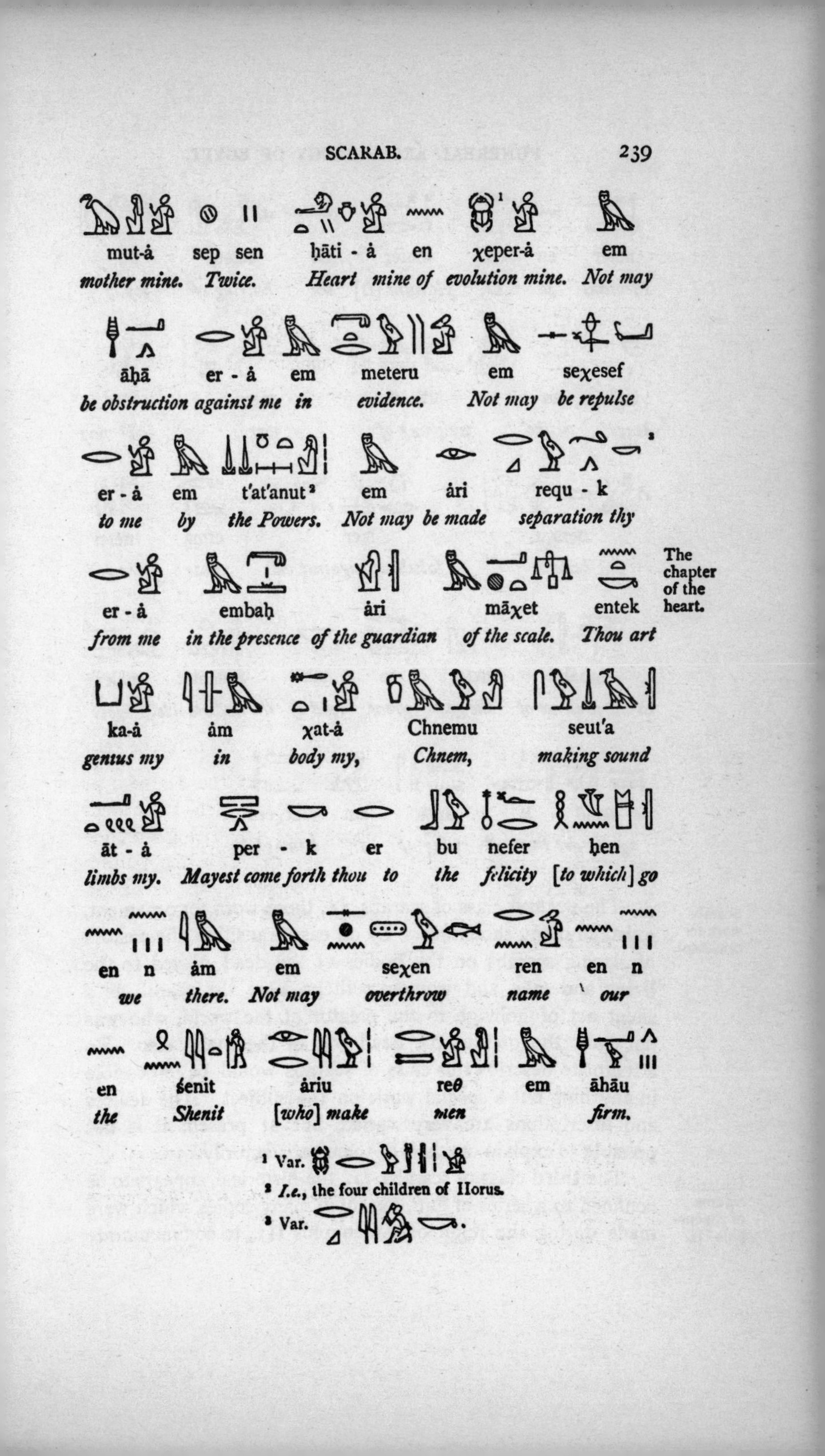

mut-à sep sen ḥāti - à en χeper-à[1] em
*mother mine. Twice. Heart mine of evolution mine. Not may*

āḥā er - à em meteru em seχesef
*be obstruction against me in evidence. Not may be repulse*

er - à em t'at'anut[2] em àri requ - k[3]
*to me by the Powers. Not may be made separation thy*

er - à embaḥ àri māχet entek
*from me in the presence of the guardian of the scale. Thou art*

The chapter of the heart.

ka-à àm χat-à Chnemu seut'a
*genius my in body my, Chnem, making sound*

āt - à per - k er bu nefer ḥen
*limbs my. Mayest come forth thou to the felicity [to which] go*

en n àm em seχen ren en n
*we there. Not may overthrow name our*

en šenit àriu reθ em āhāu
*the Shenit [who] make men firm.*

[1] Var.

[2] *I.e.*, the four children of Horus.

[3] Var.

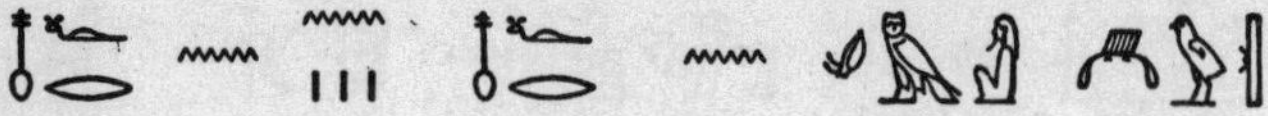

nefer en n nefer en setem āu

*Pleasant to us, pleasant* [*is*] *the hearing of joy of*

àb en ut'ā meṭu em

*heart at the weighing of words. Not may*

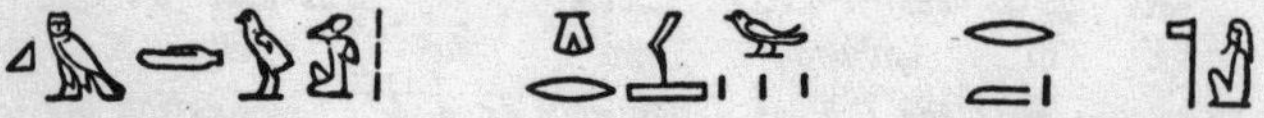

qemṭu ḳer erma neter

*be told falsehood* [*against me*] *near the god,*

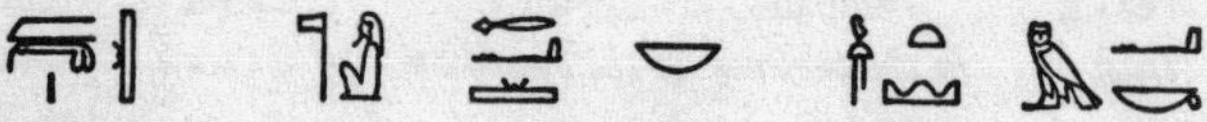

embaḥ neter āa neb Àmentet māk

*in the presence of the god great, lord of the underworld. How*

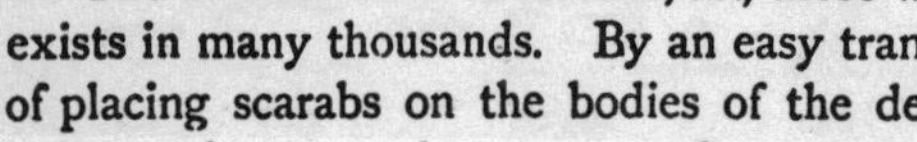

θenθ - k unθà em mātχeru

*great art thou rising up in triumph!"*

The **second** class of scarabs, *i.e.*, those worn for ornament, exists in many thousands. By an easy transition, the custom of placing scarabs on the bodies of the dead passed to the living, and men and women perhaps wore the scarab as a silent act of homage to the creator of the world, who was not only the god of the dead but of the living also. To attempt to describe this class of scarabs would be impossible in anything but a special work on the subject. The devices and inscriptions are very varied, but at present it is not possible to explain one half of them satisfactorily.

**Scarabs worn for ornament.**

The **third** class of scarabs, *i.e.*, the historical, appears to be confined to a series of four, extant in many copies, which were made during the reign of Amenophis III., to commemorate

**Historical scarabs of Amenophis III.**

certain historical events. They are of considerable interest, and the texts inscribed upon them refer to :—

I. The slaughter of 102 lions by Amenophis III., during the first ten years of his reign ; the text reads :—

1. 

ānχ Ḥeru ka neχt χā em maāt
*May live the Horus, bull powerful, diademed with law,*

2. 

. . . . . semen hepu sekerḥ taui
{*lord of North and South*}, *establisher of laws, pacifier of the two lands,*

Ḥeru nub āa χepeś ḥu sati
*Horus the golden, mighty of valour, smiter of foreign lands,*

4. 

suten net Neb-maāt-Rā se Rā en χat-f
{*King of the North and South,*} *Neb-maāt-Rā, son of the sun, of body his,*

5. 

Åmen-ḥetep ḥeq Uast ṭā ānχ suten ḥemt θi
*Amenḥetep, prince of Thebes, giver of life,* [*and*] *royal spouse Thi.*

er χet mau ån en ḥen-f em satet-f
*In respect of lions, brought majesty his from shooting his*

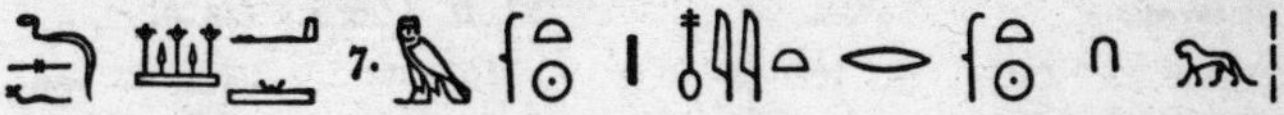

t'esef śaā em renpit uā neferit er renpit met' mau lions
*own, beginning from year first up to year tenth, lions*

Historical scarabs of Amenophis III.

8. 

ḥesau śaā sen
*fierce, one hundred and two.*

II. The limits of the Egyptian Empire, and the names of the parents of Thi, wife of Amenophis III.; the text reads:—

1. 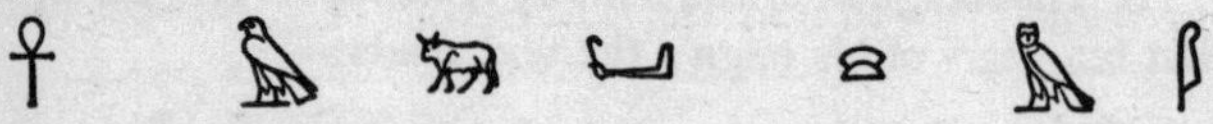

ānχ Ḥeru ka neχt χā em maāt
*May live the Horus, bull powerful, diadmed with law*

Historical scarabs of Amenophis III.

2 

. . . . semen hepu sekerḥ taui
{*lord of the North and South,*} *establisher of laws, pacifier of the two lands,*

3. 

Ḥeru nub āa χepeś ḥu Sati
*Horus the golden, mighty of valour, smiter of foreign lands,*

suten net Neb-maāt-Rā se Rā Åmen-ḥetep ḥeq Uast
{*King of the North and South,*} *Neb-maāt-Rā, son of the Sun,* {*Åmen-ḥetep prince of Thebes,*}

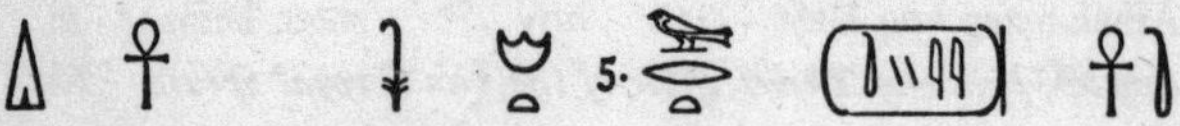

ṭā ānχ suten ḥemt urt θi ānχθ
*giver of life,* [*and*] *royal spouse, mighty lady, Thi, living one—*

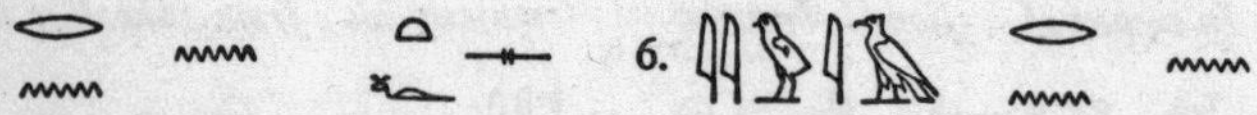

ren en tef - s Iuåa ren en
*the name of father her* [*was*] *Iuåa, the name of*

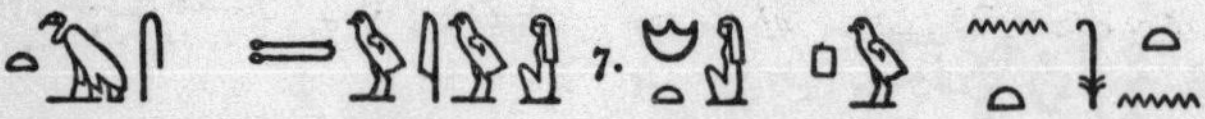

mut-s θuåu ḥemt pu ent suten
*mother her* [*was*] *Thuau— the wife to wit of the king*

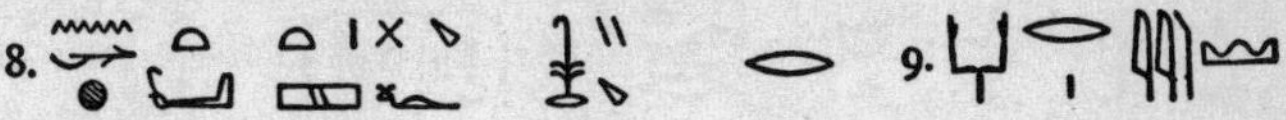

ne$\chi$t — teś-f — resi — er — Karei

*powerful. Frontier his south [is] as far as Karei,*[1] *[frontier]*

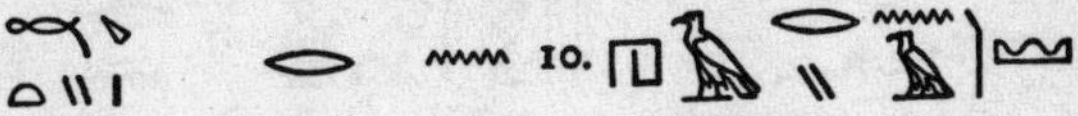

meḥt — er — N - harina

*north [his is] as far as Neharina.*[2]

III. The arrival of the bride of Amenophis III. in Egypt from Mesopotamia, with three hundred and seventeen of her women; the text reads:—[3]

Historical scarabs of Amenophis III.

renpit met' $\chi$er ḥen en Ḥeru ka ne$\chi$t $\chi$ā

*Year tenth under the majesty of Horus, bull powerful, diademed*

em maāt . . . . . semen hepu sekerḥ

*with law,* {*lord of North and South,*} *establisher of laws, pacifier of*

taui Ḥeru nub āa $\chi$epeś ḥu

*the two lands, Horus the golden, mighty of valour, smiter of*

Sati suten net neb āri $\chi$et

*foreign countries,* {*King of the North and South,*} *the lord making things,*

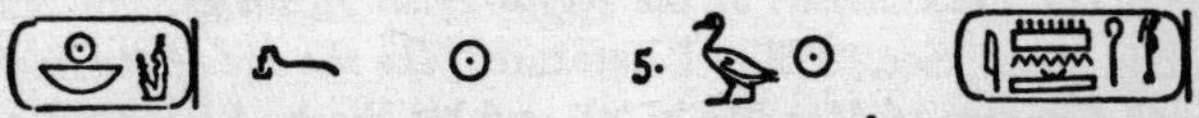

Neb-maāt-Rā, setep Rā se Rā Āmen-ḥetep ḥeq Uast

*Neb-maāt-Rā, chosen of the sun, son of the Sun,* {*Āmen-ḥetep, prince of Thebes,*}

[1] The land south of Nubia. [2] *I.e.*, ܒܝܬ ܢܗܪܝܢ Mesopotamia.

[3] Published by Brugsch, *Aeg. Zeitschrift*, 1880, p. 82.

ţā   ānχ   suten   ḥemt   urt   6.   θi   ānχθ

*giver of life, royal spouse, mighty lady,   Thi,   the living one—*

Historical
scarabs
of Ameno-
phis III.

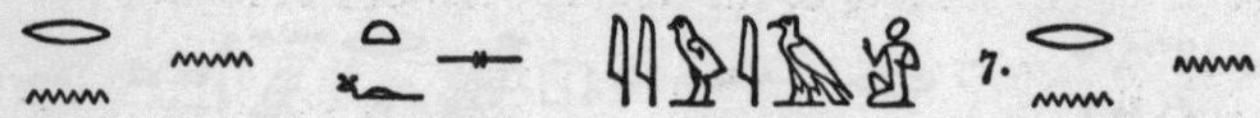

ren   en   tef-s   Iuȧa   7.   ren   en

*the name   of   father her [was]   Iuȧa,   the name   of*

mut-s   θuȧa   bait   ȧn - it   en

*mother her [was]   Thuȧa.   A wonderful thing they brought   to*

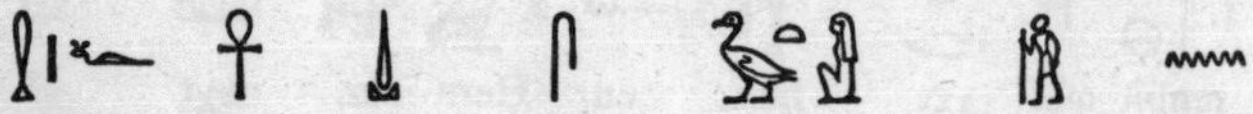

ḥen-f   ānχ   ut'a   senb   set   ser   en

*majesty his, life, strength, health, the daughter of the prince of*

Neherna   9.   Saθȧrna   Kirḳipa

*Mesopotamia,   Satharna,   Kirḳipa*

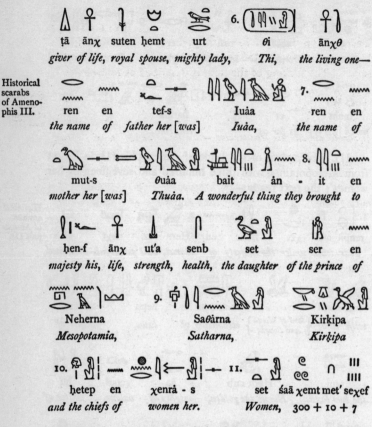

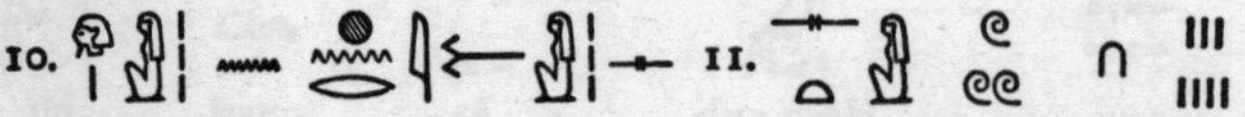

10.   ḥetep   en   χenrȧ - s   11.   set   śaā χemt met' seχef

*and the chiefs of   women her.   Women,   300 + 10 + 7*

IV. The construction of the lake of Queen Thi in the
eleventh year of the reign of Amenophis. The text of this
scarab was first published in Rosellini, *Monumenti Storici*, tav.
xliv. No. 2. It was partly translated by Rosellini, then by
Hinks (in *Transactions of the Royal Irish Academy*, vol. xxi.
Dublin, 1848, Sec. "Polite Literature," *On the age of the Eigh-
teenth Dynasty of Manetho*, p. 7), and by Birch, *Records of the
Past*, Vol. XII. p. 41. The text printed below is corrected
from Stern's copy in *Aeg. Zeitschrift*, 1887, p. 87, note 2. The
scarab is dated in the first day, the third month of sowing [1]

---

[1] Hathor.

of the eleventh year of Amenophis III., . The first few lines of the inscription containing the king's titles are the same as the beginning lines of the scarabs of the series. The making of the tank is described as follows:—

Historical scarabs of Amenophis III.

utu ḥen-f árit mer en suten ḥemt
*Ordered majesty his the making of a lake for the royal spouse,*

urt θi em ṭemȧ-s en T'āru[1] ....
*mighty lady, Thi in town her (?) of T'āru ....*

āu - f meḥ āb - f meḥ
*Length its [was] cubits* 3000 + 600, *breadth its cubits* 600.

ȧri en ḥen - f ḥeb tep śet em
*Made majesty his festival of the entrance of the waters on*

ȧbeṭ χemt śat hru met'-sas χent ḥen - f en
*month third of sowing,*[2] *day sixteen. Sailed majesty his in*

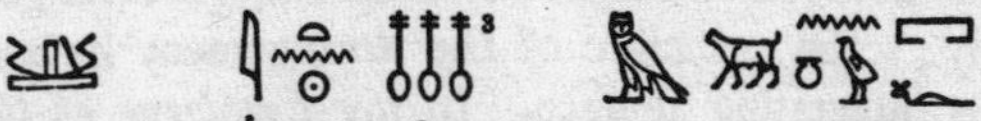

uȧa Āten - neferu[3] em - χennu-f
*the boat* {"*Āten-neferu*" (i.e., "*Disk of Beauties*")} *within it.*

Inscriptions on scarabs.

Of the inscriptions found on scarabs by far the greater number consists of the names of kings. Names of priests and ladies who took part in the services connected with the

[1]  T'āruχa (?).

[2] Hathor.

[3] Stern 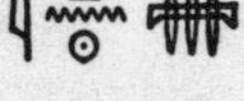 *ȧten teχen*, "disk of saffron."

various gods are common enough; so also are those of the singers of Åmen-Rā. Scarabs inscribed with the names of kings are important historically, because sometimes they form nearly the only memorials of kings and royal personages, and they fill up gaps in the lists of kings of Egypt of whom, otherwise, nothing would be known. The names of the kings most commonly found are Thothmes III., Amenophis III. and Rameses II., and of these that of Thothmes III. is the commonest. The use of the scarab by the Egyptians to denote the idea of resurrection is probably as old as their settlement in the Nile Valley, and scarabs are found inscribed with the names of nearly every king of every dynasty, beginning with that of Menå, the first king of the first dynasty, and ending with that of the Roman Emperor Antoninus.

Publication of Catalogue of Scarabs by Birch.

The first published classification of scarabs was made by the late Dr. Birch in his *Catalogue of the collection of Egyptian Antiquities at Alnwick Castle*,[1] pp. 103–167, 236–242, in which he described 565 objects of this class. The arrangement he followed in this subdivision was:—1. Names of mythological personages and emblems. 2. Historical inscriptions, names of kings, and historical representations. 3. Titles of officers.

Loftie's *Essay*.

In 1884, the Rev. W. J. Loftie published his *Essay of Scarabs*,[2] which contained a description of his collection[3] of 192 scarabs, inscribed with royal names, and excellent drawings of each. His collection, like those of the Museum of the Louvre and the British Museum, was arranged chronologically;[4] the principle of the arrangement he explained in his interesting preface. In my *Catalogue of the Egyptian Collection of the Harrow School Museum*,[5] pp. 14–29, I gave a description of nearly one hundred and fifty scarabs, and translations of most of the inscriptions.

Murray and Smith.

In 1888 a catalogue of the scarabs and scaraboids from Egypt, Kamiros, and

[1] Printed by the Duke of Northumberland for private distribution, London, 1880.

[2] London, small 4to., no date.

[3] Purchased by the Trustees of the British Museum in 1890.

[4] Loftie, *op. cit.*, p. xxxi.

[5] Harrow, 1887.

Tharros was published by Dr. A. S. Murray and Mr. Hamilton Smith, in their *Catalogue of Gems*, pp. 46–58. In 1889 Mr. Flinders Petrie published a collection [1] of drawings of 2,363 scarabs, with a few pages of introduction. The idea of this work was excellent, but the plates should have contained a tolerably complete set of examples of scarabs, carefully indexed. The title *Historical Scarabs* was a misnomer, for the only, strictly speaking, historical scarabs known, the series of the four of Amenophis III., were omitted.

**Persistence of certain names upon scarabs.**

Scarabs inscribed with certain kings' names were made and worn as much as a thousand years after the death of the kings whose names they bear. This fact is indisputable, and if any proof were required it is furnished by the scarabs dug up at Naucratis by Mr. Petrie. From the scarab-moulds found there, and the material from which they are made, and from the design and workmanship, it is clear that the scarabs of Naucratis are not older than the VIIth century B.C.; yet many of them bear the prenomens of Thothmes III., Seti I. and Rameses II.,[2] etc. As the paste of which these are made is identical with that of scarabs bearing the names of kings of the XXVIth dynasty, there is no possible doubt about this fact. Scarabs inscribed with the names of two kings furnish another proof. Thus in the British Museum, Nos. 4033 and 4035 bear the names of Thothmes III. and Seti I.; No. 16,580 bears the names of Thothmes I., Thothmes III., and Seti I.; No. 17,126 (a plaque) bears the names of Thothmes III. and Rameses II.; No. 17,138 bears the names of Thothmes III. and Rameses III.; No. 16,837 bears the names of Thothmes III. and Rameses IX.; and No. 16,796 bears the names of Thothmes III. and Psammetichus. That scarabs of a late period are found in tombs of the VIth, XIIth and XVIIIth dynasties is not to be wondered at, for tombs were used over and over again for burial by families who lived hundreds of years after they were first hewn out, and who had no connexion whatever with the people who

**Double names.**

**Exact dating of scarabs impossible.**

[1] *Historical Scarabs; A series of Drawings from the Principal Collections. Arranged Chronologically.* London, 1889.

[2] *Naucratis*, London, 1886, Plate XXXVII., No. 63, etc., Pl. XXXVIII., No. 182.

were first buried in them. When a scarab is found bound up in a mummy, the date of which can be ascertained from the inscriptions upon it, that scarab can be used with advantage as an authority by which to compare other scarabs;[1] when, however, a scarab is dug up with a lot of miscellaneous stuff it is of little value for the purpose of comparison. From the lowest depths of the VIth and XIIth dynasty tombs at Aswân, scarabs have been dug up which could not have been a day older than the XXVIth dynasty, if as old. In some of these tombs, carefully closed with beautifully fitting blocks of stone, were found also red terra-cotta jars inscribed in hieratic which could not have been a day older than the XIXth dynasty, yet the inscriptions on the walls proved beyond a doubt that the tombs were made for officials who lived during the XIIth dynasty. It must then be clearly understood that the objects found in a tomb do not, necessarily, belong to the period of the tomb itself, and all the evidence known points to the fact that it is nearly impossible to arrange a collection of scarabs chronologically, except so far as the order of the names is concerned. Comparatively little is known about the various local manufactures of scarabs, or of their characteristics, and hundreds of examples of them exist which can neither be read nor explained nor understood.

**Chronological arrangement of names possible.**

**Scarabs of Ialysos, Kamiros, and Tharros.**

What has been said of the scarabs of Naucratis applies equally to those found at Ialysos and Kamiros in Rhodes, and at Tharros in Sardinia, places associated with the Phœnicians or Carthaginians. At Ialysos, faïence and steatite scarabs are rare. Of the three found there preserved in the British Museum, two are steatite and one is of faïence. One of the examples in steatite is fractured, whereby the design or inscription is rendered illegible, and the other is inscribed with  *tet*, emblem of stability, on each side of which is an uræus 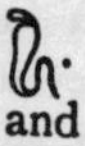. The example in faïence measures 1½ inch in length, and is inscribed with the prenomen of Åmen-ḥetep III., 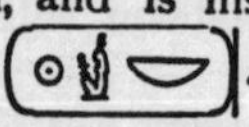.[2] Scarabs are rare in Kamiros

[1] Such a scarab, however, may quite well be *older* than the mummy upon which it is found.

[2] Brit. Mus. Reg. Nos. 72-3-15, 110; 70-10-3, 130 and 131.

also, so far as concerns the tombs, and in those in which black and red vases were obtained no scarabs were found; many specimens were, however, found in a well on the Acropolis,[1] and among them were some inscribed with the prenomen of Thothmes III.,[2] having all the characteristics of those of the XXVIth dynasty found at Naucratis. The scarabs found at Tharros do not go farther back than the period of Carthaginian supremacy, that is, not farther than the middle of the VIth century B.C.[3] A steatite scarab, found at Thebes in Bœotia, inscribed with ☥ *ānch* "life," and a winged gryphon wearing the crowns of Upper and Lower Egypt, belongs to the same period.[4]

**Impression of scarabs found at Nineveh.**

At Kouyunjik there were found two pieces of clay, of the same colour and substance as that employed by Assurbanipal for the tablets of his library, bearing impressions of an Egyptian king slaughtering his enemies, and hieroglyphic inscriptions, probably from a scarab. The king holds a club or weapon in his raised left hand, and his right holds some instrument which rests on the heads of a number of captives. The inscriptions read *neter nefer Shabaka neb àri χet*, "Beautiful god, Shabaka, the lord, maker of things" (the first king of the XXVth dynasty, about B.C. 700). Behind the king are the signs *sa* "protection," ☥ *ānch* "life," and *ḥa* "increase [of power]." In front of the king is the speech of some god *ṭā-nà nek set nebu*, "I give to thee all foreign lands." The Brit. Mus. Registration Nos. of these interesting objects are 51–9–2, 43, and 81–2–4, 352; as there is on the former also the impression of the seal of an Assyrian king, it has been thought[5] that the impression

[1] No. 132 in Table-Case E in the Kouyunjik Gallery.
[2] Murray, *Catalogue of Gems*, p. 13.
[3] Brit. Mus. Reg. Nos. 64–10–7, 895, 915, 1998.
[4] Murray, *op. cit.*, p. 13, and King, *Antique Gems and Rings*, Vol. I. p. 124.
[5] See Layard, *Nineveh and Babylon*, London, 1867, pp. 173, 174.

formed the seal of a treaty between the kings of Egypt and Assyria. Shabaka (Sabaco) was a contemporary of Sennacherib, B.C. 705–681.

Use of scarab by Phœnicians.

The Phœnicians borrowed the use of the scarab from Egypt, and as their country was overrun by Shalmaneser II., King of Assyria B.C. 860–825, and by many of his successors, it is only natural that the scarab inscribed with devices to suit the Assyrian market should find its way to Nineveh and Babylon, the Phœnician adopting in return the form of gem commonly used by the Assyrians for seals. A good example of the Phœnicio-Assyrian scarab is No. 1029, exhibited in the table-case in the Phœnician Room of the British Museum. It is made of green jasper, and measures 1¾ in. in length. On the base is inscribed a man, who stands adoring a seated deity; above is a seven-rayed star, and between them is ☥ *ānch*, "life." Beneath is inscribed in Phœnician characters, להודו ספרא, "Belonging to Hôdô the Scribe." For other examples see the specimens exhibited in the same case. As an example of the adoption of the chalcedony cone by the Phœnicians, see No. 1022, on which is inscribed a man at a fire altar and the name Palzîr-shemesh in Phœnician characters. The scarab in relief,[1] with outstretched wings inlaid with blue, red and gold carved upon an ivory panel found at Abu Habbah, about five hours' ride to the south-west of Bagdad, together with a number of miscellaneous ivory objects, is a proof of the knowledge of the scarab in Mesopotamia. That the panel was not carved by an Egyptian workman is very evident.[2] Scaraboids in agate and crystal, etc., are a small but very interesting class; at times the device is purely Egyptian, and the inscriptions in Phœnician letters are the only additions by the Phœnicians. Brit. Mus. Nos. 1024 and 1036 are tolerably good examples of them. The former is inscribed on the base with three hawks with outspread wings, and two of them have disks on

Use of scarab in Babylonia.

[1] See Table-Case G in the Nimroud Gallery.

[2] The two rectangular weights (?) found at Nimroud by Sir A. H. Layard (*Nineveh and Babylon*, London, 1867, p. 64) have each, on one face, the figure of a scarab inlaid in gold in outline; the work is excellent, and is a fine example of Phœnician handicraft.

their heads; these, of course, represent the hawk of Horus. The Phœnician inscription gives the name Eliâm. The latter is inscribed with a beetle in a square frame, and on the right and left is an uræus ; each end of the perpendicular sides of the frame terminates in *ānch*, and above and below it is a figure of Rā, or Horus, hawk-headed, holding a sceptre . The name, inscribed in Phœnician characters, is "Mersekem." In 1891, while carrying on excavations at Dêr, a place about three and a half hours to the south-west of Bagdad, I obtained a steatite scarab inscribed with an uræus , *ānch* , and an illegible sign, together with an oval green transparent Gnostic gem inscribed with the lion-headed serpent **XNOYBIC**. Both objects were probably brought from Lower Egypt, and belong to a period after the birth of Christ.[1]

Scarabs in Babylonia.

Dr. Birch describes in *Nineveh and Babylon* (London, 1853, pp. 281, 282) a series of eleven scarabs which Sir Henry Layard dug up at Arbân, a mound situated on the western bank of the Khabûr, about two and a half days' journey north of Dêr on the Euphrates, and about ten miles east of the 'Abd el-'Azîz hills. With one exception they are all made of steatite, glazed yellow or green or blue. Two of them are inscribed with the prenomen of Thothmes III. (Nos. 304, 309)[2]; one bears the prenomen of Amenophis III. (No 320), with the titles "beautiful god, lord of two lands, crowned in every land"; one is inscribed *men Cheperà àt Àmen*, "established of Cheperà, emanation of Àmen" (No. 322); two are inscribed (No. 303) and (No. 318), and belong to the same period; one is inscribed with a hawk-headed lion and a hawk (No. 273); one bears the legend, "beautiful lord, lord of two lands," *i.e.*, the North and South (No. 321); one is inscribed with a human-headed

Scarabs found at Arbân.

Scarabs found at Arbân.

[1] The numbers are G. 475 and 24,314.

[2] These interesting objects are exhibited in the Assyrian and Babylonian Room, in the Northern Gallery of the British Museum.

beetle, with outstretched wings, in the field are uræi and 𓋹𓋹 of beautiful workmanship (No. 302); and one is inscribed with 𓁹 𓂾 and an uræus 𓆗 having 𓋹 on its head (No. 307). The scarab in hæmatite (No. 313) is inscribed with the figure of a king seated on a throne, and a man standing before him in adoration; between them is 𓋹. With the exception of this last scarab, it is pretty certain that all belong to the period of the XVIIIth dynasty, for they have all the appearance of such antiquity, and they possess all the delicacy of workmanship found upon scarabs of this time. The design on the hæmatite scarab appears to be a copy from an Egyptian scarab executed by a foreign workman, but it may be that the hardness of the material made the task of engraving so difficult, that the character of the design was altered in consequence. The presence of these scarabs at Arbân is not difficult to account for. Thothmes I., one of the early kings of the XVIIIth dynasty, carried his victorious arms into Mesopotamia, and set up a tablet to mark the boundary of the Egyptian territory at a place called Nî, on the Euphrates, and the authority of the Egyptians in that land was so great that when Thothmes III. arrived there several years after, he found the tablet still standing. The kings who immediately succeeded Thothmes I. marched into this land, and that their followers should take up quarters on the fertile banks of the Khabûr, and leave behind them scarabs and other relics, is not to be wondered at. The antiquities found at Arbân are of a very miscellaneous character, and, among other things, include an Assyrian colossus inscribed "Palace of Meshezib-Marduk the king" (B.C. 700), and a Chinese glass bottle[1] inscribed with a verse of the Chinese poet KEĬN-TAU, A.D. 827–831; it is possible that the scarabs described above may have been brought there at a period subsequent to the XVIIIth dynasty, but, in any case, the objects themselves appear to belong to this period.

**Use of scarab by the Gnostics.**

The Gnostics inscribed the scarab on the gems worn by them, and partly adopted the views concerning it held by the

[1] British Museum, No. N. 1380.

Egyptians. On an oval slab of green granite,[1] in the British Museum, is inscribed a scarab encircled by a serpent having his tail in his mouth. The same design is found on another oval,[2] but the beetle has a human head and arms; above the head are rays, and above that the legend ЄΙΛΑΜΨ; to the right is a star, to the left a star and crescent, and beneath the hind legs three stars.

The scarab is an antiquity which is readily bought from the native of Egypt by modern travellers of every nationality; it is easily carried, and is largely worn as an ornament by ladies in their necklaces, bracelets and rings, and by men in pins and rings. As the number of visitors to Egypt has been steadily increasing for many years past, it follows of necessity that the demand for scarabs has increased also, and the price of these objects has risen in proportion. The late Sir Gardner Wilkinson, during one of his visits to Egypt, anchored his *dhahabiyyeh*[3] opposite Ḳûrnah at Thebes, and in the afternoon a native brought him a bag full of scarabs, many hundreds in number, which he had that day taken out of the ground in a tomb from under the coffin of a mummy. These scarabs were of a fine green colour and made of steatite; they were all inscribed with the name and titles of Thothmes III. Sir Gardner Wilkinson bought a *handful* of these for an English pound, but each scarab might now easily be sold for two pounds. The supply of scarabs varies year by year, some years but few are to be had, and some years they are very common. The supply cannot be inexhaustible, although the demand for them appears to be so. The native has discovered that the European not only wants scarabs, but that he wants scarabs inscribed with the names of particular kings; and as these are not always forthcoming, he has found out the way to make them. The imitation of scarabs by the modern native of Egypt began about sixty years ago. At first the number produced was few, and they were so clumsily made that it was soon apparent that they were forgeries. In later

Modern manufacture of scarabs.

Modern manufacture of scarabs.

[1] G. 455, Table-Case N, Fourth Egyptian Room.

[2] G. 483, Table-Case N, Fourth Egyptian Room.

[3] Arab. ذَهَبِيَّة.

days, however, the native has brought skill and thought to bear upon the matter, and he sets about his work in a systematic way. He has seen what the old faïence scarabs are made of, and he can now make a paste very much like that of which they are made. From the old broken *ushabtiu* figures, scarabs and beads, he chips off the thin layer of green or blue covering for his use. A large number of genuine moulds for scarabs have been found, and from these and others which he makes like them, he turns out large numbers of scarabs ready for glazing. For glaze he uses the pieces which he has collected from broken genuine scarabs, etc., and he spreads this over the paste with a blow-pipe. When he wishes to make steatite scarabs he obtains the steatite from the mountains where the ancient Egyptians found it. There is a large amount of artistic skill in many natives, and with a little practice they are able to cut very good scarabs. The discoloration of the genuine scarab is easily imitated by keeping them in wet sand, earth and ashes, and if he wants to glaze them he makes use of the same method as in glazing his paste forgeries. For inscriptions he usually follows slavishly those inscribed on genuine scarabs, of which he keeps a good supply. In this matter, however, he is greatly helped by the act of an English traveller, who wrote out for one of these imitators a list of all the most important kings of Egypt! which he now imitates with great success. He sells hundreds, perhaps even thousands, of his scarabs yearly, and many of them bring a high price. One has only to see the excellent way in which some of the natives can make a fine and correct reproduction in stone from a sculpture in a tomb or temple, to understand how well the native can imitate such things. Colours and other materials and tools can now be easily obtained in Egypt, and through the support of numerous purchasers who have bought readily for some years past, the production of forgeries of antiquities in general, and of scarabs in particular,[1] has become

Process of modern manufacture of scarabs.

[1] And this, notwithstanding the statement, "Generally speaking, forgeries—except of one or two obvious kinds—are very rare, and there is nothing like the amount of doubt in the matter which is often supposed to exist." Petrie, *Historical Scarabs*, p. 6.

a very profitable business. At more than one place in Egypt scarabs, bronze figures, etc., etc., have been so well imitated that experts were deceived and purchased them. Genuine *ushabtiu* figures and bronze statues of gods are cast in moulds found among the ruins of ancient Egyptian towns, wooden Ptaḥ-Seker-Ȧusȧr figures and boats are made from the planks of old coffins, and as it is evident that the substance itself is genuine, the unwary collector is thrown off his guard. In certain dealers' houses at Thebes and elsewhere, the visitor will always find a large assortment of forgeries, even on the tables set apart for genuine antiquities, and he will be able to compare and judge for himself.

Modern manufacture of antiquities.

The reverence shown by the Egyptians to the scarab, as an emblem of the Creator, was not shared by neighbouring nations. Thus Physiologus, after describing how scarabs roll up their eggs in balls of dung, and how they push them backwards, and how the young having come to life feed upon the dung in which they are hatched, goes on to say that we may learn of a certainty that scarabs are heretics[1] who are polluted by the filth of heresies; that these balls, which are formed of filth and nastiness, and which they roll backwards and not forwards, are the evil thoughts of their heresies, which are formed of wickedness and sin, and which they roll against mankind, until they become children of error, and by being participators in the filth of their heresies they become other beings and like unto them. See Land, *Anecdota*

Physiologus on the scarabæus.

[1] The ignorance of the habits and manner of life of the scarabæus which is displayed by certain Syrian writers upon natural history is marvellous; here is a specimen: "The scarabæus receiveth conception through its mouth, and when it cometh to bring forth, it giveth birth to its young through its ears. It hath the habit of stealing, and wherever it findeth small things and things of gold and silver it taketh and hideth them in its hole. And if pulse be found in the house it taketh [it] and mixeth [it] up with [other] things, chick-peas with beans, and beans with lentils, rice with millet and wheat, and everything which it findeth it mixeth up together in the place where it hideth itself. It thus doeth the work of the cooks who mix such things together to make to stumble those who buy pulse at the shops. And if any man taketh note of it and smiteth it, it taketh its vengeance upon [his] clothing. If having collected pieces of money and taken them forth to the race-course or to play with them, they be taken away from it, it wandereth about and turneth hither and thither, and if it findeth them not it straightway killeth itself." Ahrens, *Das Buch der Naturgegenstände*, text, p. 41, translation, p. 62.

*Syriaca*, tom. IV. p. 77, cap. 56. Bar-Hebraeus, commenting in ܐܘܨܪ ܐܪ̈ܙܐ, on Psalm lxxviii. 45, and referring to the words ܫܕܪ ܒܗܘܢ ܥܪܒܐ ܘܐܟܠ ܐܢܘܢ (Heb., בָּהֶם עָרֹב יְשַׁלַּח, he sent among them the gad-fly, LXX., 'Εξαπέστειλεν εἰς αὐτοὺς κυνόμυιαν), "he sent against them crowds of insects and they devoured them," includes the scarab (ܚܡܣܦܣܐ, plur. ܚܡ̈ܣܦܣܐ; ܚܡܣܦܣܬܐ, plur. ܚܡ̈ܣܦܣܝܬܐ) among noxious creatures like dog-flies, scorpions, ants, etc. . ܗ̇ . ܥܪܒܐ ܘܥܩܪ̈ܒܐ ܘܫܘ̈ܫܡܢܐ ܘܩܘܪ̈ܩܣܐ ܘܚܡ̈ܣܦܣܝܬܐ ܘܕ̈ܒܒܐ ܘܩܠ̈ܡܐ ܘܦ̈ܪܥܘܫܐ . ܘܒܩ̈ܐ ܕܡܚܒܠܝܢ ܟܠܡܐ ܕܐܟ̈ܠܐ ܀

## AMULETS.

**The Buckle of Isis.**

I. The **Buckle** or Tie. This amulet, called by the Egyptians *θet*, is one of the commonest objects found among collections of Egyptian amulets. It was most commonly made of red jasper, carnelian, red porphyry, red glass or faïence, and sycamore wood; sometimes it was made entirely of gold, and sometimes, when it was made of substances other than gold, it was set in gold, or covered over with gold leaf. Buckles are usually uninscribed, but frequently when two or more are found together the 156th chapter of the Book of the Dead is engraved on them. The buckle was placed on the neck of the mummy, which it was supposed to protect; the red material of which it was made represented the blood of Isis. The formula which is inscribed on buckles reads :—

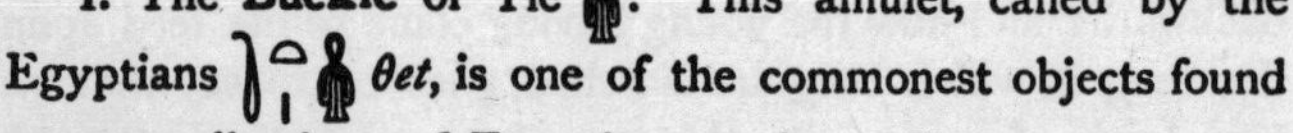

| Re | en | θet | ent | χenemet | ṭāṭā | er | χeχ |
|---|---|---|---|---|---|---|---|
| *Chapter* | *of* | *the buckle* | *of* | *red jasper* | *placed* | *on* | *the neck* |

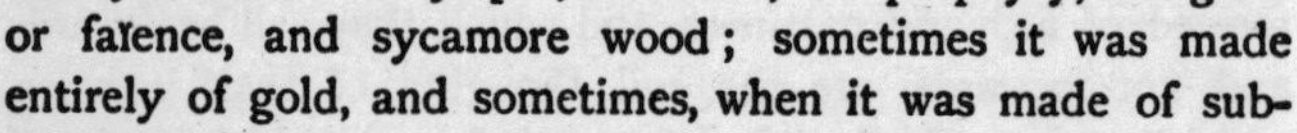

| en | χu | senef | ent | Åuset | ḥekau |
|---|---|---|---|---|---|
| *of* | *the deceased.* | *The blood* | *of* | *Isis,* | *the incantations* |

ent Åuset χut ent Åuset ut'at em

*of Isis, the power of Isis, a charm for the*

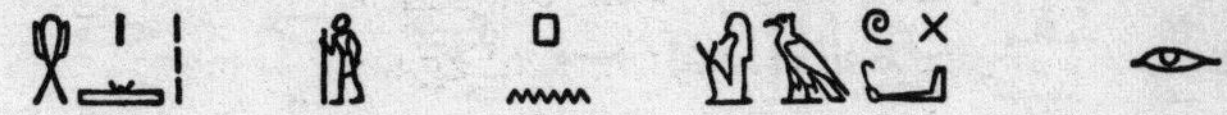

sa ur pen sau åri

*protection of mighty one this, protecting [him from] the doing of*

betaut - f pu[1]

*what to him is hateful.*

The rubric of this chapter reads:—

Rubric of 156th chapter of Book of the Dead.

t'eṭ-tu re pen ḥer θet ent χenem

*Is to be said chapter this over a buckle of red jasper*

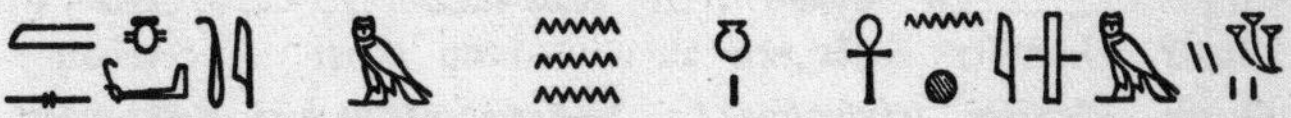

mes - θå em māu nu ānχåm

*anointed with water of* āncham *flowers,*

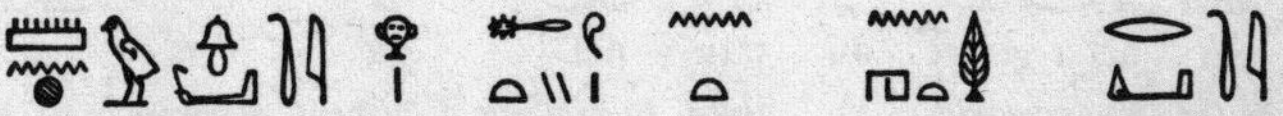

menχu - θå ḥer χati ent nehet erṭā - θå

*made of the heart of a sycamore tree, and placed*

er χeχ en χu pen år åritu - nef

*on the neck of deceased person this. If makes one*

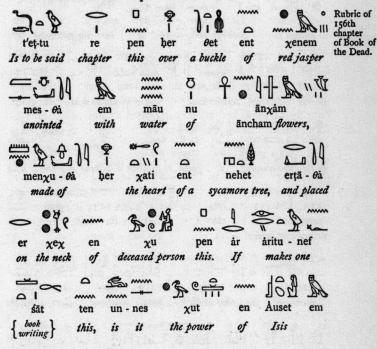

śāt ten un - nes χut en Åuset em

{*book writing*} *this, is it the power of Isis*

[1] See Birch, *The Amulet of the Tie*, *Aeg. Zeit.*, 1871, p. 13: and Maspero, *Mémoire sur Quelques Papyrus du Louvre*, p. 8.

sau - f ḥāā Ḥeru se Åuset maa - f
*protecting him, rejoices Horus, son of Isis, when sees he*

su ȧn t'erȧ en uat nebt er-ef
*it, not is blocked way any against him,*

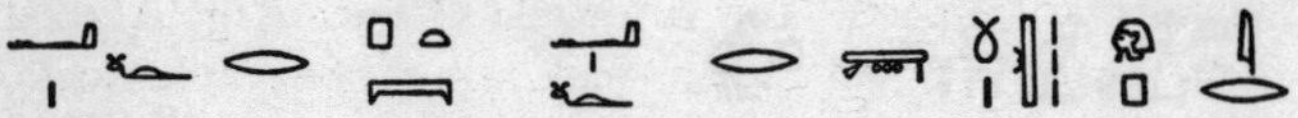

ā - f er pet ā - f er ta . . . . . . ȧr
*hand his is to heaven, hand his is to earth. . . . . . If*

reχ - tu śāt ten un - nef em śes en
*known is book this, is he in the following of*

Åusȧr Un-nefer maātχeru ȧu untu - nef sebau
*Osiris Unnefer, triumphant! Are opened to him the gates*

em neter-χertet ȧu ṭātu - nef χa ta em
*of the underworld, is given to him an allotment of ground with*

pertu beti em Seχet - Åan - re unen
*wheat and barley in Sechet - Aanre, is*

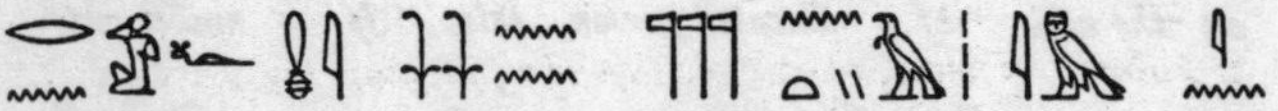

ren-f mȧ enen neteru enti ȧm ȧn
*name his like that of those gods who are there, say the*

Ḥeru Śesu aseχ - sen
*Horus followers, they [who] reap.*

**The ṭeṭ of Osiris.**

II. The Ṭeṭ . This object, which represents a mason's table and not a Nilometer, as a religious emblem symbolizes Osiris the lord of Ṭeṭṭu, great god of the underworld. The meaning of the word *ṭeṭ* is "firmness, stability, preservation," etc. The ṭeṭ had on it sometimes the plumes, disk and horns, , and was painted on mummies and tombs. The amulet itself was placed on the neck of the mummy which it was supposed to protect. Ṭeṭs are made of faïence, gold, wood gilded, carnelian, lapis-lazuli, and many other substances, although the rubric of the 155th chapter, of which  is the vignette, states that they are to be made of gold. This chapter is entitled :—

**The Chapter of the ṭeṭ**

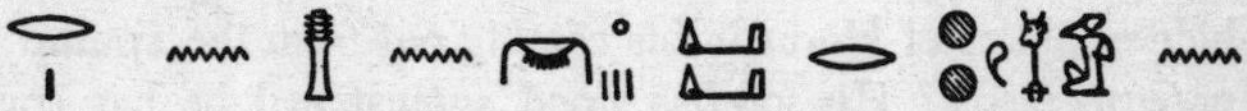

re en ṭeṭ en nub ṭāṭā er χeχ en
"*Chapter of a ṭeṭ of gold placed on the neck of*

χu
*the deceased.*"

and reads :—

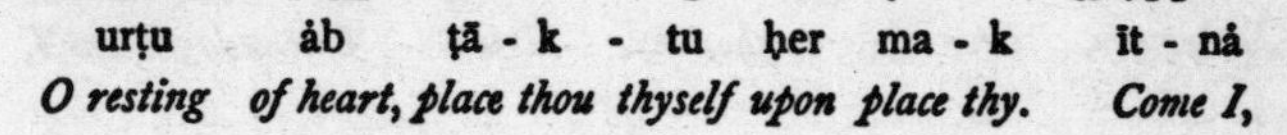

uben - k - nek urṭu - àb pen pesṭ - k nek
"*Rise up thou, O resting of heart this, shine thou,*

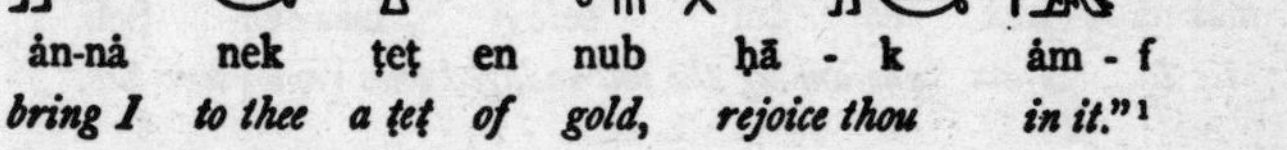

urṭu àb ṭā - k - tu ḥer ma - k ìt - nà
*O resting of heart, place thou thyself upon place thy. Come I,*

àn-nà nek ṭeṭ en nub ḥā - k àm - f
*bring I to thee a ṭeṭ of gold, rejoice thou in it.*"[1]

[1] *Papyrus of Ani*, pl. 33; the text given by Naville, *Das Todtenbuch*, Bl. clxxx., differs from this.

This chapter was to be "said over a ṭeṭ of gold, made of the heart of sycamore wood, which was to be placed on the neck of the mummy." The ṭeṭ enabled the deceased to enter in through the gates of the underworld, and if this chapter were known by him, he would "rise up as a perfect soul in the underworld, he would not be repulsed at the gates there, and cakes would be given to him, and joints of meat from the altars of Rā."

The Vulture of Isis.

III. The **Vulture** . According to the rubric of the 157th chapter of the Book of the Dead, a vulture of gold was to be placed on the neck of the mummy on the day of the funeral; it was supposed to carry with it the protection of "Mother" Isis. The chapter reads, "Isis has come, she has gone round about the towns, she has sought out the hidden places of Horus in his coming out from the swamp of papyrus reeds. His son has stood against evil, he has come into the divine boat, he has commanded the princes of the world, he has made a great fight, he makes mention of what he has done, he has caused himself to be feared and established terror of him. His mother, the mighty lady, makes his protection and brings (?) him to Horus." Amulets of the vulture inscribed with this chapter are very rare.

IV. The **Collar**  *useχ*. The rubric of the 158th chapter of the Book of the Dead orders a collar of gold to be laid upon the neck of the deceased on the day of the funeral. It was to be inscribed:—

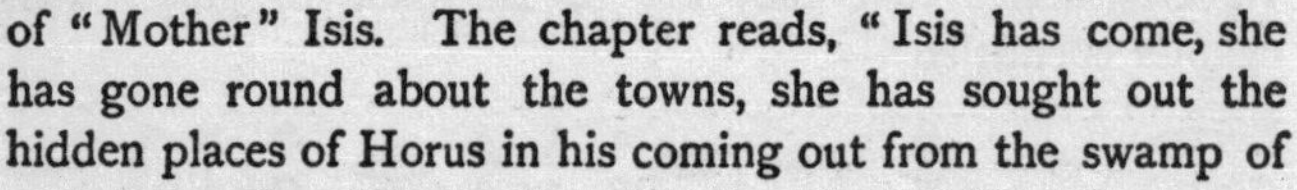

àtf-à sent-à mut - à Àuset sefeχi - uà

*Father my, sister my, mother my, Isis! Unbandaged am I,*

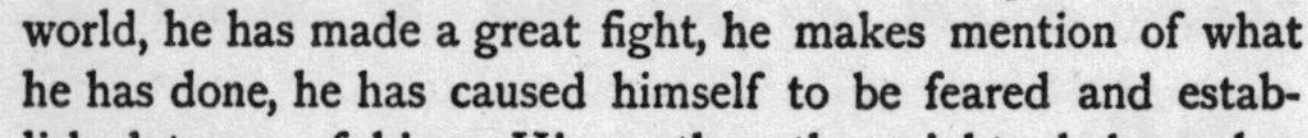

maa-uà nuk uā àm sefeχi maa-sen Seb

*see I. I am one among the unbandaged ones* [*who*] *see Seb.*

Amulet collars are found made of red jasper, carnelian, etc.

The papyrus sceptre of Thoth.

V. The **"Papyrus Sceptre"** *uat'*. This amulet is usually made of mother-of-emerald or of faïence like unto it in colour, and the hieroglyphic word which it represents, *uat'*, means "verdure, flourishing, greenness," and the like; it was placed on the neck of the deceased, and indicated the eternal youth which it was hoped he would enjoy in the underworld. This amulet was sometimes inscribed with the 159th chapter of the Book of the Dead, where it is described as *uat' en nešem*, "an *uat'* of mother-of-emerald." The next chapter says that a rounded tablet, on which is a figure of the in relief, is to be placed on the neck of the deceased; it was supposed to be given to him by Thoth, and to protect his limbs.

VI. The **Pillow** *urs.*[1] This amulet is usually made of hæmatite, and is generally uninscribed; it is a model of the large pillows of wood, alabaster and stone which are placed under the heads of mummies to "lift them up." When inscribed the text is a version of that of the 166th chapter of the Book of the Dead.

No. 20,647 in the British Museum reads:—

The Chapter of the Pillow.

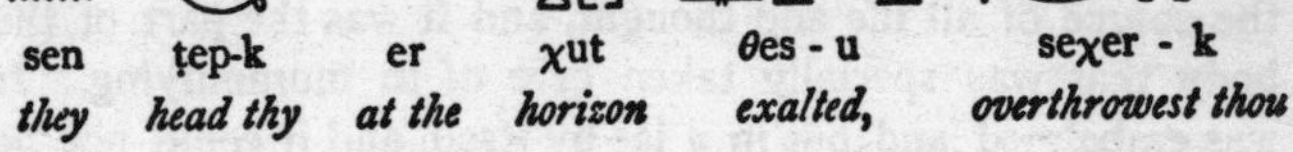

| θes - tu | mentu | st'erθ | seres - |
|---|---|---|---|
| *Rise up from* | *non-existence,* | *O prostrate one.* | *Watch over* |

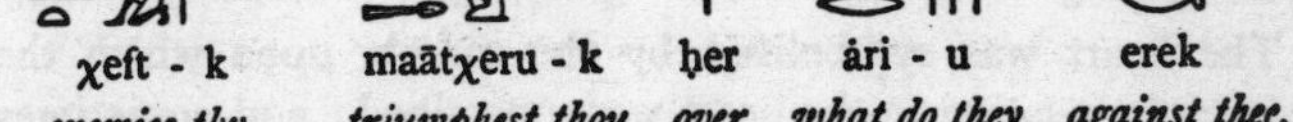

| sen | ṭep-k | er | χut | θes - u | seχer - k |
|---|---|---|---|---|---|
| *they* | *head thy* | *at the* | *horizon* | *exalted,* | *overthrowest thou* |

| χeft - k | maātχeru - k | ḥer | ȧri - u | erek |
|---|---|---|---|---|
| *enemies thy,* | *triumphest thou* | *over* | *what do they* | *against thee,* |

[1] See Birch, *The Chapter of the Pillow*, in *Aeg. Zeit.*, 1868, pp. 52–54.

utu er ari nek Ḥeru net′ tef - f

*[as] has commanded to be done for thee Horus, the avenger of father his*

Ȧusȧr pen āṭ - k ṭepu nu χeft - k ȧn

*Osiris this. Cuttest off thou heads of enemies thy, not*

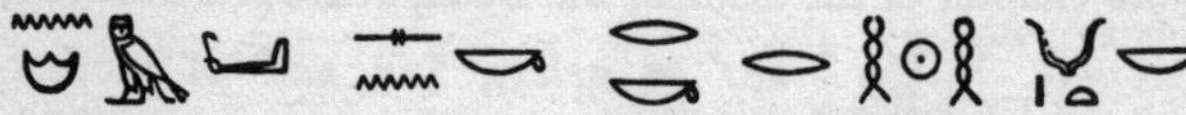

neḥem - sen k erek er ḥeḥ ȧpt - k

*shall carry away they from thee for ever head (?) thy!*

māk śāṭ Ȧusȧr ȧri em peru ṭepu

*Verily slaughter Osiris maketh at the coming forth of the heads*

nu χeft - f ȧn neḥem - sen [ṭep] f er - f

*of enemies his, not may remove they [head] his from him*

er ḥeḥ

*for ever!*

VII. The **Heart** *ȧb.* Amulets of the heart are made of carnelian, green jasper, basalt, lapis-lazuli, and many other kinds of hard stone. The heart was considered to be the source of all life and thought, and it was the part of the body that was specially taken care of in mummifying. It was embalmed and put in a jar by itself, and it could not be replaced in the body until it had undergone judgment by being weighed in the balance against , representing "Law." The heart was symbolised by the scarab, upon which the formulæ relating to the heart were inscribed; and sometimes a heart amulet was inscribed with one of the chapters of the heart on one side, and a scarab on the other (B.M. No. 8003).

Sometimes the heart is human-headed, with the hands crossed over it (B.M. 15,598), and sometimes a figure of the soul, in the shape of a hawk with outstretched wings, is inlaid on one side of it (B.M. No. 8005). The chapters in the Book of the Dead which refer to the heart are the 26th, the "Chapter of giving to a person his heart in the underworld"; the 27th, 28th, 29th A, "Chapter of not allowing the heart of a person to be taken away from him in the underworld"; 29 B, "Chapter of a heart of carnelian;" 30 A, and 30 B, "Chapter of not allowing the heart of a person to be turned away from him in the underworld." The most important chapter of the heart, and that most commonly found, 29 B, is translated in that portion of this Catalogue which describes the green basalt heart in the Fitzwilliam Museum; for the text of the others see Naville, *Das Todtenbuch*, Bll. XXXVII.–XLIII.; and for translations see Birch, *On formulas relating to the heart*, in *Aeg. Zeit.*, 1866, pp. 69, 1867, pp. 16, 54; and Pierret, *Le Livre des Morts*, pp. 103–114. An interesting example of the heart amulet is described by Birch[1]; on one side are *Net*, "Neith" and the *bennu* bird, , with the legend *Nuk ba χeperȧ*, "I am the soul of Cheperȧ," and on the other is the common chapter of the heart. The *bennu* bird or phœnix was an emblem of the resurrection.

The Chapter of the Heart.

VIII. The **Amulet of Life** *ānχ*. This object is found in every material used by the Egyptians for making amulets, and formed a very common ornament for the living and the dead. Necklaces were frequently composed of pendants made in forms of , , and , and sometimes *neferu* "good luck," were added.

IX. The "**Symbolic Eye**" or , *ut'at*. This amulet was made of glazed faïence, wood, granite, hæmatite, carnelian, lapis-lazuli, gold, silver, and many other materials. Ut'ats are either right or left, and they are also made double or quadruple; they are sometimes made in

[1] *Catalogue of Egyptian Antiquities in Alnwick Castle*, p. 224.

hollow-work, and are sometimes ornamented with a number of others in relief. Some have on their obverse a head of Hathor (B.M. No. 7357) or a figure of Bes (B.M. No. 21,547); on their reverse they frequently have names of kings, private persons, or gods. They are sometimes made with wings, and have an arm and hand holding 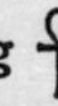 "life," projecting (B.M. No. 7378); and some have a ram and two lions on them in relief.

**The amulet of the *ut'at*.**

The two ut'ats, right and left, represented the two eyes of the sun , the one symbolising the northern half of the sun's daily course, and the other the southern half; they also represented the sun and moon. On sepulchral boxes the ut'ats are often accompanied by *neferu* . The vignette of the 163rd chapter of the Book of the Dead contains two ut'ats, winged, with human legs, and the vignette of the 167th, or "Chapter of bringing the ut'at," is ; the 140th chapter was to be recited over an ut'at made of lapis-lazuli, and offerings were to be made to it. The word *ut'a*  means "to be in good health, safe, preserved and happy," and the popularity of this amulet in Egypt was probably due to the fact that those who wore it, whether living or dead, were supposed to be safe and happy under the protection of the eye of Rā.

**Miscellaneous amulets.**

X. The amulet **Nefer**  or "Good Luck," was commonly made of glazed faïence or of carnelian, and was much used by the Egyptians for necklaces.

XI. The amulet **Sam**  or 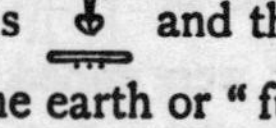 represented "union"; sometimes it is made thus 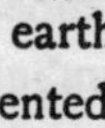 and then probably represents *sam-ta*, the union with the earth or "funeral."

XII. The amulet **Chut**  represented the disk of the sun on the horizon, and was often made of jasper or hard stone.

XIII. The amulet **Shen**  represented the orbit of the sun, and is made of lapis-lazuli and of carnelian. It is often found on sepulchral stelæ and boxes, but its exact use is unknown.

XIV, XV. The amulet of the **Tesher** crown represented the crown of Lower Egypt; and **Ḥet'** represented the crown of Upper Egypt.

Miscellaneous amulets.

XVI. The amulet of the **Menàt** signified "joy" and "health," and perhaps "life."[1] It is always worn by Ptaḥ at the back of his neck, and it is frequently an emblem of the goddess Hathor.

XVII. The **Cartouche** is thought by Pierret (*Dict. d'Archéologie Egyptienne*, p. 118) to be nothing more than an elongated seal (see No. XIII), and to represent natural reproduction and eternity.

XVIII. The amulet **Neha** or represented "protection"; it was made chiefly of hæmatite, and is found in the breast of the mummy.

XIX. The amulet of the **Serpent's head** is made of stone, red jasper, or paste to imitate red jasper, and carnelian. It was placed on mummies to prevent their being bitten by snakes and other reptiles in the underworld. The 34th chapter of the Book of the Dead, entitled, "Chapter of not allowing a person to be bitten in the underworld by a serpent," is sometimes found engraved upon this amulet. In later times glass and faïence models of serpents , , were worn by men and women round the neck; they were probably connected in some way with Isis.

XX. The amulet of the **Disk and Plumes** probably represented the head-dress of Seker, the god of the resurrection; the feathers often occur without the disk. The use of this amulet is unknown.

XXI. The **Frog** represents "myriads." This amulet is made of steatite, jasper of various colours, faïence, etc.; it

[1] For a discussion on this amulet see Lefébure, *Trans. Soc. Bib. Arch.*, 1891, pp. 333-349.

is often found with and , and was probably placed with these on the neck of the mummy, although examples are known which were taken from the chest. The frog-headed goddess Ḥeqt is a form of the goddess Hathor, the wife of Chnemu; she was considered to be connected with the resurrection. On lamps of the Greek and Roman periods found in Egypt the frog often appears on the upper part, and one is known [1] which has the legend **ЄΓѠ ЄΙΜΙ ΑΝΑCΤΑCΙC**, "I am the resurrection." The use of this amulet appears not to be older than the XVIIIth dynasty.

The frog emblem of the resurrection.

XXII. The **Stairs** or . This amulet is usually made of glazed faïence, but the use of it is unknown to me. In the vignette of the 110th chapter of the Book of the Dead it is figured placed in a boat (Naville, *Das Todtenbuch*, Bl. CXXIII.); in the 22nd chapter the deceased says, "I am Osiris, lord of Re-stau (the passages of the tomb), and of those who are at the top of the stairs"; and in the 85th chapter the deceased says, "I am the lord of the stairs, I have made my nest on the borders of the sky."

XXIII. The amulet of the two **Fingers,** the index and medius, is found in the interior of mummies, and is generally made of hæmatite or obsidian. The use of the amulet is unknown to me.

Ring amulets.

In every Egyptian collection of importance a large number of rings, having a gap in each, will be found; they are made of gold, red jasper, obsidian, red glazed faïence, shell, stone, and glass. Those made of gold have a small ring at each end for a wire to pass through (?), and they may thus have been used as earrings or pendants for necklaces; on the other hand they may have been used as amulets. Some believe that they were used as buttons.

## Figures of Gods.

The gold, silver, bronze, wooden and faïence **figures of gods** in Egyptian collections may be reckoned by thousands, and they vary in size from half an inch to fifteen inches or

[1] Figured in Lanzone, *Dizionario*, p. 853.

more. Bronze statues were usually cast in moulds, in one or more pieces, the core being made of sand or earth. When cast in pieces the limbs were soldered together and the edges smoothed with a file or scraper. The core is frequently found inside the statue, where it was left by the workmen to strengthen the casting. Figures of gods in gold are comparatively few, the gods most often represented in this metal being Åmen-Rā, Chensu, and Nefer-Åtmu; figures of these gods were also made of silver and plated with gold, and a figure of the god Set, made of bronze plated with gold, is also known (B.M. No. 18,191). Bronze figures of gods were sometimes inlaid with gold, and the eyes were made of gold or silver with obsidian pupils. Glazed faïence figures of gods are very common, and certain gods were made of this substance, which up to the present have rarely been met with in bronze. They were usually cast from moulds, and follow fairly closely the design and patterns of the bronze figures; they do not occur earlier than the XXVth or XXVIth dynasty, and although wretched copies of them were made for hundreds of years after, they do not appear to have continued in use among all classes of people in Egypt. It may be mentioned in passing that the natives of Egypt at the present day make use of the old moulds, found chiefly in Upper Egypt, to cast figures of the gods in gold and silver which they sell to the traveller as genuine antiquities.

**Method of manufacture.**

Figures of the gods of Egypt are found among the ruins of houses and in temples and tombs. According to M. Mariette[1] those found among the ruins of towns are of two kinds: 1, those placed in a niche, cut in the form of a shrine, which represented the divinity to the service of which the inhabitants of the house were attached, and before which, on certain days, offerings were laid; 2, those which were placed in crevices of the walls of the inner chambers of the house, and which were supposed to be able by magical influence to protect the inhabitants of the house from spells and the results of incantations, and from other malignant influences. The use of this latter class of statues or small

**Uses of bronze figures.**

[1] *Catalogue Général des Monuments d'Abydos*, p. 1.

figures is as old as the XVIIIth dynasty, at least. The figures of gods found in temples are very numerous and are votive. The Egyptians seem to have believed that the gods inhabited statues or figures, made in their honour, and on this account they often made them very beautiful, so that they might form worthy habitations for them. On certain days prayers were said before them, and offerings were made to them. As figures of many different gods are found in the same temple, it follows that a worshipper wishing to place a figure of a god in a temple was not bound to offer one of the god to whom the temple was dedicated; supposing the temple to be one of Ptaḥ, he could offer a figure of Rā, or Chnemu, or of any god he pleased. Figures of gods were supposed to answer questions, for it will be remembered that when Chensu was asked if he would go to the land of Bechten to cure a daughter of the prince of that land of her sickness, he inclined his head in assent. When he arrived in that land, he held a conversation with the demon that possessed the maiden, and when the demon agreed to come out from her, provided thát a feast were made in his honour, the god through his priest, assented. Figures of gods other than Osiris, Isis, and Nephthys are not commonly found in tombs; it is true that many examples in faïence are found in the wrappings of mummies, but in these cases they were simply used as amulets like the buckle, ṭeṭ, pillow and many others. Figures of gods made of every sort of material were also buried in the sand around temples and tombs with the view of guarding them from every evil influence. The following is a list of the most important of the gods and goddesses of whom figures were made in bronze and glazed faïence:—

Funereal bronzes.

**Åmen-Rā**  and Mut and Chensu formed the great triad of Thebes; the word *Åmen* means "hidden." Åmen was said to be the son of Ptaḥ, and he seems to have usurped the attributes of all the other gods. Before the expulsion of the Hyksos by Se-qenen-Rā his position was that of the local god of Thebes; subsequently he became the national god of Egypt. He was said to be the maker of things above and of things below, and to have more forms

Åmen the national god of Egypt.

than any other god. He made the gods, and stretched out the heavens, and founded the earth; he was lord of eternity and maker of everlasting. The Egyptians affirmed of him that he was ONE, the ONLY ONE. In bronze figures he stands upon a plinth, he holds the sceptre  in his left hand, and on his head he wears the disk and feathers ; at times he holds a scimitar (B.M. Nos. 28, 29). He is also represented seated on a throne, and the throne was sometimes placed inside a shrine, the top of which was ornamented with uræi, winged disk, etc., and the sides and back with hollow-work figures of Isis, Nephthys, and Osiris (B.M. No. 11,013). On the pedestals he is called "Åmen-Rā, lord of the thrones of the world, the president of the Apts (*i.e.*, Karnak), lord of heaven, prince of Thebes."  . He is, at times, one of a triad consisting of Åmen, Åmsu, and Rā (B.M. No. 18,681). The faïence figures of this god are similar to

Åmen-Rā.

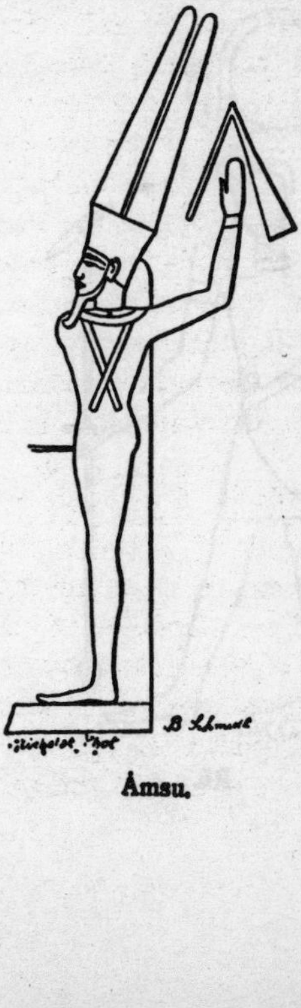

Åmsu.

the bronze , and he appears together with the other members of his triad, Mut and Chensu.

The god of procreation.

**Ȧmes** or **Ȧmsu** , , commonly read "Chem," is a form of Ȧmen-Rā, and represented "generation" or the productive power in nature: figures of him, in bronze and faïence, , are tolerably numerous.

Different forms of Rā.

**Rä** , the Sun-god, was also the creator of gods and men; his emblem was the sun's disk. His worship was very ancient, and he was said to be the offspring of Nut, or the sky. He assumed the forms of several other gods, and is at times represented by the lion, cat, and hawk. In papyri and on bas-reliefs he has the head of a hawk, and wears a disk, in front of which is an uræus . When he rose in the morning he was called Ḥeru-chuti or **Harmachis**; and at night, when he set, he was called Ȧtmu, or "the closer."

Rā.

Ḥeru (Horus).

During the night he was supposed to be engaged in fighting Āpepi, the serpent, who, at the head of a large army of fiends, personifications of mist, darkness, and cloud, tried to overthrow him. The battle was renewed daily, but Rā always conquered, and appeared day after day in the sky. Bronze and faïence figures of this god represent him hawk-headed and wearing disk and uræus.

Rā the warrior.

**Menthu-Rā** in bronze figures is hawk-headed, and wears the disk, in front of which are two uræi, and plumes; at times figures have two hawk's heads on a single body.

**Horus**, the morning sun, son of Isis and Osiris, is usually called "the avenger of his father," in reference to his defeat of Set. Figures in bronze and faïence represent him hawk-headed and wearing the crown of Upper and Lower Egypt. This god was distinguished in name only from Ḥeru-ur, the elder brother of Osiris.

The god of youth.

**Harpocrates**, or Ḥeru-pa-Chraṭ, the morning

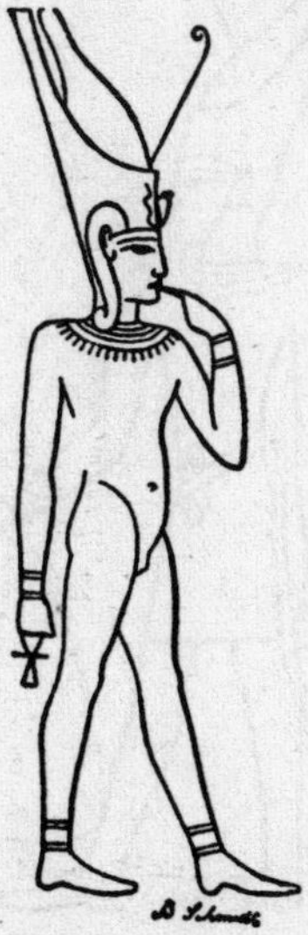

**Ḥeru-pa-chraṭ (Harpocrates).**

**Chensu.**

sun, in bronze or faïence wears the crown of Upper and Lower Egypt, or the triple crown, or the plumes, or is quite bald; over the right shoulder a lock of hair falls, and the tip of a finger of the right hand rests on his lips. He is represented naked, as being in the lap of his mother Isis.

**Chensu** was associated with Åmen-Rā and Mut in the Theban triad, and was god of the moon. In bronze figures he is human-headed, and wears a crescent and disk; in faïence figures he is made like a mummy, and holds sceptres of different shapes in his hands. His second name was Nefer-ḥetep, and he was worshipped with great honour at Thebes. **Chensu-pa-chraṭ** has all the attributes of Harpocrates, and figures of him in bronze are not rare. A very fine specimen is B.M. No. 11,045

Different forms of Chensu.

**Tmu**, or **Åtmu** the "Closer" of the day or night, usually represents the night-sun. He

The night-Sun.

Chensu Nefer-Ḥetep.

Åtmu.

wears the crowns of Upper and Lower Egypt; in the right hand he holds 𓋹, and in the left [hieroglyph]. **Nefer-Åtmu,** the son of Ptaḥ and Sechet or Bast, represents the power of the heat of the rising sun. Figures of this god were made in gold, silver, bronze, and faïence. In metal, he stands upright, wearing lotus flowers and plumes on his head, in his right hand he holds [hieroglyph] and in the left 𓋹. Sometimes each shoulder is inlaid in gold with an *ut'at* (B.M. No. 22,921). In faïence he has the same head-dress, but stands on a lion; in faïence, too, he is often accompanied by his mother Sechet or Bast (B.M. Nos. 250*b*, 260*a*).

**The oldest god of Egypt.**

**Ptaḥ** 𓊪𓏏𓎛[hieroglyph], the "Opener," perhaps the oldest of all the gods of Egypt, was honoured with a temple and worshipped at Memphis from the time of the Ist dynasty. He is said to be the father of the gods, who came forth from his eye, and of men, who came forth from his mouth.

**Nefer-Åtmu.**

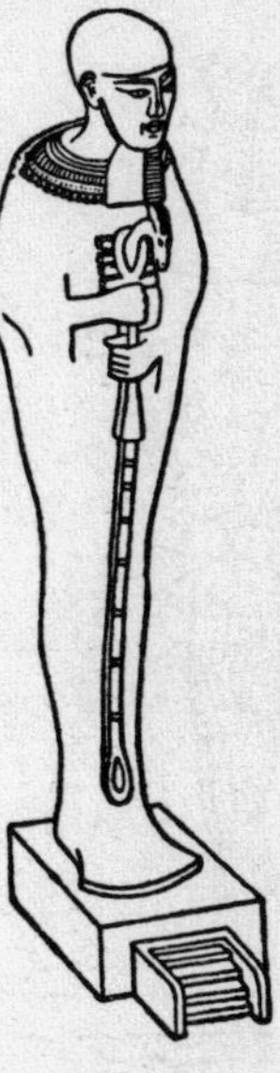

**Ptaḥ.**

He is represented in the form of a mummy, and he holds a sceptre composed of *usr*, "strength," *ānch*, "life," and *ṭeṭ*, "stability." Bronze and faïence figures of this god are tolerably common, and resemble each other in form and design. At the back of his neck he wears the *menȧt*.

**The god of the resurrection.**

With reference to his connexion with the resurrection and the nether world, he is called **Ptaḥ-Seker-Ȧusȧr,** and is represented as a little squat boy, with bent legs, and his hands on his hips. Sometimes he has his feet on the head of a crocodile; on the right side stands Isis, on the left Nephthys, at his back is a human-headed hawk emblematic of the soul, on each shoulder is a hawk, and on his head is a beetle, the emblem of Cheperȧ, the self-begotten god. In faïence figures of this god are very common, but in bronze they are rare.

**Imouthis the scribe.**

**Ī-em-ḥetep**, the Imouthis of the Greeks, was the first-born son of Ptaḥ and Nut. He is represented

**Ptaḥ-Tatenen.**

**Ī-em-ḥetep.**
**(Imouthis).**

both standing and seated, holding a sceptre in the right hand, and in the left; at times he holds on his knees an open roll, upon which is inscribed his name. The bronze figures of this god are usually of very fine workmanship, often having the inscriptions inlaid in gold; in faïence, figures of this god are very rare.

The "mould-er" of man.

**Chnemu**, the "Moulder," the *Χνουμις*, *Χνούβις*, *Χνουβι*, *Κνήφ* or *Κνουφις* of the Greeks, is one of the oldest gods of Egypt, and was especially worshipped in Nubia, at Philæ, where he is represented making man out of clay on a potter's wheel, and at Elephantine. Like Åmen-Rā he is said to be the father of the gods,[1] and

**Chnemu.** **Cheperà.** **Teḥuti (Thoth).**

[1] Father of the fathers of the gods, the lord who evolveth from himself, maker of heaven, earth, the underworld, water, and mountains

with this god and Ptaḥ and Cheperȧ he shared the name of "creator of men." Chnemu put together the scattered limbs of the dead body of Osiris, and it was he who created the beautiful woman who became the wife of Bata in the Tale of the Two Brothers. In bronze and faïence, figures of this god represent him with the head of a ram, and wearing plumes, ; these figures are tolerably common.

Thoth the accurate scribe of the gods.

**Thoth,** in Egyptian **Teḥuti** , the "Measurer," was the scribe of the gods, the measurer of time and inventor of numbers. In the judgment hall of Osiris he stands by the side of the balance holding a palette and reed ready to record the result of the weighing of the heart as announced by the dog-headed ape who sits on the middle of the beam of the scales. In bronze figures he is represented with the head of an ibis, but he has upon it sometimes horns and plumes. In faïence figures he has also the head of an ibis, and occasionally he holds an *ut'at* between his hands in front of him (B. M. No. 490*a*).

**Set** or **Sut** , Gr. *Σήθ*, was one of the sons of Seb and Nut, and was brother of Osiris, and husband of Nephthys. His worship dates from the Vth dynasty, and he continued to be a most popular god in Egypt until the XIXth dynasty; kings delighted to call themselves "beloved of Set," and to be compared to him for valour when the records of their battles were written down. He probably represented the destructive power of the sun's heat. Between the XXIInd and XXVth dynasties a violent reaction set in against this god, his statues and figures were smashed, his effigy was hammered out from the bas-reliefs and stelæ in which it appeared, and from being a beneficent god, and a companion of Ȧmen and his brother-gods, he became the personification of all evil, and the opponent of all good. His persistent enmity of Osiris will be mentioned below. Set, or Sutech, was chosen by the Hyksos for their god. Bronze figures of Set are very rare indeed. The British Museum possesses two examples, Nos. 18,191 and 22,897; each represents the god standing upright, in each he has the characteristic animal's

The murderer of Osiris and opponent of Horus.

head, and wears the crown of Upper and Lower Egypt, ; each figure was originally gilded, and each has a hole drilled in a projecting piece of metal, from which it was suspended and worn. When I bought the larger figure it was bent double, evidently by a violent blow, given probably when the reaction against this god's worship set in. Faïence figures of Set I have never seen.

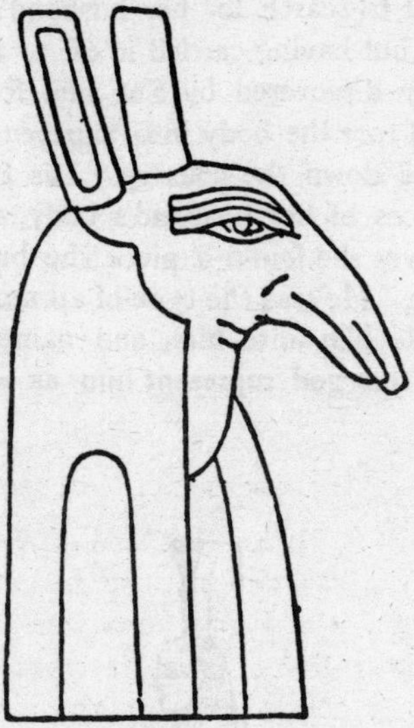

**Set.**

**Ȧusȧr (Osiris).**

**Osiris**, in Egyptian *Ȧusȧr* , the great god and king of the underworld, the judge of the dead, was the son of Seb and Nut, and husband of Isis; he was murdered by his brother Set, who was in turn slain by Horus, the son of Osiris, and the "avenger of his father." According to Plutarch (*De Iside et Osiride*, xii.–xx.) Osiris was the wise and good king of Egypt, who spent his life in civilizing his subjects and in improving their condition. Having brought them out of degradation and savagery, he set out to do the like for the other nations of the world. Upon his return his brother Set,

**Plutarch's story of Osiris.**

together with seventy-two other people, and the queen of Ethiopia, made a conspiracy against him. They invited him into a banqueting room, and by an artful device made Osiris get into a box which Set had previously caused to be made to fit him. As soon as Osiris had lain down in it, the conspirators nailed the cover on it, and having poured molten lead over it, they carried it by river to the sea, the waves of which washed it up at Byblos. As soon as Isis heard of what had happened, she set out to search for her husband's body, and eventually found it; but having carried it off to another place, it was accidentally discovered by Set, who forthwith broke open the chest, and tore the body into fourteen pieces, which he scattered up and down the country. Isis then set out to search for the pieces of her husband's body, and she found all but one; wherever she found a piece she buried it, and built a temple over it. He was the type of all mummies, and the deceased is made like unto him, and named after him. Bronze figures of this god represent him as a mum-

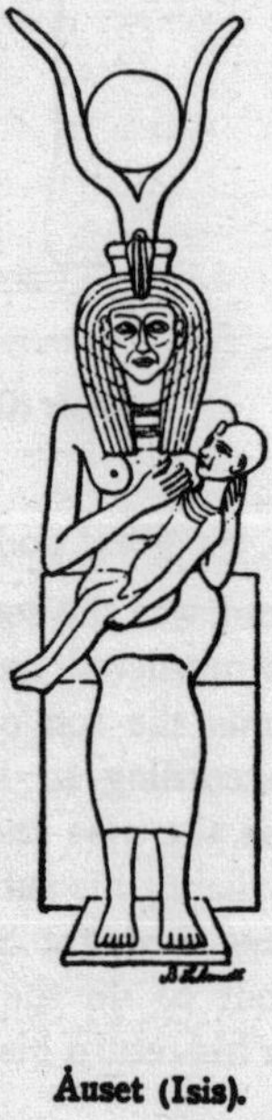

Åuset (Isis).

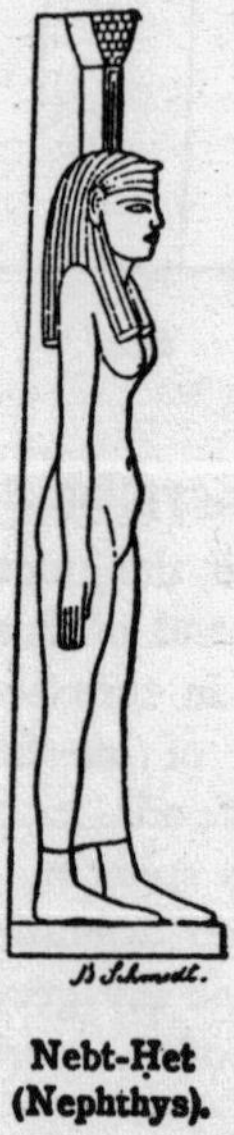

Nebt-Ḥet (Nephthys).

mified figure wearing the crown, in his right hand he holds the whip, and in the left the crook. Figures of this god in faïence are not very common.

The family of Osiris.

**Isis**, in Egyptian *Àuset*, was a daughter of Seb and Nut; she married her brother Osiris. Bronze figures represent her 1, standing and wearing upon her head, and 2, seated suckling her naked child Horus, who is sitting on her knees, at her left breast, and wearing disk and horns upon her head. In faïence many figures of both kinds are found. In funereal scenes Isis stands at the foot of the bier mourning the deceased.

**Nephthys**, in Egyptian *Nebt-ḥet*, was also a daughter of Seb and Nut; she married her brother Set. Bronze figures, which are not common, represent her standing draped in a long tunic, and wearing on her head; in faïence, figures of this goddess are very numerous, and follow the style and design of those in bronze. A number of rectangular faïence pendants have been found in which Isis, Nephthys and Harpocrates or Horus stand side by side.

**Anubis**, in Egyptian *Ànpu*, was, according to some legends, the son of Nephthys and Osiris, who mistook that goddess for Isis; elsewhere he is said to be the son of Rā. He is always represented as having the head of a jackal, and he is one of the chief gods of the dead and the netherworld. He presided over the embalming of the mummy, he led the mummy into the presence of Osiris, and watched over the ceremony of weighing the heart, and he is often represented standing by the bier with one hand laid on the mummy. The belief that this god acted in this capacity survived for some centuries after Christ, and a remarkable proof of this fact is given by a light green, glazed faïence plaque in the British Museum, No. 22,874. On the obverse Anubis, jackal-headed, in relief, stands by the side of a bier in the shape of a lion, also in relief; on the reverse, in relief,

The god of the tomb.

Persistence of Pagan beliefs among the Copts.

are two lines of inscription in Coptic which read, ⲁⲥ ⲓⲏⲥ ⲉ ⲧⲱⲛⲕ, "May she hasten to arise." At each end is a pierced projection whereby the plaque was fastened to the mummy. The plaque is an interesting example of the survival of ancient Egyptian ideas among the Egyptians after they had embraced Christianity. Anubis is sometimes confused with *Ȧp-uat*, "the opener of the ways," another jackal-headed god, and the attributes of the one are ascribed

**Ȧnpu (Anubis).**

**Shu.**

to the other. Bronze and faïence figures of this god represent him standing and having the head of a jackal.

**Sunlight and moisture.**

**Shu**, in Egyptian , was the first-born son of Rā and Hathor, and brother of Tefnut; he is supposed to symbolise the air or sun-light, and in papyri and on coffins he is represented in the form of a man, standing with both arms raised, lifting up Nut, or the sky, from the embrace of Seb the earth. In bronze and faïence figures he is in the form of a man kneeling on his right knee and supporting the sun's disk and horizon with his upraised arms on his shoulders. There is in the British Museum (No. 11,057) a fine example of an ægis in bronze with the heads of Shu and **Tefnut,** , his sister, upon it. Shu is bearded and wears two pairs of plumes upon his head; Tefnut has the head of a lion and wears a disk and uræus; B.M. No. 389 is an example of these gods in faïence. Standing figures of Shu, in faïence, have sometimes on his head.

**Ḥāpi** , the god of the Nile, is depicted as a man, sitting or standing, holding a table or altar on which are vases for libations, , and lotus flowers and fruits, he also has a clump of lotus flowers upon his head. **The Nile-god.** The British Museum possesses a figure of this god, No. 11,069, which represents him standing upright, with a table of

**Ḥāpi, the god of the Nile.**

**The Apis Bull.**

offerings of plants, fruits and flowers before him. On his head he wears , and in front is an *ut'at* .

Antiquity of Apis worship.

**Apis** or **Ḥāpi** , "the second life of Ptaḥ," and the incarnation of Osiris, was the name given to the sacred bull of Memphis, where the worship of this god was most ancient, having been introduced from Heliopolis by Kakau, a king of the IInd dynasty. He is variously called "the son of Ptaḥ," "the son of Tmu," "the son of Osiris," and "the son of Seker." In bronze Ḥāpi is sometimes represented in the form of a man with a bull's head, between the horns of which are a disk and an uræus wearing a disk. Usually, however, he is in the form of a bull having a disk and an uræus between the horns; on the back above the shoulders is engraved a vulture with outstretched wings, and on the back, over the hind quarters, is a winged scarab. The bull usually stands on a rectangular pedestal, on the sides of which are inscribed the name and titles of the person who had the bull made; on the same pedestal is frequently a figure of this person kneeling in adoration before him. Figures of Apis in bronze are commoner than those in faïence. According to Herodotus (II. 27–29) Apis was the calf of a cow incapable of conceiving another offspring; "and the Egyptians say, that lightning descends upon the cow from heaven, and that from thence it brings forth Apis. This calf, which is called Apis, has the following marks: it is black, and has a square spot of white on the forehead; and on the back the figure of an eagle; and in the tail double hairs; and on the tongue a beetle."

Description of the Apis bull.

When Apis was dead he was called Ausȧr Ḥāpi or 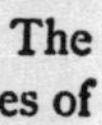 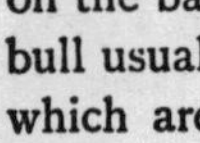, or **Serapis** by the Greeks, and he is represented on coffins in the form of a bull with disk and uræus on his head; on his back is the mummy of the deceased, above which the soul in the form of a hawk is seen hovering. The place where the Apis bulls that lived at Memphis were buried was called the **Serapeum**, and Mariette discovered at Ṣaḳḳȧrah their tombs, dating from the time of Amenophis III. down to that of the Roman Empire. Above each tomb of an Apis bull was built a chapel, and it was the series of chapels which formed the Serapeum properly so called.

The **Mnevis** bull, , worshipped at Heliopolis, is thought by some to represent the same symbolism, and to be identical in form with Apis ; he is called the "renewing of the life of Rā."

**The gods of the Cardinal points.**

**Mesthȧ, Ḥāpi, Ṭuamāutef and Qebḥsennuf,** the four children of Horus (see *Canopic Jars*, p. 194), are common in glazed faïence, but rare in bronze.

**Sati** , together with **Ānqet**  and Chnemu, formed the triad of Elephantine, and she seems to resemble Nephthys in some of her attributes. She usually stands upright, holding ☥ in her right hand, and  in her left. The British Museum possesses one example, No. 110, in bronze, in which she is represented seated. On her head she wears the crown of Upper Egypt, in the front of which is an

The Mnevis Bull.

Mesthȧ.

uræus; a pair of horns follows the contour of the white crown, and above them is a star. No. 11,143 is a fine bronze figure of a woman, standing upright upon a pedestal; the right arm hangs by her side, but the left arm is bent, and her hand, holding an object, is laid upon her breast. She has the same head-dress as No. 110, and I believe her to be the same goddess, although she is labelled Hesi-Sept. [Isis-Sothis or the Dog Star.] Dr. Birch probably had some reason for thus labelling it, but it is unknown to me. The British Museum possesses one example also in faïence, No. 13,664, in which the goddess stands upright.

Other forms of Isis.

**Sebek** 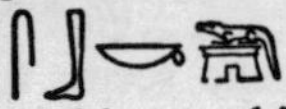 represented the destroying power of the sun, and his worship is as old as the XIIIth dynasty. The British Museum possesses one example of this god in bronze, No. 22,924, in which he stands upright, and has the head of a crocodile surmounted with disk, plumes and uræi, which have disks and horns .

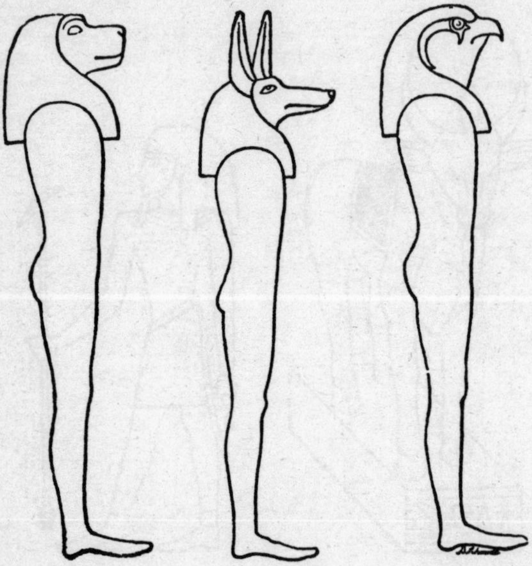

Ḥāpi. Ṭuamāutef. Qebḥsennuf.

**Ȧnḥer**, "the leader of the celestial regions," which Shu supports, is usually represented wearing plumes, and holding a dart; he is at times called *neb māb*, "lord of the dart." The British Museum possesses a glazed faïence pendant, No. 11,335, upon which this god is represented in relief, standing upright and wearing plumes; in his right hand he holds and in the left the sceptre. This sceptre is usually composed of , , and arranged perpendicularly one above the other. He is sometimes called *Ȧn-ḥer Shu se Rā*, "Ȧn-ḥer Shu, the son of Rā."

**Bes**, a god whose worship in Egypt dates from a very remote period, seems to have possessed a double character. He is represented as a grotesque person with horns and eyes on a level with the top of his head, his tongue hangs out, and he has bandy legs. He wears a crown of

Sati

Anqet

feathers on his head, and a leopard's skin thrown round his body. As a warrior, or the god of war, he is armed with a shield and sword, and sometimes he has a bow; he was also the god of music and the dance, and in this character he is represented as a tailed creature, half man, half animal, playing a harp, or striking cymbals together and dancing. It is thought that he symbolized the destructive power of nature, and in this capacity he is identified in the Book of the Dead with Set; as the god of joy and pleasure figures of him are carved upon the *kohl* jars, and other articles used by Egyptian ladies in their toilet. The worship of this god seems to have been introduced into Egypt from *Neter ta*, *i.e.*, the land which was situated by the eastern bank of the Nile, supposed by the Egyptians to be the original home of the gods. Figures of this god in bronze and faïence are very common, and they represent him as described above. Faïence figures were made as much as fourteen inches long,

**The various aspects of Bes.**

**Worship of Bes of foreign origin.**

Sebek.

Ȧnḥeru.

and were sometimes in relief and sometimes "in the round." The British Museum possesses a large mould (No. 20,883) used for making flat figures, presented by F. G. Hilton Price, F.S.A., who obtained it from Bubastis; it also possesses a beautiful figure in the round in blue glazed faïence (No. 28,112), about fourteen inches high. A remarkable example of the use of the head and face of this god is furnished by a bronze bell in the British Museum (No. 6374). The plumes on his head form the handle, and the head, hollowed out, forms the bell. Bronze and faïence statues of this god, to which have been added the distinguishing characteristics of many other gods, also exist. B.M. No. 17,169 is a bronze ithyphallic bird with two pairs of outstretched wings and the legs of a man, from the knees of which spring serpents, the arms of a man, and the head of Bes. Above the wings is a second pair of outstretched arms, with clenched fists, and on each side of his head, in relief, are the heads of a ram, a dog-headed ape, a crocodile, and a hawk (?). Above the head are two pairs of horns, two pairs of uræi and two pairs of plumes, between which is a disk. In this figure are united the attributes of Àmen-Rā, Àmsu, Horus, Chnemu, Sebek, and other gods. No. 1205, a bronze cast from a genuine bronze, makes this polytheistic figure stand upon crocodiles; the whole group is enclosed within a serpent having his tail in his mouth. A very interesting example of a similar kind of figure in faïence is described by Lanzone in his *Dizionario*, p. 211, tav. lxxx., and compare B.M. No. 11,821. It need hardly be said that such figures belong to a very late period, and they are found imitated on gems inscribed for the Gnostics; see B.M. Nos. G. 10, 11, 12, 151, 205, etc. On the Metternich stele Bes is represented in much the same way as in the bronze figures,

Various forms of Bes.

**Bes.**

but in the pair of outstretched arms and hands he holds sceptres of , , , knives, , etc., and in those which hang by his side he holds  and ; he has on his head in addition eight knives and the figure  "myriads of years." He stands on an oval in which are a lion, two serpents, a jackal, crocodile, scorpion, hippopotamus and tortoise. This scene is repeated very accurately on a Gnostic lapis-lazuli plaque in the British Museum, No. 12, on the back of which is an address to ΙΑω ΣΑΒΑωΘ = יָהּ צְבָאוֹת with whom this polytheistic deity was identified. Figures of the god Bes are common on gems and seals other than Egyptian, and on a small Babylonian cylinder in the possession of Sir Charles Nicholson he is represented in the form in which he ordinarily occurs . On a red carnelian cylinder in the British Museum (Reg. No. $\frac{49}{\frac{6-23}{10}}$) he is engraved, full face, wearing plumes, and holding a lotus flower in each hand; on each side of him is a male bearded figure, with upraised hands and arms, supporting a winged disk. This seal was inscribed for Arsaces, and belongs to the Persian period.

Bes in Babylonian art.

**Sechet** , also written , was the wife of Ptaḥ, and was, in this capacity, the mother of Nefer-Åtmu and Ī-em-ḥetep; she was the second person of the triad of Memphis. She represented the violent heat of the sun and its destroying power, and in this capacity destroyed the souls of the wicked in the underworld. In bronze and faïence figures she has the head of a lion, upon which she wears the disk and uræus, and she holds  in her right hand and  in her left; she is sometimes seated, when her hands are laid upon her knees.

**Bast**  represents the heat of the sun in its softened form as the producer of vegetation. She has often the head of a lion, but, properly speaking, the head of a cat is her distinguishing characteristic; in her right hand she holds a sistrum, on her left arm she carries a basket, and in her left hand she holds an ægis. She was chiefly worshipped at Bubastis, Pa-Bast, where a magnificent temple was built in her honour. Bronze figures of this goddess are tolerably numerous, and she is represented, both sitting and standing, wearing the disk and uræus on her head. In faïence, standing figures hold a sceptre (B.M. No. 236), or (B.M. No. 233), or an ægis (B.M. No. 11,297); when seated she often holds a sistrum, B.M. No. 272; a fine large example of the goddess seated is B.M. No. 277. Such figures are sometimes inscribed with the prayer, "may she grant all life and power, all health, and joy of heart," , or, "I am Bast, the lady of life,"

*The Lady of Bubastis.*

Bast.

**Menḥit** represented the power of light or heat, or both; in faïence she is represented as an upright woman, walking, having a lion's head, upon which she wears a disk and uræus; in her right hand is , and in her left

**Mut** , the "mother," was the wife of Åmen, and the second member of the Theban triad; she is called the "lady of Åsher," , the name given to a district to the south of the great temple of Åmen-Rā at Karnak, where her temple was situated. She symbolized Nature, the mother of all things. In bronze and faïence figures she is represented as a woman, seated or standing, wearing a head-dress in the form of a vulture, surmounted by the crowns of Upper and Lower Egypt; she holds in her right hand, and in her left.

*The universal mother.*

**Net** , or Neith, the "Weaver" or "Shooter," was a counterpart of the goddess Mut, and was also identified with

*The Lady of Saïs.*

Hathor; she wears the crown of Lower Egypt on her head, and she is often represented armed with bow and arrows. In bronze and faïence figures of this goddess are tolerably common.

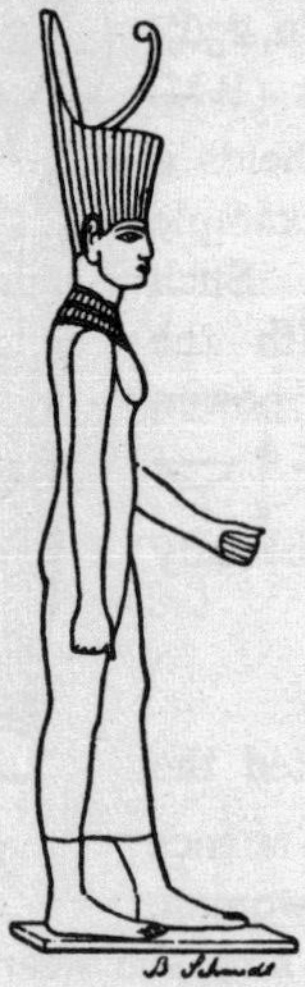

Net (Neith).

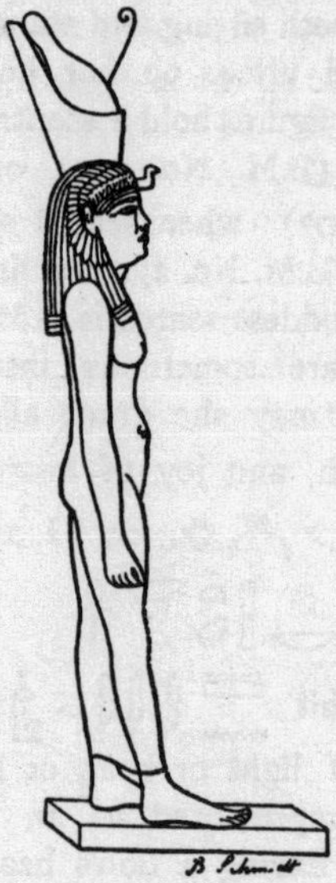

Mut.

The goddess of Right.

Maāt , the "daughter of Rā and mistress of the gods," symbolized Law, and she is always represented with *maāt*, emblematic of Law, upon her head; in papyri two Maāt are shown together, each wearing , but sometimes this feather alone takes the place of the head. In figures of bronze, lapis-lazuli, and faïence she is represented sitting down.

Hathor, in Egyptian , or Ḥet-Ḥert, the "house of Horus," is identified with Nut, the sky, or place in which she brought forth and suckled Horus; she was the wife of Ȧtmu, a form of Rā. She is represented as a woman cow-headed, with horns and a disk between them, and shares with Isis and Mut many of their attributes.[1] She is often represented as a cow coming forth from the mountain of the west. The worship of Hathor is exceedingly ancient, and she was supposed to be the goddess of beauty, love, and joy, and the benefactress of the world. The forms[2] in which she is depicted on the monuments are as numerous as the aspects from which she could be regarded. Full length figures of this goddess in bronze and faïence are comparatively few,[3] but plaques and pendants of faïence upon which her head is inscribed or painted are common.

The goddess of fine art.

For a fine example in bronze of Hathor, cow-headed, wearing horns, disk, uræus and plumes, see B.M. No. 22,925. The British Museum also possesses two interesting bronze hollow-work portions of menàts in which Hathor is represented in

Maāt.

Ḥet-Ḥeru (Hathor).

[1] A list of the gods with whom she is identified is given in Lanzone, *Dizionario*, p. 863, 864.

[2] On a pendant, B.M. No. 302, she is represented at full length, in relief.

[3] For a fine example, see B.M. No. 22,925.

profile. No. 20,760 shows the goddess wearing an uræus on her forehead, and four uræi on her head; she has the usual head-dress of women falling over her shoulders. Beneath is a Hathor-headed sistrum, with pendent uræi, resting on . Beneath in an oval is the cow of Hathor, wearing ,

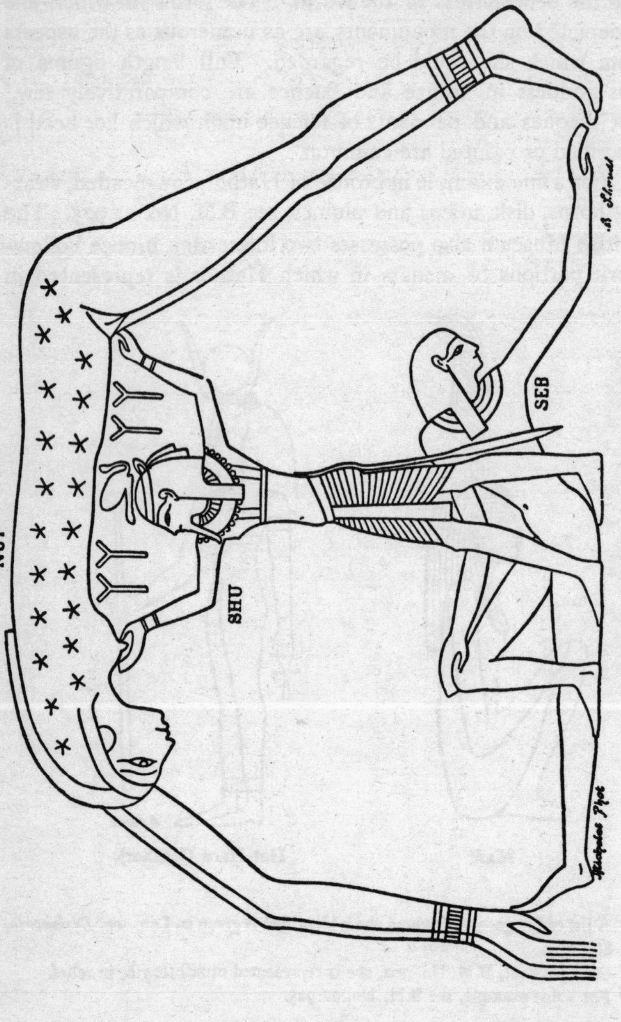


The god Shu lifting up Nut from Seb.

standing in a boat. Above, on each side, is an uræus. One wears the crown of Upper Egypt, , and the other wears the crown of Lower Egypt. This beautiful object was found at Dêr el-Baḥari, and is inscribed with the prenomen of Amenophis III. (). No. 300 represents the goddess with a vulture head-dress, wearing . Below, in relief, are a figure of the goddess, and a floral ornament; it is inscribed , "Hathor, lady of heaven."

Nu was the god of the sky and the husband of Nut.

The goddess of the sky.

Nut , the sky, the wife of Seb, and mother of Osiris, Isis, Set, Nephthys, Anubis, Shu, and Tefnut, was represented by a woman having a vase of water on her head, and holding in her right hand and in her left. She was painted on the outside of coffins, and was supposed

Nut. Seb.

to protect with her wings the deceased within. Figures of this goddess in bronze or faïence are unknown to me.

**Seb**, was the husband of Nut, the sky, and father of Osiris, Isis, and the other gods of that cycle; figures of this god in bronze or faïence are unknown to me.

**Serq**, daughter of Rā, wife of Horus, and identified with Sesheta and Isis, symbolized the scorching heat of the sun. A bronze figure in the Louvre (see Pierret, *Panthéon Egyptien*, p. 17; Lanzone, *Dizionario*, tav. ccclxii.), gives her the body of a scorpion, and the head of a woman wearing disk and horns, by which she is identified with Isis. There is a similar figure in the British Museum, No. 11,629, on the base of which is inscribed, "Isis, Giver of Life," and a small bronze scorpion. B.M. No. 18,667 also gives her the head and arms of a woman with disk and horns. The figures of this goddess, other than bronze, are usually made of lapis-lazuli.

Serq.

**Maȧḥes** is represented as a man, lion-headed, wearing a disk and uræus; a few figures of this god in faïence are known.*

* See Lanzone, *Dizionario*, p. 272.

**Neḥeb-ka** is a god mentioned in the Book of the Dead (chap. xvii. 61; chap. xxx. 3, etc.), and pictures of him are found upon coffins. In bronze figures he has the body of a man, and the head of a serpent; in wood he has the body of an animal, and the head of a serpent, and holds in his paws (B.M. No. 11,779), in faïence he has an animal's body and a serpent's head, and either holds outstretched in his paws (B.M. No. 11,795), or raises them to his mouth (B.M. No. 1197). He sometimes wears plumes and horns.

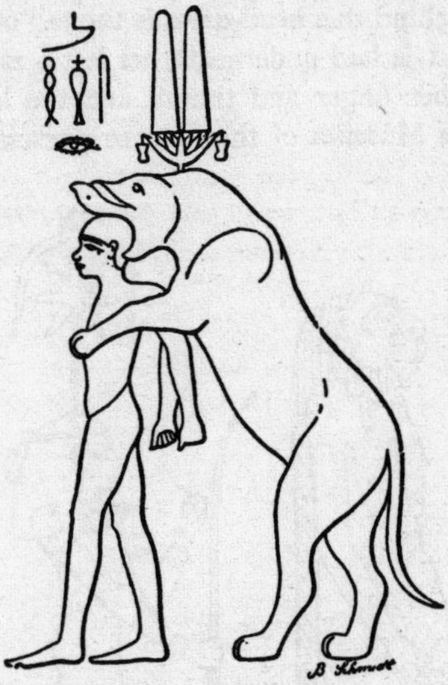


**Maàḥes.**

**Seker.**

**Seker** or Socharis, a form of the night-sun, is represented as a man, hawk-headed, holding , and in his hands; for Ptaḥ-Seker-Àusàr figures, see page 215.

**Polytheistic figures of gods.**

There are among the Egyptian gods in the British Museum two examples (Nos. 1419 and 22,930) of a polytheistic figure of considerable interest. They have hawks' ithyphallic[1] bodies, human legs and feet, each of which stands on a crocodile, and human hands and arms; the front of the head is in the form of a jackal's head, surmounted by plumes and disk, and the back is in the form of a ram's head, surmounted by a disk and uræus. In the right hand is a whip , and in the left an object which I cannot identify. Each group stands on a pedestal with a circle formed by a serpent having his tail in his mouth. These figures have much in common with those described under the name Bes, and may be variant forms of this god.

Another figure of interest is No. 24,385, which represents a seated woman, with the head of a sheep, surmounted by disk, uræus, and horns; behind this head-dress is the tail of a scorpion. The right hand is laid underneath her left breast, which she touches with her finger and thumb, and the left rests upon her knee. The Museum of the Louvre possesses

Ta-urt (Thoueris). Thoueris, lion-headed. Sefech-Aabu, or Sesheta.

[1] In No. 22,930, the hawk's body is more distinct, and has a head, surmounted by a disk, and the feathers of the tail rest upon a hippopotamus.

a similar figure with the addition of a naked child whom she holds upon her knees, and whom she is about to suckle. Lanzone (*Dizionario*, p. 841, for the figure see tav. cccxi.) thinks that the sheep and scorpion headed god represents Isis, and the child, Horus.

**Ta-urt** , or Thoueris, was the wife of Set, and she is usually represented in bronze and faïence with the head and body of a hippopotamus, the hind-quarters of a lion, and the tail of a crocodile. On her head she wears a modius which is sometimes surmounted by a disk, horns, and plumes .

**Sefeχ-Āabu** or **Sesheta** is a form of the goddess Hathor which was worshipped in Hermopolis, and was also adored in Memphis from the earliest dynasties.

## Figures of Animals, Birds and Reptiles, Sacred to the Gods.

The **figures of animals** found in the temples, tombs and ruined houses of Egypt may, like those of the gods, be divided into three classes:—1. Votive; 2. Those worn as amulets either by the living or dead; 3. Those which stood in houses. They are made of bronze, steatite, basalt, faïence, wood, wood gilded, lapis-lazuli, wax, and many other materials. Those in bronze, stone, and wood were usually made for temples, and to stand in tombs; those in faïence, lapis-lazuli, and other precious stones were placed on the bead-work, or under the folds of the wrappings of mummies, or were worn suspended to necklaces, by the living; those placed in the walls of houses, but which are not sufficiently well distinguished to give many details, were usually made of faïence cast in moulds. The animals and reptiles of which figures are most commonly found are:—

Animals sacred to the gods.

1. **Ape**, dog-headed, 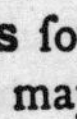, wearing disk and crescent, sacred to Thoth and Chensu. Figures in bronze, stone, wood and faïence, in which he is represented sitting, sometimes on a pedestal with steps, or standing, are common; sometimes

he holds  (B.M. No. 1442), and sometimes a goat (B.M. No. 11,910).

2. **Hippopotamus** , *Ta-urt*, Thoueris, standing on the hind-quarters of a lion, and holding the tail of a crocodile; figures in bronze and faïence are common. The most beautiful example of this composite animal in green basalt is preserved in the Museum at Gîzeh, a cast of which is exhibited in the Egyptian Gallery of the British Museum, No. 1075.

3. **Cow,** sacred to Hathor, with disk between her horns, .

4. **Lion** , couchant or running, sacred to Horus. Examples are very common in faïence. Frequently the body of the lion has a lion's head at each end of it, and sometimes there is a lion's head at one end, and a bull's head at the other; on the back, between the two heads, is the disk of the sun, , the whole representing the sun on the horizon . The two heads, facing in opposite directions, are supposed to represent the south and north, *i.e.*, the sun's course daily. An example in which each lion's head has two faces, one looking towards the south and the other towards the north, is figured in Lanzone, *Dizionario*, tav. cvi.

5. **Sphinx** , couchant or sitting on his haunches, sacred to Harmachis. Figures in bronze and faïence are tolerably common.

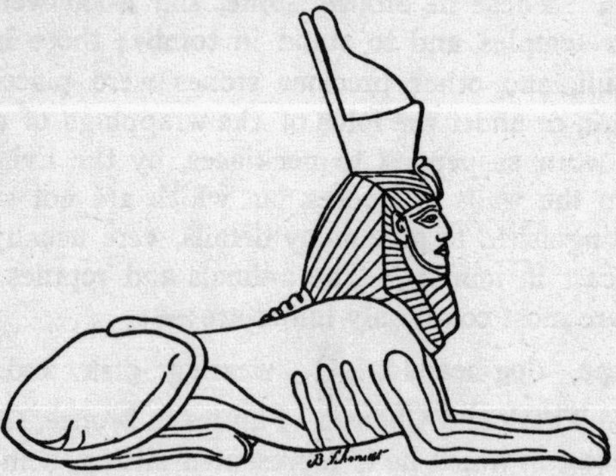

**Sphinx.**

6. **Bull**, sacred to Apis or Mnevis, having disk and uræus between his horns, and the figures of a vulture with outspread wings and a winged scarab on his back. Figures in bronze and stone are more common than in faïence.

7. **Ram,** , sacred to Chnemu or Åmen-Rā; figures in bronze and faïence are tolerably common.

Animals sacred to the gods.

8. **Cat**, sacred to Bast, lady of Bubastis. Large votive figures of the cat were made of bronze and wood, the eyes being inlaid with obsidian and gold; B.M. No. 22,927 has the eyes, and a large number of the hairs of the body, inlaid with gold. The smaller figures worn for ornament by the votaries of Bast are made of bronze, stone, rock-crystal, faïence, &c.; in the smaller figures the cat is represented with one, two, or more kittens, and the top of the sceptre is often ornamented with a cat.

9. **Jackal**, sacred to Ånpu (Anubis), or to Åp-uat. In bronze figures, which are plentiful, he stands on a pedestal which fitted on to the top of a sceptre or staff; faïence figures are not very common. A large number of wooden models from the top of sepulchral boxes are known.

10. **Hare**, sacred to Osiris Unnefer; figures in faïence are common.

11. **Sow**, sacred to Set (?), was the abomination of Horus, according to the 112th chapter of the Book of the Dead; figures of this animal in faïence are fairly common. B.M. No. 11,897 has a head at each end of its body.

12. **Hippopotamus**, sacred to Set or Typhon; many large and beautiful examples of this animal in glazed faïence and steatite exist in public and private collections.

13. **Stag**. Figures in which the animal is represented with its legs tied together ready for sacrifice are known in bronze, *e.g.*, B.M. No. 1696.

14. **Hedgehog**, a few examples of which, in bronze and faïence, are known.

15. **Shrew-mouse,** sacred to Horus (?), examples of which are commoner in bronze than in faïence.

16. **Ichneumon.** Examples in bronze, in which the animal wears disk and horns and plumes, are known, but figures in faïence are rare.

17. **Crocodile**, sacred to Sebek; examples in bronze and faïence are fairly common.

Birds sacred to the gods.

18. **Vulture**, sacred to Mut; figures of this bird in bronze and faïence are few.

19. **Hawk**, sacred to Horus; votive figures are made of bronze, stone, and wood, and the hawk wears either the crown of Upper or Lower Egypt, or both crowns united. In smaller figures worn for ornament, it wears a disk (B.M. No. 1889) or, (B.M. No. 1850), or plumes (B.M. No. 1859); it is often man-headed, when it represents the soul, , and sometimes two hawks are on one pedestal, and each has the head of a man. A form of Horus, worshipped in Arabia under the name of **Sepṭ**, is often found in hard stone and wood; figures made of the latter material are generally found on the small chests which cover the portions of human bodies placed in the pedestals of Ptaḥ-Seker-Ȧusȧr figures. When complete they have plumes on their heads.

20. **Ibis**, sacred to Thoth; figures in bronze and faïence are not rare.

21. **Frog** and **Toad.** Figures of both reptiles are common in bronze and faïence.

22. **Fish**. The five kinds of fish of which figures in bronze and faïence are known are the Oxyrhynchus, Phagrus, Latus, Silurus, and the Lepidotus; of these the Oxyrhynchus, Silurus, and Lepidotus are the commonest. The Oxyrhynchus fish, B.M. No. 1953, has on its back horns, disk, and uræus; fish were sacred to Hathor, Isis, Mut, and other goddesses.

23. **Scorpion**, sacred to Serqet. Figures in bronze have often a woman's head on which are horns and disk, and if mounted, the sides of the base have inscriptions upon them which show that the scorpion was regarded as Isis–Serqet. Faïence figures of this reptile are tolerably numerous.

**Uræus** or serpent, sacred to or emblem of **Meḥen**, , or **Merseḳer**, ; figures in bronze and faïence are not rare.

**Scarab**, emblem of the god Cheperȧ (see p. 234). The largest scarab known is preserved in the British Museum (Southern Egyptian Gallery, No. 74), and is made of green granite; it was probably a votive offering in some temple, and was brought from Constantinople, whither it was probably taken after the Roman occupation of Egypt. The scarabs worn for ornament round the neck, and in finger-rings, were made of gold, silver, every kind of precious stone known to the Egyptians, and faïence. B.M. No. 11,630 is an interesting example of a horned scarab; B.M. No. 2043, in faïence, has the head of a hawk, and B.M. No. 12,040 has the head of a bull.

## Figures of Kings and Private Persons.

Figures of kings and private persons were placed in temples or tombs either by the persons they represented, or by those who wished to do honour to them. Figures of kings occupied prominent places in the temples, and services were performed before them, and offerings made to them as to the gods, among the number of whom kings were supposed to have entered. The Rosetta Stone states (ll. 39–42) that the priests of all Egypt decreed that a figure or statue of Ptolemy V. Epiphanes, should be placed in the most conspicuous part of every temple, that the priests should thrice daily perform services before it, and that sacred decorations should be placed upon it. The custom of placing such figures in temples and tombs is as old as the IVth dynasty at least, for many examples of this period are known; as we are certain that religious services were held in tombs during

Uses of statues.

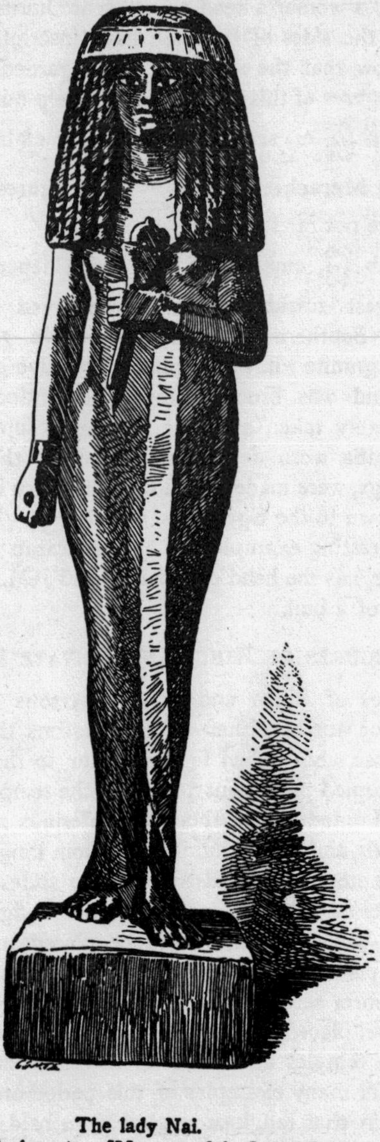

The lady Nai.
XIXth dynasty. [Museum of the Louvre].

the earlier dynasties, figures of deceased persons must have been placed in them, and it would seem that the custom is as old as the settlement of the Egyptians in Egypt. Votive figures of the gods were rarely colossal, but figures of kings were made of every size, and their heights vary from a few inches to several feet; the colossi of Amenophis III., of Ḥeru-em-Ḥeb, and of Rameses II., are examples of the extreme size to which figures of kings attained. In the earlier dynasties there can be no doubt that the artist endeavoured to make the form and features of the figure exactly like the person for whom it was made; how well they succeeded is evident from the most cursory examination of the figures of the first six dynasties exhibited in European museums, or in the Museum of Gîzeh, which is particularly

Votive statues.

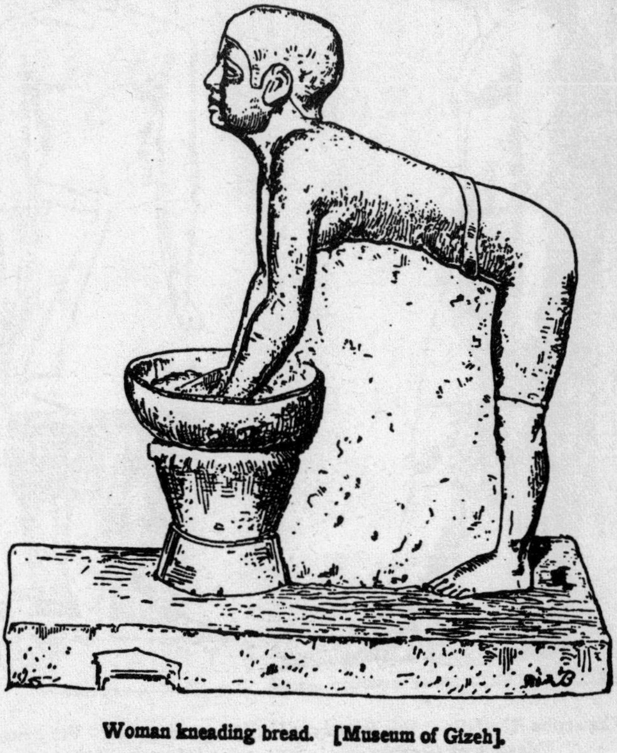

**Woman kneading bread. [Museum of Gizeh].**

rich in figures of this period. The famous Shêkh el-Beled is what may well be termed a "speaking likeness," and the other figures of that date show that he is not a solitary success of the Egyptian artist. In later times conventional representation was adopted in forming the figure, with the result that the sculptor lost the art of portraiture once and for all. Figures were made of granite, basalt, and other hard stones, limestone, gold, silver, bronze, wood, steatite, faïence, and terra-cotta. Standing figures have the arms placed at the sides of the body ,and the hands usually hold a roll; sometimes, however,

The scribe Kha-f-Rā. Vth dynasty. [Museum of Gizeh].

Limestone statue. Vth dynasty. [Museum of Gizeh].

they hold a sceptre, or weapon, or flowers, or ☥, and figures made in the form of Osiris have the hands crossed over the breast. Figures kneeling or sitting on the ground hold with both hands tablets or altars, or shrines engraved with funereal inscriptions, before them; figures seated on thrones or chairs have the hands laid flat on the knees. All figures were draped, and the pedestals or plinths on which they stood were usually inscribed with the names and titles of the persons for whom they were made; at times the various

Statue of Ti. Vth dynasty.
[Museum of Gîzeh]

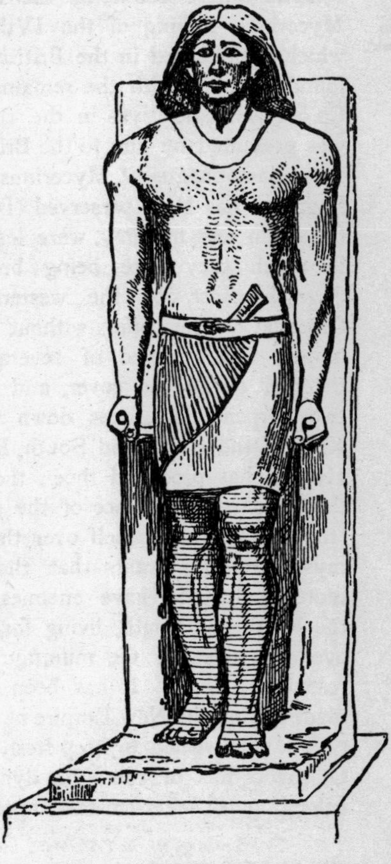

Statue of Rā-Nefer. Vth dynasty.
[Museum of Gîzeh]

members of the deceased's family were sculptured in relief, with their names on the seat. Groups of two or more figures, husband and wife, brother and sister, father, mother and child, were placed in tombs, and from the biographical notices inscribed upon them many valuable historical facts have been gleaned.

## COFFINS.

Egyptian coffins are usually made of wood, but under the Ptolemies and Romans hard stone came into use.

Oldest coffin in the world.

The oldest coffin in the world is probably that of Mycerinus, a king of the IVth dynasty, about B.C. 3633, which is preserved in the British Museum, No. 6647; it was found, together with the remains of a wrecked mummy, by Colonel Howard Vyse in the third pyramid of Gîzeh, and was presented by him to the British Museum in 1837. The stone sarcophagus of Mycerinus, of which only a very small fragment has been preserved (B.M. No. 6646), and parts of the coffin and mummy, were lost by the wreck of the ship in which they were being brought to England, on the Spanish coast, on the western side of the Strait of Gibraltar. The coffin, without paintings, had originally a human face, formed of several pieces of wood pegged together on to the cover, and the well-cut inscription in two perpendicular lines down the cover reads: "Osiris, King of the North and South, Men-kau-Rā, living for ever. Heaven has produced thee; thou wast conceived by Nut; thou comest of the race of the god Seb. Thy mother Nut (the sky) spreads herself over thee in her form of heavenly mystery. She grants that thou shalt be a god; never more shalt thou have enemies, O Men-kau-Rā, King of the North and South, living for ever." On the cover, just over the knees of the mummy, are two raised projections resembling knees. It has been stated[1] that this coffin was made during the New Empire at the expense of some pious person who wished to keep fresh the memory of Mycerinus. Of the coffins of the VIth dynasty, the fragments of that belonging to Seker-em-sa-f[2] appear to be the only remains;

[1] See *Aegyptische Zeitschrift*, 1892, p. 94.

[2] Maspero, *Guide du Visiteur au Musée de Boulaq*, p. 311.

but it is tolerably certain that coffins during the first six dynasties were made of plain wood, that they had a human face, and that the inscriptions were short and cut into the cover.

**Coffins about B.C. 2500.**

Coffins during the XIth and XIIth dynasties are usually rectangular in form, with a cover consisting of one flat plank about 2½ inches thick. Both coffin and cover are very rough, and the paintings consist of large stripes of blue, red, white, green, and yellow colours, interspersed with lotus flowers and pictures of funereal offerings, sometimes very rudely drawn. Many of the coffins of this period are, however, of the greatest interest, and B.M. 6654 and 6655 are good typical examples. The former is inscribed on the outside with one line of well-cut hieroglyphics, and is inlaid with ; the inside of the coffin and both inside and outside of the cover are inscribed in hieratic with a number of chapters of the Book of the Dead of the period of the Ancient Empire; this coffin was made for an official called Amamu.[1] The latter, made for Mentu-ḥetep, is of the same form, and is also inscribed in hieratic with chapters from the Book of the Dead.[2] At the same period, coffins with human faces were also made; they were formed of rough pieces of wood, badly put together, and are characterised by a rude, gaudy style of ornamentation. A striking contrast to these is the gilded wooden coffin of Ȧn-ȧntef, B.M. No. 6652, a king of the XIth dynasty, who ruled at Thebes about B.C. 2500. The hardwood face is beautifully carved, and is intended to be a portrait of the deceased; the eyes and eyelids are made of black, white, and blue obsidian, inlaid; the feather work and star ornaments on the coffin appear to have originated at this period. The ordinary ornamentation of coffins at this period is a large collar, beneath which are figures of the uræus and vulture, emblematic of dominion over the north and south, and under the feet are kneeling figures of Isis and Nephthys, who mourn the dead Osiris.

**Ornamentation of early coffins.**

The coffins of the period between the XIIth and the

[1] A facsimile of the text and an English translation were published by Birch, *Coffin of Amamu*, London, 1886.

[2] For facsimiles of other hieratic texts on coffins of the XIth dynasty, see Lepsius, *Aelteste Texte des Todtenbuchs*, Berlin, 1867.

XVIIIth dynasties are imitations of those with the gilded featherwork and bright colours of the XIth and XIIth dynasties; at this period many articles of furniture, vases, etc., were placed in the mummy chamber, either near the coffin or arranged by the walls.

Coffins about about B.C. 1700.

During the XVIIIth dynasty coffins were made very much larger, and were painted inside and outside in black; the face is either gilded or coloured a bright red, the eyes are often inlaid; on the breast is a vulture, and the inscriptions, which divide the lower half of the cover into a series of rectangular sections, are painted in yellow.

With the XIXth dynasty there appears a class of coffin very beautiful to behold. Inside and outside both coffin and cover are profusely decorated with scenes of all kinds, large figures of gods and genii, vignettes from the Book of the Dead with appropriate inscriptions, and a number of emblems and decorations formed of rows of amulets, all painted in the brightest colours, and covered with a bright, yellow, shining varnish. Immediately over the mummy of a royal person, or of a wealthy man, was laid a slightly convex covering of wood, made in the form of a mummy, painted with the scenes alluded to above, and varnished. On the inside of this covering the boat of the sun, the mummy with plants growing out from it, and other scenes were traced in yellow, on a mauve or purple ground. The mummy and this covering were placed in a coffin with a cover having a human face, and the hands, in relief, were crossed upon the breast. The lower part was ornamented with scenes in which the deceased is represented adoring various gods in shrines; these scenes are divided into two groups by one or more perpendicular lines of inscription which record the name and titles of the deceased. This coffin, with the mummy and its wooden covering, was then placed inside a larger coffin, upon the outside and inside of which were painted scenes similar to those on the inner coffin, but with less attention to details. The inside of the cover of the outer coffin was often left blank. A very fine example of a set of two coffins, and the wooden covering of the mummy, is that of Nesi-pa-ur-shefi, which is described in detail in the "Catalogue of the Egyptian

The finest coffins made about B.C 1400.

Antiquities in the Fitzwilliam Museum." A third, and even a fourth, coffin was sometimes used for one mummy.

The coffins of the XXth dynasty are good imitations of the best examples of the XIXth dynasty; the paintings are, however, neither so fine nor so carefully executed.

**Coffins about B.C. 600.**

From the XXIst to the XXVIth dynasty coffins exhibit many varieties of decoration; they are sometimes painted black, or the wood is left altogether in its natural colour, and the faces are often red. Sometimes they are painted with inscriptions in many colours on a white ground, and the scenes on the covers are divided into two groups by perpendicular inscriptions between them. Faces of coffins of this period are also flesh coloured and gilded, and the eyes, made of obsidian, are inlaid between eyelids of the same material or of bronze. Notwithstanding the fact that mummies of this period are protected by cartonnage cases, they are laid in two and even three coffins. Akhmîm coffins of this period are covered with rows of gods and elaborate collars, and are profusely inscribed with extracts from the Book of the Dead; the mummies inside them have gilded masks and are usually covered with a network of glazed faïence bugle beads, upon which are laid figures of Nut and the four children of Horus in smaller bead work. These coffins belong to a class which has little in common either with those of Memphis or Thebes. Favourite scenes on coffins from the XXIInd to the XXVIth dynasties are the weighing of the heart, and the soul visiting the body.

**Decay of the manufacture of coffins.**

After the XXVIth dynasty the art of coffin making degenerated, and as a result the examples of this period known to us exhibit rough and careless work, the scenes of the weighing of the heart, etc., spread right across the cover, and the inscriptions show that the copyist had very little or no knowledge of their meaning. On the other hand very handsome coffins, in the form of a man, in granite and basalt, became fashionable, and the high polish and beauty of the cutting of the figures, inscriptions, etc., show that although the art of mummifying was decaying, and the national religion of Egypt changing, attempts were made to imitate ancient art in its best forms.

Græco-Roman coffins and their decoration.

Under the Ptolemies and Romans the forms of coffins and their decorations altered very much. Coffins are now made of thin pieces of wood, and are usually rectangular in shape, and the inscriptions upon them, like those on coffins of the earlier dynasties, are rarely extracts from the Book of the Dead. Sandals, pillows, red pottery, and papyri were often buried with the dead at this epoch. Stone coffins, covered with figures and inscriptions, are also common, but they are found chiefly in Lower Egypt. In the early centuries of our era, the decay of the art of making coffins followed that of mummifying, and the coffins are large, badly shaped and ugly, the inscriptions upon them are copies of old formulæ, but so carelessly written and so full of mistakes that they are unintelligible. The custom of laying mummies in old tombs increased greatly, and chapels, serdâbs, pits and sarcophagi-chambers were alike used for piling up mummies by hundreds and thousands; and one single roll of papyrus or parchment laid in a tomb contained the names of all those who were buried there. This was practically the end of the Egyptian system of mummifying and burial. Within a hundred years of the preaching of Christianity at Alexandria by St. Mark, a large part of the population of Egypt had become Christian; the resurrection of the body of Christ made the Egyptians hope for the resurrection of their own bodies, and though they could not eradicate from themselves all traces of their old belief, they abandoned gradually the making of their dead into mummies, and were content to lay their bodies in the earth, wrapped in linen cloths only, to await revivification.

Coffins of all periods were closed by dowels, let into cavities in the sides and cover, through which pegs of wood were driven; these were covered with plaster and painted, and were thus invisible.

## SARCOPHAGI.

Sarcophagi of the Ancient Empire.

Egyptian **sarcophagi** are made of black or green basalt, granite, agglomerate and limestone. During the first six dynasties they are rectangular, and the cover is either flat like a plank, or vaulted. Running round the edge of the inside of the cover is a projection about two inches deep, which is carefully chiselled to fit a hollow corresponding in size in the sarcophagus, and after the cover was lowered upon it, a layer of fine cement was run in between, and the sarcophagus became hermetically sealed. Not content with this, holes were drilled sideways through the cover and the sarcophagus, and into these pegs of wood were driven. Covers have usually at each end one or more projections, whereby it is easy to lift them; the magnificent sarcophagus of Chufu-ānch (IVth dynasty), preserved at Gîzeh,[1] has two rounded projections at each end of the cover. The sarcophagus of Mycerinus (IVth dynasty) found in his pyramid at Gîzeh resembled a small building; it was beautifully sculptured, but was absolutely without ornament. Sarcophagi of this period have their sides made to represent the openings, vestibules, and doors of maṣṭabas, and the inscriptions upon them usually contain only the names and titles of their owners, and prayers that sepulchral gifts may be made to the deceased on the specified festivals. Of the sarcophagi of the VII–Xth dynasties nothing is known.

Sarcophagi of the Middle Empire.

During the XIth and XIIth dynasties, rectangular wooden coffins seem to have superseded, in some measure, stone sarcophagi, royal examples of which of this period are unknown. A granite sarcophagus of this period at Florence resembles in form, style of inscription, etc., those of the first six dynasties.

Sarcophagi from the XIIIth to the XVIIth dynasty are unknown.

In the XVIIIth dynasty the sarcophagi of Memphis are in the form of a mummy, and are made of granite; they are very sparingly ornamented. A perpendicular line of inscription runs from the breast to the feet, and the surface of the cover on each side of it is divided by three or more lines of inscription at right angles to it into sections on which are inscribed figures of gods. The sarcophagus of Ai is a good example of the work of this period.[2]

[1] For a cast see B.M. No: 1111.
[2] For a scale drawing and inscriptions, see Lepsius, *Denkmäler*, Bl. 113 d–g.

In the XIXth dynasty sarcophagi become somewhat smaller, but otherwise differ very little from those of the preceding dynasty. They are usually made of granite, but alabaster, as in that of Seti I., was also used. This magnificent object and its cover were inscribed inside and out with scenes and inscriptions from the "Book of being in the Underworld," inlaid with a pigment of a light greenish-blue colour. The cover was broken in trying to open it, but the sarcophagus itself is intact, and is preserved in Sir John Soane's Museum; the inscriptions were published by Bonomi, *Sarcophagus of Oi Meneptah*, London, 1864, and for translations see *Records of the Past*, vol. X., pp. 79 ff. The chief idea which underlies these scenes is that, just as the life of a man is identified with the course of the sun by day, so the life of the soul after death is identified with the passage of the sun in the nether-world, through which he was supposed to travel during the night. The scenes represent the various parts of the nether-world, and the beings who dwell in them: Isis and Nephthys, Horus the son of Isis and Osiris, Seb and Nut, the four children of Horus, are all inscribed on sarcophagi of this period, and all were supposed to assist in protecting the deceased, who was identified with Osiris. In this dynasty, large, painted, wooden sarcophagi, in the form of mummies, are also common at Thebes.

**Sarcophagus of Seti I.**

In the XXth dynasty, granite was much used for sarcophagi, but the form has changed, and the deceased is represented lying on the cover. He wears a thick, square beard, his hands are freed from their bandages, and hold in them 𓋹, 𓊽, and 𓎬; beneath the long tunic the feet appear, and on the sides of the sarcophagus are figures of the four children of Horus and of other funereal gods. A most interesting example of this period is the sarcophagus of Rameses III., which is made in the form of a cartouche 𓍷; the cover is preserved in the Fitzwilliam Museum (for a description of it see the *Catalogue*), and the sarcophagus is in the Museum of the Louvre. On the head, outside, is the figure of Nephthys, with outstretched wings, emblematic

**Cover of Sarcophagus of Rameses III.**

of her protection of Osiris; the inscriptions give the names and titles of the king, and refer to the course of the sun in the nether-world. On the other side, by the feet, is Isis, also with outstretched wings; on one side is Åp-uat, and on the other Anubis, each jackal-headed. The two sides are ornamented with scenes and inscriptions referring to the passage of the sun, who is being towed along in his boat through the various divisions of the nether-world by their gods, and to his attack, defeat, and slaughter of Āpepi, his chief enemy. Two scenes at the feet, in which Neith and Isis promise to put together the limbs of Osiris, complete the ornamentation of the outside.[1] At the head, inside, are the solar disk, a mummy with a disk and star on his head, and a head of a goddess on each side holding out an arm, the hand of which supports a being who pours out water on the head of the deceased in the form of a mummy. On the sides are figures of an ithyphallic god, hawks, etc., forming scenes from the "Book of being in the Under-world." At the foot is the god Cheperȧ in a disk around which are twined the folds of a serpent; above is the head of a ram being adored by figures of the king, by the sides of which are the cartouches of Rameses III. On the bottom of the sarcophagus is the figure of Hathor, goddess of Amenta, with wings outstretched to receive the deceased.

The sarcophagi of the XXVIth dynasty are usually rectangular, and are made of green and black basalt, and variegated hard stone. Many of the scenes and inscriptions upon them are copied from sarcophagi of the XIXth and XXth dynasties, but long extracts from the Book of the Dead are characteristic of this period, and some sarcophagi are covered entirely with such funereal inscriptions,[2] with the exception of the spaces occupied by the figures of the deceased and Nut, on the outside and inside of the cover respectively, and the figure of Hathor on the bottom inside.

Sarcophagi of the New Empire.

[1] For a fuller description of this sarcophagus see De Rougé, *Notice des Monuments au Musée du Louvre*, Paris, 1872, pp. 173–175, and Seyffarth, *Beiträge*, 2–5, Bl. 6.

[2] *E.g.*, the sarcophagus of Ānch-nes-nefer-ȧb-Rā, B.M. No. 32.

Such sarcophagi are beautifully sculptured, carefully inscribed, and the attention given to detail is marvellous.

After the XXVIth dynasty sarcophagi are sometimes rounded at the head, and the covers have human faces; they are ornamented with rows of figures of gods, the four children of Horus, a number of genii of the netherworld, and inscriptions which state that they have taken the deceased under their protection. Rectangular sarcophagi which taper slightly towards the feet, and are narrower at the base than at the top, are also common.

In the XXXth dynasty massive sarcophagi of granite, basalt and agglomerate, highly polished and beautifully sculptured, become very plentiful; they are found chiefly in Lower Egypt. The inscriptions and scenes upon them are extracts, more or less complete, from the "Book of being in the Under-world," and, in arrangement, they greatly resemble those of the earlier dynasties; a fine example of this period is the sarcophagus of Nectanebus I., B.M. No. 10.

Sarcophagi of the Græco-Roman period.

Under the rule of the Ptolemies and Romans wooden sarcophagi became very common; they consisted of two parts, viz., the board upon which the deceased in his coffin was laid, and the rectangular, vaulted cover, which is, at times, as much as eighteen inches high. The planks from which the covers are made are rarely more than an inch thick, and they are let into four rectangular uprights, which are often made of a hard wood with a fine texture. The vaulted cover has, at times, a gilded hawk upon the top, and a cornice running round the four sides; it was fastened to the board, upon which the coffin stood, by its uprights, one at each corner, which, projecting slightly below the lower edge of the sides, fitted into four rectangular cavities cut in the board. The inside and outside of the vaulted cover are painted in gaudy colours with figures of the gods, the signs of the Zodiac, and inscriptions in hieroglyphics; when the deceased was a Greek, his name and that of his father were also inscribed in Greek. The mummies which belong to such coffins are covered over with a linen cloth on which is painted the god Osiris, with the features of the deceased, wearing the *atef* crown, and holding  and ; on each side of him are two of the children of Horus. The scenes and inscriptions on the sarcophagi of this period show that the people of Egypt had ceased to attach any importance to their meaning, and they appear simply as funereal decorations, without which the sarcophagi would have been incomplete.

## THE EGYPTIAN TOMBS.

The extreme care which the Egyptians took to preserve the bodies of their dead would have been all in vain, if they had not provided secure resting places for their mummies. To guard the mummy intact and ready for the return of the soul, it was necessary to provide tombs which should be safe from the attacks of human beings and from the prowlings of wild animals, and also out of the reach of the infiltration of the waters of the Nile, or of the inundation itself. If the preservation of a mummy was regarded as a sacred duty to be performed by the relatives of the deceased, who were morally bound to show all honour to it, and to spend their money freely on whatever was necessary for its adornment, it follows of a necessity that a house or tomb meet for the habitation of the *ka*, and for the soul after it had been decreed triumphant in the judgment hall of Osiris, must also be provided. The size and beauty of a tomb and its furniture depended, as much as the making of the mummy, upon the means at the disposal of the relatives of a deceased person. Every person in Egypt knew perfectly well that to ensure the resurrection of his body, after the pure soul had returned to inhabit it, it was necessary that every part of it should be preserved in a fitting state, but nevertheless, every person was not able to afford the costly embalming, and the still more costly furniture and tomb and procession which were, no doubt, held by the wealthy to be absolutely necessary for "living a second time." The burial of the very poor of Egypt must have been much the same in all times and in all dynasties. The body, having been salted only, was laid in the sand to a depth of three or four feet, without covering, without ornament, and even without a coffin; sometimes even the salting was

**Double purpose of the Egyptian tomb.**

Drying qualities of Egyptian sand.

dispensed with. The drying up qualities of the sand of Egypt are very remarkable. Some few years ago Sir C. Holled Smith, K.C.B., while making some excavations among the ruins of a temple at Wâdy Ḥalfah, on the west bank of the river, dug up a box, which, having been opened, was seen to contain the body of a European; on making inquiries he found that an English engineer had died there about a dozen years before. The hair and beard and features were unaltered as far as appearance went, but the skin had dried up like parchment, and the body had become much smaller. In tombs of the lower classes of the Ancient

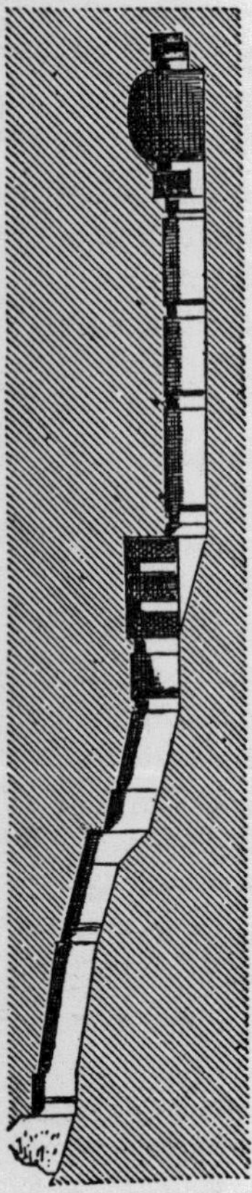

Section of the tomb of Rameses II.

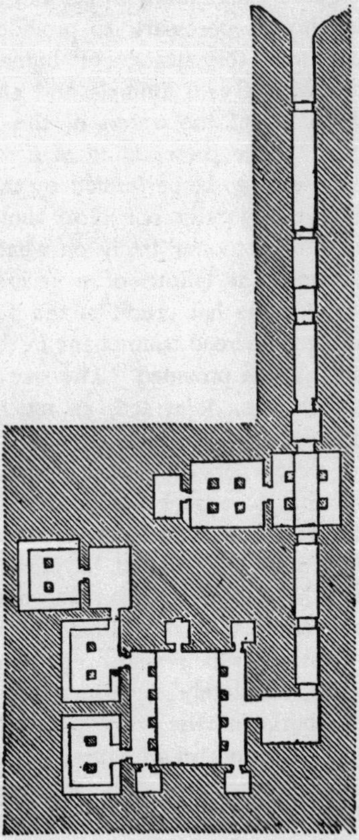

Plan of the tomb of Rameses II.

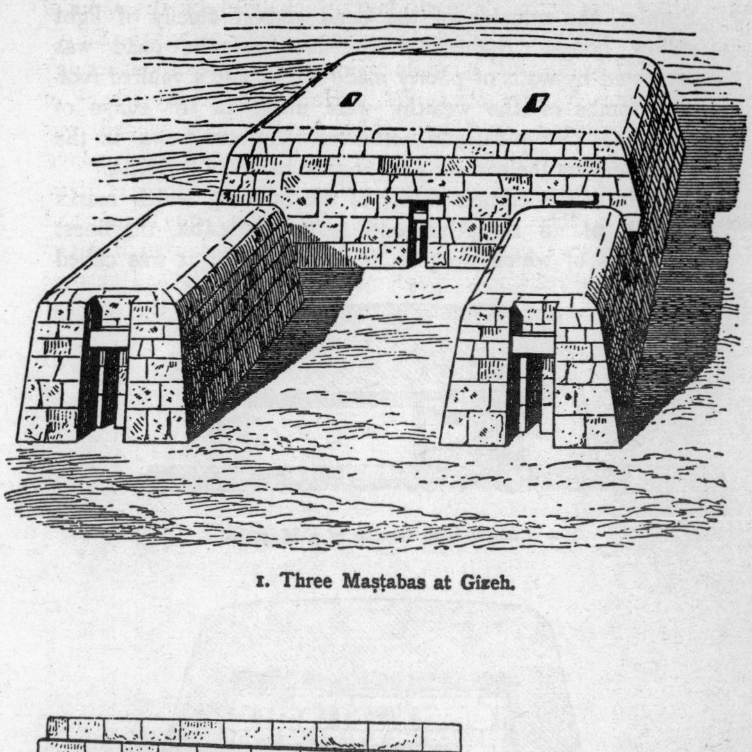

1. Three Maṣṭabas at Gizeh.

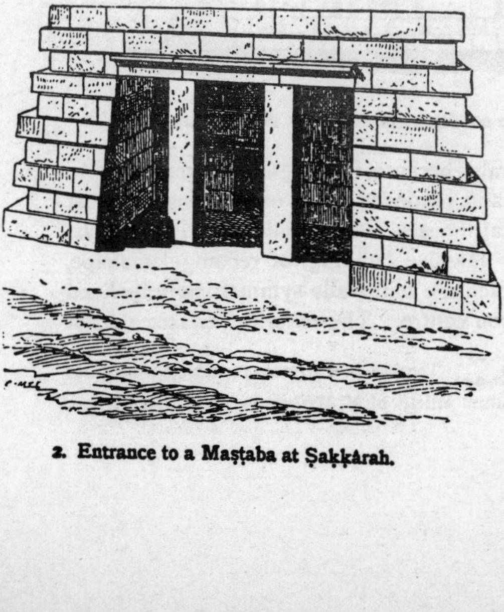

2. Entrance to a Maṣṭaba at Ṣaḳḳârah.

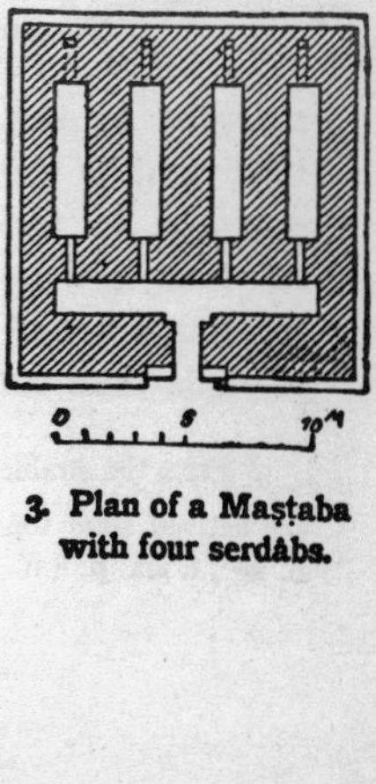

3. Plan of a Maṣṭaba with four serdâbs.

Empire, the remains of the dead consist chiefly of light yellow bones. Sometimes the body of the dead was protected by walls of poorly made bricks, and a vaulted roof. The tombs of the wealthy were made in the shape of maṣṭabas, pyramids, and series of chambers hewn in the mountains on the eastern and western banks of the Nile.

The maṣṭaba tomb.

One of the earliest forms of the building which marks the site of an Egyptian tomb is the **maṣṭaba**,[1] the finest examples of which were built at Ṣaḳḳârah; it was called

4. Longitudinal section of a Maṣṭaba.

5. Transverse section of the chamber of a Maṣṭaba.

maṣṭaba by the Arabs because its length, in proportion to its height, is great, and reminded them of the long, low seat common in Oriental houses, and familiar to them. The maṣṭaba is a heavy massive building, of rectangular shape, the four sides of which are four walls symmetrically inclined towards their common centre. The exterior surfaces are not

[1] From the Arabic مَصْطَبَة. The facts here given on the subject of maṣṭabas are derived from the excellent articles of M. Mariette in *Revue Archéologique*, S. 2me, t. xix. p. 8 ff.

flat, for the face of each course of masonry, formed of stones laid vertically, is a little behind the one beneath it, and if these recesses were a little deeper, the external appearance of each side of the building would resemble a flight of steps. The stones which form the maṣṭabas are of a moderate size, and with the exception of those used for the ceiling and architrave, have an average height of 18 or 20 inches. The height and length of the maṣṭaba vary; the largest measures about 170 feet long by 86 feet wide, and the smallest about 26 feet long by 20 feet wide; they vary in height from 13 to 30 feet. The ground at Ṣaḳḳârah is formed of calcareous rock covered to the depth of a few feet with sand; the foundations of the maṣṭabas are always on the solid rock. The plan of the maṣṭaba is a rectangle, and the greater axis of the rectangle is, without exception, in the direction from north to south. Moreover, at the pyramids of Gîzeh, where the maṣṭabas are arranged symmetrically, the plan of their arrangement is like a chess-board, the squares of which are uniformly elongated towards the north. Maṣṭabas then are oriented astronomically towards the true north, and in the cases where they are a few degrees out, this difference must be attributed not to design but to negligence. It has been asserted that maṣṭabas are only unfinished pyramids, but properly considered, it is evident that they form a class of buildings by themselves, and that they have nothing in common with the pyramid, save in respect of being oriented towards the north, this orientation being the result, not of a studied imitation of the pyramid, but of a religious intention, which at this early period influenced the construction of all tombs, whatever their external form. The maṣṭabas at Ṣaḳḳârah are built of stone and brick; the stone employed is of two kinds, the one being very hard, and of a bluish-grey colour, and the other being comparatively soft, and of a yellowish colour. The bricks also are of two kinds, the

Plan and position of maṣṭabas.

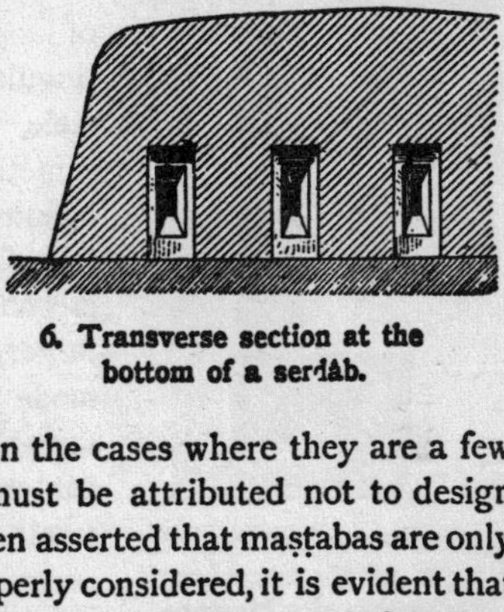

6. Transverse section at the bottom of a serdâb.

Orientation of maṣṭabas.

one yellowish, and the other black; both sorts were sun-dried only. The bricks of a yellowish colour seem to have been used entirely during the earliest dynasties, and the black ones only appear with the second half of the IVth dynasty. However carefully the outside of the maṣṭaba was built, the inside is composed of sand, pieces of stone thrown in without design or arrangement, rubble, rubbish, etc., and but for the outside walls holding all together many of them must have perished long since. The eastern face of the maṣṭaba is the most important, for, four times out of five, the entrance is in it; it is sometimes, but very rarely, bare. Some yards from the north-east corner is, at times, a very high, narrow opening, at the bottom of which the masonry of the maṣṭaba itself assumes the form of long vertical grooves, which distinguish the stelæ of this epoch; a stele, with or without inscription, sometimes takes the place of this opening. At a distance of some feet from the south-east corner is generally another opening, but larger, deeper and more carefully made; at the bottom of this is sometimes a fine inscribed calcareous stone stele, and sometimes a small architectural façade, in the centre of which is a door. When the eastern face has the opening at the south-east corner which has just been described, the maṣṭaba has no interior chamber, for this opening takes its place. When the maṣṭaba has the façade in the place of the opening, there is a chamber within. When the entrance to the maṣṭaba is made on the north side, the façade is brought back to the end of a kind of vestibule, and at the front of this vestibule are set up two monolithic columns, without abacus, and without base, which support the architrave, which supports the ceiling. The entrance to the maṣṭaba is

7. The upper chamber, the pit, and the sarcophagus chamber of a Maṣṭaba.

The stele in maṣtabas.

sometimes made from the south, but never from the west; the top of the maṣṭaba is quite flat.

The interior of the complete maṣṭaba consists of three parts, the chamber, the serdâb, and the pit. Having entered the **Chamber** by the door in the side, it is found to be either without any ornamentation whatever, or to be covered with sculptures. At the bottom of the chamber usually facing the **The maṣṭaba chamber.**

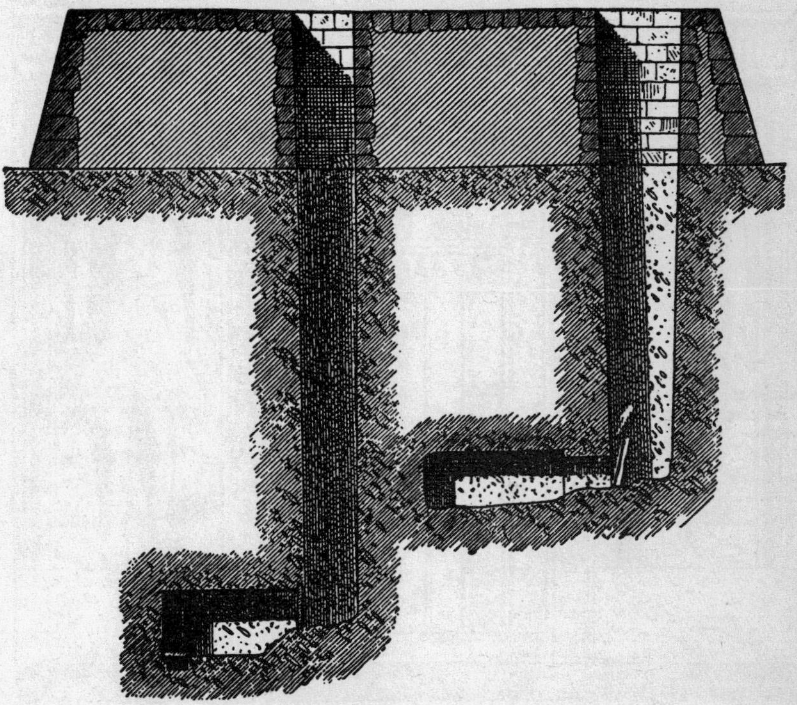

**8. Maṣṭaba at Gîzeh with double pit.**

east, is a stele, which, whether the walls are inscribed or not, is always inscribed. At the foot of the stele, on the bare ground, is often a table of offerings made of granite, alabaster, or calcareous stone; two obelisks, or two supports for offerings, are often found at each side of this table. Besides these things the chamber has no furniture, and it rarely has a door.

Not far from the chamber, oftener to the south than to the north, and oftener to the north than to the west, is a lofty but narrow nook hidden in the thickness of the masonry, and built with large stones; this nook is called the **Serdâb.**[1] Sometimes the serdâb has no communication whatever with the other parts of the maṣṭaba, but sometimes a rectangular passage, so

Use of the serdâb.

**9. Figures in relief in a Maṣṭaba at Gîzeh. Vth dynasty.**

narrow that the hand can only be inserted with difficulty, leads from the serdâb into the chamber; in the serdâb statues of the deceased were placed and the narrow passage served

[1] A *serdâb*, سرداب, strictly speaking, is a lofty, vaulted, subterranean chamber, with a large opening in the north side to admit air in the hot weather.

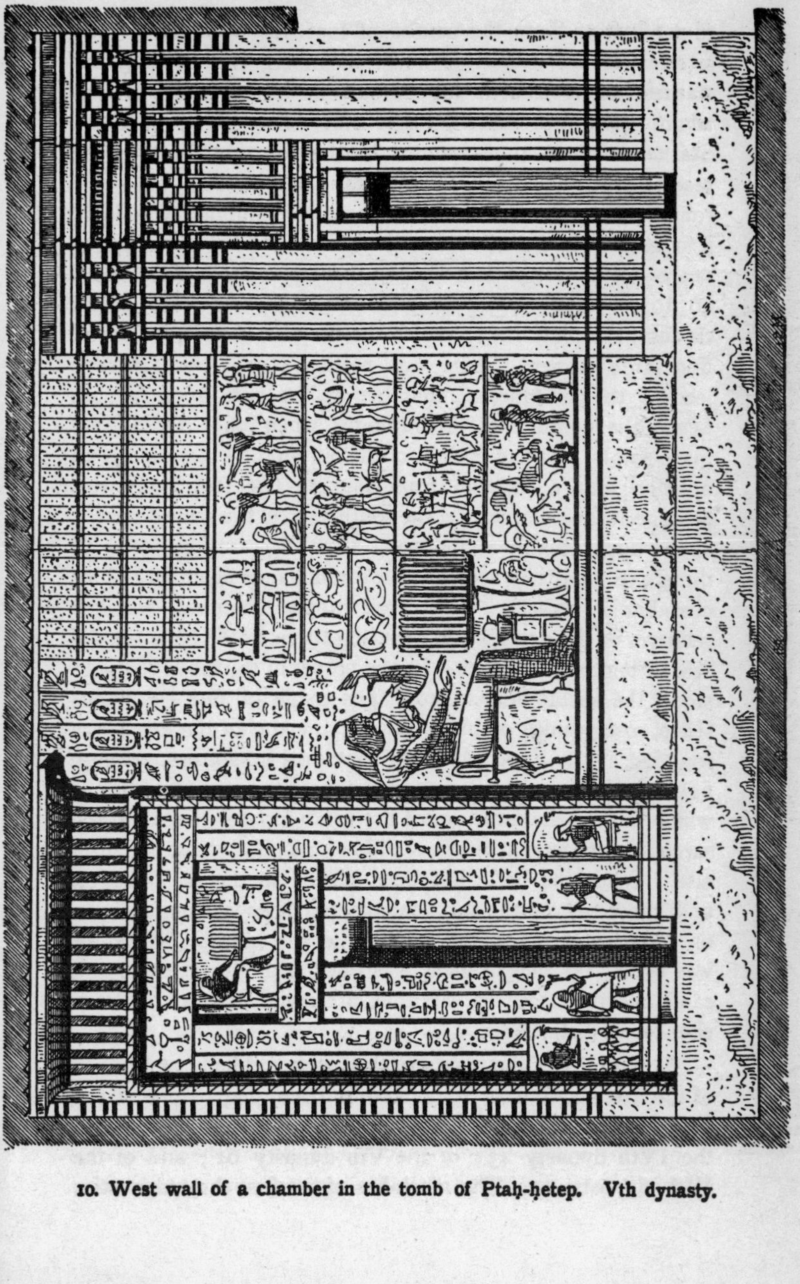

10. West wall of a chamber in the tomb of Ptaḥ-ḥetep. Vth dynasty.

to conduct to them the smoke of incense or perfume. The interior of the serdâb is never inscribed, and nothing but statues, inscribed with the names and titles of the persons whom they represented, have ever been found in them. Statues were at times placed in the court in front of the maṣṭaba. The pit, square or rectangular in form, but never round, leads to the chamber where the mummy was laid; it is situated in the middle of the greater axis of the maṣṭaba nearer to the north than the south, and varies in depth from 40 to 80 feet. The top part of the pit where it passes through the platform on which the maṣṭaba stands, is built of fine large stones. There was neither ladder nor staircase, leading to the funereal chamber at the bottom of the pit, hence the coffin and the mummy when once there were inaccessible. At the bottom of the pit, on the south side, is an opening into a passage from four to five feet high; this passage leads obliquely to the south-east, in the same direction as the upper chamber, and soon after increases in size in all directions, and thus becomes the sarcophagus chamber. This chamber is exactly under the upper chamber, and the relatives of the deceased in standing there, would have the deceased beneath their feet. In one corner of the lower chamber stood the rectangular sarcophagus made of fine calcareous stone, rose granite or black basalt; the top of the cover was rounded. The upper chamber contained no statues, *ushabtiu* figures, amulets, canopic jars, nor any of the numerous things which formed the furniture of the tomb in later times; in the sarcophagus were, at times, a pillow or a few vases, but little else. When the body had been placed in the sarcophagus, and the cover of the sarcophagus had been cemented down on it, the entrance to the passage at the bottom of the pit was walled up, the pit itself was filled with stones, earth and sand, and the deceased was thus preserved from all ordinary chances of disturbance.

**The maṣṭaba pit and sarcophagus chamber.**

**Characteristics of the earliest maṣṭabas.**

The tombs of the maṣṭaba class stop suddenly at the end of the first six dynasties; of tombs belonging to one of the first three dynasties, M. Mariette found 4 at Ṣaḳḳârah; of the IVth dynasty 43; of the Vth dynasty 61; and of the VIth dynasty 25. The maṣṭabas of the first three dynasties have but one upper chamber, which is built of brick, the stelæ are very deeply cut, the hieroglyphics and the figures are in relief, and display more vigour than at any other time; the inscriptions are terse, and the use of phonetic signs less common than in later times. These tombs can hardly be said to be oriented at all, for they are, at times, as much as twelve degrees west of the true north. In the second half of the IVth dynasty, maṣṭabas have a size and extent hitherto unknown; they are either built entirely of black brick or of stone. Their orientation becomes accurate, the figures and hieroglyphics are well executed, the formulæ become fixed, and the statues in the serdâbs, which are very numerous, unite the vigour of those of the first half of the IVth with the delicacy of those of the Vth dynasty. The famous wooden statue of the Shêkh el-Beled belongs to this time. In the Vth dynasty maṣṭabas are not so large, but they are always built of stone; inside there are more chambers than one, approached by long passages, and the statues are not so characteristic as those of the latter half of the IVth dynasty. The maṣṭabas of the VIth dynasty show a decided decadence, and lose their fine proportions; the figures are in light relief, the formulæ become longer, and the chambers are built of brick and covered with thin sculptured slabs of stone.

**Ornamentation of the maṣṭaba.**

The walls of the upper chambers of maṣṭabas were frequently covered with scenes which, according to M. Mariette, are without any representation of divinities and religious emblems, the names of deities, and characters employed in the course of writing naturally excepted. The inscription which asks the god Anubis to grant a happy burial to the deceased, after a long and happy old age, to make his way easy for him on the roads in the underworld, and to grant the bringing to the tomb a perpetual supply of funereal gifts, is inscribed in bold hieroglyphics over the entrances to the tomb, and upon the most conspicuous places on the stelæ in the upper chamber. The scenes depicted on the walls of the maṣṭabas are divided by Mariette into three classes: 1, Biographical, 2, Sepulchral, and 3, those relating to funereal gifts. Biographical scenes are found in tombs of all periods. The deceased is represented hunting or fishing, taking part in pleasure excursions by water, and listening to music played before him accompanied by the dancing of women; he is also represented as overseer of a number of building operations in which many workmen are employed. It is tolerably certain that these scenes are not fictitious, and that they were painted while the person who hoped to occupy the tomb was still alive, and could direct the labours of the artist. The prayer that the deceased might enter his tomb after a

Scenes and inscriptions.

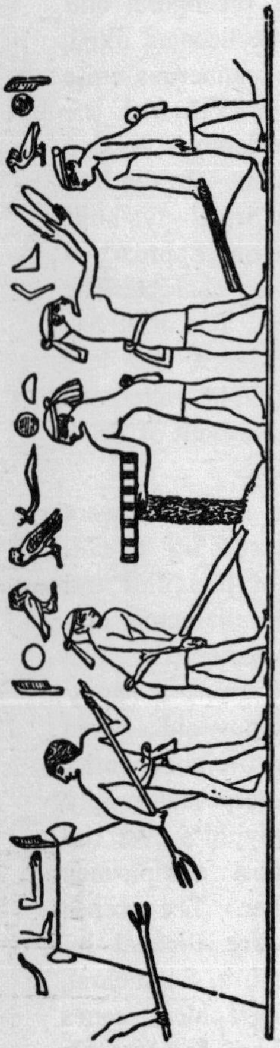

Winnowing Wheat. From a Vth dynasty Tomb at Ṣakkârah.

Netting Wild Fowl. From a Vth dynasty Tomb at Ṣakkârah.

long and prosperous life has a significance which it could not possess if the tomb were made after his death. The sepulchral scenes refer to the passage of the mummy in a boat to Amenta. The scenes relating to sepulchral gifts

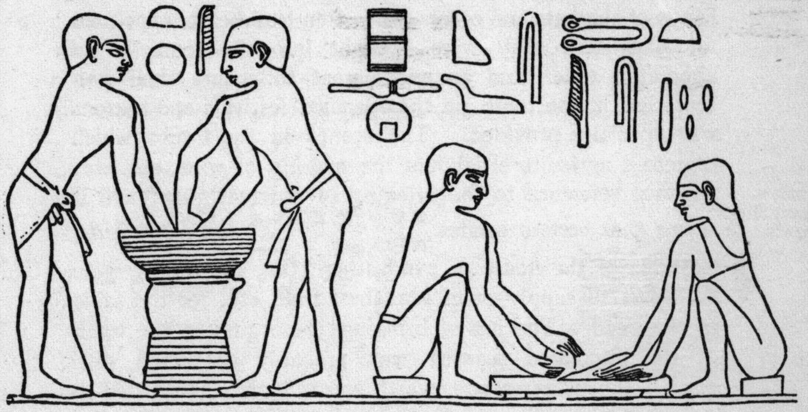

Bakers making Bread. From a Vth dynasty Tomb at Ṣaḳḳârah.

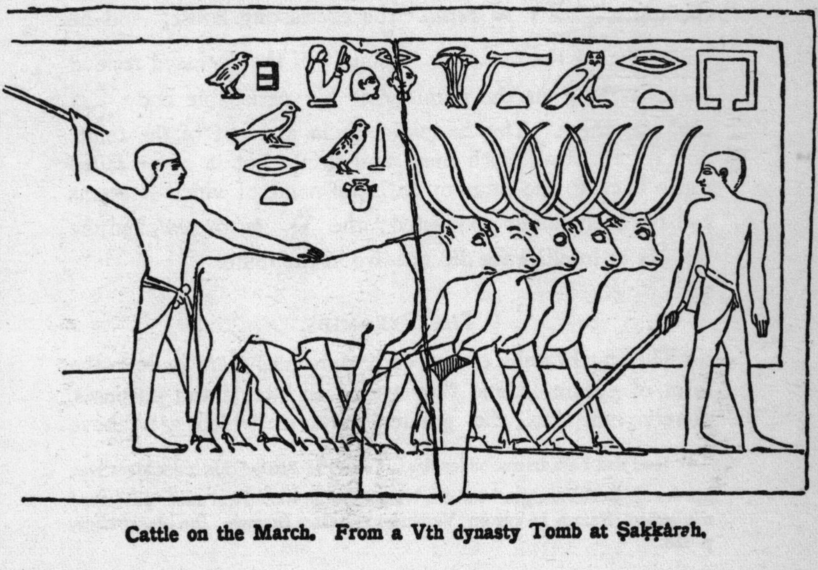

Cattle on the March. From a Vth dynasty Tomb at Ṣaḳḳârah.

represent the deceased, having colossal proportions compared with the other figures, sitting or standing with a round table before him, upon which fruits, flowers, vegetables, ducks, haunches of beef, etc., etc., are placed. These offerings are sometimes carried in before the deceased on the head or hands of servants and others, who often lead beasts appointed for slaughter; they were brought into the tomb in an appointed order, and an endowment to ensure their presentation in the tomb on the specified festivals and seasons was specially provided. The scenes in the tombs which represent agricultural labours, the making of wine, etc., etc., all have reference to the bringing of funereal gifts; and it seems that certain estates *nut ent pa t'etta*, "estates of the house of everlasting" (*i.e.*, the tomb), were set apart to supply palm branches, fruit, etc., for the table of the dead. The act of bringing these gifts to the tomb at the appointed seasons was probably connected with some religious ceremony, which seems to have consisted in pouring out libations and offering incense, bandages, etc., by the *cher ḥeb* or priest. The Egyptian called the tomb *pa t'etta*, "the everlasting house," and he believed that the *ka* or "genius" of the deceased resided there as long as the mummy of his perishable body, *cha*, was there. The *ka* might go in and out of the tomb, and refresh itself with meat and drink, but it never failed to go back to the mummy with the name of which it seems to have been closely connected;[1] the *ba* or *soul*, and the *chu* or intelligence did not live in the tomb.

**Endowment of tombs.**

## THE PYRAMIDS.

The royal tombs of the early dynasties were built in the form of **pyramids**, and they are, to all intents and purposes, merely maṣṭabas, the greater parts of which are above

[1] Herz und Leib vereint bilden das oder die Persönlichkeit des Menschen, das dem Individuum eigenthümliche Wesen, die ihn von andern unterscheidet und mit seinem Namen in engster Verbindung steht. Brugsch, *Die Aegyptologie*, p. 181.

ground; they consist of the chamber in which funereal gifts were offered, the passage and the sarcophagus chamber. The actual pyramid contained the passage and the sarcophagus chamber, but although the chamber, sometimes called temple or chapel, in which funereal gifts were offered, was a building separate from the pyramid, it nevertheless formed an integral part of the pyramid plan. On the western bank of the Nile, from Abu Roâsh on the north to Mêdûm on the south, is a slightly elevated tract of land, about twenty-five miles long, on the edge of the Libyan desert, on which stand the

Pyramids are tombs.

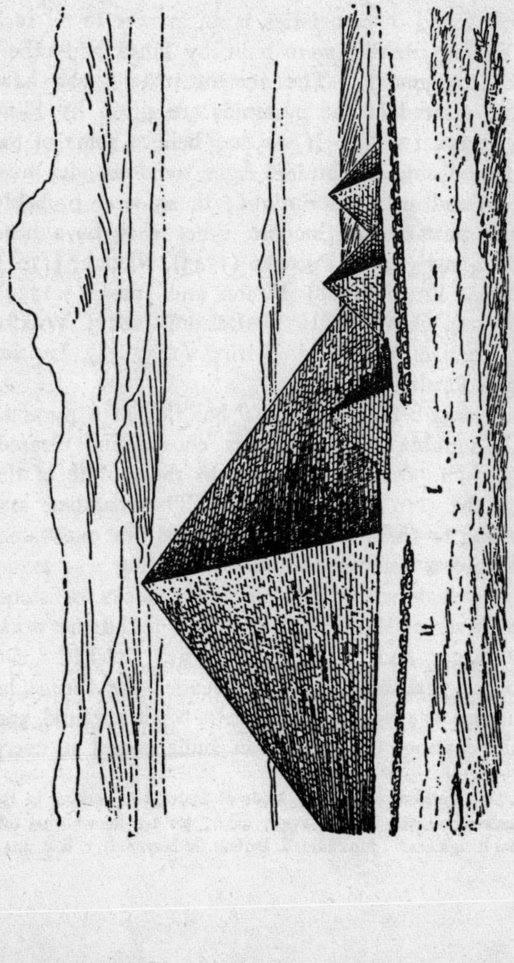

The Great Pyramid and the three Small Pyramids.

pyramids of Abu Roâsh, Gîzeh, Zâwyet el-'Aryân, Abuṣîr, Ṣaḳḳârah, and Dahshûr. Other places in Egypt where pyramids are found are El-lâhûn in the Fayyûm, and Kullah near Esneh. The pyramids built by the Ethiopians at Meroë and Gebel Barkal are of a very late date (B.C. 600–100) and are mere copies, in respect of form only, of the pyramids in Egypt. There is no evidence whatever to show that they were built for purposes of astronomical observations, and the theory that the Great Pyramid was built to serve as a standard of measurement is ingenious but worthless. The significant fact, so ably pointed out by Mariette, that pyramids are only found in cemeteries, is an answer to all such theories. Tomb-pyramids were built by kings and others until the XIIth dynasty. The ancient writers who have described and treated of the pyramids are given by Pliny (Nat. Hist., xxxvi. 12, 17). If we may believe some of the writers on them during the Middle Ages, their outsides must have been covered with inscriptions; these were probably of a religious nature.[1] In modern times they have been examined by Shaw (1721), Pococke (1743), Niebuhr (1761), Davison (1763), Bruce (1768), Denon and Jumard (1799), Hamilton (1801), Caviglia (1817), Belzoni (1817), Wilkinson (1831), Howard Vyse and Perring (1837–38), Lepsius (1842–45), and Petrie (1881).

**The building of a pyramid.**

It appears that before the actual building of a pyramid was begun, a suitable rocky site was chosen and cleared, a mass of rock if possible being left in the middle of the area to form the core of the building. The chambers and galleries leading to them were next planned and excavated. Around the core a truncated pyramid building was made, the angles of which were filled up with blocks of stone. Layer after layer of stone was then built round the work, which grew larger and larger until it was finished. Dr. Lepsius thought that when a king ascended the throne, he built for himself a small but complete tomb-pyramid, and that a fresh coating of stone was built round it every

[1] "...... their surfaces exhibit all kinds of inscriptions written in the characters of ancient nations which no longer exist. No one knows what this writing is or what it signifies." Mas'ûdi (ed. Barbier de Meynard), t. ii. p. 404.

year that he reigned; that when he died the sides of the pyramid were like long flights of steps, which his successor filled up with right-angled triangular blocks of stone; and that the door of the pyramid was walled up after the body of its builder had been laid in it, and thus it became a finished tomb. The explanation of Dr. Lepsius may not be correct, but at least it answers satisfactorily more objections than do the views of other theorists on this matter. It has been pointed out that near the core of the pyramid the work is more carefully executed than near the exterior, that is to say, as the time for the king's death approached the work was more hurriedly performed.

During the investigations made by Lepsius in and around the pyramid area, he found the remains of about seventy-five pyramids, and noticed that they were always built in groups.

**Violation of pyramids by the Persians.**

The pyramids of Gîzeh were opened by the Persians during the fifth and fourth centuries before Christ; it is probable that they were also entered by the Romans. Khalif Mâmûn (A.D. 813–833) entered the Great Pyramid, and found that others had been there before him. The treasure which is said to have been discovered there by him is probably fictitious. Once opened, it must have been evident to every one what splendid quarries the pyramids formed, and very few hundred years after the conquest of Egypt by the Arabs, they were laid under contribution for stone to build mosques, etc., in Cairo. At the end of the twelfth century Melik el-Kâmil made a mad attempt to destroy the pyramid built by Mycerinus; but after months of toil he only succeeded in stripping off the covering from one of the sides. It is said that Muḥammad 'Ali was advised to undertake the senseless task of destroying them all. The most important pyramids and groups of pyramids are the following:—

## THE GREAT PYRAMID.

This, the largest of the three pyramids at Gîzeh, was built by Chufu  or Cheops, the second king of the IVth dynasty, B.C. 3733, who called it  *Chut*. His name was found written in red ink upon the blocks of stone inside it. All four sides measure in greatest length about 755 feet each, but the length of each was originally about 20 feet more; its height now is 451 feet, but it is said to have been originally about 481 feet. The stone used in the construction of this pyramid was brought from Turra and Moḳaṭṭam, and the contents amount to 85,000,000 cubic feet. The flat space at the top of the pyramid is about thirty feet square, and the view from it is very fine.

Pyramid of Cheops.

The entrance (A) to this pyramid is, as with all pyramids, on the north side, and is about 43 feet above the ground. The passage A B C is 320 feet long, $3\frac{1}{4}$ feet high, and 4 feet wide; at B is a granite door, round which the path at D has been made. The passage at D E is 125 feet long, and the large hall E F is 155 feet long and 28 feet high; the passage E G leads to the pointed-roofed Queen's Chamber H, which measures about 17 × 19 × 20 feet. The roofing in of this chamber is a beautiful piece of mason's work. From the large hall E F there leads a passage 22 feet long, the antechamber in which was originally closed by four granite doors, remains of which are still visible, into the King's Chamber, J, which is lined with granite, and measures about 35 × 17 × 19 feet. The five hollow chambers K, L, M, N, O were built above the King's Chamber to lighten the pressure of the superincumbent mass. In chamber O the name Chufu was found written The air shafts P and Q measure 234 feet × 8 inches × 6 inches, and 174 feet × 8 inches × 6 inches respectively. A shaft from E to R leads down to the subterranean chamber S, which measures 46 × 27 × $10\frac{1}{2}$ feet. The floor of the King's Chamber, J, is about 140 feet from the level of the base of the pyramid, and the chamber is a little to the south-east of the line drawn from T to U. Inside the chamber lies the empty, coverless, broken, red granite sarcophagus of Cheops, measuring $7\frac{1}{2}$ × $3\frac{1}{4}$ × $3\frac{1}{3}$ feet. The account of the building of this pyramid is told by Herodotus[1] as follows: "Now, they told me, that to the reign of Rhampsinitus there was a perfect distribution

[1] Bk. ii. 124–126.

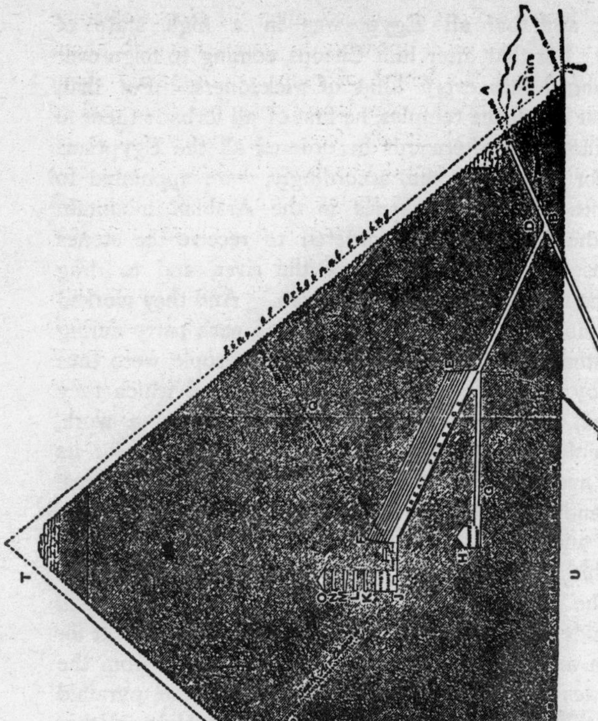

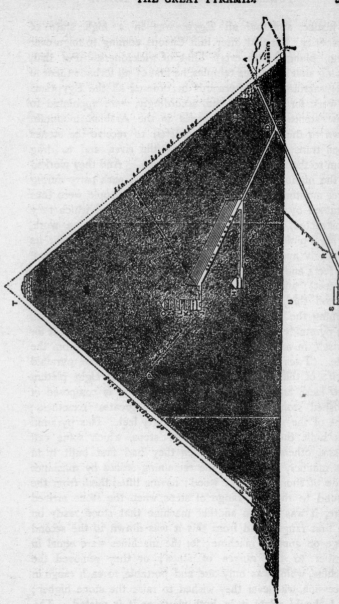

**Section of the Pyramid of Cheops at Gizeh. From Vyse, "Pyramids of Gizeh," Vol. I. p. 2.**

Herodotus on the building of the Great Pyramid.

of justice, and that all Egypt was in a high state of prosperity; but that after him Cheops, coming to reign over them, plunged into every kind of wickedness. For that, having shut up all the temples, he first of all forbade them to offer sacrifice, and afterwards he ordered all the Egyptians to work for himself; some, accordingly, were appointed to draw stones from the quarries in the Arabian mountain down to the Nile, others he ordered to receive the stones when transported in vessels across the river, and to drag them to the mountain called the Libyan. And they worked to the number of 100,000 men at a time, each party during three months. The time during which the people were thus harassed by toil, lasted ten years on the road which they constructed, along which they drew the stones, a work, in my opinion, not much less than the pyramid; for its length is five stades (3,021 feet), and its width ten orgyæ (60 feet), and its height, where it is the highest, eight orgyæ (48 feet); and it is of polished stone, with figures carved on it: on this road then ten years were expended, and in forming the subterraneous apartments on the hill, on which the pyramids stand, which he had made as a burial vault for himself, in an island, formed by draining a canal from the Nile. Twenty years were spent in erecting the pyramid itself: of this, which is square, each face is eight plethra (820 feet), and the height is the same; it is composed of polished stones, and jointed with the greatest exactness; none of the stones are less than thirty feet. This pyramid was built thus; in the form of steps, which some call crossæ, others bomides. When they had first built it in this manner, they raised the remaining stones by machines made of short pieces of wood: having lifted them from the ground to the first range of steps, when the stone arrived there, it was put on another machine that stood ready on the first range; and from this it was drawn to the second range on another machine; for the machines were equal in number to the ranges of steps; or they removed the machine, which was only one, and portable, to each range in succession, whenever they wished to raise the stone higher; for I should relate it in both ways, as it is related. The highest parts of it, therefore, were first finished, and afterwards they completed the parts next following; but last of all they finished the parts on the ground, and that were lowest. On the pyramid is shown an inscription, in Egyptian characters, how much was expended in radishes, onions, and garlic, for the workmen; which the interpreter,[1] as I well remember, reading the inscription, told me amounted to 1,600 talents of silver. And if this be really the case, how much more was probably expended in iron tools, in bread, and in clothes for the labourers, since they occupied in building the works the time which I mentioned, and no short time besides, as I think, in cutting and drawing the stones, and in forming the subterraneous excavation. [It is related] that Cheops reached such a degree of infamy, that being in want of money, he prostituted his own daughter in a brothel, and ordered her to extort, they did not say how much; but she exacted a certain sum of money, privately, as much as her father ordered her; and contrived to leave a monument of herself, and asked every one that came in to her to give her a stone towards the edifice she designed: of these stones they said the pyramid was built that stands in the middle of the three, before the great pyramid, each side of which is a plethron and a half in length." (Cary's translation.)

Herodotus on the building of the Great Pyramid.

## THE SECOND PYRAMID.

The second pyramid at Gîzeh was built by Chā-f-Rā, , or Chephren, the third king of the IVth dynasty, B.C. 3666, who called it , *ur*. His name has not been found inscribed upon any part of it, but the fragment of a marble sphere inscribed with the name of Chā-f-Rā,

[1] Herodotus was deceived by his interpreter, who clearly made up a translation of an inscription which he did not understand. William of Baldensel, who lived in the fourteenth century, tells us that the outer coating of the two largest pyramids was covered with a great number of inscriptions arranged in lines. (Wiedemann, *Aeg. Geschichte*, p. 179.) If the outsides were actually inscribed, the text must have been purely religious, like those inscribed inside the pyramids of Pepi, Tetà, and Unàs.

which was found near the temple, close by this pyramid, confirms the statements of Herodotus and Diodorus Siculus, that Chephren built it. A statue of this king, now in the Gîzeh Museum, was found in the granite temple close by. This pyramid appears to be larger than the Great Pyramid because it stands upon a higher level of stone foundation; it was cased with stone originally and polished, but the greater part of the outer casing has disappeared. An ascent of this pyramid can only be made with difficulty. It was first explored in 1816 by Belzoni (born 1778, died 1823), the discoverer of the tomb of Seti I. and of the temple of Rameses II. at Abu Simbel. In the north side of the pyramid are two openings, one at the base and one about 50 feet above it. The upper opening leads into a corridor 105 feet long, which descends into a chamber $46\frac{1}{2} \times 16\frac{1}{3} \times 22\frac{1}{2}$ feet, which held the granite sarcophagus in which Chephren was buried. The lower opening leads into a corridor about 100 feet long, which, first descending and then ascending, ends in the chamber mentioned above, which is usually called Belzoni's Chamber. The actual height is about 450 feet, and the length of each side at the base about 700 feet. The rock upon which the pyramid stands has been scarped on the north and west sides to make the foundation level. The history of the building of the pyramid is thus stated by Herodotus[1]: "The Egyptians say that this Cheops reigned fifty years; and when he died, his brother Chephren succeeded to the kingdom; and he followed the same practices as the other, both in other respects, and in building a pyramid; which does not come up to the dimensions of his brother's, for I myself measured them; nor has it subterraneous chambers; nor does a channel from the Nile flow to it, as to the other; but this flows through an artificial aqueduct round an island within, in which they say the body of Cheops is laid. Having laid the first course of variegated Ethiopian stones, less in height than the other by forty feet, he built it near the large pyramid. They both stand on the same hill, which is about 100 feet high. Chephren, they said, reigned fifty-six years. Thus 106 years are reckoned, during

Pyramid of Chephren.

Pyramid of Chephren.

[1] Bk. ii. 127.

which the Egyptians suffered all kinds of calamities, and for this length of time the temples were closed and never opened. From the hatred they bear them, the Egyptians are not very willing to mention their names; but call the pyramids after Philition, a shepherd, who at that time kept his cattle in those parts." (Cary's translation.)

## THE THIRD PYRAMID.

The third pyramid at Gîzeh was built by Men-kau-Rā, , the fourth king of the IVth dynasty, about B.C. 3633, who called it , *Ḥer.* Herodotus and other ancient authors tell us that Men-kau-Rā, or Mycerinus, was

Pyramid of Mycerinus.

buried in this pyramid, but Manetho states that Nitocris, a queen of the VIth dynasty, was the builder. There can be, however, but little doubt that it was built by Mycerinus, for the sarcophagus and the remains of the inscribed coffin of this king were found in one of its chambers by Howard Vyse in 1837. The sarcophagus, which measured 8 × 3 × 2½ feet, was lost through the wreck of the ship in which it was sent to England, but the venerable fragments of the coffin are preserved in the British Museum, and form one of the most valuable objects in the famous collection of that institution. The formula on it is one which is found upon coffins down to the latest period, but as the date of Mycerinus is known, it is possible to draw some interesting and valuable conclusions from the fact that it is found upon his coffin. It proves that as far back as 3,600 years before Christ the Egyptian religion was established on a firm base, that the doctrine of immortality was already deeply rooted in the human mind. The art of preserving the human body by embalming was also well understood and generally practised at that early date.

Pyramid of Mycerinus.

The pyramid of Men-kau-Rā, like that of Chephren, is built upon a rock with a sloping surface; the inequality of the surface in this case has been made level by building up courses of large blocks of stones. Around the lower part the remains of the old granite covering are visible to a depth of from 30 to 40 feet. It is unfortunate that this pyramid has been so much damaged; its injuries, however, enable the visitor to see exactly how it was built, and it may be concluded that the pyramids of Cheops and Chephren were built in the same manner. The length of each side at the base is about 350 feet, and its height is variously given as 210 and 215 feet. The entrance is on the north side, about thirteen feet above the ground, and a descending corridor about 104 feet long, passing through an ante-chamber, having a series of three granite doors, leads into one chamber about 44 feet long. In this chamber is a shaft which leads down to the granite-lined chamber about 20 feet below, in which were found the sarcophagus and wooden coffin of Mycerinus, and the remains of a human body. It is thought that, in spite of the body of Mycerinus being buried in this pyramid, it was left unfinished at the death of this king, and that a succeeding ruler of Egypt finished the pyramid and made a second chamber to hold his or her body. At a short distance to the east of this pyramid are the ruins of a temple which was probably used in connexion with the rites performed in honour of the dead king. In A.D. 1196 a deliberate and systematic attempt was made to destroy this pyramid by the command of the Muḥammadan ruler of Egypt. The account of the character of Mycerinus and of his pyramid as given by Herodotus is as follows: "They said that after him, Mycerinus,[1] son of Cheops, reigned over Egypt; that the conduct of his father was displeasing to him; and that he opened the temples, and permitted the people, who were worn down to the last extremity, to return to their employments, and to sacrifices; and that he made the most just decisions of all their kings. On this account, of all the kings that ever reigned in Egypt, they praised him most, for he both judged well in other respects, and moreover, when any man complained of his decision, he used to make him some present out of his own treasury and pacify his anger. . . . . . . This king also left a pyramid much less than that of his father, being on each side 20 feet short of three plethra; it is quadrangular, and built half way up of

**Pyramid of Mycerinus.**

[1] Bk. ii. 129, 134.

Ethiopian stone. Some of the Grecians erroneously say that this pyramid is the work of the courtesan Rhodopis; but they evidently appear to me ignorant who Rhodopis was; for they would not else have attributed to her the building such a pyramid, on which, so to speak, numberless thousands of talents were expended; besides, Rhodopis flourished in the reign of Amasis, and not at this time; for she was very many years later than those kings who left these pyramids.' (Cary's translation.)

In one of the three small pyramids near that of Mycerinus the name of this king is painted on the ceiling.

## THE PYRAMIDS OF ABU ROÂSH.

These pyramids lie about six miles north of the Pyramids of Gîzeh, and are thought to be older than they. Nothing remains of one except five or six courses of stone, which show that the length of each side at the base was about 350 feet, and a passage about 160 feet long leading down to a subterranean chamber about 43 feet long. A pile of stones close by marks the site of another pyramid; the others have disappeared. Of the age of these pyramids nothing certain is known. The remains of a causeway about a mile long leading to them are still visible.

## THE PYRAMIDS OF ABUṢIR.

**Other pyramids of the Vth dynasty.**

These pyramids, originally fourteen in number, were built by kings of the Vth dynasty, but only four of them are now standing, probably because of the poorness of the workmanship and the careless way in which they were put together. The most northerly pyramid was built by

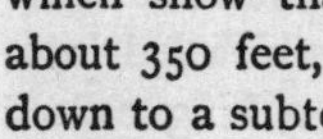

Saḥu-Rā, the second king of the Vth dynasty, B.C. 3333; its actual height is about 120 feet, and the length of each side at the base about 220 feet. The blocks of stone in the sepulchral chamber are exceptionally large. Saḥu-Rā made war in the peninsula of Sinai, he

founded a town near Esneh, and he built a temple to Sechet at Memphis.

The pyramid to the south of that of Saḥu-Rā was built by  "*Usr-en-Rā, son of the Sun, Ȧn.*" This king, like Saḥu-Rā, also made war in Sinai. The largest of these four pyramids is now about 165 feet high and 330 feet square; the name of its builder is unknown. Abuṣir is the Busiris of Pliny.

## THE STEP PYRAMID OF ṢAḲḲÂRAH.

This pyramid is generally thought to have been built by the fourth king of the Ist dynasty (called Uenephes by Manetho, and  Ȧta in the tablet of Abydos), who is said to have built a pyramid at Kochome (*i.e.*, Ka-Kam) near Ṣaḳḳârah. Though the date of this pyramid is not known accurately, it is probably right to assume that it is older than the pyramids of Gîzeh. The door which led into the pyramid was inscribed with the name of a king called Rā-nub, and M. Mariette found the same name on one of the stelæ in the Serapeum. The steps of the pyramid are six in number, and are about 38, 36, 34½, 32, 31 and 29½ feet in height; the width of each step is from six to seven feet. The lengths of the sides at the base are: north and south 352 feet, east and west 396 feet, and the actual height is 197 feet. In shape this pyramid is oblong, and its sides do not exactly face the cardinal points. The arrangement of the chambers inside this pyramid is quite peculiar to itself.

The oldest pyramid.

The PYRAMID OF UNȦS , better known as "Maṣṭabat el-Far'ûn," *i.e.*, "Pharaoh's Maṣṭaba," called in Egyptian Nefer-ȧs-u, lies to the south-east of the Step Pyramid, and was reopened and cleared out in 1881 by M. Maspero, at the expense of Messrs. Thomas Cook and Son. Its original height was about 62 feet, and the length of each side at the base 220 feet. Owing to the broken blocks of sand which lie round about it, Vyse was unable to give exact measurements. Several attempts had been

Pyramids inscribed with funereal texts.

made to break into it, and one of the Arabs who took part in one of these attempts, "Aḥmed the Carpenter," seems to have left his name inside one of the chambers in red ink. It is probable that he is the same man who opened the Great Pyramid at Gîzeh, A.D. 820. A black basalt sarcophagus, from which the cover had been dragged off, an arm, a shin bone, and some ribs and fragments of the skull from the mummy of Unȧs were found in the sarcophagus chamber. The walls of the two largest chambers and two of the corridors are inscribed with ritual texts and prayers of a very interesting character. Unȧs, the last king of the Vth dynasty, reigned about thirty years. The Maṣṭabat el-Far'ûn was thought by Mariette to be the tomb of Unȧs, but some scholars thought that the "blunted pyramid" at Dahshûr was his tomb, because his name was written upon the top of it.

The PYRAMID OF TETȦ , called in Egyptian Ṭeṭ-ȧsu, lies to the north-east of the Step Pyramid, and was opened in 1881. The Arabs call it the "Prison Pyramid," because local tradition says that it is built near the ruins of the prison where Joseph the patriarch was confined. Its actual height is about 59 feet; the length of its sides at the base is 210 feet, and the platform at the top is about 50 feet. The arrangement of the chambers and passages and the plan of construction followed is almost identical with that of the pyramid of Unȧs. This pyramid was broken into in ancient days, and two of the walls of the sarcophagus chamber have literally been smashed to pieces by the hammer blows of those who expected to find treasure inside them. The inscriptions, painted in green upon the walls, have the same subject matter as those inscribed upon the walls of the chambers of the pyramid of Unȧs. According to Manetho, Tetȧ, the first king of the VIth dynasty, reigned about fifty years, and was murdered by one of his guards.

The PYRAMID OF PEPI I., or  "Rā-meri, son of the Sun, Pepi," lies to the south-east of the

Step Pyramid, and forms one of the central group of pyramids at Ṣaḳḳârah, where it is called the Pyramid of Shêkh Abu Manṣûr; it was opened in 1880. Its actual height is about 40 feet, and the length of the sides at the base is about 250 feet; the arrangement of the chambers, etc., inside is the same as in the pyramids of Unȧs and Tetȧ, but the ornamentation is slightly different. It is the worst preserved of these pyramids, and has suffered most at the hands of the spoilers, probably because having been constructed with stones which were taken from tombs ancient already in those days, instead of stones fresh from the quarry, it was more easily injured. The granite sarcophagus was broken to take out the mummy, fragments of which were found lying about on the ground; the cover too, smashed in pieces, lay on the ground close by. A small rose granite box, containing alabaster jars, was also found in the sarcophagus chamber. The inscriptions are, like those inscribed on the walls of the pyramids of Unȧs and Tetȧ, of a religious nature; some scholars see in them evidence that the pyramid was usurped by another Pepi, who lived at a much later period than the VIth dynasty. The pyramid of Pepi I., the second king of the VIth dynasty, who reigned, according to Manetho, fifty-three years, was called in Egyptian by the same name as Memphis, *i.e.*, Men-nefer, and numerous priests were attached to its service.

## THE PYRAMIDS OF DAHSHÛR.

The Blunted Pyramid.

These pyramids, four of stone and two of brick, lie about three and a half miles to the south of Maṣṭabat el-Far'ûn. The largest stone pyramid is about 326 feet high, and the length of each side at the base is about 700 feet; beneath it are three subterranean chambers. The second stone pyramid is about 321 feet high, and the length of its sides at the base is 620 feet; it is usually called the "Blunted Pyramid," because the lowest parts of its sides are built at one angle, and the completing parts at another. The larger of the two brick pyramids is about 90 feet high, and the length of the sides at the base is about 350 feet; the smaller is about 156 feet high, and the length of its sides at the base is about 343 feet.

## THE PYRAMID OF MEDÛM.

Tombs of Early and Middle Empire identical in plan.

This pyramid, called by the Arabs *El-Haram el-Kaddab*, or "the False Pyramid," is probably so named because it is unlike any of the other pyramids known to them; it is said to have been built by Seneferu , the first king of the IVth dynasty, but there is no indisputable evidence that he was the builder. The pyramid is about 115 feet high, and consists of three stages: the first is 70, the second 20, and the third about 25 feet high. The stone for this building was brought from the Moḳaṭṭam hills, but it seems never to have been finished; as in all other pyramids, the entrance is on the north side. When opened in modern times the sarcophagus chamber was found empty, and it would seem that this pyramid had been entered and rifled in ancient days.

## TOMBS OF THE THEBAN EMPIRE.

Egyptian tombs belonging to a period subsequent to the maṣṭabas and pyramids, *i.e.*, about the XIIth dynasty, usually have the three characteristic parts of these forms of tomb, viz., the chapel, the passage to the sarcophagus chamber, and the sarcophagus chamber itself excavated in the solid rock; sometimes, however, the chapel or chamber in which the relatives of the deceased assembled from time to time, is above ground and separate from the tomb, as in the case of the pyramid. Tombs having the chapel separate are the oldest, and the best examples are found at Abydos.[1] On a brick base about 50 feet by 35 feet, and four or five feet high, rose a pyramid to a height of about 30 feet; theoretically such a tomb was supposed to consist of chapel,

[1] Abydos étant surtout une nécropole du Moyen Empire, c'est la petite pyramide qui y domine. Des centaines de ces monuments, disposés sans ordre, hérissaient la nécropole et devaient lui donner un aspect pittoresque bien différent de l'aspect des nécropoles d'un autre temps. Mariette, *Abydos*, tom. II. Paris, 1880, p. 39.

Tombs at Abydos.

passage and pit, but at Abydos, owing to the friable nature of the rock, these do not exist, and the mummy was laid either in the ground between the foundations, or in the masonry itself, or in a chamber which projected from the building and formed a part of it, or in a chamber beneath. This class of tomb is common both at Thebes and Abydos. Tombs hewn entirely out of the solid rock were used at all periods, and the best examples of these are found in the mountains behind Asyûṭ, at Beni-Ḥasân, at Thebes, and at Aswân. The tombs at Beni-Ḥasân are about fifteen in number, and they all belong to the XIIth dynasty; they have preserved the chief characteristics of the maṣṭabas at Ṣaḳḳârah, that is to say, they consist of a chamber and a shaft leading down to a corridor, which ends in the chamber containing the sarcophagus and the mummy. The tombs rise tier above tier, and follow the course of the best layers of stone; the most important here are those of Ameni and Chnemu-ḥetep, which are remarkable for possessing columns somewhat resembling those subsequently called Doric, hewn out of the solid rock. The columns inside the tomb have sixteen sides.

Tombs at Beni-Ḥasân.

The bold headland which rises up in the low range of hills which faces the whole of the island of Elephantine, just opposite to the modern town of Aswân, has been found to be literally honeycombed with tombs, tier above tier, of various epochs. In ancient days there was down at the water's edge a massive stone quay, from which a broad, fine double staircase, cut in the living rock, ascended to a layer of firm rock about 150 feet higher. At Thebes and at Beni-Ḥasân, where such staircases must have existed, they have been destroyed, and only the traces remain to show that they ever existed. At Aswân it is quite different, for the whole of this remarkable staircase is intact. It begins at the bottom of the slope, well above the highest point reached by the waters of the Nile during the inundation, and following the outward curve of the hill, ends in a platform in front of the highest tombs. Between each set of steps which form the staircase is a smooth slope, up which the coffins and sarcophagi were drawn to the tomb by the men who walked up the steps at each side. At the bottom of the staircase the steps are only a few inches

Tombs at Aswân.

deep, but towards the top they are more than a foot. On each side of the staircase is a wall which appears to be of later date than the staircase itself, and about one-third of the way up there is a break in each wall, which appears to be a specially constructed opening leading to passages on the right and left respectively. The walls probably do not belong to the period of the uppermost tier of tombs, and appear to have been made during the rule of the Greeks or Romans.

**Tombs of the VIth dynasty at Aswân.**

In the hill of the tombs at Aswân there are three distinct layers of stone which have been chosen by the ancient Egyptians for the purpose of excavating tombs. The finest and thickest layer is at the top, and this was chosen principally by the architects of the VIth dynasty for the sepulchres of the governors of Elephantine. The tombs here belong to the VIth and XIIth dynasties, and of the former period the most interesting is that of Sabben, which is situated at the top of the staircase. Sabben was an official who lived in the time of Pepi II., whose cartouche 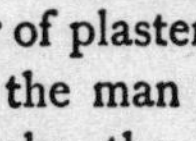 Nefer-ka-Rā is found on the right hand side of the doorway. The entrance to this tomb is made through a rectangular opening, in which is a small doorway about one-third of the height of the opening, that is to say through a door within a door. The walls inside were covered with a thin layer of plaster, and upon them were painted scenes in the life of the man who was buried there.

**Tombs of the XIIth dynasty at Aswân.**

Of the XIIth dynasty tombs, the most interesting is that of Se-renput, in the front of which there originally stood a portico. The scarped rock was ornamented with inscriptions, rows of cattle, etc., etc., and passing through the doorway, a chamber or chapel having four rectangular pillars was reached. A passage, in the sides of which were niches having figures in them, leads to a beautifully painted shrine in which was a black granite seated figure of the deceased; thus the serdâb and the stele of the maṣṭaba became united. On the right hand side was a tunnel, which, winding as it descended, led to the sarcophagus chamber which was situated exactly under the shrine containing the figure of the deceased. Se-renput lived in the time of Usertsen I., and was an officer in the service of this king when he marched into Ethiopia; thus the date of the tomb is well known.[1] Like the tombs of the VIth dynasty the walls inside were covered with a layer of plaster upon which scenes and inscriptions were painted.

Tombs of the XIIth and XVIIIth dynasties similar in plan.

During the XVIIIth dynasty tombs on the plan of the rock-hewn tombs of the XIIth dynasty were commonly built, but the inscriptions, which in ancient days were brief, now become very long, and the whole tomb is filled with beautifully painted scenes representing every art and trade, every agricultural labour, and every event in the life of the deceased. The biography of the deceased is given at great length; if a soldier, the military expeditions in which he took part are carefully depicted, and appropriate hieroglyphic descriptions are appended; the tribute brought to the king from the various countries is depicted with the most careful attention to the slightest detail of colour and form. The mummy chamber was made exactly under the chapel, but the position of the pit which led to it varied. Under the XVIIIth and XIXth dynasties the tombs of kings and private persons possessed a size and magnificence which they never attained either before or since. The finest specimens of these periods are the famous Tombs of the Kings which are hewn in the living rock in the eastern and western valleys at Thebes; those in the latter valley belong to the XVIIIth dynasty, and those in the former belong to the XIXth dynasty. The royal tombs here consist of long inclined planes, with chambers at intervals, receding into the mountains; according to Strabo these tombs were forty in number, but at the time of the death of M. Mariette, only about twenty-five were known. The tomb which we may consider to have been the model during the palmy days of the XVIIIth and XIXth dynasties, is that of Seti I.; the walls of the staircases and chambers are covered with inscriptions and scenes from the "Book of being in the

Bibân el-Mulûk.

[1] For a full account of this tomb, see my paper in *Proc. Soc. Bib. Arch.*, November, 1887, p. 33 ff. A tomb of great importance was discovered at Aswân in 1892 by Signor E. Schiaparelli, who published the hieroglyphic text with a commentary in his valuable paper *Una Tomba Egiziana Inedita della VIa Dinastia*, Roma, 1892.

Underworld," and their excellence and beauty is such that they cannot be too highly praised. Under this king, Egyptian funereal art seems to have been at its culminating point, for neither sculptor nor painter appears to have produced anything so fine after this date. The tomb is entered by means of two flights of steps, at the bottom of which is a passage terminating in a small chamber. Beyond this are two halls having four and two pillars respectively, and to the left are the passages and small chambers which lead to the large six-pillared hall and to the vaulted chamber in which stood the sarcophagus of Seti I. Here also is an inclined plane which descends into the mountain for a considerable distance; from the level of the ground to the bottom of this incline the depth is about 150 feet; the length of the tomb is nearly 500 feet. The designs on the walls were first sketched in outline in red, and the alterations by the master designer or artist were made in black; this tomb was never finished. Each chamber in this tomb has its peculiar ornamentation, and there is little doubt that each chamber had its peculiar furniture; it is thought that many articles of furniture, pieces of armour, weapons, etc., etc., were broken intentionally when they were placed in the tomb.[1] Of the tombs belonging to the period between the XXth and the XXVIth dynasty, nothing need be said, for they call for no special notice; in the XXVIth dynasty, however, the renaissance of Egyptian art naturally showed itself in the tombs of the period, and in some few instances an attempt was made to reproduce tombs after the plan and with the elegance of those of the XIXth dynasty. It must be noticed that the inscriptions on the walls are of a funereal character, and consist usually of a series of chapters of the Book of the Dead.

The tomb of Seti I.

The renaissance.

That the tombs described above are those of wealthy people goes without saying; it now remains to refer to the tombs of the extremely poor. They were sometimes buried in the crevices of the rocks, and at other times in the desert, either near the great necropolis of the town or in

[1] On les tuait de la sorte afin que leur âme allât servir l'âme de l'homme dans l'autre monde. Maspero, *L'Archéologie Egyptienne*, p. 159.

The tombs of the poor.

solitary places. A cave or hollow in the mountains afforded a place of sepulture unto many, and numerous rock caves exist in the mountains to the west of Thebes and other places, where the mass of decayed mummies and bones is several feet deep, and where skulls and skeletons, some with their skins shrivelled upon them, and others with bare bones, line the sides up to the ceiling. Sometimes pits were dug as common graves for the whole town, and sometimes the pit and passage of a forsaken tomb served to accommodate hundreds of bodies. The absence of valuable furniture and ornaments rendered the bodies of the poor of no account to the pillager of tombs, and the inaccessible situation of the places where they were buried made it unlikely that they would be disturbed that others might be put in their places. The funereal furniture of the poor consisted of very little more than what they wore day by day, and, provided they were protected by a few amulets and figures of the gods in faïence to guard them against the attacks of evil-disposed demons, and by a scarab, the emblem of the resurrection and the new life, they probably laid down the burden of this life with as firm a hope in the mercy of Osiris as did the rich man in the maṣṭaba or pyramid.

Graeco-Roman tombs.

Under the Ptolemies and the Roman Emperors the arrangement of the tombs changes greatly; the outer chapel or chamber disappears entirely, and the character of everything appertaining to the service of the tomb shows that a great change has taken place in the religious views of the people, for although ancient forms and observances are kept up, it is clear that the spirit which gave them life has been forgotten.

Egyptian tombs used by Christian monks.

In the early centuries of the Christian era the tombs in the mountains of Egypt formed dwelling-places for a number of monks and ascetics, and it would seem that the statues and other objects in them suffered at their hands. An instance of the use of a rock-hewn tomb by Pisentios, Bishop of Coptos, is made known to us by an encomium on this saint by his disciple John.[1] The tomb in which

[1] For the Coptic text and a French translation, see Amélineau, *Etude sur le Christianisme en Egypte au Septième Siècle*, Paris, 1887.

Pisentios lived was rectangular in shape, and was fifty-two feet wide; it had six pillars and contained a large number of mummies. The coffins were very large and profusely decorated, and one of the mummies was clothed in silk, and his fingers and toes were mummified separately; the names of those buried there were written on a small parchment roll (ⲛ̄ ⲟⲩⲧⲟⲙⲁⲣⲓⲟⲛ ⲛ̄ ϫⲱⲙ ⲙ̄ ⲙⲉⲙⲃⲣⲁⲛⲟⲛ). Pisentios conversed with one of the mummies, who begged the saint to pray for his forgiveness; when Pisentios had promised him that Christ would have mercy upon him, the mummy lay down in his coffin again.

## EGYPTIAN WRITING MATERIALS.

The writing materials chiefly used by the ancient Egyptians consisted of papyrus, palette, reeds, and colours.

The **papyrus** was called  *thuf*,  *ḥai*, 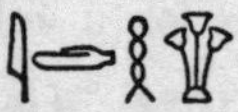 *āṭeḥ*, etc., and was made from the byblus hieraticus, or *Cyperus papyrus*, which grew in the marshes and pools near the Nile. The height of the plant was from twelve to fifteen feet, and the largest diameter of its triangular stalk was about four or six inches. The roots were used for firewood, parts of the plant were eaten, and other and coarser parts were made into paper, boats, ropes, mats, etc., etc. It will be remembered that the boat in which Isis set out to seek for Osiris was made of papyrus,[1] and the "ark of bulrushes"[2] in which Moses was laid was probably made of the same material. When it was intended to make paper from the plant, the outer rind was removed, and the stalk was divided with a flat needle into layers. These layers, the length of which depended upon the width of the roll to be made, and the width upon the thickness of the stalk of the plant from which they were taken, were then laid upon a table, side by side, and upon these another series of layers was laid in a horizontal direction, and a thin solution of gum was then run between them; the two series of layers thus united were

**Preparation of papyrus for writing purposes.**

[1] Plutarch, *De Iside et Osiride*, Squire's translation, p. 22.
[2] Exodus ii. 3.

pressed and afterwards dried. It is clear that by joining a number of such sheets of papyrus together, a roll of almost any length could be made. The quality of the papyrus depended entirely upon the class of plant used in its manufacture. The colour of the papyri that have come down to us varies greatly, from a rich brown to a whitish-grey; the texture of some is exceedingly coarse, and of others fine and silky. The width of papyri varies from six to seventeen inches, and the longest papyrus known (Harris, No. 1, B.M. 9999) measures 135 feet in length. The finest hieroglyphic papyri of the Book of the Dead are about fifteen inches in width, and when they contain a tolerably full number of chapters, are from eighty to ninety feet long. The papyri upon which contracts in Greek and Demotic are written are of a coarse fibre, and vary from ten to fourteen inches in width; their lengths vary from one to ten feet. The usual width of papyri employed for literary compositions is about eight inches. The common name for a roll of papyrus was *t'amā*, Copt. ϫⲱⲙ, "a book." Papyrus letters and legal documents were fastened by being tied round with a piece of papyrus string, and upon this a piece of clay was laid, which, being impressed with a ring or scarab, formed a seal, called in Egyptian *t'ebāt*. The British Museum possesses among its seals impressions in clay of the seal of Shabaka, found at Kouyunjik (see p. 249); a seal (No. 5585) ascribed to Shashanq by Dr. Birch (in Layard, *Babylon and Nineveh*, London, 1853, p. 1857), which reads ; an oval seal (No. 5584) bearing the name of a private person and the prenomen of Amāsis II. ; and an oval seal (No. 5583), bearing the name of Naifāarut, the first king of the XXIXth dynasty.

**Dimensions of papyri.**

The **palette** of the Egyptian scribe, called *mesthȧ*, was made of basalt (B.M. No. 12,778), calcareous stone inlaid with lapis-lazuli (B.M. No. 24,576), and ivory (B.M. No. 5524), but more commonly of wood. In shape it was rectangular, and its size varied from 10 in. × 2 in. to 16 in. × $2\frac{1}{2}$ in.; its thickness was usually $\frac{3}{8}$ of an inch. At one end were circular, or oval, hollows to hold ink, the former being in the shape of 𓍶, and the latter of a cartouche 𓍷. About a third of the length of the palette from this end a sloping groove was cut, which from about the middle of the palette to the other end had an equal depth, for holding the reeds for writing. These were kept in their place either by a piece of wood gummed into the palette about a third of the way above the groove, or by a piece of wood, forming a bridge, under which the reeds could pass freely, and which was left uncut when the groove was made. A sliding cover over the longer part of the groove protected the ends of the reeds from damage. The hollows in the palette for holding the ink are usually two in number, one for red ink and one for black; these being the colours most commonly used for writing upon papyri. Some palettes have as many as a dozen hollows, and these probably belonged to scribes whose business it was to ornament papyri with scenes painted in many colours. The dates of palettes can often be determined with accuracy because, in addition to the name of the owner, the name of the king in whose reign he lived is given. Thus B.M. No. 12,784 was made in the reign of Amāsis I., B.M. 5513 in that of Amenophis III., and B.M. 5514 in that of Rameses II.; from these three examples we see that the form of the palette changed very little in a whole dynasty. The inscriptions upon palettes were usually in hieroglyphics, but B.M. No. 5524, made of ivory, is inscribed in hieratic, and B.M. No. 5517, made of wood, also has upon it an inscription in hieratic. The palette of a scribe was sometimes placed in the tomb with its owner (see in the *Papyrus of Ani*, pl. 7, where it lies under the bier), and votive palettes are known, as for example B.M. No. 12,778. This object is made of green basalt, and at the end where the coloured inks were placed is a scene in outline in which the deceased is represented making an offering to Osiris, behind whom stand a goddess and Thoth. The places for the ink are outlined, but not hollowed out, and the groove is only cut a part of the length; the reeds which still remain are fastened in with plaster, and it is perfectly clear that this

**Royal palettes.**

palette was never used by a scribe. On each side is an inscription in hieroglyphics, which records the name and titles of the deceased, and which prays that appropriate sepulchral meals may be given to the deceased, and that he may enter in, and come out from the underworld, without repulse, whenever he pleases. Inscriptions on palettes are often dedications to the god Thoth, "lord of divine words." Stone and faïence palettes with eight, ten, or twelve small vases for ink were also used.

**The Egyptian pen.**

The **reed**, in Egyptian 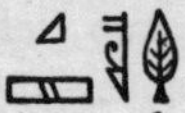 *qesh*, Copt. ⲕⲁϣ, with which the Egyptian wrote, was about ten inches long, $\frac{1}{16}$th or $\frac{1}{8}$th of an inch in diameter; the end used for writing was bruised to make the fibres flexible, and not cut. After the XXVIth dynasty an ordinary reed, similar to that which the Arabs and other Oriental nations use for writing at the present day, was employed, and the end was cut like a quill, or steel pen. The average sized palette will hold about ten writing reeds easily.

The **ink** which the Egyptian used was made of mineral and vegetable substances, mixed with a little gum and water. The substance which coloured the ink, black, red, blue, green, white, or yellow, was carefully rubbed down on a rectangular slab of granite, basalt, or marble, with a hard stone muller, and then thrown into a vessel, where the necessary quantity of water and gum was added to make it the consistency of moderately thin cream. The professional scribe probably carried about with him pieces of colour similar to the specimens in blue, green, and red which are preserved in European museums, and rubbed down a little at a time according to his need. The green and blue colours are preparations from copper, which can, I understand, be successfully imitated at the present time; fine examples are B.M. 5565, 5571 *c*, and small prepared lumps of colour exhibited in bronze bowl, B.M. 5556. The red and bronze colours were preparations from red ochre mixed with chalk; an interesting example of the former is B.M. No. 18,337, and of the latter B.M. No. 5572.

## EGYPTIAN WRITING.

The system of writing employed by the people called Egyptians was probably entirely pictorial either at the time when they first arrived in Egypt, or during the time that they still lived in their original home. We, however, know of no inscription in which pictorial characters alone are used, for the earliest specimens of their writing known to us contain alphabetical characters. The Egyptians had three kinds of writing—Hieroglyphic, Hieratic, and Demotic; soon after the preaching of Saint Mark at Alexandria, the Christian population made use of the Greek alphabet, with the addition of certain characters which they borrowed from the demotic; this method of writing was called Coptic.

**Great antiquity of hieroglyphic writing.**

**Hieroglyphics,** from the Greek *ἱερογλυφικός*, were commonly employed for inscriptions upon temples, tombs, coffins, statues, and stelæ, and many copies of the Book of the Dead were written in them. The earliest hieroglyphic inscription at present known is found on the monument of Sherá, parts of which are preserved in the Ashmolean Museum at Oxford and in the Gîzeh Museum; it dates from the IInd dynasty. Hieroglyphics were used in Egypt for writing the names of Roman Emperors and for religious purposes until the third century after Christ, at least.

**Oldest hieroglyphic inscription.**

**Hieratic,** from the Greek *ἱερατικός*, was a style of cursive writing much used by the priests in copying literary compositions on papyrus; during the XIth or XIIth dynasty wooden coffins were inscribed in hieratic with religious texts. The oldest document in hieratic is the famous Prisse papyrus, which records the counsels of Ptaḥ-ḥetep to his son; the composition itself is about a thousand years older than this papyrus, which was probably inscribed about the XIth dynasty. Drafts of inscriptions were written upon flakes of calcareous stone in hieratic, and at a comparatively early date hieratic was used in writing copies of the Book of the Dead. Hieratic was used until about the fourth century after Christ.

**Oldest hieratic inscription.**

**Demotic,** from the Greek *δημοτικός*, is a purely conventional modification of hieratic characters, which preserve little of their original form, and was used for social and business purposes; in the early days of Egyptian decipherment it was called **enchorial**, from the Greek *ἐγχώριος*. The demotic writing appears to have come into use about B.C. 900, and it survived until about the fourth century after Christ. In the time of the Ptolemies three kinds of writing were inscribed side by side upon documents of public importance, hieroglyphic, Greek, and Demotic; examples are the stele of Canopus, set up in the ninth year of the reign of Ptolemy III. Euergetes I., B.C. 247–222, at Canopus, to record the benefits which this king had conferred upon his country, and the famous Rosetta Stone, set up at Rosetta in the eighth year of the reign of Ptolemy V. Epiphanes (B.C. 205–182), likewise to commemorate the benefits conferred upon Egypt by himself and his family, etc., etc. On the Rosetta Stone hieroglyphic writing is called 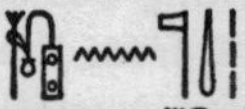 *nā en neter met*, "writing of divine words," Demotic,  *nā en šāi*, "writing of letters," and Greek 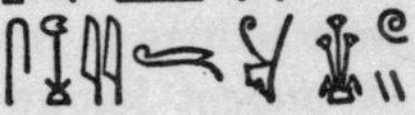 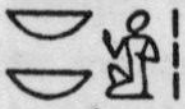 *seχai en Ḥaui-nebu*, "writing of the Greeks."

**The various kinds of writing used in Egypt.**

A century or two after the Christian era Greek had obtained such a hold upon the inhabitants of Egypt, that the native Christian population, the disciples and followers of Saint Mark, were obliged to use the Greek alphabet to write down the Egyptian, that is to say **Coptic**, translation of the books of the Old and New Testaments, but they borrowed six signs from the demotic forms of ancient Egyptian characters to express the sounds which they found unrepresented in Greek. These signs are—

ϣ =  SH; ϥ =  F;
ϧ =  CH; ϩ =  Ḥ;
ϫ =  TCH, like Turk. چ; ϭ =  K.

**Coptic writing.**

The knowledge of the ancient hieroglyphics was fast dying out, and the phonetic values of many of those in use at this period were altered. The name Copt is derived from قبط, the Arabic form of the Coptic form of the Greek name for

Egyptian, Αἰγύπτιος. The Coptic language is, at base, a dialect of ancient Egyptian; many of the nouns and verbs found in the hieroglyphic texts remain unchanged in Coptic, and a large number of others can, by making proper allowance for phonetic decay and dialectic differences, be identified without difficulty.

**Dialects of Coptic.**

The Coptic dialect of Upper Egypt, called "Sahidic" (from Arab. صعيد), or Theban, was the older and richer dialect; that of Lower Egypt was called Boheiric, from the province of Boheirâ in the Delta. The latter dialect has been wrongly called Bashmuric, and as it appears to have been exclusively the language of Memphis, it has obtained generally the name "Memphitic"; the dialect of Bushmur on the Lake of Menzaleh appears to have become extinct about A.D. 900, and to have left no traces of itself behind. The Coptic translation of the Bible was considered by Renaudet, Wilkins, Woide, and George, to be as old as the second century of our era; more modern scholars, however, are inclined to assert that it is not older than the eighth century. For an account of the revival of Coptic studies in Europe, see Quatremère, *Recherches Critiques et Historiques sur la Langue et la Littérature de l'Egypte*, Paris, 1808, and for a list of the printed literature of the Copts, see Stern, *Koptische Grammatik*, pp. 441–447. The recognition of the fact that a knowledge of Coptic is most valuable as a preliminary to the study of hieroglyphics, probably accounts for the large and increasing share of the attention of scholars which this language receives.

## Mummies of Animals, Reptiles, Birds, and Fishes.

The most common of the animals, reptiles, birds, and fishes which the Egyptians regarded as emblems of or sacred to the gods, and therefore mummified with great reverence and care, were:—Bull, Antelope, Jackal, Hippopotamus, Cat, Monkey or Ape, Crocodile, Ichneumon, Hedgehog, Shrew-mouse, Ibis, Hawk, Frog, Toad, Scorpion, Beetle, Snake, and the Latus, Oxyrhynchus and Silurus fishes.

**Apis Bull,** in Egyptian  *Ḥāp*, mummies are tolerably common; they were mummified with great honour, and buried in sarcophagi at Ṣaḳḳârah. The oldest are probably those of the XVIIIth dynasty.

**Antelope,** in Egyptian  *ḳaḥes* or 
 *maḥet'*, mummies are rare; a good specimen is B.M. No. 6783*a*.

**Cat,** in Egyptian  *mäu*, mummies are very common, and exhibit many methods of bandaging with linen of two colours; they were placed in bronze or wooden cases, made in the form of a cat, the eyes of which were inlaid with obsidian, rock-crystal, or coloured paste. Wooden cat-cases often stand on pedestals, and are painted white, green, etc. Mummified kittens were placed in rectangular bronze or wooden cases, which, at times, are surmounted with figures of cats. Diodorus says (I., 83) that when a cat died all the inmates of the house shaved their eyebrows as a sign of mourning, and although the statement by the same writer that the Egyptians slew a Roman who had accidentally killed a cat may be somewhat exaggerated, there is no doubt that the animal sacred to Bast was treated with great respect in Egypt, and that dead bodies of the animals were sent to be buried, after embalmment, to Bubastis. The cat was fed with specially prepared bread soaked in milk, and chopped fish.

Greek legends concerning the cat.

Mummies of animals, etc.

**Crocodile,** in Egyptian  *emsuḥ*, mummies of a large size are not common; small crocodiles, lizards, and other members of that family were embalmed and placed in rectangular bronze or wooden cases, the tops of which were frequently surmounted by a figure of this reptile in relief.

**Ichneumon** mummies were placed in bronze cases, made in the shape of this animal.

**Shrew-mice** mummies are not common; they were placed in rectangular bronze cases, surmounted by a figure of this animal.

**Ibis**, in Egyptian *habu*, mummies, embalmed, and buried in earthenware jars, stopped with plaster, are very common.

The **Hawk**, in Egyptian *bàk*, when mummified, was placed either in a rectangular bronze case or in a bronze case in the form of a hawk.

**Frogs**, in Egyptian *ḥeqet*, and **Toads**, when embalmed, were placed in cases made of bronze or steatite.

**Scorpion**, in Egyptian *Serq*, mummies are very rare; they were placed in rectangular cases, inscribed with the name of Isis-Serq, which were surmounted by figures of the scorpion, with the head of a woman wearing disk and horns (B.M. No. 11,629).

**Beetle**, in Egyptian or *χeper*, rarely *āбeb*, mummies were deposited in cases of wood (B.M. No. 8654*a*) or stone (B.M. No. 2880).

**Mummies of reptiles, etc.**

**Snake** mummies are very common, and were either placed in rectangular bronze or wooden cases, or wrapped in many bandages and laid in pits. Bronze snake-cases usually have a figure of the snake coiled up in relief upon them, but sometimes the head, which is human and erect, wears the double crown and uræus (B.M. No 6881*c*); one example having the head of a hawk is also known (B.M. No. 6879). The uræus serpent, in Egyptian *Ārārt*, was the most commonly mummified.

**Fish** were mummified largely, and were either placed singly in cases of bronze or wood, or several were bandaged up in a bundle and laid in a pit prepared for the purpose. Many fish were known to the Egyptians, and the commoner sorts were *ànnu* = φάγρος, *āba*, *uḥeb*, *meḥi*, *nārt*, *barei*, *baḳa*, and *betu*; the usual name for fish in general was

 *rem.* The  *abṭu* and the  *ȧnt* were mythological fishes which accompanied the boat of the Sun.

## Cippi of Horus.

These curious and interesting objects are made of basalt and other kinds of hard stone, and calcareous stone; they are in the shape of a rounded tablet, and vary in size from 3 in. × 2 in., to 20 in. × 16 in.; the Metternich stele is, however, very much larger. The scenes engraved upon them represent the triumph of light over darkness, the victory of good over evil, and cippi were used as talismans by those who were initiated into the mysteries of magic, to guard them from the attacks of noxious beasts, and from the baneful influence of Set, the god of all evil. To give an idea of these magical objects, a description of an example, in a good state of preservation, now in the British Museum (No. 957*a*) is here appended.[1] On the front, in relief, is a figure of Horus, naked, standing upon two crocodiles, which are supported by a projecting ledge at the foot of the stele. Horus has the lock of hair, emblematic of youth, on the right side of his head, and above him, resting on the top of his head, is a head of Bes, also in relief. His arms hang at a little distance from his sides; in the right hand he holds two serpents, a scorpion, and a ram or stag,

Scenes on a cippus of Horus.

and in the left two serpents, a scorpion, and a lion. On the right is a sceptre, upon which stands the hawk of Horus wearing horns, disk and feathers,[2] and on the left is a lotus-headed sceptre with plumes and two *menȧts*[3] (see p. 265). To the right and to the left of the god, outside the sceptres, are eight divisions; those on the right represent:—

1. Oryx, with a hawk on his back, in front is inscribed 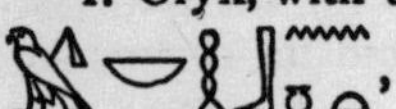, "Horus, lord of Ḥebennu," *i.e.*, the metropolis of the sixteenth nome of Upper Egypt.

[1] A faulty copy is given in Wilkinson, *The Ancient Egyptians*, Vol. III., pl. XXXIII.

[2] The inscription reads 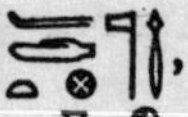, "Beḥuṭet, great god."

[3] The inscription reads, .

2. Ibis-headed god, Thoth, , "lord of Chemennu, lord of divine words," and the god Ḥer-shef , hawk-headed, wearing the triple crown .

3. "Ḥeka, lord of enchantments," , hawk-headed, holding a serpent in each hand; "Neith, mighty lady, divine mother, lady of Saïs" .

4. Hawk-headed god, mummified, wearing disk and holding a serpent in each hand; the inscription is "Chensu, lord of Sam-beḥuṭet."

5. Isis, , with the body of a hippopotamus, holding a snake; on her head she wears a disk and horns.

6. Ptaḥ, in the form of a squat child standing on a pedestal with four or five steps; the inscription is *Ptaḥ ser āa*, "Ptaḥ, prince, mighty ......"

7. The goddess Serqet, scorpion-headed, holding a serpent with both hands; the inscription is "Serqet, lady of life."

8. Goddess, wearing disk and serpent, , on her head, standing between two serpents; the inscription reads "Nebt ḥetep." Scenes on a cippus of Horus.

The eight scenes on the left hand side of Horus represent:—

1. Goddess, having a disk and two scorpions on her head, which is in the form of two serpents' heads, standing on a crocodile; she holds a serpent in her right hand, and a serpent and a scorpion in the left; on the crocodile's head is a bird. The inscription reads, .

2. Crocodile, with disk and horns, on a stand; behind it a serpent Usert, . The inscription reads, "great god......"

3. Isis suckling Horus among papyrus plants, under a canopy formed by two serpents, called Nechebet and Uatchet , wearing the crown of Upper and Lower

Egypt respectively; under each serpent is a scorpion. The inscription reads , "Isis, lady of Cheb."

4. Crocodile-headed god Sebek 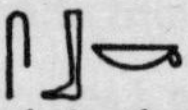 seated. This scene is rendered incomplete by a break in the cippus.

5. Hawk-headed god wearing the crown of Lower Egypt, and holding a serpent in his hands; he is called 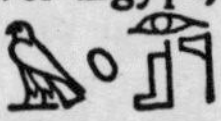 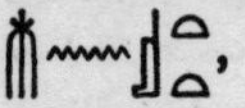, "Horus, son of Osiris, born of Isis."

6. Hawk of Horus , wearing horns and plumes , standing on ; behind him is  *šen*, and a goddess, wearing disk and horns, and having the body of a scorpion, called "Isis-Serqet" 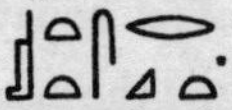.

7. Horus, in the form of a boy, holding  over his left shoulder, seated on a crocodile, under a canopy formed by two serpents; the inscription reads, 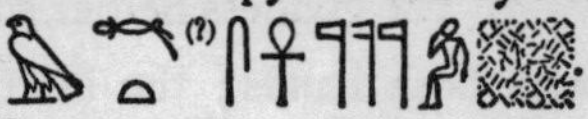

8. The goddess Uatchet 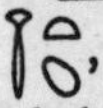, wearing crown of Lower Egypt, on a papyrus sceptre; behind her Ḥu  and Sau , each holding a knife.

Above the two crocodiles on which Horus stands are two small scenes in each of which is a crocodile, one being on a stand; that to the right of Horus has on his head  and that on the left ; the former is called , "Hidden is his name," and the latter 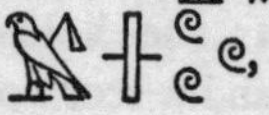, "Horus in Uu."

The inscription, which covers the front and base of the pedestal and back and sides of the cippus, contains an invocation to the god from whom the person for whom it was made seeks to gain power.

**Late date of cippi of Horus.**

Cippi of Horus belong probably to the period which followed soon after the end of the rule of the XXVIth dynasty over Egypt, and the inscriptions on them are badly executed. They are generally found broken in half, or if not broken, the head of Horus has been hammered to deface the features; these injuries probably date from ancient times.

**The Metternich stele.**

The largest and finest specimen of the cippi of Horus is that preserved in the Museum of Metternich Castle at Königswarth in Bohemia. It was found in the beginning of this century at Alexandria during the building of a fountain in a Franciscan convent there, and was given to Prince Metternich by Muḥammad 'Ali in 1828. It is made of a hard, dark-green stone upon which the figures of the gods and the inscriptions are finely and beautifully cut. The inscriptions have much in common with the magical texts inscribed upon papyri in London, Turin, and Paris, and are of great interest; this stele was made for Nectanebus I., about B.C. 370. A fac-simile of the stele and the text was published with a German translation and notes by W. Golenischeff, *Die Metternichstele .... zum ersten Mal herausgegeben*, Leipzig, 1877. A long article is devoted to the consideration of the cippi of Horus by Lanzone, *Dizionario*, pp. 583–594; and see Birch in Arundale and Bonomi, *Gallery of Antiquities*, p. 39 ff.

## The Egyptian Year.[1]

The ancient Egyptians had:—I. The vague, or civil year, which consisted of 360 days; it was divided into twelve months of thirty days each, and five intercalary days[2] were added at the end. II. The Sothic year of 365¼ days. The first year of a Sothic period began with the rising of Sirius or the dog-star, on the 1st of the month Thoth, when it coincided with the beginning of the inundation. III. The solar year, which was practically the same as the civil year, and which was a quarter of a day shorter than the Sothic year, an error which corrected itself in 1460 fixed years or 1461 vague years. The true year was estimated approximately by the conjunction of the sun with Sirius. Dr. Brugsch

[1] The whole subject of the origin of the Egyptian year has recently been discussed with excellent results in *Nature*, Vol. XLV., 1892, p. 487, by Prof. N. Lockyer; and Vol. XLVI., p. 104 ff.

[2] Called in Egyptian 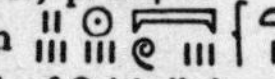, "five days over the year." The first was called the "birth of Osiris," the second "the birth of Horus," the third "the birth of Set," the fourth "the birth of Isis," and the fifth the "birth of Nephthys." The Greeks called these days, ἐπαγόμεναι ἡμέραι πέντε, and the Copts ⲡⲓⲁⲃⲟⲧ ⲛⲕⲟⲩϫⲓ, "the little month."

thinks (*Egypt under the Pharaohs*, Vol. II., p. 17) that as early as B.C. 2500 *four* different forms of the year were already in use, and that the "little year" corresponded with the lunar year, and the "great year" with a lunar year having intercalated days.[1] The divisions of time of the Egyptians were 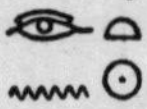 *ȧnt*, "one-sixtieth of a second,"  *ḥat*, "second,"  *at*, "minute,"  *unnut*, "hour,"  *hru*, "day,"  *ȧbeṭ*, "month," 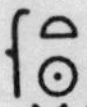 *renpit*, "year,"  *sed*, "period of thirty years,"  *ḥen*, "period,"  *ḥeḥ*, "millions of years," 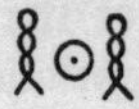 *ḥeḥ*, and  *t'etta*, "immeasurable time," or "eternity." The Egyptian week consisted of ten days .

[1] See Lepsius, *Die Chronologie der Aegypter*, p. 147 ff.

## EGYPTIAN MONTHS.

| | | | Hieroglyphic Name. | Coptic Names. Sahidic. | Coptic Names. Memphitic. | Greek. | Arabic. | God of the Month. |
|---|---|---|---|---|---|---|---|---|
| April | *26 | Months 1-4 of the season of inundation. | | ⲡⲁϣⲱⲛⲥ | ⲡⲁϣⲱⲛⲥ | Παχών | بشنس | *Chensu.* |
| May | 26 | | | ⲡⲁⲱⲛⲉ | ⲡⲁⲱⲛⲓ | Παϋνί | بؤونه | *Chenthi* (*a name of Horus*). |
| June | 25 | | | ⲉⲡⲏⲫ | ⲉⲡⲏⲡ | Ἐπιφί | ابيب | *Peteti.* |
| July | 25 | | | ⲙⲉⲥⲱⲣⲏ | ⲙⲉⲥⲱⲣⲏ | Μεσορί | مسرى | *Ḥeru-χuti* (Harmachis). |
| August | 29 | Months 1-4 of the season of sowing. | | ⲑⲟⲟⲩⲑ | ⲑⲱⲟⲩⲧ | Θωῦθ | توت | *Techi* (Thoth). |
| September | 28 | | | ⲡⲁⲟⲡⲉ | ⲡⲁⲱⲡⲓ | Φαωφί | بابه | *Ptaḥ resu àneb-f* (Ptaḥ of Memphis). |
| October | 28 | | | ϩⲁⲑⲱⲣ | ⲁⲑⲱⲣ | Ἀθύρ | هتور | *Ḥet-Ḥeru* (Hathor). |
| November | 27 | | | ⲭⲟⲓⲁϩⲕ | ⲭⲟⲓⲁⲕ | Χοιάκ | كيهك | *Sechet.* |
| December | 27 | Months 1-4 of the season of coming forth, or growing. | | ⲧⲱⲃⲉ | ⲧⲱⲃⲓ | Τυβί | طوبه | *Àmsu.* |
| January | 26 | | | ⲙϣⲓⲣ | ⲙⲉⲭⲓⲣ | Μεχίρ | امشير | *Rekḥ-ur.* |
| February | 25 | | | ⲡⲁⲣⲙϩⲁⲧ | ⲫⲁⲙⲉⲛⲱⲑ | Φαμενώθ | برمهات | *Rekḥ sheràu.* |
| March | 27 | | | ⲡⲁⲣⲙⲟⲩⲧⲉ | ⲫⲁⲣⲙⲟⲩⲑⲓ | Φαρμουθί | برموده | *Rennutet.* |

* The days for the beginnings of these months were first fixed at Alexandria about B.C. 30.

## Egyptian and Coptic Numbers.

| | Hieroglyphic. | | | Coptic. | Masculine. | Feminine |
|---|---|---|---|---|---|---|
| ½ | | | *ma*[1] | | ⲫⲁϣⲓ, ϫⲟⲥ, ϭⲟⲥ | |
| ⅔ | | | *neb* | | | |
| 1 | \| | = | *uā* (fem. *uāt*) | ⲁ̅ | ⲟⲩⲁⲓ[2] | ⲟⲩⲓ |
| 2 | \|\| | = | *sen* | ⲃ̅ | ⲥⲛⲁⲩ | ⲥⲛⲟⲩϯ |
| 3 | \|\|\| | = | *xemt* | ⲅ̅ | ϣⲟⲙⲧ | ϣⲟⲙϯ |
| 4 | \|\|\|\| | = | *åfṭ*, or *fṭu* | ⲇ̅ | ϥⲧⲱⲟⲩ | ϥⲧⲟⲉ |
| 5 | \|\|\|\|\| | = | *ṭua* | ⲉ̅ | ϯⲟⲩ | ϯⲉ |
| 6 | \|\|\|\|\|\| | = | *sås* | ⲋ̅ | ϭⲟⲩ | ⲥⲟⲉ |
| 7 | \|\|\|\|\|\|\| | = | *sexef* | ⲍ̅ | ϣⲁϣϥ | ϣⲁϣϥⲓ |
| 8 | \|\|\|\|\|\|\|\| | = | *xemennu* | ⲏ̅ | ϣⲙⲏⲛ | ϣⲙⲏⲛⲓ |
| 9 | \|\|\| \|\|\| \|\|\| | = | *paut* and *pesṭ* | ⲑ̅ | ⲯⲓⲧ | ⲯⲓϯ |
| 10 | ∩ | = | *met* | ⲓ̅ | ⲙⲏⲧ | ⲙⲏϯ |
| 15 | ∩\|\|\|\|\| | = | *met ṭua* | ⲓ̅ⲉ̅ | ⲙⲉⲧϯⲟⲩ | |
| 20 | ∩∩ | = | *t'aut* | ⲕ̅ | ϫⲱⲧ | ϫⲟⲩⲱⲧⲉ |
| 30 | ∩∩∩ | = | *māb* | ⲗ̅ | ⲙⲁⲃ | |
| 40 | ∩∩∩∩ | = | *ḥement* | ⲙ̅ | ϩⲙⲉ | |
| 50 | ∩∩∩∩∩ | | *ṭaiu* | ⲛ̅ | ⲧⲉⲟⲩⲓ | |
| 60 | ∩∩∩ ∩∩∩ | | *sau* | ⲝ̅ | ⲥⲉ | |

[1] See Eisenlohr, *Ein mathematisches Handbuch der alten Aegypter*, Leipzig, 1877, p. 15 ff.

[2] For the variants see Stern, *Koptische Grammatik*, p. 131 ff.

| | | | | |
|---|---|---|---|---|
| 70 | 𓎉𓎉𓎉𓎉𓎉𓎉𓎉 | = | *sefex* | ō ϣⲃⲉ |
| 80 | 𓎉𓎉𓎉𓎉𓎉𓎉𓎉𓎉 | = | *xemennui* | π̄ ϩⲙⲉⲛⲉ |
| 90 | 𓎉𓎉𓎉𓎉𓎉𓎉𓎉𓎉𓎉 | | | ϥ̄ ⲡⲓⲥⲧⲉⲟⲩⲓ |
| 100 | 𓍢 | = | *śaā* | ρ̄ ϣⲉ |
| 200 | 𓍢𓍢 | = | *śetau* | ⲥ̄[1] ⲥⲛⲁⲩ ⲛ̄ ϣⲉ |
| 1000 | 𓆼 | = | *xa* | ⲁ̳ ϣⲟ |
| 10,000 | 𓂭 | = | *t'āb* | ī ⲑⲃⲁ |
| 100,000 | 𓆐 | = | *ḥefennu* | ⲣⲁ̄ ϣⲉ ⲛ̄ ϣⲟ |
| 1,000,000 | 𓁨 | = | *ḥeḥ* | ⲁⲁ̄ ϣⲟ ⲛ̄ ϣⲟ |

[1] ⲧ̄ = 300, ⲩ̄ = 400, ⲫ̄ = 500, ⲭ̄ = 600, ⲯ̄ = 700 ⲱ̄ = 800, ⳁ = 900.

# A List of the Commonest Hieroglyphic Signs and their Phonetic Values.[1]

## A.

a 

an 

as 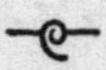

at 

aṭ 

## Á.

á 

áa 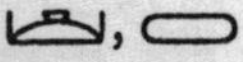

áau 

áāḥ 

áb 

ábeṭ 

áp 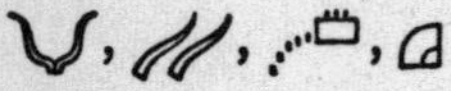

áf 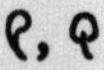

áfeṭ 

áusár 

áuset 

ám 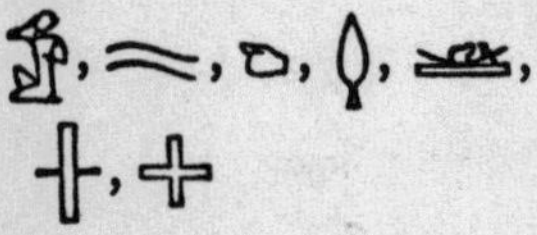

ámaχ 

ámen 

áment 

ámsu 

án 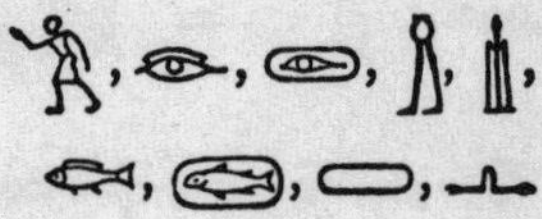

áneb 

ánem 

áner 

ár 

ári 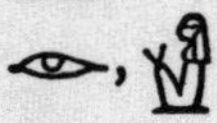

áru 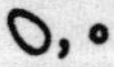

ás 

át 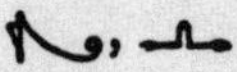

áteḥ 

áter 

áθi 

[1] This list does not contain the values assigned to certain of the hieroglyphics in the Greek and Roman periods.

## Ā.

ā

āa

āu

āb

āba

āp

āper

āf

ām

ān

ānχ

ār

ārq

āḥā

āḥet

āχ

āṭ

āq

## I.

i

iā

## I.

I

## B.

b

ba

bȧ

bener

bennu

beḥ

beḥa

beḥutet

bāḥ

beχ

bes

beti

## B—*continued.*

betu 

beṭ 

bek 

bȧk 

beq 

## P.

p 

pa 

pāt 

paut 

pāpā 

per 

peḥ 

peχ 

pesṭ 

peś 

pet 

peteḥ 

peṭ 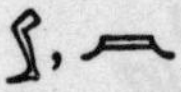

peḳ 

## F.

f 

fa 

fent 

## U.

u 

ua 

uas 

uat 

uat′ 

uā 

uār 

uaḥ 

uu 

un 

ur 

usr 

useχ 

uś 

**U**—*continued.*

ut

uteb

uθes

uṭen

ut'a

ut'eb

**M.**

m

ma

maa

maā

må

mā

māu

mār

māk

men

menåt

meni

menχ

mer

meḥ

mes

mesen

met

mut

mat'a

**N.**

n

nā

nār

nu

neb

nub

nef

## N—*continued.*

nefer 

nem 

nemmat 

enen 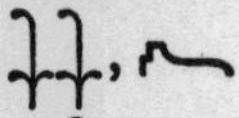

nini 

ner 

neh 

neḥ 

neḥem 

neχeb 

neχt 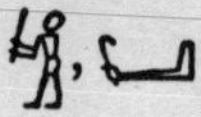

nes 

nest 

net 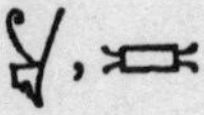

nut 

net' 

net'em 

neter 

neqer 

## R.

r *or* l 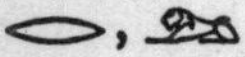

rā 

ru 

remen 

ren 

renp 

rer 

reχ 

res 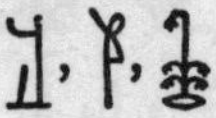

reṭ 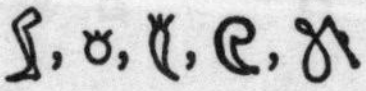

## H.

h  ha  heb 

hen  hru 

## Ḥ.

ḥ  ḥa  ḥā 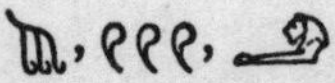 ḥāā 

## Ḥ—*continued.*

ḥāp
ḥu
ḥeb
ḥep
ḥefen
ḥem
ḥen
ḥenk
ḥer

ḥrȧ
ḥeḥ
ḥes
ḥeseb
ḥesep
ḥet
ḥet′
ḥetep
ḥetem
ḥeter
ḥeka

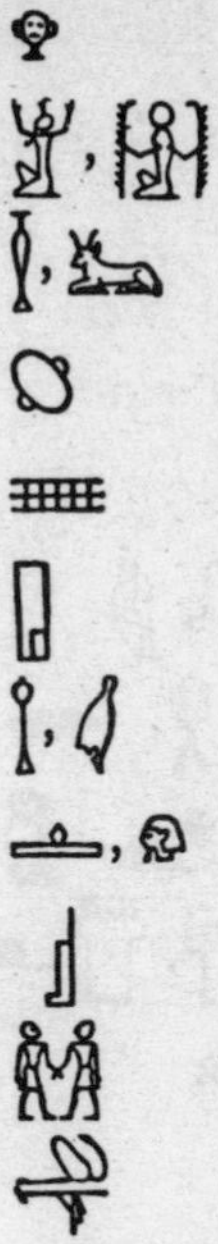

ḥeq

## χ or CH.

χ
χa
χai
χā
χi
χu
χabes
χeb
χep

χeper
χepeś
χem
χemt
χen
χnem
χent
χer

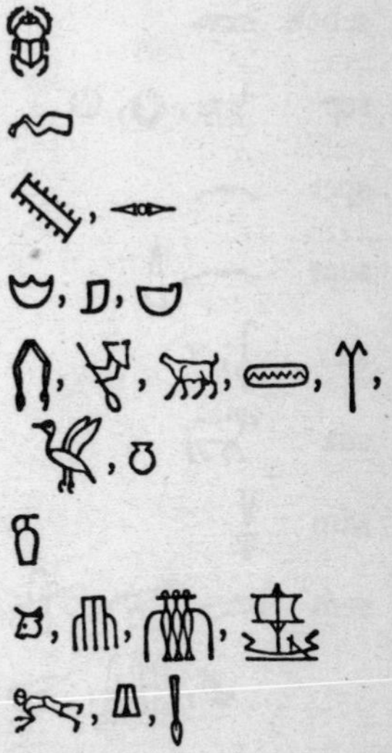

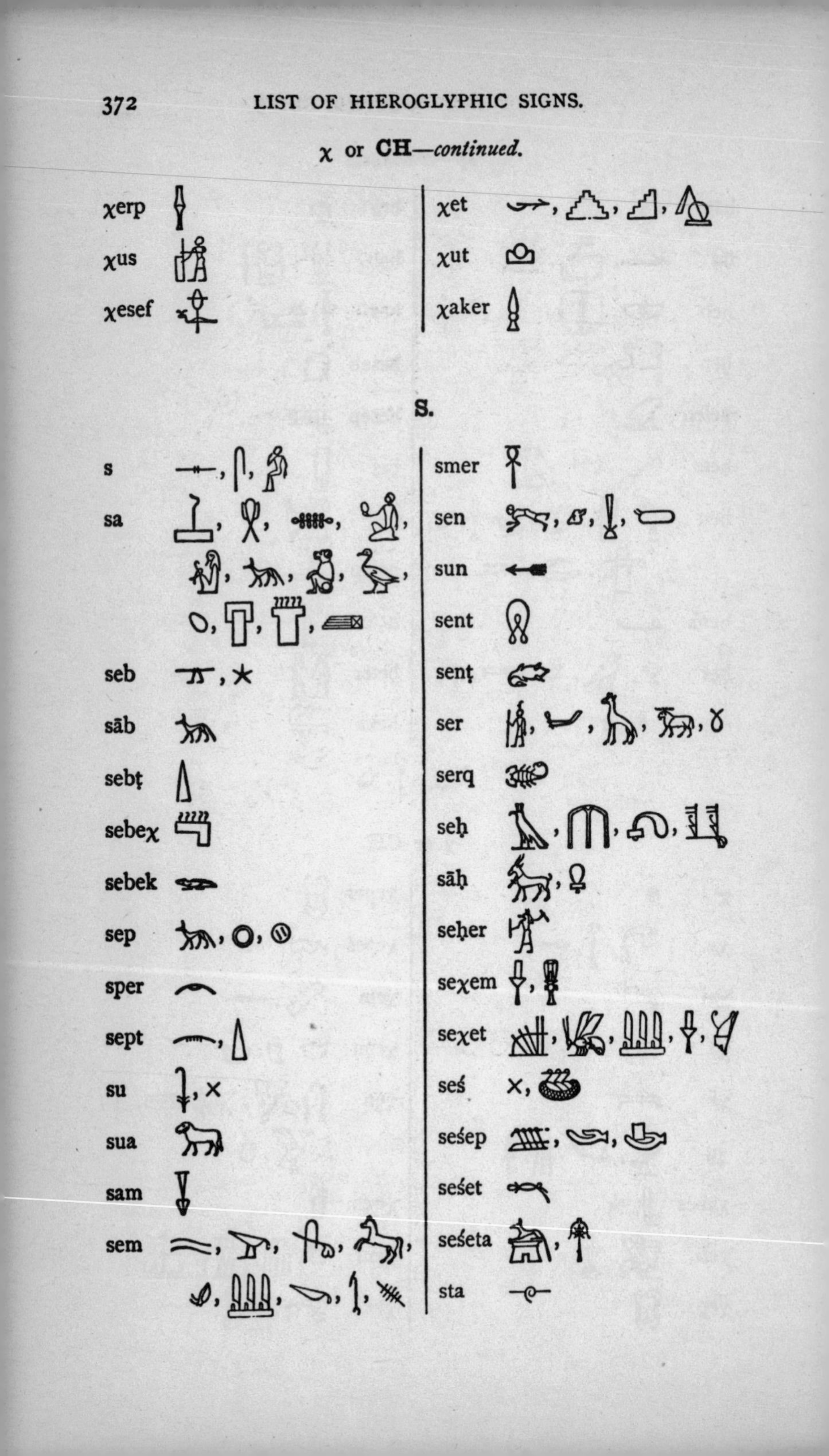

## χ or **CH**—*continued.*

χerp

χus

χesef

χet

χut

χaker

## S.

s

sa

seb

sāb

sebṭ

sebeχ

sebek

sep

sper

sept

su

sua

sam

sem

smer

sen

sun

sent

senṭ

ser

serq

seḥ

sāḥ

seḥer

seχem

seχet

seś

seśep

seśet

seśeta

sta

## S—*continued.*

sati

set

seṭ

set'eb

setep

setem, set'em

sek

seq

## SH.

ś

śa

śā

śu

śeps

śep

śem

śef

śemer

śen

śeråu

śes

śāṭ

## T.

t

ta

taui

tå

ti

teb

tep

tef

tem

ten

ter

trå

teh

teḥ

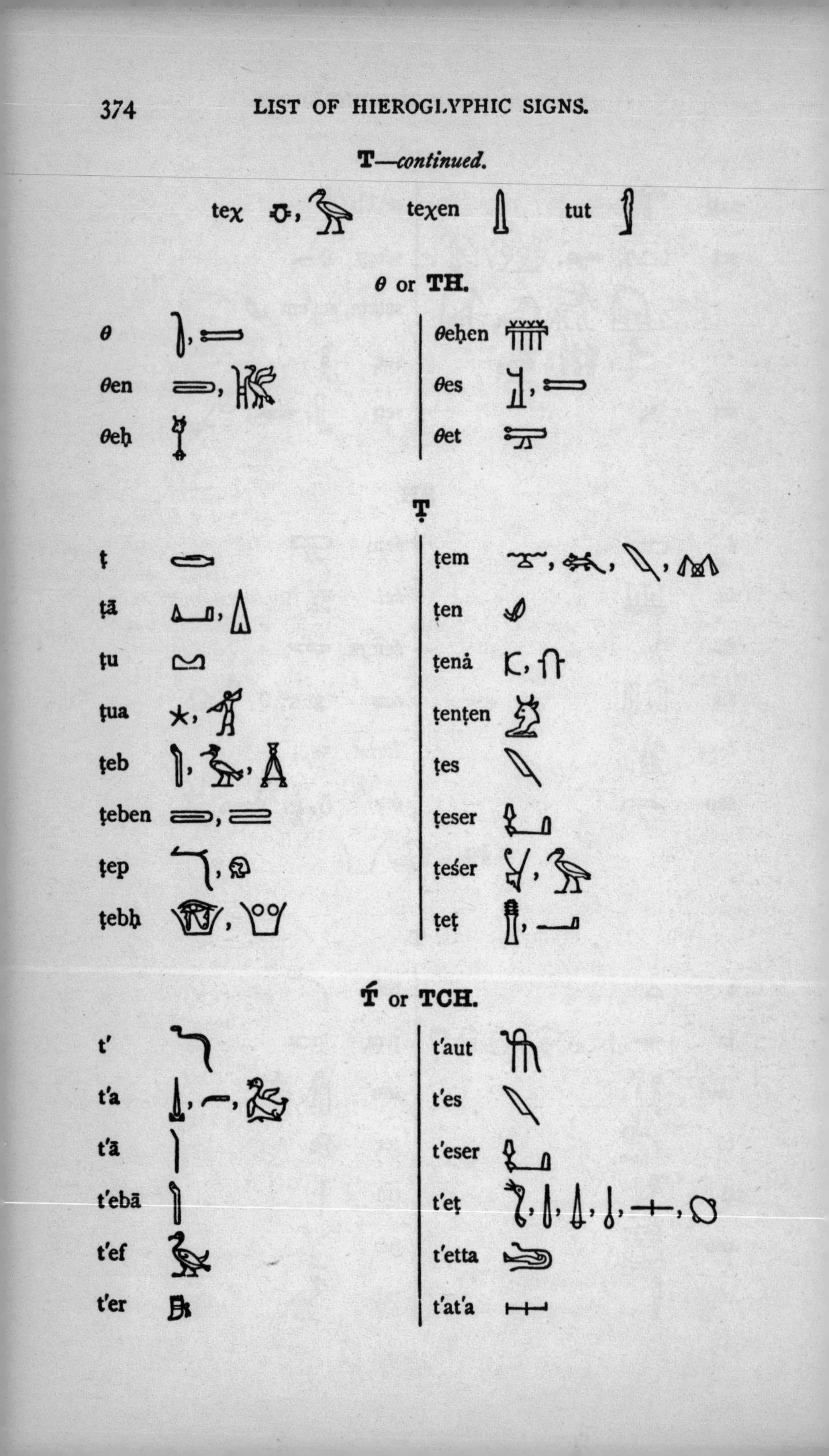

## T—*continued.*

teχ, teχen, tut

## θ or TH.

θ
θen
θeḥ
θeḥen
θes
θet

## Ṭ

ṭ
ṭā
ṭu
ṭua
ṭeb
ṭeben
ṭep
ṭebḥ
ṭem
ṭen
ṭenȧ
ṭenṭen
ṭes
ṭeser
ṭeśer
ṭeṭ

## Ť or TCH.

t'
t'a
t'ā
t'ebā
t'ef
t'er
t'aut
t'es
t'eser
t'eṭ
t'etta
t'at'a

## K.

k  ka  kep 

kat  katu 

## Q.

q 

qa 

qebḥ 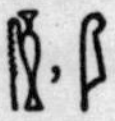

qem 

qemā 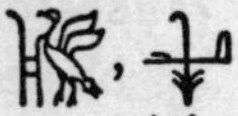

qen 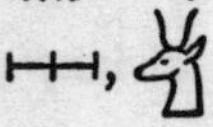

qenbet 

qens 

qenṭ 

qer 

qers 

qes 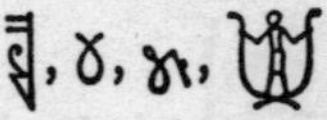

qeṭ 

## Ḳ.

ḳ  ḳa  ḳeb  ḳer 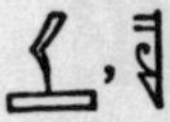

## A List of the Commonest Determinatives.

| Character. | Determinative of. |
|---|---|
|  | to cry, to call |
|  | to address, to adore |
|  | to exalt, to rejoice |
|  | to turn back |
|  | to dance |
|  | to skip |
|  | to bow down |
|  | to make an agreement |
|  | form, image, mummy, to establish |
|  | majesty, dignity |
|  | old age |

| Character. | Determinative of. |
|---|---|
|  | to beat, to strike |
|  | joy |
|  | to plough |
|  | to make an offering |
|  | to sow |
|  | to bear, to carry |
|  | wickedness, enemy |
|  | to build |
|  | to support |
|  | to pierce |
|  | to run |
|  | to pour out a libation |
|  | man |
|  | to eat, to think, to speak |
|  | inertness, to rest |
|  | to hide, be hidden |
|  | libationer |

| Character. | Determinative of. |
|---|---|
|  | millions of years |
|  | to write |
|  | dead body |
|  | overthrow, defeat |
|  | soldier |
|  | child, youth, growth |
|  | king, prince |
|  | ancestor, the blessed dead |
|  | divinity |
|  | Osiris |
|  | Ptaḥ |
|  | Ptaḥ-tenen |
|  | Ȧmsu |
|  | Ȧmen |
|  | Shu |
|  | Chensu |
|  | Rā |
|  | Ḥeru (Horus) |
|  | Ȧnpu (Anubis) |
|  | Chnemu |
|  | Ḥāpi (Nile) |

| Character. | Determinative of. |
|---|---|
|  | Set |
|  | Teḥuti (Thoth) |
|  | Bes |
|  | woman, goddess |
|  | Åuset (Isis) |
|  | Nebt-ḥet (Nephthys) |
|  | Ḥet-Ḥert (Hathor) |
|  | Nut |
|  | Maāt |
|  | Sechet |
|  | Bast |
|  | Sesheta |
|  | Serqet |
|  | pregnancy |
|  | birth |
|  | to suckle |
|  | to dandle |
|  | head, chief, best |
|  | head-dress, skin, colour, grief |
|  | to see, to watch, to sleep |

| Character. | Determinative of. |
|---|---|
|  | eye painted with *kohl* |
|  | to weep, to grieve |
|  | eye of Horus |
|  | eyes of Sun and Moon |
|  | eyebrows |
|  | ear, to listen |
|  | nose, to smell, joy |
|  | lips |
|  | teeth |
|  | blood |
| 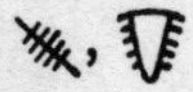 | back-bone, to cut |
|  | breast |
| 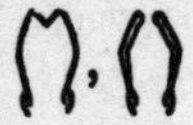 | to embrace |
|  | to prohibit, negation, want, need |
| 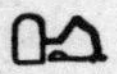 | battle, to fight |
|  | to seize, to beat, to strike |
|  | to write, paint |
| 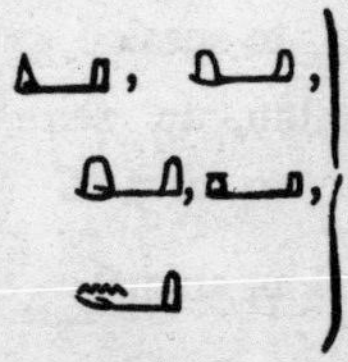 | to make an offering, or gift |

| Character. | Determinative of. | Character. | Determinative of. |
|---|---|---|---|
|  | to grasp |  | to shoot |
|  | finger |  | flesh and bone, heir, offspring |
| 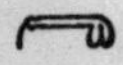 | phallus, the front of, male |  | tail, end |
|  | testicles |  | all actions attributed to Set |
|  | to walk, stand, to enter |  | birds, to fly |
|  | to turn back, to return |  | to hover, to stop |
|  | leg, foot, to run |  | small size, wickedness |
|  | foot and leg |  | wing, to fly |
|  | to break into |  | egg, feminine gender |
|  | knee |  | fish |
|  | flesh |  | crocodile, destruction |
|  | animals |  | serpent |
|  | birth |  | goddess, uræus |
|  | the front |  | tree |
|  | behind, power, to arrive at | 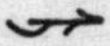 | wood |
|  | throat, to breathe, to eat |  | flower |
|  | horn, to resist, to attack |  | sweetness, pleasure |
|  | to taste, to eat, to speak |  | year, time, growth |
|  | talon, to seize, to carry off |  | field |
| 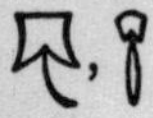 | skin, animal | | |

| Character. | Determinative of. |
|---|---|
| 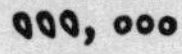 | grain |
| 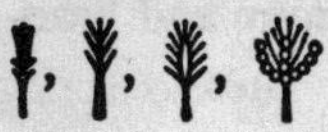 | wheat, barley, *etc.* |
|  | store house, granary |
|  | vineyard |
|  | sky |
| 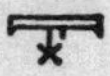 | night, darkness |
|  | rain, storm, cloud |
|  | sun, time |
|  | light, brilliance |
|  | moon |
|  | star, god |
| 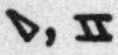 | earth, land |
|  | mountain |
|  | foreign land, foreign people |
|  | island, sea-coast |
|  | nome, district |
|  | town |
|  | road, to travel |
| 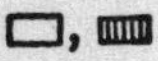 | stone |
|  | metal |
|  | metal |
|  | water, river, to wash |
|  | liquid |
| 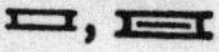 | a collection of water |
| 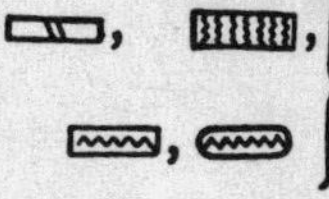 | lake, basin of water |
|  | house |
|  | pylon |
|  | wall |
|  | to overturn |
| 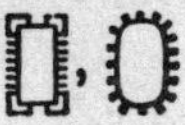 | a fortified place |
|  | angle |
|  | staircase |
| 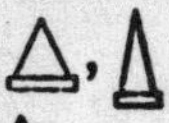 | pyramid |
|  | obelisk |
|  | tablet |
|  | to establish |
|  | festival |
|  | door, to open |
| | a bolt |
|  | funereal coffer |
| 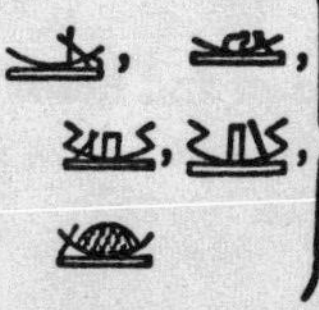 | boat |

| Character. | Determinative of. |
|---|---|
|  | boat of Seker |
| 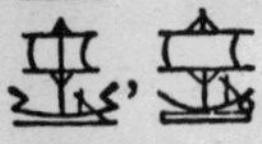 | to sail up the river |
|  | wind, breath |
|  | to steer |
|  | seat |
|  | bier, dead person, mummy |
|  | pillow |
|  | to bandage |
|  | seat, throne |
| 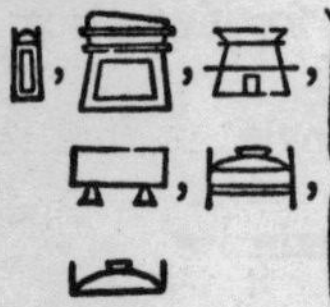 | funereal box, tomb, sarcophagus |
|  | bandages |
|  | fan |
|  | mirror |
|  | scales |
| 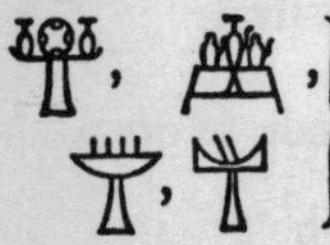 | altar, table |
| 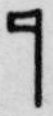 | divinity |
|  | crown and head-dress |

| Character. | Determinative of. |
|---|---|
| 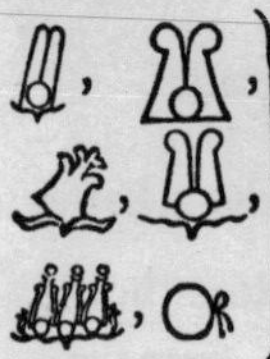 | crown and head-dress |
|  | collar |
|  | buckle, tie |
|  | tongue, to taste |
|  | ring |
|  | to seal |
| 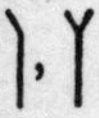 | to arrive, foreign people |
| 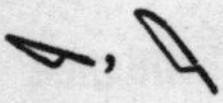 | to cut, to wound |
|  | block and hatchet |
| 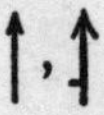 | weapon |
|  | arrow |
|  | chariot |
| 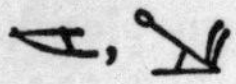 | to plough |
|  | cord, to bandage, to wrap |
| 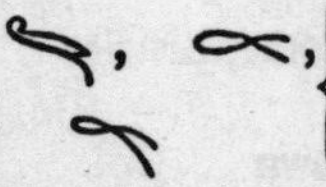 | book, to write, to read, knowledge |
|  | oil, perfume |
|  | libation |
| 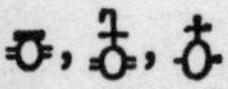 | oil, perfume, wine |
|  | milk |

| Character. | Determinative of. |
|---|---|
|  | vase |
|  | offering |
|  | the heart, intelligence |
|  | offering |
| 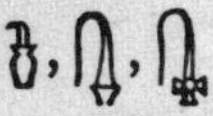 | fire, to burn |
|  | incense |
|  | vase |
| 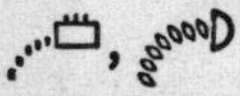 | pouring out |
| 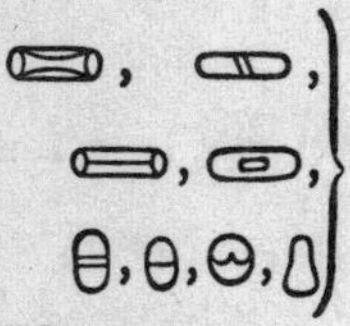 | cake, bread |
|  | scribe, writing |

| Character. | Determinative of. |
|---|---|
|  | book, writing, picture, account, thought, abstract idea |
| 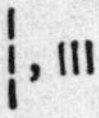 | plural |
|  | to repeat |
|  | to add, to increase |
| 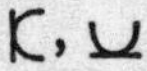 | half, to divide |
| 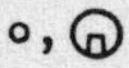 | death, wickedness |
|  | name |
|  | to stink, to embalm |
|  | scent |
|  | a cutting tool, to make to shine, bone |

# INDEX.

The principal references are indicated by blacker-faced type.